Ralph Waldo Emerson

Prose Works of Ralph Waldo Emerson

Ralph Waldo Emerson

Prose Works of Ralph Waldo Emerson

ISBN/EAN: 9783744687324

Printed in Europe, USA, Canada, Australia, Japan

Cover: Foto ©Thomas Meinert / pixelio.de

More available books at **www.hansebooks.com**

THE

PROSE WORKS

OF

RALPH WALDO EMERSON.

NEW AND REVISED EDITION.

IN THREE VOLUMES.

VOL. III.

BOSTON:

HOUGHTON, OSGOOD AND COMPANY.

The Riverside Press, Cambridge.

1880.

CONTENTS OF VOL. III.

SOCIETY AND SOLITUDE.

LETTERS AND SOCIAL AIMS.

SOCIETY AND SOLITUDE.

SOCIETY AND SOLITUDE.

I FELL in with a humorist, on my travels, who had in his chamber a cast of the Rondanini Medusa, and who assured me that the name which that fine work of art bore in the catalogues was a misnomer, as he was convinced that the sculptor who carved it intended it for Memory, the mother of the Muses. In the conversation that followed, my new friend made some extraordinary confessions. "Do you not see," he said, "the penalty of learning, and that each of these scholars whom you have met at S——, though he were to be the last man, would, like the executioner in Hood's poem, guillotine the last but one?" He added many lively remarks, but his evident earnestness engaged my attention, and, in the weeks that followed, we became better acquainted. He had good abilities, a genial temper, and no vices; but he had one defect, — he could not speak in the tone of the people. There was some paralysis on his will, such that, when he met men on common terms, he spoke weakly, and from the point, like a flighty girl. His consciousness of the fault made it worse. He envied every drover and lumberman in the tavern their manly speech. He coveted Mirabeau's *don terrible de la familiarité*, believing that he whose sympathy goes lowest is the man from whom kings have the most to fear. For himself, he declared that he could not get enough alone to write a letter to a friend. He left the city; he hid himself in pastures. The solitary river was not solitary enough; the sun and moon put him out. When he bought a house, the first thing he did was to plant trees. He could not enough conceal himself. Set a hedge here; set oaks there, —trees behind trees; above all, set evergreens, for they will keep a secret all the year round. The most agreeable compliment you could pay him was, to imply that you had not observed him in a house or a

street where you had met him. Whilst he suffered at being
seen where he was, he consoled himself with the delicious
thought of the inconceivable number of places where he was
not.   All he wished of his tailor was to provide that sober
mean of color and cut which would never detain the eye for a
moment.   He went to Vienna, to Smyrna, to London.   In all
the variety of costumes, a carnival, a kaleidoscope of clothes,
to his horror he could never discover a man in the street who
wore anything like his own dress.   He would have given his
soul for the ring of Gyges.   His dismay at his visibility had
blunted the fears of mortality.   "Do you think," he said, " I
am in such great terror of being shot, — I, who am only waiting to shuffle off my corporeal jacket, to slip away into the back
stars, and put diameters of the solar system and sidereal orbits between me and all souls, — there to wear out ages in
solitude, and forget memory itself, if it be possible?"   He
had a remorse running to despair, of his social *gaucheries*, and
walked miles and miles to get the twitchings out of his face,
the starts and shrugs out of his arms and shoulders.   God
may forgive sins, he said, but awkwardness has no forgiveness
in heaven or earth.   He admired in Newton, not so much his
theory of the moon, as his letter to Collins, in which he for-
bade him to insert his name with the solution of the problem
in the " Philosophical Transactions " : "It would perhaps increase my acquaintance, the thing which I chiefly study to
decline."

These conversations led me somewhat later to the knowledge
of similar cases, and to the discovery that they are not of very
infrequent occurrence.   Few substances are found pure in nature.   Those constitutions which can bear in open day the
rough dealing of the world must be of that mean and average
structure, — such as iron and salt, atmospheric air, and water.
But there are metals, like potassium and sodium, which, to be
kept pure, must be kept under naphtha.   Such are the talents
determined on some specialty, which a culminating civilization
fosters in the heart of great cities and in royal chambers.
Nature protects her own work.   To the culture of the world,
an Archimedes, a Newton is indispensable ; so she guards them
by a certain aridity.   If these had been good fellows, fond of
dancing, port, and clubs, we should have had no " Theory of
the Sphere," and no " Principia."   They had that necessity of
isolation which genius feels.   Each must stand on his glass
tripod, if he would keep his electricity.   Even Swedenborg,

whose theory of the universe is based on affection, and who reprobates to weariness the danger and vice of pure intellect, is constrained to make an extraordinary exception : " There are also angels who do not live consociated, but separate, house and house ; these dwell in the midst of heaven, because they are the best of angels."

We have known many fine geniuses with that imperfection that they cannot do anything useful, not so much as write one clean sentence. 'T is worse, and tragic, that no man is fit for society who has fine traits. At a distance, he is admired ; but bring him hand to hand, he is a cripple. One protects himself by solitude, and one by courtesy, and one by an acid, worldly manner, — each concealing how he can the thinness of his skin and his incapacity for strict association. But there is no remedy that can reach the heart of the disease, but either habits of self-reliance that should go in practice to making the man independent of the human race, or else a religion of love. Now he hardly seems entitled to marry ; for how can he protect a woman who cannot protect himself ?

We pray to be conventional. But the wary Heaven takes care you shall not be, if there is anything good in you. Dante was very bad company and was never invited to dinner. Michel Angelo had a sad, sour time of it. The ministers of beauty are rarely beautiful in coaches and saloons. Columbus discovered no isle or key so lonely as himself. Yet each of these potentates saw well the reason of his exclusion. Solitary was he ? Why, yes ; but his society was limited only by the amount of brain Nature appropriated in that age to carry on the government of the world. "If I stay," said Dante, when there was question of going to Rome, "who will go ? and if I go, who will stay ?"

But the necessity of solitude is deeper than we have said, and is organic. I have seen many a philosopher whose world is large enough for only one person. He affects to be a good companion ; but we are still surprising his secret, that he means and needs to impose his system on all the rest. The determination of each is *from* all the others, like that of each tree up into free space. 'T is no wonder, when each has his whole head, our societies should be so small. Like President Tyler, our party falls from us every day, and we must ride in a sulky at last. Dear heart ! take it sadly home to thee, — there is no co-operation. We begin with friendships, and all our youth is a reconnoitring and recruiting of the holy fraternity they shall combine for the salvation of men. But so the remoter stars seem a nebula of united light; yet there is no group which a telescope will not resolve, and the dearest friends are separated by impassable gulfs. The co-operation is involuntary, and is put upon us by the Genius of Life, who reserves this as a part of his prerogative. 'T is fine for us to talk, we sit and muse, and are serene and complete; but the moment we meet with anybody, each becomes a fraction.

Though the stuff of tragedy and of romances is in a moral union of two superior persons, whose confidence in each other for long years, out of sight, and in sight, and against all appearances, is at last justified by victorious proof of probity to gods and men, causing joyful emotions, tears and glory, — though there be for heroes this *moral union*, yet, they, too, are as far off as ever from an intellectual union, and the moral union is for comparatively low and external purposes, like the co-operation of a ship's company or of a fire-club. [But how insular and pathetically solitary are all the people we know! Nor dare they tell what they think of each other, when they meet in the street. We have a fine right, to be sure, to taunt men of the world with superficial and treacherous courtesies!

Such is the tragic necessity which strict science finds underneath our domestic and neighborly life, irresistibly driving each adult soul as with whips into the desert, and making our warm covenants sentimental and momentary. We must infer that the ends of thought were peremptory, if they were to be secured at such ruinous cost. They are deeper than can be told, and belong to the immensities and eternities. They reach down to that depth where society itself originates and disappears, — where the question is, Which is first, man or men? — where the individual is lost in his source.

But this banishment to the rocks and echoes no metaphysics can make right or tolerable. This result is so against nature, such a half-view, that it must be corrected by a common sense and experience. "A man is born by the side of his father, and there he remains." A man must be clothed with society, or we shall feel a certain bareness and poverty, as of a displaced and unfurnished member. He is to be dressed in arts and institutions, as well as in body garments. Now and then a man exquisitely made can live alone, and must; but coop up most men, and you undo them. "The king lived and ate in his hall with men, and understood men," said Selden. When a young barrister said to the late Mr.

Mason, " I keep my chamber to read law," — " Read law ! "
replied the veteran, "'t is in the court-room you must read
law." Nor is the rule otherwise for literature. If you would
learn to write, 't is in the street you must learn it. Both for
the vehicle and for the aims of fine arts, you must frequent
the public square. The people, and not the college, is the
writer's home. A scholar is a candle which the love and desire of all men will light. Never his lands or his rents, but
the power to charm the disguised soul that sits veiled under
this bearded and that rosy visage is his rent and ration. His
products are as needful as those of the baker or the weaver.
Society cannot do without cultivated men. As soon as the
first wants are satisfied, the higher wants become imperative.

'T is hard to mesmerize ourselves, to whip our own top ;
but through sympathy we are capable of energy and endurance. Concert fires people to a certain fury of performance
they can rarely reach alone. Here is the use of society : it is
so easy with the great to be great ; so easy to come up to an
existing standard ; — as easy as it is to the lover to swim to
his maiden through waves so grim before. The benefits of
affection are immense ; and the one event which never loses
its romance is the encounter with superior persons on terms
allowing the happiest intercourse.

It by no means follows that we are not fit for society, because *soirées* are tedious, and because the *soirée* finds us tedious. A backwoodsman, who had been sent to the university,
told me that, when he heard the best bred young men at the
law school talk together, he reckoned himself a boor; but
whenever he caught them apart, and had one to himself alone,
then they were the boors, and he the better man. And if we
recall the rare hours when we encountered the best persons,
we then found ourselves, and then first society seemed to
exist. That was society, though in the transom of a brig, or
on the Florida Keys.

A cold, sluggish blood thinks it has not facts enough to the
purpose, and must decline its turn in the conversation. But
they who speak have no more, — have less. 'T is not new
facts that avail, but the heat to dissolve everybody's facts.
Heat puts you in right relation with magazines of facts.
The capital defect of cold, arid natures is the want of animal
spirits. They seem a power incredible, as if God should raise
the dead. The recluse witnesses what others perform by
their aid, with a kind of fear. It is as much out of his pos-

sibility as the prowess of Cœur-de-Lion or an Irishman's day's-
work on the railroad. 'T is said the present and the future
are always rivals. Animal spirits constitute the power of the
present, and their feats are like the structure of a pyramid.
Their result is a lord, a general, or a boon companion. Before
these, what a base mendicant is Memory with his leathern
badge ! But this genial heat is latent in all constitutions,
and is disengaged only by the friction of society. As Bacon
said of manners, " To obtain them, it only needs not to despise them," so we say of animal spirits, that they are the
spontaneous product of health and of a social habit. " For
behavior, men learn it, as they take diseases, one of another."

But the people are to be taken in very small doses. If
solitude is proud, so is society vulgar. In society, high advantages are set down to the individual as disqualifications.
We sink as easily as we rise, through sympathy. So many
men whom I know are degraded by their sympathies, their
native aims being high enough, but their relation all too tender
to the gross people about them. Men cannot afford to live
together on their merits, and they adjust themselves by their
demerits, — by their love of gossip, or by sheer tolerance and
animal good-nature. They untune and dissipate the brave
aspirant.

The remedy is, to reinforce each of these moods from the
other. Conversation will not corrupt us, if we come to the
assembly in our own garb and speech, and with the energy of
health to select what is ours and reject what is not.) Society
we must have ; but let it be society, and not exchanging
news, or eating from the same dish. Is it society to sit in
one of your chairs ? I cannot go to the houses of my nearest
relatives, because I do not wish to be alone. Society exists
by chemical affinity, and not otherwise.

Put any company of people together with freedom for conversation, and a rapid self-distribution takes place, into sets
and pairs. The best are accused of exclusiveness. It would
be more true to say, they separate as oil from water, as children from old people, without love or hatred in the matter,
each seeking his like ; and any interference with the affinities
would produce constraint and suffocation. All conversation is
a magnetic experiment. I know that my friend can talk elo-
quently ; you know that he cannot articulate a sentence : we
have seen him in different company. Assort your party,
or invite none. Put Stubbs and Coleridge, Quintilian and

Aunt Miriam, into pairs, and you make them all wretched. 'T is an extempore Sing-Sing built in a parlor. Leave them to seek their own mates, and they will be as merry as sparrows.

A higher civility will re-establish in our customs a certain reverence which we have lost. What to do with these brisk young men who break through all fences, and make themselves at home in every house? I find out in an instant if my companion does not want me, and ropes cannot hold me when my welcome is gone. One would think that the affinities would pronounce themselves with a surer reciprocity.

Here again, as so often, Nature delights to put us between extreme antagonisms, and our safety is in the skill with which we keep the diagonal line. Solitude is impracticable, and society fatal. We must keep our head in the one and our hands in the other. The conditions are met, if we keep our independence, yet do not lose our sympathy. These wonderful horses need to be driven by fine hands. We require such a solitude as shall hold us to its revelations when we are in the street and in palaces ; for most men are cowed in society, and say good things to you in private, but will not stand to them in public. But let us not be the victims of words. Society and solitude are deceptive names. It is not the circumstance of seeing more or fewer people, but the readiness of sympathy, that imports ; and a sound mind will derive its principles from insight, with ever a purer ascent to the sufficient and absolute right, and will accept society as the natural element in which they are to be applied.

CIVILIZATION.

CIVILIZATION.

A CERTAIN degree of progress from the rudest state in which man is found, — a dweller in caves, or on trees, like an ape, — a cannibal, and eater of pounded snails, worms, and offal, — a certain degree of progress from this extreme is called Civilization. It is a vague, complex name, of many degrees. Nobody has attempted a definition. Mr. Guizot, writing a book on the subject, does not. It implies the evolution of a highly organized man, brought to supreme delicacy of sentiment, as in practical power, religion, liberty, sense of honor, and taste. In the hesitation to define what it is, we usually suggest it by negations. A nation that has no clothing, no iron, no alphabet, no marriage, no arts of peace, no abstract thought, we call barbarous. And after many arts are invented or imported, as among the Turks and Moorish nations, it is often a little complaisant to call them civilized.

Each nation grows after its own genius, and has a civilization of its own. The Chinese and Japanese, though each complete in his way, is different from the man of Madrid or the man of New York. The term imports a mysterious progress. In the brutes is none ; and in mankind to-day the savage tribes are gradually extinguished rather than civilized. The Indians of this country have not learned the white man's work ; and in Africa, the negro of to-day is the negro of Herodotus. In other races the growth is not arrested ; but the like progress that is made by a boy "when he cuts his eye-teeth," as we say, — childish illusions passing daily away, and he seeing things really and comprehensively, — is made by tribes. It is the learning the secret of cumulative power, of advancing on one's self. It implies a facility of association, power to compare, the ceasing from fixed ideas. The Indian is gloomy and distressed when urged to depart from his habits and traditions. He is overpowered by the gaze of the white, and his eye sinks. The occasion of one of these starts of growth is always some novelty that astounds the mind, and provokes it to dare to change. Thus there is a Cadmus, a Pytheas, a Manco Capac at the beginning of each improvement, — some superior foreigner importing new and wonderful arts, and teaching them. Of course, he must not know too much, but must have the sympathy, language, and gods of those he would inform. But chiefly the sea-shore has been the point of departure to knowledge, as to commerce. The most advanced nations are always those who navigate the most. The power which the sea requires in the sailor makes a man of him very fast, and the change of shores and population clears his head of much nonsense of his wigwam.

Where shall we begin or end the list of those feats of liberty and wit, each of which feats made an epoch of history? Thus, the effect of a framed or stone house is immense on the tranquillity, power, and refinement of the builder. A man in a cave or in a camp, a nomad, will die with no more estate than the wolf or the horse leaves. But so simple a labor as a house being achieved, his chief enemies are kept at bay. He is safe from the teeth of wild animals, from frost, sunstroke, and weather; and fine faculties begin to yield their fine harvest. Invention and art are born, manners and social beauty and delight. 'Tis wonderful how soon a piano gets into a log-hut on the frontier. You would think they found it under a pine-stump. With it comes a Latin grammar, — and one of those tow-head boys has written a hymn on Sunday. Now let colleges, now let senates take heed! for here is one who, opening these fine tastes on the basis of the pioneer's iron constitution, will gather all their laurels in his strong hands.

When the Indian trail gets widened, graded, and bridged to a good road, there is a benefactor, there is a missionary, a pacificator, a wealth bringer, a maker of markets, a vent for industry. Another step in civility is the change from war, hunting, and pasturage to agriculture. Our Scandinavian forefathers have left us a significant legend to convey their sense of the importance of this step. "There was once a giantess who had a daughter, and the child saw a husbandman ploughing in the field. Then she ran and picked him up with her finger and thumb, and put him and his plough and his oxen into her apron, and carried them to her mother, and said, 'Mother, what sort of a beetle is this that I found wriggling in the sand?' But the mother said, 'Put it away, my child ; we must begone out of this land, for these people will dwell in it.'" Another success is the post-office, with its educating energy augmented by cheapness and guarded by a certain religious sentiment in mankind ; so that the power of a wafer or a drop of wax or gluten to guard a letter, as it flies over sea, over land, and comes to its address as if a battalion of artillery brought it, I look upon as a fine metre of civilization.

The division of labor, the multiplication of the arts of peace, which is nothing but a large allowance to each man to choose his work according to his faculty,— to live by his better hand, — fills the State with useful and happy laborers ; and they, creating demand by the very temptation of their productions, are rapidly and surely rewarded by good sale : and what a police and ten commandments their work thus becomes. So true is Dr. Johnson's remark that "men are seldom more innocently employed than when they are making money."

The skilful combinations of civil government, though they usually follow natural leadings, as the lines of race, language, religion, and territory, yet require wisdom and conduct in the rulers, and in their result delight the imagination. "We see insurmountable multitudes obeying, in opposition to their strongest passions, the restraints of a power which they scarcely perceive, and the crimes of a single individual marked and punished at the distance of half the earth." *

Right position of woman in the State is another index. Poverty and industry with a healthy mind read very easily the laws of humanity, and love them : place the sexes in right relations of mutual respect, and a severe morality gives that essential charm to woman which educates all that is delicate, poetic, and self-sacrificing, breeds courtesy and learning, conversation and wit, in her rough mate ; so that I have thought a sufficient measure of civilization is the influence of good women.

Another measure of culture is the diffusion of knowledge, overrunning all the old barriers of caste, and, by the cheap press, bringing the university to every poor man's door in the newsboy's basket. Scraps of science, of thought, of poetry are in the coarsest sheet, so that in every house we hesitate to burn a newspaper until we have looked it through.

The ship, in its latest complete equipment, is an abridg-

* Dr. Thomas Brown.

ment and compend of a nation's arts: the ship steered by
compass and chart, — longitude reckoned by lunar observation and by chronometer, — driven by steam; and in wildest
sea-mountains, at vast distances from home,

> " The pulses of her iron heart
> Go beating through the storm."

No use can lessen the wonder of this control, by so weak a
creature, of forces so prodigious.   I remember I watched, in
crossing the sea, the beautiful skill whereby the engine, in its
constant working, was made to produce two hundred gallons
of fresh water out of salt water, every hour, — thereby sup-
plying all the ship's want.

The skill that pervades complex details; the man that
maintains himself; the chimney taught to burn its own
smoke; the farm made to produce all that is consumed on
it; the very prison compelled to maintain itself and yield a
revenue; and, better still, made a reform school, and a manu-
factory of honest men out of rogues, as the steamer made
fresh water out of salt, — all these are examples of that tendency to combine antagonisms, and utilize evil, which is the
index of high civilization.

Civilization is the result of highly complex organization.   In
the snake, all the organs are sheathed: no hands, no feet, no
fins, no wings.   In bird and beast, the organs are released,
and begin to play.   In man, they are all'unbound, and full of
joyful action.   With this unswaddling he receives the absolute
illumination we call Reason, and thereby true liberty.

.Climate has much to do with this melioration.   The highest
civility has never loved the hot zones.   Wherever snow falls,
there is usually civil freedom.   Where the banana grows, the
animal system is indolent and pampered at the cost of higher
qualities: the man is sensual and cruel.   But this scale is not
invariable.   High degrees of moral sentiment control the unfavorable influences of climate; and some of our grandest
examples of men and of races come from the equatorial regions,
— as the genius of Egypt, of India, and of Arabia.

These feats are measures or traits of civility; and temperate
climate is an important influence, though not quite indispensable, for there have been learning, philosophy, and art in
Iceland, and in the tropics.   But one condition is essential to
the social education of man, namely, morality.   There can be
no high civility without a deep morality, though it may not
always call itself by that name, but sometimes the point of

honor, as in the institution of chivalry; or patriotism, as in the Spartan and Roman republics; or the enthusiasm of some religious sect which imputes its virtue to its dogma; or the cabalism, or *esprit de corps*, of a masonic or other association of friends.

The evolution of a highly-destined society must be moral; it must run in the grooves of the celestial wheels. It must be catholic in aims. What is *moral?* It is the respecting in action catholic or universal ends. Hear the definition which Kant gives of moral conduct: "Act always so that the immediate motive of thy will may become a universal rule for all intelligent beings."

Civilization depends on morality. Everything good in man leans on what is higher. This rule holds in small as in great. Thus, all our strength and success in the work of our hands depend on our borrowing the aid of the elements. You have seen a carpenter on a ladder with a broad-axe chopping upward chips from a beam. How awkward! at what disadvantage he works! But see him on the ground, dressing his timber under him. Now, not his feeble muscles, but the force of gravity brings down the axe; that is to say, the planet itself splits his stick. The farmer had much ill-temper, laziness, and shirking to endure from his hand-sawyers, until one day he bethought him to put his saw-mill on the edge of a waterfall; and the river never tires of turning his wheel: the river is good-natured, and never hints an objection.

We had letters to send: couriers could not go fast enough, nor far enough; broke their wagons, foundered their horses; bad roads in spring, snowdrifts in winter, heats in summer; could not get the horses out of a walk. But we found out that the air and earth were full of Electricity; and always going our way, — just the way we wanted to send. *Would he take a message?* Just as lief as not; had nothing else to do; would carry it in no time. Only one doubt occurred, one staggering objection, — he had no carpet-bag, no visible pockets, no hands, not so much as a mouth, to carry a letter. But, after much thought and many experiments, we managed to meet the conditions, and to fold up the letter in such invisible compact form as he could carry in those invisible pockets of his, never wrought by needle and thread, — and it went like a charm.

I admire still more than the saw-mill the skill which, on the sea-shore, makes the tides drive the wheels and grind corn, and which thus engages the assistance of the moon, like a hired hand, to grind, and wind, and pump, and saw, and split stone, and roll iron.

Now that is the wisdom of a man, in every instance of his labor, to hitch his wagon to a star, and see his chore done by the gods themselves. That is the way we are strong, by borrowing the might of the elements. The forces of steam, gravity, galvanism, light, magnets, wind, fire, serve us day by day, and cost us nothing.

Our astronomy is full of examples of calling in the aid of these magnificent helpers. Thus, on a planet so small as ours, the want of an adequate base for astronomical measurements is early felt, as, for example, in detecting the parallax of a star. But the astronomer, having by an observation fixed the place of a star, by so simple an expedient as waiting six months, and then repeating his observation, contrived to put the diameter of the earth's orbit, say two hundred millions of miles, between his first observation and his second, and this line afforded him a respectable base for his triangle.

All our arts aim to win this vantage. We cannot bring the heavenly powers to us, but, if we will only choose our jobs in directions in which they travel, they will undertake them with the greatest pleasure. It is a peremptory rule with them, that *they never go out of their road.* We are dapper little busybodies, and run this way and that way superserviceably ; but they swerve never from their foreordained paths, — neither the sun, nor the moon, nor a bubble of air, nor a mote of dust.

And as our handiworks borrow the elements, so all our social and political action leans on principles. To accomplish anything excellent, the will must work for catholic and universal ends. A puny creature walled in on every side, as Daniel wrote, —

> " Unless above himself he can
> Erect himself, how poor a thing is man ! "

but when his will leans on a principle, when he is the vehicle of ideas, he borrows their omnipotence. Gibraltar may be strong, but ideas are impregnable, and bestow on the hero their invincibility. " It was a great instruction," said a saint in Cromwell's war, " that the best courages are but beams of the Almighty." Hitch your wagon to a star. Let us not fag in paltry works which serve our pot and bag alone. Let us not lie and steal. No god will help. We shall find all their teams going the other way, — Charles's Wain, Great Bear, Orion, Leo, Hercules : every god will leave us. Work rather for those interests which the divinities honor and promote, — justice, love, freedom, knowledge, utility.

If we can thus ride in Olympian chariots by putting our works in the path of the celestial circuits, we can harness also evil agents, the powers of darkness, and force them to serve against their will the ends of wisdom and virtue. Thus, a wise government puts fines and penalties on pleasant vices. What a benefit would the American government, not yet relieved of its extreme need, render to itself, and to every city, village, and hamlet in the States, if it would tax whiskey and rum almost to the point of prohibition! Was it Bonaparte who said that he found vices very good patriots? — " he got five millions from the love of brandy, and he should be glad to know which of the virtues would pay him as much." Tobacco and opium have broad backs, and will cheerfully carry the load of armies, if you choose to make them pay high for such joy as they give and such harm as they do.

~~and~~ modes; and the true test of civilization is, not the census, nor the size of cities, nor the crops, — no, but the kind of man the country turns out. I see the vast advantages of this country, spanning the breadth of the temperate zone. I see the immense material prosperity, — towns on towns, states on states, and wealth piled in the massive architecture of cities, quartz-mountains dumped down in New York to be repiled architecturally alongshore from Canada to Cuba, and thence westward to California again. But it is not New York streets built by the confluence of workmen and wealth of all nations, though stretching out towards Philadelphia until they touch it, and northward until they touch New Haven, Hartford, Springfield, Worcester, and Boston, — not these that make the real estimation. But, when I look over this constellation of cities which animate and illustrate the land, and see how little the government has to do with their daily life, how self-helped and self-directed all families are, — knots of men in purely natural societies, — societies of trade, of kindred blood, of habitual hospitality, house and house, man acting on man by weight of opinion, of longer or better-directed industry, the refining influence of women, the invitation which experience and permanent causes open to youth and labor, — when I see how much each virtuous and gifted person, whom all men consider, lives affectionately with scores of excellent people who are not known far from home, and perhaps with great reason reckons these people his superiors in virtue, and in the symmetry and force of their qualities, I see what cubic values America has, and in these a better certificate of civilization than great cities or enormous wealth.

In strictness, the vital refinements are the moral and intellectual steps. The appearance of the Hebrew Moses, of the Indian Buddh, — in Greece, of the Seven Wise Masters, of the acute and upright Socrates, and of the Stoic Zeno, — in Judæa, the advent of Jesus, — and in modern Christendom, of the realists Huss, Savonarola, and Luther, are causal facts which carry forward races to new convictions, and elevate the rule of life. In the presence of these agencies, it is frivolous to insist on the invention of printing or gunpowder, of steam-power or gas-light, percussion-caps and rubber-shoes; which are toys thrown off from that security, freedom, and exhilaration which a healthy morality creates in society. These arts add a comfort and smoothness to house and street life; but a purer morality, which kindles genius, civilizes 'civilization; casts backward all that we held sacred into the profane, as the flame of oil throws a shadow when shined upon by the flame of the Bude-light. Not the less the popular measures of progress will ever be the arts and the laws.

But if there be a country which cannot stand any one of these tests, — a country where knowledge cannot be diffused without perils of mob-law and statute-law, where speech is not free, — where the post-office is violated, mail-bags opened, and letters tampered with, — where public debts and private debts outside of the State are repudiated — where liberty is attacked in the primary institution of social life, — where the position of the white woman is injuriously affected by the outcry of the black woman, — where the arts, such as they have, are all imported, having no indigenous life, — where the laborer is not secured in the earnings of his own hands, — where suffrage is not free or equal, — that country is, in all these respects, not civil, but barbarous; and no advantages of soil, climate, or coast can resist these suicidal mischiefs.

Morality and all the incidents of morality are essential; as, justice to the citizen, and personal liberty. Montesquieu says: "Countries are well cultivated, not as they are fertile, but as they are free"; and the remark holds not less but more true of the culture of men, than of the tillage of land. And the highest proof of civility is, that the whole public action of the State is directed on securing the greatest good of the greatest number.

ART.

ART.

ALL departments of life at the present day,—Trade, Politics, Letters, Science, or Religion,— seem to feel, and to labor to express, the identity of their law. They are rays of one sun; they translate each into a new language the sense of the other. They are sublime when seen as emanations of a Necessity contradistinguished from the vulgar Fate, by being instant and alive, and dissolving man, as well as his works, in its flowing beneficence. This influence is conspicuously visible in the principles and history of Art.

On one side in primary communication with absolute truth through thought and instinct, the human mind on the other side tends, by an equal necessity, to the publication and embodiment of its thought, modified and dwarfed by the impurity and untruth which, in all our experience, injure the individuality through which it passes. The child not only suffers, but cries; not only hungers, but eats. The man not only thinks, but speaks and acts. Every thought that arises in the mind, in its rising aims to pass out of the mind into act; just as every plant, in the moment of germination, struggles up to light. Thought is the seed of action; but action is as much its second form as thought is its first. It rises in thought, to the end that it may be uttered and acted. The more profound the thought, the more burdensome. Always in proportion to the depth of its sense does it knock importunately at the gates of the soul, to be spoken, to be done. What is in, will out. It struggles to the birth. Speech is a great pleasure, and action a great pleasure; they cannot be forborne.

The utterance of thought and emotion in speech and action may be conscious or unconscious. The sucking child is an unconscious actor. The man in an ecstasy of fear or anger is an unconscious actor. A large part of our habitual actions are unconsciously done, and most of our necessary words are unconsciously said.

The conscious utterance of thought, by speech or action, to any end, is Art. From the first imitative babble of a child to the despotism of eloquence, from his first pile of toys or chip bridge to the masonry of Minot Rock Light-house or the Pacific Railroad, from the tattooing of the Owhyhees to the Vatican Gallery, from the simplest expedient of private prudence to the American Constitution, from its first to its last works, Art is the spirit's voluntary use and combination of things to serve its end. / The Will distinguishes it as spiritual action. Relatively to themselves, the bee, the bird, the beaver, have no art ; for what they do, they do instinctively ; but relatively to the Supreme Being, they have. And the same is true of all unconscious action : relatively to the doer, it is instinct ; relatively to the First Cause, it is Art. In this sense, recognizing the Spirit which informs Nature, Plato rightly said, " Those things which are said to be done by Nature are indeed done by Divine Art." Art, universally, is the spirit creative. It was defined by Aristotle, " The reason of the thing, without the matter."

If we follow the proper distinction of works according to their aim, we should say, the Spirit, in its creation, aims at use or at beauty, and hence Art divides itself into the Useful and the Fine Arts.

The useful arts comprehend not only those that lie next to instinct, as agriculture, building, weaving, &c., but also navigation, practical chemistry, and the construction of all the grand and delicate tools and instruments by which man serves himself ; as language, the watch, the ship, the decimal cipher ; and also the sciences, so far as they are made serviceable to political economy.

When we reflect on the pleasure we receive from a ship, a railroad, a dry-dock ; or from a picture, a dramatic representation, a statue, a poem, we find that these have not a quite simple, but a blended origin. We find that the question, What is Art? leads us directly to another,— Who is the artist? and the solution of this is the key to the history of Art.

I hasten to state the principle which prescribes, through different means, its firm law to the useful and the beautiful arts. The law is this. The universal soul is the alone crea-

tor of the useful and the beautiful ; therefore, to make anything useful or beautiful, the individual must be submitted to
the universal mind.

In the first place, let us consider this in reference to the
useful arts. Here the omnipotent agent is Nature ; all human
acts are satellites to her orb. Nature is the representative of
the universal mind, and the law becomes this,— that Art must
be a complement to nature, strictly subsidiary. It was said,
in allusion to the great structures of the ancient Romans,—
the aqueducts and bridges,— that "their Art was a Nature
working to municipal ends." That is a true account of all
just works of useful art. Smeaton built Eddystone Light-
house on the model of an oak-tree, as being the form in nature
best designed to resist a constant assailing force. Dollond
formed his achromatic telescope on the model of the human
eye. Duhamel built a bridge by letting in a piece of stronger
timber for the middle of the under surface, getting his hint
from the structure of the shin-bone.

The first and last lesson of the useful arts is, that Nature
tyrannizes over our works. They must be conformed to her
law, or they will be ground to powder by her omnipresent activity. Nothing droll, nothing whimsical will endure. Nature is ever interfering with Art. You cannot build your
house or pagoda as you will, but as you must. There is a
quick bound set to your caprice. The leaning tower can only
lean so far. The verandah or pagoda roof can curve upward
only to a certain point. The slope of your roof is determined
by the weight of snow. It is only within narrow limits that
the discretion of the architect may range : gravity, wind, sun,
rain, the size of men and animals, and such like, have more
to say than he. It is the law of fluids that prescribes the
shape of the boat, — keel, rudder, and bows, — and, in the
finer fluid above, the form and tackle of the sails. Man
seems to have no option about his tools, but merely the necessity to learn from Nature what will fit best, as if he were
fitting a screw or a door. Beneath a necessity thus almighty,
what is artificial in man's life seems insignificant. He seems
to take his task so minutely from intimations of nature, that
his works become as it were hers, and he is no longer free.

But if we work within this limit, she yields us all her
strength. All powerful action is performed by bringing the
forces of nature to bear upon our objects. We do not grind
corn or lift the loom by our own strength, but we build a mill

in such position as to set the north wind to play upon our instrument, or the elastic force of steam, or the ebb and flow of
the sea.   So in our handiwork, we do few things by muscular
force, but we place ourselves in such attitudes as to bring the
force of gravity, that is, the weight of the planet, to bear
upon the spade or the axe we wield.   In short, in all our op-
erations we seek not to use our own, but to bring a quite infinite force to bear.

Let us now consider this law as it affects the works that
have beauty for their end ; that is, the productions of the
Fine Arts.   Here again the prominent fact is subordination
of man.   His art is the least part of his work of art.   A
great deduction is to be made before we can know his proper
contribution to it.

Music, Eloquence, Poetry, Painting, Sculpture, Architecture.
This is a rough enumeration of the Fine Arts.   I omit Rhetoric, which only respects the form of eloquence and poetry.
Architecture and eloquence are mixed arts, whose end is sometimes beauty and sometimes use.

It will be seen that in each of these arts there is much
which is not spiritual.   Each has a material basis, and in each
the creating intellect is crippled in some degree by the stuff
on which it works.   The basis of poetry is language, which is
material only on one side.   It is a demi-god.   But being applied primarily to the common necessities of man, it is not
new-created by the poet for his own ends.

The basis of music is the qualities of the air and the vibrations of sonorous bodies.   The pulsation of a stretched
string or wire gives the ear the pleasure of sweet sound, before yet the musician has enhanced this pleasure by concords
and combinations.

Eloquence, as far as it is a fine art, is modified how much
by the material organization of the orator, the tone of the
voice, the physical strength, the play of the eye and countenance.   All this is so much deduction from the purely spiritual pleasure, — as so much deduction from the merit of
Art, — and is the attribute of Nature.

In painting, bright colors stimulate the eye, before yet they
are harmonized into a landscape.   In sculpture and in architecture, the material, as marble or granite, and in architecture
the mass, are sources of great pleasure, quite independent
of the artificial arrangement.   The art resides in the model, in
the plan ; for it is on that the genius of the artist is expended,

not on the statue or the temple. Just as much better as is the polished statue of dazzling marble than the clay model, or as much more impressive as is the granite cathedral or pyramid than the ground-plan or profile of them on paper, so much more beauty owe they to Nature than to Art.

There is a still larger deduction to be made from the genius of the artist in favor of Nature than I have yet specified.

A jumble of musical sounds on a viol or a flute, in which the rhythm of the tune is played without one of the notes being right, gives pleasure to the unskilful ear. A very coarse imitation of the human form on canvas, or in wax-work, — a coarse sketch in colors of a landscape, in which imitation is all that is attempted, — these things give to unpractised eyes, to the uncultured, who do not ask a fine spiritual delight, almost as much pleasure as a statue of Canova or a picture of Titian. And in the statue of Canova, or the picture of Titian, these give the great part of the pleasure ; they are the basis on which the fine spirit rears a higher delight, but to which these are indispensable.

Another deduction from the genius of the artist is what is conventional in his art, of which there is much in every work of art. Thus how much is there that is not original in every particular building, in every statue, in every tune, painting, poem, or harangue ! — whatever is national or usual ; as the usage of building all Roman churches in the form of a cross, the prescribed distribution of parts of a theatre, the custom of draping a statue in classical costume. Yet who will deny that the merely conventional part of the performance contributes much to its effect ?

One consideration more exhausts, I believe, all the deductions from the genius of the artist in any given work. This is the adventitious. Thus the pleasure that a noble temple gives us is only in part owing to the temple. It is exalted by the beauty of sunlight, the play of the clouds, the landscape around it, its grouping with the houses, trees, and towers in its vicinity. The pleasure of eloquence is in greatest part owing often to the stimulus of the occasion which produces it, — to the magic of sympathy, which exalts the feeling of each by radiating on him the feeling of all.

The effect of music belongs how much to the place, — as the church, or the moonlight walk ; or to the company ; or, if on the stage, to what went before in the play, or to the expectation of what shall come after.

In poetry, "It is tradition more than invention that helps the poet to a good fable." The adventitious beauty of poetry may be felt in the greater delight which a verse gives in happy quotation than in the poem.

It is a curious proof of our conviction that the artist does not feel himself to be the parent of his work, and is as much surprised at the effect as we, that we are so unwilling to impute our best sense of any work of art to the author. The highest praise we can attribute to any writer, painter, sculptor, builder, is, that he actually possessed the thought or feeling with which he has inspired us. We hesitate at doing Spenser so great an honor as to think that he intended by his allegory the sense we affix to it. We grudge to Homer the wide human circumspection his commentators ascribe to him. Even Shakspeare, of whom we can believe everything, we think indebted to Goethe and to Coleridge for the wisdom they detect in his Hamlet and Antony. Especially have we this infirmity of faith in contemporary genius. We fear that Allston and Greenough did not foresee and design all the effect they produce on us.

Our arts are happy hits. We are like the musician on the lake, whose melody is sweeter than he knows, or like a traveller, surprised by a mountain echo, whose trivial word returns to him in romantic thunders.

In view of these facts, I say that the power of Nature predominates over the human will in all works of even the fine arts, in all that respects their material and external circumstances. Nature paints the best part of the picture; carves the best part of the statue; builds the best part of the house; and speaks the best part of the oration. For all the advantages to which I have adverted are such as the artist did not consciously produce. He relied on their aid, he put himself in the way to receive aid from some of them; but he saw that his planting and his watering waited for the sunlight of Nature, or were vain.

Let us proceed to the consideration of the law stated in the beginning of this essay, as it affects the purely spiritual part of a work of art.

As, in useful art, so far as it is useful, the work must be strictly subordinated to the laws of Nature, so as to become a sort of continuation, and in no wise a contradiction of Nature; so, in art that aims at beauty, must the parts be subordinated to Ideal Nature, and everything individual abstracted, so that it shall be the production of the universal soul.

The artist who is to produce a work which is to be admired, not by his friends or his townspeople or his contemporaries, but by all men, and which is to be more beautiful to the eye in proportion to its culture, must disindividualize himself, and be a man of no party, and no manner, and no age, but one through whom the soul of all men circulates, as the common air through his lungs. He must work in the spirit in which we conceive a prophet to speak, or an angel of the Lord to act; that is, he is not to speak his own words, or do his own works, or think his own thoughts, but he is to be an organ through which the universal mind acts.

In speaking of the useful arts, I pointed to the fact that we do not dig, or grind, or hew, by our muscular strength, but by bringing the weight of the planet to bear on the spade, axe, or bar. Precisely analogous to this, in the fine arts, is the manner of our intellectual work. We aim to hinder our individuality from acting. So much as we can shove aside our egotism, our prejudice, and will, and bring the omniscience of reason upon the subject before us, so perfect is the work. The wonders of Shakspeare are things which he saw whilst he stood aside, and then returned to record them. The poet aims at getting observations without aim; to subject to thought things seen without (voluntary) thought.

In eloquence, the great triumphs of the art are, when the orator is lifted above himself; when consciously he makes himself the mere tongue of the occasion and the hour, and says what cannot but be said. Hence the term *abandonment*, to describe the self-surrender of the orator. Not his will, but the principle on which he is horsed, the great connection and crisis of events, thunder in the car of the crowd.

In poetry, where every word is free, every word is necessary. Good poetry could not have been otherwise written than it is. The first time you hear it, it sounds rather as if copied out of some invisible tablet in the Eternal mind, than as if arbitrarily composed by the poet. The feeling of all great poets has accorded with this. They found the verse, not made it. The muse brought it to them.

In sculpture, did ever anybody call the Apollo a fancy piece? Or say of the Laocoon how it might be made different? A masterpiece of art has in the mind a fixed place in the chain of being, as much as a plant or a crystal.

The whole language of men, especially of artists, in reference to this subject, points at the belief that every work of art, in proportion to its excellence, partakes of the precision of fate : no room was there for choice, no play for fancy ; for in the moment, or in the successive moments, when that form was seen, the iron lids of Reason were unclosed, which ordinarily are heavy with slumber. The individual mind became for the moment the vent of the mind of humanity.

There is but one Reason. The mind that made the world is not one mind, but *the* mind. Every man is an inlet to the same, and to all of the same. And every work of art is a more or less pure manifestation of the same. Therefore we arrive at this conclusion, which I offer as a confirmation of the whole view, that the delight which a work of art affords seems to arise from our recognizing in it the mind that formed Nature again in active operation.

It differs from the works of Nature in this, that they are organically reproductive. This is not, but spiritually it is prolific by its powerful action on the intellects of men.

Hence it follows that a study of admirable works of art sharpens our perceptions of the beauty of Nature ; that a certain analogy reigns throughout the wonders of both ; that the contemplation of a work of great art draws us into a state of mind which may be called religious. It conspires with all exalted sentiments.

Proceeding from absolute mind, whose nature is goodness as much as truth, the great works are always attuned to moral nature. If the earth and sea conspire with virtue more than vice, — so do the masterpieces of art. The galleries of ancient sculpture in Naples and Rome strike no deeper conviction into the mind than the contrast of the purity, the severity, expressed in these fine old heads, with the frivolity and grossness of the mob that exhibits and the mob that gazes at them. These are the countenances of the first-born, — the face of man in the morning of the world. No mark is on these lofty features, of sloth, or luxury, or meanness, and they surprise you with a moral admonition, as they speak of nothing around you, but remind you of the fragrant thoughts and the purest resolutions of your youth.

Herein is the explanation of the analogies which exist in all the arts. They are the reappearance of one mind, working in many materials to many temporary ends. Raphael paints wisdom, Handel sings it, Phidias carves it, Shakspeare writes it, Wren builds it, Columbus sails it, Luther preaches it, Washington arms it, Watt mechanizes it. Painting was called "silent poetry;" and poetry, "speaking painting." The laws of each art are convertible into the laws of every other.

Herein we have an explanation of the necessity that reigns in all the kingdom of Art.

Arising out of eternal Reason, one and perfect, whatever is beautiful rests on the foundation of the necessary. Nothing is arbitrary, nothing is insulated in beauty. It depends for ever on the necessary and the useful. The plumage of the bird, the mimic plumage of the insect, has a reason for its rich colors in the constitution of the animal. Fitness is so inseparable an accompaniment of beauty, that it has been taken for it. The most perfect form to answer an end is so far beautiful. We feel, in seeing a noble building, which rhymes well, as we do in hearing a perfect song, that it is spiritually organic; that is, had a necessity, in nature, for being, was one of the possible forms in the Divine mind, and is now only discovered and executed by the artist, not arbitrarily composed by him.

And so every genuine work of art has as much reason for being as the earth and the sun. The gayest charm of beauty has a root in the constitution of things. The Iliad of Homer, the songs of David, the odes of Pindar, the tragedies of Æschylus, the Doric temples, the Gothic cathedrals, the plays of Shakspeare, all and each were made not for sport, but in grave earnest, in tears and smiles of suffering and loving men.

Viewed from this point, the history of Art becomes intelligible, and, moreover, one of the most agreeable studies. We see how each work of art sprang irresistibly from necessity, and, moreover, took its form from the broad hint of Nature. Beautiful in this wise is the obvious origin of all the known orders of architecture; namely, that they were the idealizing of the primitive abodes of each people. There was no wilfulness in the savages in this perpetuating of their first rude abodes. The first form in which they built a house would be the first form of their public and religious edifice also. This form becomes immediately sacred in the eyes of their children, and, as more traditions cluster round it, is imitated with more splendor in each succeeding generation.

In like manner, it has been remarked by Goethe that the granite breaks into parallelopipeds, which broken in two, one part would be an obelisk; that in Upper Egypt the inhabitants would naturally mark a memorable spot by setting up so conspicuous a stone. Again, he suggested, we may see in any stone wall, on a fragment of rock, the projecting veins of harder stone, which have resisted the action of frost and water which has decomposed the rest. This appearance certainly gave the hint of the hieroglyphics inscribed on their obelisk. The amphitheatre of the old Romans, — any one may see its origin who looks at the crowd running together to see any fight, sickness, or odd appearance in the street. The first-comers gather round in a circle; those behind stand on tip-toe; and farther back they climb on fences or window-sills, and so make a cup of which the object of attention occupies the hollow area. The architect put benches in this, and in-closed the cup with a wall, — and, behold a coliseum!

It would be easy to show of many fine things in the world, — in the customs of nations, the etiquette of courts, the con-stitution of governments, — the origin in quite simple local necessities. Heraldry, for example, and the ceremonies of a coronation, are a dignified repetition of the occurrences that might befall a dragoon and his footboy. The College of Cardi-nals were originally the parish priests of Rome. The leaning towers originated from the civil discords which induced every lord to build a tower. Then it became a point of family pride, — and for more pride the novelty of a leaning tower was built.

This strict dependence of Art upon material and ideal Nature, this adamantine necessity which underlies it, has made all its past, and may foreshow its future history. It never was in the power of any man, or any community, to call the arts into being. They come to serve his actual wants, never to please his fancy. These arts have their origin always in some enthusiasm, as love, patriotism, or religion. Who carved the marble? The believing man, who wished to sym-bolize their gods to the waiting Greeks.

The Gothic cathedrals were built when the builder and the priest and the people were overpowered by their faith. Love and fear laid every stone. The Madonnas of Raphael and Titian were made to be worshipped. Tragedy was instituted for the like purpose, and the miracles of music: all sprang out of some genuine enthusiasm, and never out of dilettanteism and holidays. Now they languish, because their purpose is merely exhibition. Who cares, who knows what works of art our government have ordered to be made for the Capitol? They are a mere flourish to please the eye of persons who have associations with books and galleries. But in Greece, the Demos of Athens divided into political factions upon the merits of Phidias.

In this country, at this time, other interests than religion and patriotism are predominant, and the arts, the daughters of enthusiasm, do not flourish. The genuine offspring of our ruling passions we behold. Popular institutions, the school, the reading-room, the telegraph, the post-office, the exchange, the insurance-company, and the immense harvest of economical inventions, are the fruit of the equality and the boundless liberty of lucrative callings. These are superficial wants; and their fruits are these superficial institutions. But as far as they accelerate the end of political freedom and national education, they are preparing the soil of man for fairer flowers and fruits in another age. For beauty, truth, and goodness are not obsolete; they spring eternal in the breast of man; they are as indigenous in Massachusetts as in Tuscany or the Isles of Greece. And that Eternal Spirit, whose triple face they are, moulds from them forever, for his mortal child, images to remind him of the Infinite and Fair.

ELOQUENCE.

ELOQUENCE.

IT is the doctrine of the popular music-masters, that whoever can speak can sing. So, probably, every man is eloquent once in his life. Our temperaments differ in capacity
of heat, or, we boil at different degrees. One man is brought
to the boiling-point by the excitement of conversation in the
parlor. The waters, of course, are not very deep. He has a two-
inch enthusiasm, a patty-pan ebullition. Another requires the
additional caloric of a multitude, and a public debate; a third
needs an antagonist, or a hot indignation; a fourth needs a
revolution; and a fifth, nothing less than the grandeur of
absolute ideas, the splendors and shades of Heaven and Hell.

But because every man is an orator, how long soever he may
have been a mute, an assembly of men is so much more sus-
ceptible. The eloquence of one stimulates all the rest, some
up to the speaking-point, and all others to a degree that makes
them good receivers and conductors, and they avenge themselves for their enforced silence by increased loquacity on their
return to the fireside.

The plight of these phlegmatic brains is better than that of
those who prematurely boil, and who impatiently break silence
before their time. Our county conventions often exhibit a
small-pot-soon-hot style of eloquence. We are too much re-
minded of a medical experiment where a series of patients are
taking nitrous-oxide gas. Each patient, in turn, exhibits
similar symptoms, — redness in the face, volubility, violent
gesticulation, delirious attitudes, occasional stamping, an alarming loss of perception of the passage of time, a selfish enjoyment of his sensations, and loss of perception of the sufferings
of the audience.

Plato says, that the punishment which the wise suffer, who
refuse to take part in the government, is, to live under the

government of worse men ; and the like regret is suggested to all the auditors, as the penalty of abstaining to speak, — that they shall hear worse orators than themselves.

But this lust to speak marks the universal feeling of the energy of the engine, and the curiosity men feel to touch the springs. Of all the musical instruments on which men play, a popular assembly is that which has the largest compass and variety, and out of which, by genius and study, the most wonderful effects can be drawn. An audience is not a simple addition of the individuals that compose it. Their sympathy gives them a certain social organism, which fills each member, in his own degree, and most of all the orator, as a jar in a battery is charged with the whole electricity of the battery. No one can survey the face of an excited assembly, without being apprised of new opportunity for painting in fire human thought, and being agitated to agitate. How many orators sit mute there below ! They come to get justice done to that ear and intuition which no Chatham and no Demosthenes has begun to satisfy.

The Welsh Triads say, " Many are the friends of the golden tongue." Who can wonder at the attractiveness of Parliament, or of Congress, or the bar, for our ambitious young men, when the highest bribes of society are at the feet of the successful orator ? He has his audience at his devotion. All other fames must hush before his. He is the true potentate ; for they are not kings who sit on thrones, but they who know how to govern. The definitions of eloquence describe its attraction for young men. Antiphon the Rhamnusian, one of Plutarch's ten orators, advertised in Athens " that he would cure distempers of the mind with words." No man has a prosperity so high or firm but two or three words can dishearten it. There is no calamity which right words will not begin to redress. Isocrates described his art as " the power of magnifying what was small and diminishing what was great," — an acute but partial definition. Among the Spartans, the art assumed a Spartan shape ; namely, of the sharpest weapon. Socrates says : " If any one wishes to converse with the meanest of the Lacedæmonians, he will at first find him despicable in conversation ; but, when a proper opportunity offers, this same person, like a skilful jaculator, will hurl a sentence worthy of attention, short and contorted, so that he who converses with him will appear to be in no respect superior to a boy." Plato's definition of rhetoric is, "the art of ruling the minds of men." The Koran says, "A mountain may change its place, but a man will not change his disposition"; yet the end of eloquence is, — is it not? — to alter in a pair of hours, perhaps in a half-hour's discourse, the convictions and habits of years. Young men, too, are eager to enjoy this sense of added power and enlarged sympathetic existence. The orator sees himself the organ of a multitude, and concentrating their valors and powers :

> "But now the blood of twenty thousand men
> Blushed in my face."

That which he wishes, that which eloquence ought to reach, is, not a particular skill in telling a story, or neatly summing up evidence, or arguing logically, or dexterously addressing the prejudice of the company, — no, but a taking sovereign possession of the audience. Him we call an artist who shall play on an assembly of men as a master on the keys of the piano, — who, seeing the people furious, shall soften and compose them, shall draw them, when he will, to laughter and to tears. Bring him to his audience, and, be they who they may, — coarse or refined, pleased or displeased, sulky or savage, with their opinions in the keeping of a confessor, or with their opinions in their bank-safes, — he will have them pleased and humored as he chooses ; and they shall carry and execute that which he bids them.

This is that despotism which poets have celebrated in the "Pied Piper of Hamelin," whose music drew like the power of gravitation, — drew soldiers and priests, traders and feasters, women and boys, rats and mice, ; or that of the minstrel of Meudon, who made the pall-bearers dance around the bier. This is a power of many degrees, and requiring in the orator a great range of faculty and experience, requiring a large composite man, such as nature rarely organizes ; so that, in our experience, we are forced to gather up the figure in fragments, here one talent, and there another.

The audience is a constant metre of the orator. There are many audiences in every public assembly, each one of which rules in turn. If anything comic and coarse is spoken, you shall see the emergence of the boys and rowdies, so loud and vivacious that you might think the house was filled with them. If new topics are started, graver and higher, these roisters recede ; a more chaste and wise attention takes place. You would think the boys slept, and that the men have any degree of profoundness. If the speaker utter a noble sentiment, the attention deepens, a new and highest audience now listens, and the audiences of the fun and of facts and of the understanding are all silenced and awed.   There is also something excellent in every audience, — the capacity of virtue. They are ready to be beatified.   They know so much more than the orator, — and are so just !   There is a tablet there for every line he can inscribe, though he should mount to the highest levels.   Humble persons are conscious of new illumination ; narrow brows expand with enlarged affections ; — delicate spirits, long unknown to themselves, masked and muffled in coarsest fortunes, who now hear their own native language for the first time, and leap to hear it.   But all these several audiences, each above each, which successively appear to greet the variety of style and topic, are really composed out of the same persons ; nay, sometimes the same individual will take active part in them all, in turn.

This range of many powers in the consummate speaker, and of many audiences in one assembly, leads us to consider the successive stages of oratory.

Perhaps it is the lowest of the qualities of an orator, but it is, on so many occasions, of chief importance, — a certain robust and radiant physical health ; or, — shall I say? — great volumes of animal heat.   When each orator feels himself to make too large a part of the assembly, and shudders with cold at the thinness of the morning audience, and with fear lest all will heavily fail through one bad speech, mere energy and mellowness are then inestimable.   Wisdom and learning would be harsh and unwelcome, compared with a substantial cordial man, made of milk, as we say, who is a house-warmer, with his obvious honesty and good meaning, and a hue-and-cry style of harangue, which inundates the assembly with a flood of animal spirits, and makes all safe and secure, so that any and every sort of good speaking becomes at once practicable.   I do not rate this animal eloquence very highly ; and yet as we must be fed and warmed before we can do any work well, — even the best, — so is this semi-animal exuberance, like a good stove, of the first necessity in a cold house.

Climate has much to do with it, — climate and race.   Set a New-Englander to describe any accident which happened in his presence.   What hesitation and reserve in his narrative ! He tells with difficulty some particulars, and gets as fast as he can to the result, and, though he cannot describe, hopes to suggest the whole scene.   Now listen to a poor Irishwoman recounting some experience of hers. Her speech flows like a river, — so unconsidered, so humorous, so pathetic, such justice done to all the parts! It is a true transubstantiation, — the fact converted into speech, all warm and colored and alive, as it fell out. Our Southern people are almost all speakers, and have every advantage over the New England people, whose climate is so cold that 't is said we do not like to open our mouths very wide. But neither can the Southerner in the United States, nor the Irish, compare with the lively inhabitant of the south of Europe. The traveller in Sicily needs no gayer melodramatic exhibition than the *table d' hôte* of his inn will afford him in the conversation of the joyous guests. They mimic the voice and manner of the person they describe; they crow, squeal, hiss, cackle, bark, and scream like mad, and, were it only by the physical strength exerted in telling the story, keep the table in unbounded excitement. But in every constitution some large degree of animal vigor is necessary as material foundation for the higher qualities of the art.

But eloquence must be attractive, or it is none. The virtue of books is, to be readable, and of orators, to be interesting; and this is a gift of Nature; as Demosthenes, the most laborious student in that kind, signified his sense of this necessity when he wrote, "Good Fortune," as his motto on his shield. As we know, the power of discourse of certain individuals amounts to fascination, though it may have no lasting effect. Some portion of this sugar must intermingle. The right eloquence needs no bell to call the people together, and no constable to keep them. It draws the children from their play, the old from their arm-chairs, the invalid from his warm chamber : it holds the hearer fast; steals away his feet, that he shall not depart,— his memory, that he shall not remember the most pressing affairs,— his belief, that he shall not admit any opposing considerations. The pictures we have of it in semi-barbarous ages, when it has some advantages in the simpler habit of the people, show what it aims at. It is said that the Khans, or story-tellers, in Ispahan and other cities of the East, attain a controlling power over their audiences, keeping them for many hours attentive to the most fanciful and extravagant adventures. The whole world knows pretty well the style of these improvisators, and how fascinating they are, in our translations of the "Arabian Nights." Scheherezade tells these stories to save her life, and the delight of young Europe and young America in them proves that she fairly earned it.

And who does not remember in childhood some white or black
or yellow Scheherezade, who, by that talent of telling endless
feats of fairies and magicians, and kings and queens, was more
dear and wonderful to a circle of children than any orator in
England or America is now? The more indolent and imaginative complexion of the Eastern nations makes them much more
impressible by these appeals to the fancy.

These legends are only exaggerations of real occurrences, and
every literature contains these high compliments to the art of
the orator and the bard, from the Hebrew and the Greek down
to the Scottish Glenkindie, who

> " harpit a fish out o' saut-water,
> Or water out of a stone,
> Or milk out of a maiden's breast
> Who bairn had never none."

Homer specially delighted in drawing the same figure. For
what is the " Odyssey " but a history of the orator, in the
largest style, carried through a series of adventures furnishing
brilliant opportunities to his talent? See with what care and
pleasure the poet brings him on the stage. Helen is pointing out
to Priam, from a tower, the different Grecian chiefs. "The
old man asked : 'Tell me, dear child, who is that man, shorter
by a head than Agamemnon, yet he looks broader in his
shoulders and breast. His arms lie on the ground, but he,
like a leader, walks about the bands of the men. He seems to
me like a stately ram, who goes as a master of the flock.'
Him answered Helen, daughter of Jove : 'This is the wise
Ulysses, son of Laertes, who was reared in the state of craggy
Ithaca, knowing all wiles and wise counsels.' To her the prudent Antenor replied again : 'O woman, you have spoken
truly. For once the wise Ulysses came hither on an embassy,
with Menelaus, beloved by Mars. I received them, and entertained them at my house. I became acquainted with the
genius and the prudent judgments of both. When they mixed
with the assembled Trojans, and stood, the broad shoulders of
Menelaus rose above the other ; but, both sitting, Ulysses was
more majestic. When they conversed, and interweaved stories
and opinions with all, Menelaus spoke succinctly,— few but
very sweet words, since he was not talkative, nor superfluous
in speech, and was the younger. But when the wise Ulysses
arose, and stood, and looked down, fixing his eyes on the
ground, and neither moved his sceptre backward nor forward,
but held it still, like an awkward person, you would say it was

some angry or foolish man ; but when he sent his great voice forth out of his breast, and his words fell like the winter snows, not then would any mortal contend with Ulysses ; and we, beholding, wondered not afterwards so much at his aspect.' " * Thus he does not fail to arm Ulysses at first with this power of overcoming all opposition by the blandishments of speech. Plutarch tells us that Thucydides, when Archidamus, king of Sparta, asked him which was the best wrestler,— Pericles or he,— replied, " When I throw him, he says he was never down, and he persuades the very spectators to believe him." Philip of Macedon said of Demosthenes, on hearing the report of one of his orations, " Had I been there, he would have persuaded me to take up arms against myself" ; and Warren Hastings said of Burke's speech on his impeachment, " As I listened to the orator, I felt for more than half an hour as if I were the most culpable being on earth."

In these examples, higher qualities have already entered ; but the power of detaining the ear by pleasing speech, and addressing the fancy and imagination, often exists without higher merits. Thus separated, as this fascination of discourse aims only at amusement, though it be decisive in its momentary effect, it is yet a juggle, and of no lasting power. It is heard like a band of music passing through the streets, which converts all the passengers into poets, but is forgotten as soon as it has turned the next corner ; and unless this oiled tongue could, in Oriental phrase, lick the sun and moon away, it must take its place with opium and brandy. I know no remedy against it but cotton-wool, or the wax which Ulysses stuffed into the ears of his sailors to pass the Sirens safely.

There are all degrees of power, and the least are interesting, but they must not be confounded. There is the glib tongue and cool self-possession of the salesman in a large shop, which, as is well known, overpower the prudence and resolution of housekeepers of both sexes. There is a petty lawyer's fluency, which is sufficiently impressive to him who is devoid of that talent, though it be, in so many cases, nothing more than a facility of expressing with accuracy and speed what everybody thinks and says more slowly, without new information, or precision of thought, — but the same thing, neither less nor more. It requires no special insight to edit one of our country newspapers. Yet whoever can say off currently, sentence by sentence, matter neither better nor

* Iliad, III. 191.

worse than what is there printed, will be very impressive to our easily pleased population. These talkers are of that class who prosper, like the celebrated schoolmaster, by being only one lesson ahead of the pupil. Add a little sarcasm, and prompt allusion to passing occurrences, and you have the mischievous member of Congress. A spice of malice, a ruffian touch in his rhetoric, will do him no harm with his audience. These accomplishments are of the same kind, and only a degree higher, than the coaxing of the auctioneer, or the vituperative style well described in the street-word "jawing." These kinds of public and private speaking have their use and convenience to the practitioners; but we may say of such collectively, that the habit of oratory is apt to disqualify them for eloquence.

One of our statesmen said, " The curse of this country is eloquent men." And one cannot wonder at the uneasiness sometimes manifested by trained statesmen, with large experience of public affairs, when they observe the disproportionate advantage suddenly given to oratory over the most solid and accumulated public service. In a Senate or other business committee, the solid result depends on a few men with working talent. They know how to deal with the facts before them, to put things into a practical shape, and they value men only as they can forward the work. But a new man comes there, who has no capacity for helping them at all is insignificant, and nobody in the committee, but has a talent for speaking. In the debate with open doors, this precious person makes a speech, which is printed, and read all over the Union, and he at once becomes famous, and takes the lead in the public mind over all these executive men, who, of course, are full of indignation to find one who has no tact or skill, and knows he has none, put over them by means of this talking-power which they despise.

Leaving behind us these pretensions, better or worse, to come a little nearer to the verity, — eloquence is attractive as an example of the magic of personal ascendancy, — a total and resultant power, rare, because it requires a rich coincidence of powers, intellect, will, sympathy, organs, and, over all, good fortune in the cause. We have a half-belief that the person is possible who can counterpoise all other persons. We believe that there may be a man who is a match for events, — one who never found his match, — against whom other men being dashed are broken, — one of inexhaustible

personal resources, who can give you any odds and beat you.
What we really wish for is a mind equal to any exigency.
You are safe in your rural district, or in the city, in broad
daylight, amidst the police, and under the eyes of a hundred
thousand people. But how is it on the Atlantic, in a storm,
— do you understand how to infuse your reason into men disabled by terror, and to bring yourself off safe then? — how
among thieves, or among an infuriated populace, or among can-
nibals? Face to face with a highwayman who has every temptation and opportunity for violence and plunder, can you
bring yourself off safe by your wit, exercised through speech?
— a problem easy enough to Cæsar or Napoleon. Whenever
a man of that stamp arrives, the highwayman has found a master. What a difference between men in power of face! A
man succeeds because he has more power of eye than another,
and so coaxes or confounds him. The newspapers, every week,
report the adventures of some impudent swindler, who, by
steadiness of carriage, duped those who should have known
better. Yet any swindlers we have known are novices and
bunglers, as is attested by their ill name. A greater power of
face would accomplish anything, and, with the rest of their
takings, take away the bad name. A greater power of carrying the thing loftily, and with perfect assurance, would confound merchant, banker, judge, men of influence and power,
— poet and president, — and might head any party, unseat
any sovereign, and abrogate any constitution in Europe and
America. It was said that a man has at one step attained
vast power, who has renounced his moral sentiment, and settled it with himself that he will no longer stick at anything.
It was said of Sir William Pepperel, one of the worthies of
New England, that, "put him where you might, he commanded, and saw what he willed come to pass." Julius Cæsar
said to Metellus, when that tribune interfered to hinder him
from entering the Roman treasury, "Young man, it is easier
for me to put you to death than to say that I will;" and the
youth yielded. In earlier days he was taken by pirates.
What then? He threw himself into their ship, established
the most extraordinary intimacies, told them stories, declaimed
to them; if they did not applaud his speeches, he threatened
them with hanging, — which he performed afterwards, and in
a short time, was master of all on board. A man this is who
cannot be disconcerted, and so can never play his last card,
but has a reserve of power when he has hit his mark. With

a serene face, he subverts a kingdom. What is told of him is miraculous; it affects men so. The confidence of men in him is lavish, and he changes the face of the world, and histories, poems, and new philosophies arise to account for him. A supreme commander over all his passions and affections; but the secret of his ruling is higher than that. It is the power of Nature running without impediment from the brain and will into the hands. Men and women are his game. Where they are, he cannot be without resource. "Whoso can speak well," said Luther, "is a man." It was men of this stamp that the Grecian States used to ask of Sparta for generals. They did not send to Lacedæmon for troops, but they said, "Send us a commander;" and Pausanias, or Gylippus, or Brasidas, or Agis, was despatched by the Ephors.

It is easy to illustrate this overpowering personality by these examples of soldiers and kings; but there are men of the most peaceful way of life, and peaceful principle, who are felt, wherever they go, as sensibly as a July sun or a December frost, — men who, if they speak, are heard, though they speak in a whisper, — who, when they act, act effectually, and what they do is imitated; and these examples may be found on very humble platforms, as well as on high ones.

In old countries, a high money-value is set on the services of men who have achieved a personal distinction. He who has points to carry must hire, not a skilful attorney, but a commanding person. A barrister in England is reputed to have made thirty or forty thousand pounds *per annum* in representing the claims of railroad companies before committees of the House of Commons. His clients pay not so much for legal as for manly accomplishments, — for courage, conduct, and a commanding social position, which enable him to make their claims heard and respected.

I know very well, that, among our cool and calculating people, where every man mounts guard over himself, where heats and panics and abandonments are quite out of the system, there is a good deal of scepticism as to extraordinary influence. To talk of an overpowering mind rouses the same jealousy and defiance which one may observe round a table where anybody is recounting the marvellous anecdotes of mesmerism. Each auditor puts a final stroke to the discourse by exclaiming, "Can he mesmerize *me*?" So each man inquires if any orator can change *his* convictions.

But does any one suppose himself to be quite impregnable?

Does he think that not possibly a man may come to him who shall persuade him out of his most settled determination?— for example, good sedate citizen as he is, to make a fanatic of him, — or, if he is penurious, to squander money for some purpose he now least thinks of, — or, if he is a prudent, industrious person, to forsake his work, and give days and weeks to a new interest? No, he defies any one, every one. Ah? he is thinking of resistance, and of a different turn from his own. But what if one should come of the same turn of mind as his own, and who sees much farther on his own way than he? A man who has tastes like mine, but in greater power, will rule me any day, and make me love my ruler.

Thus it is not powers of speech that we primarily consider under this word *eloquence*, but the power that, being present, gives them their perfection, and, being absent, leaves them a merely superficial value. Eloquence is the appropriate organ of the highest personal energy. Personal ascendancy may exist with or without adequate talent for its expression. It is as surely felt as a mountain or a planet; but when it is weaponed with a power of speech, it seems first to become truly human, works actively in all directions, and supplies the imagination with fine materials.

This circumstance enters into every consideration of the power of orators, and is the key to all their effects. In the assembly, you shall find the orator and the audience in perpetual balance; and the predominance of either is indicated by the choice of topic. If the talents for speaking exist, but not the strong personality, then there are good speakers who perfectly receive and express the will of the audience, and the commonest populace is flattered by hearing its low mind returned to it with every ornament which happy talent can add. But if there be personality in the orator, the face of things changes. The audience is thrown into the attitude of pupil, follows like a child its preceptor, and hears what he has to say. It is as if, amidst the king's council at Madrid, Ximenes urged that an advantage might be gained of France, and Mendoza that Flanders might be kept down, and Columbus, being introduced, was interrogated whether his geographical knowledge could aid the cabinet, and he can say nothing to one party or to the other, but he can show how all Europe can be diminished and reduced under the king, by annexing to Spain a continent as large as six or seven Europes.

This balance between the orator and the audience is expressed in what is called the pertinence of the speaker. There is always a rivalry between the orator and the occasion, between the demands of the hour and the prepossession of the individual. The emergency which has convened the meeting is usually of more importance than anything the debaters have in their minds, and therefore becomes imperative to them. But if one of them have anything of commanding necessity in his heart, how speedily he will find vent for it, and with the applause of the assembly! This balance is observed in the privatest intercourse. Poor Tom never knew the time when the present occurrence was so trivial that he could tell what was passing in his mind without being checked for unseasonable speech; but let Bacon speak, and wise men would rather listen, though the revolution of kingdoms was on foot. I have heard it reported of an eloquent preacher, whose voice is not yet forgotten in this city, that, on occasions of death or tragic disaster, which overspread the congregation with gloom, he ascended the pulpit with more than his usual alacrity, and, turning to his favorite lessons of devout and jubilant thankfulness, — "Let us praise the Lord," — carried audience, mourners, and mourning along with him, and swept away all the impertinence of private sorrow with his hosannas and songs of praise. Pepys says of Lord Clarendon (with whom "he is mad in love"), on his return from a conference, "I did never observe how much easier a man do speak when he knows all the company to be below him, than in him; for, though he spoke indeed excellent well, yet his manner and freedom of doing it, as if he played with it, and was informing only all the rest of the company, was mighty pretty." *

This rivalry between the orator and the occasion is inevitable, and the occasion always yields to the eminence of the speaker; for a great man is the greatest of occasions. Of course, the interest of the audience and of the orator conspire. It is well with them only when his influence is complete; then only they are well pleased. Especially, he consults his power by making instead of taking his theme. If he should attempt to instruct the people in that which they already know, he would fail; but, by making them wise in that which he knows, he has the advantage of the assembly every moment. Napoleon's tactics of marching on the angle of an army, and always presenting a superiority of numbers, is the orator's secret also.

* Diary, I. 169.

The several talents which the orator employs, the splendid weapons which went to the equipment of Demosthenes, of Æschines, of Demades the natural orator, of Fox, of Pitt, of Patrick Henry, of Adams, of Mirabeau, deserve a special enumeration. We must not quite omit to name the principal pieces.

The orator, as we have seen, must be a substantial personality. Then, first, he must have power of statement, — must have the fact, and know how to tell it. In any knot of men conversing on any subject, the person who knows most about it will have the ear of the company, if he wishes it, and lead the conversation, — no matter what genius or distinction other men there present may have ; and in any public assembly, him who has the facts, and can and will state them, people will listen to, though he is otherwise ignorant, though he is hoarse and ungraceful, though he stutters and screams.

In a court of justice, the audience are impartial ; they really wish to sift the statements and know what the truth is. And in the examination of witnesses there usually leap.out, quite unexpectedly, three or four stubborn words or phrases which are the pith and fate of the business, which sink into the ear of all parties, and stick there, and determine the cause. All the rest is repetition and qualifying ; and the court and the county have really come together to arrive at these three or four memorable expressions, which betrayed the mind and meaning of somebody.

In every company, the man with the fact is like the guide you hire to lead your party up a mountain, or through a difficult country. He may not compare with any of the party in mind, or breeding, or courage, or possessions, but he is much more important to the present need than any of them. That is what we go to the court-house for, — the statement of the fact, and the elimination of a general fact, the real relation of all the parties ; and it is the certainty with which, indifferently in any affair that is well handled, the truth stares us in the face, through all the disguises that are put upon it, — a piece of the well-known human life, — that makes the interest of a court-room to the intelligent spectator.

I remember, long ago, being attracted by the distinction of the counsel, and the local importance of the cause, into the court-room. The prisoner's counsel were the strongest and cunningest lawyers in the Commonwealth. They drove the attorney for the State from corner to corner, taking his reasons

from under him, and reducing him to silence, but not to submission. When hard pressed, he revenged himself, in his turn,
on the judge, by requiring the court to define what salvage
was. The court, thus pushed, tried words, and said everything it could think of to fill the time, supposing cases, and
describing duties of insurers, captains, pilots, and miscellaneous sea-officers that are or might be, — like a schoolmaster
puzzled by a hard sum, who reads the context with emphasis.
But all this flood not serving the cuttle-fish to get away in,
the horrible shark of the district attorney being still there, grim-
ly awaiting with his "The court must define," — the poor court
pleaded its inferiority. The superior court must establish the
law for this, and it read away piteously the decisions of the
Supreme Court, but read to those who had no pity. The
judge was forced at last to rule something, and the lawyers
saved their rogue under the fog of a definition, The parts
were so well cast and discriminated, that it was an interesting
game to watch. The government was well enough represent-
ed. It was stupid, but it had a strong will and possession,
and stood on that to the last. The judge had a task beyond
his preparation, yet his position remained real : he was there
to represent a great reality, — the justice of states, which we
could well enough see beetling over his head, and which his
trifling talk nowise affected, and did not impede, since he was
entirely well-meaning.

The statement of the fact, however, sinks before the statement of the law, which requires immeasurably higher powers,
and is a rarest gift, being in all great masters one and the
same thing, — in lawyers, nothing technical, but always some
piece of common sense, alike interesting to laymen as to clerks.
Lord Mansfield's merit is the merit of common sense. It is
the same quality we admire in Aristotle, Montaigne, Cervantes, or in Samuel Johnson, or Franklin. Its application to law
seems quite accidental. Each of Mansfield's famous decisions
contains a level sentence or two, which hit the mark. His
sentences are not always finished to the eye, but are finished
to the mind. The sentences are involved, but a solid proposition is set forth, a true distinction is drawn. They come from
and they go to the sound of human understanding ; and I read
without surprise that the black-letter lawyers of the day
sneered at his " equitable decisions," as if they were not also
learned. This, indeed, is what speech is for, — to make the
statement; and all that is called eloquence seems to me of lit-

tle use, for the most part, to those who have it, but inestimable to such as have something to say.

Next to the knowledge of the fact and its law is method,
which constitutes the genius and efficiency of all remarkable
men. A crowd of men go up to Faneuil Hall; they are all
pretty well acquainted with the object of the meeting; they
have all read the facts in the same newspapers. The orator
possesses no information which his hearers have not; yet he
teaches them to see the thing with his eyes. By the new
placing, the circumstances acquire new solidity and worth.
Every fact gains consequence by his naming it, and trifles become important. His expressions fix themselves in men's
memories, and fly from mouth to mouth. His mind has some
new principle of order. Where he looks, all things fly into
their places. What will he say next? Let this man speak,
and this man only. By applying the habits of a higher style
of thought to the common affairs of this world, he introduces
beauty and magnificence wherever he goes. Such a power
was Burke's, and of this genius we have had some brilliant
examples in our own political and legal men.

Imagery. The orator must be, to a certain extent, a poet.
We are such imaginative creatures, that nothing so works on
the human mind, barbarous or civil, as a trope. Condense
some daily experience into a glowing symbol, and an audience
is electrified. They feel as if they already possessed some
new right and power over a fact, which they can detach, and
so completely master in thought. It is a wonderful aid to the
memory, which carries away the image, and never loses it. A
popular assembly, like the House of Commons, or the French
Chamber, or the American Congress, is commanded by these
two powers, — first by a fact, then by skill of statement. Put
the argument into a concrete shape, into an image, — some
hard phrase, round and solid as a ball, which they can see and
handle and carry home with them, — and the cause is half
won.

Statement, method, imagery, selection, tenacity of memory,
power of dealing with facts, of illuminating them, of sinking
them by ridicule or by diversion of the mind, rapid generalization, humor, pathos, are keys which the orator holds; and yet
these fine gifts are not eloquence, and do often hinder a man's
attainment of it. And if we come to the heart of the mystery,
perhaps we should say that the truly eloquent man is a sane
man with power to communicate his sanity. If you arm the

man with the extraordinary weapons of this art, give him a
grasp of facts, learning, quick fancy, sarcasm, splendid allusion,
interminable illustration, — all these talents, so potent and
charming, have an equal power to insnare and mislead the
audience and the orator.   His talents are too much for him,
his horses run away with him; and people always perceive
whether you drive, or whether the horses take the bits in their
teeth and run.   But these talents are quite something else
when they are subordinated and serve him; and we go to
Washington, or to Westminster Hall, or might well go round
the world, to see a man who drives, and is not run away with,
— a man who, in prosecuting great designs, has an absolute
command of the means of representing his ideas, and uses them
only to express these; placing facts, placing men; amid the
inconceivable levity of human beings, never for an instant
warped from his erectness.   There is for every man a statement possible of that truth which he is most unwilling to receive, — a statement possible, so broad and so pungent that he
cannot get away from it, but must either bend to it or die of
it.   Else there would be no such word as eloquence, which
means this.   The listener cannot hide from himself that something has been shown him and the whole world, which he did
not wish to see ; and, as he cannot dispose of it, it disposes of
him.   The history of public men and affairs in America will
readily furnish tragic examples of this fatal force.

For the triumphs of the art somewhat more must still be required ; namely, a reinforcing of man from events, so as to
give the double force of reason and destiny.   In transcendent
eloquence, there was ever some crisis in affairs, such as could
deeply engage the man to the cause he pleads, and draw all
this wide power to a point.   For the explosions and eruptions,
there must be accumulations of heat somewhere, beds of ig-
nited anthracite at the centre.   And in cases where profound
conviction has been wrought, the eloquent man is he who is
no beautiful speaker, but who is inwardly drunk with a certain belief.   It agitates and tears him, and perhaps almost
bereaves him of the power of articulation.   Then it rushes
from him as in short abrupt screams, in torrents of meaning.
The possession the subject has of his mind is so entire, that it
insures an order of expression which is the order of Nature
itself, and so the order of greatest force, and inimitable by
any art.   And the main distinction between him and other
well-graced actors is the conviction, communicated by every

word, that his mind is contemplating a whole, and inflamed by the contemplation of the whole, and that the words and sentences uttered by him, however admirable, fall from him as unregarded parts of that terrible whole which he sees, and which he means that you shall see. Add to this concentration a certain regnant calmness, which, in all the tumult, never utters a premature syllable, but keeps the secret of its means and method; and the orator stands before the people as a demoniacal power to whose miracles they have no key. This terrible earnestness makes good the ancient superstition of the hunter, that the bullet will hit its mark which is first dipped in the marksman's blood.

Eloquence must be grounded on the plainest narrative. Afterwards, it may warm itself until it exhales symbols of every kind and color, speaks only through the most poetic forms; but, first and last, it must still be at bottom a biblical statement of fact. The orator is thereby an orator, that he keeps his feet ever on a fact. Thus only is he invincible. No gifts, no graces, no power of wit or learning or illustration, will make any amends for want of this. All audiences are just to this point. Fame of voice or of rhetoric will carry people a few times to hear a speaker; but they soon begin to ask, " What is he driving at ?" and if this man does not stand for anything, he will be deserted. A good upholder of anything which they believe, a fact-speaker of any kind, they will long follow; but a pause in the speaker's own character is very properly a loss of attraction. The preacher enumerates his classes of men, and I do not find my place therein; I suspect, then, that no man does. Everything is my cousin; and whilst he speaks things, I feel that he is touching some of my relations, and I am uneasy; but whilst he deals in words, we are released from attention. If you would lift me, you must be on higher ground. If you would liberate me, you must be free. If you would correct my false view of facts, — hold up to me the same facts in the true order of thought, and I cannot go back from the new conviction.

The power of Chatham, of Pericles, of Luther, rested on this strength of character, which, because it did not and could not fear anybody, made nothing of their antagonists, and became sometimes exquisitely provoking and sometimes terrific to these.

We are slenderly furnished with anecdotes of these men, nor can we help ourselves by those heavy books in which their

discourses are reported. Some of them were writers, like
Burke ; but most of them were not, and no record at all
adequate to their fame remains. Besides what is best is lost,
— the fiery life of the moment. But the conditions for eloquence always exist. It is always dying out of famous places,
and appearing in corners. Wherever the polarities meet,
wherever the fresh moral sentiment, the instinct of freedom
and duty, come in direct opposition to fossil conservatism
and the thirst of gain, the spark will pass. The resistance to
slavery in this country has been a fruitful nursery of orators.
The natural connection by which it drew to itself a train of
moral reforms, and the slight yet sufficient party organization
it offered, reinforced the city with new blood from the woods
and mountains. Wild men, John Baptists, Hermit Peters,
John Knoxes, utter the savage sentiment of Nature in the
heart of commercial capitals. They send us every year some
piece of aboriginal strength, some tough oak-stick of a man
who is not to be silenced or insulted or intimidated by a mob,
because he is more mob than they, — one who mobs the mob,
— some sturdy countryman on whom neither money, nor
politeness, nor hard words, nor eggs, nor blows, nor brickbats,
make any impression. He is fit to meet the bar-room wits
and bullies ; he is a wit and a bully himself, and something
more : he is a graduate of the plough and the stub-hoe, and
the bushwhacker ; knows all the secrets of swamp and snow-
bank, and has nothing to learn of labor or poverty or the
rough of farming. His hard head went through, in childhood,
the drill of Calvinism, with text and mortification, so that he
stands in the New England assembly a purer bit of New England than any, and flings his sarcasms right and left. He has
not only the documents in his pocket to answer all cavils, and
to prove all his positions, but he has the eternal reason in his
head. This man scornfully renounces your civil organizations, — county, or city, or governor, or army, — is his own
navy and artillery, judge and jury, legislature and executive.
He has learned his lessons in a bitter school. Yet, if the
pupil be of a texture to bear it, the best university that can
be recommended to a man of ideas is the gauntlet of the
mobs.

He who will train himself to mastery in this science of
persuasion must lay the emphasis of education, not on popular arts, but on character and insight. Let him see that his
speech is not differenced from action ; that, when he has

spoken, he has not done nothing, nor done wrong, but has cleared his own skirts, has engaged himself to wholesome exertion. Let him look on opposition as opportunity. He cannot be defeated or put down. There is a principle of resurrection in him, an immortality of purpose. Men are averse and hostile to give value to their suffrages. It is not the people that are in fault for not being convinced, but he that cannot convince them. He should mould them, armed as he is with the reason and love which are also the core of their nature. He is not to neutralize their opposition, but he is to convert them into fiery apostles and publishers of the same wisdom.

The highest platform of eloquence is the moral sentiment. It is what is called affirmative truth, and has the property of invigorating the hearer; and it conveys a hint of our eternity, when he feels himself addressed on grounds which will remain when everything else is taken, and which have no trace of time or place or party. Everything hostile is stricken down in the presence of the sentiments; their majesty is felt by the most obdurate. It is observable that, as soon as one acts for large masses, the moral element will and must be allowed for, will and must work; and the men least accustomed to appeal to these sentiments invariably recall them when they address nations. Napoleon, even, must accept and use it as he can.

It is only to these simple strokes that the highest power belongs, — when a weak human hand touches, point by point, the eternal beams and rafters on which the whole structure of Nature and society is laid. In this tossing sea of delusion we feel with our feet the adamant; in this dominion of chance, we find a principle of permanence. For I do not accept that definition of Isocrates, that the office of his art is, to make the great small and the small great; but I esteem this to be its perfection, — when the orator sees through all masks to the eternal scale of truth, in such sort that he can hold up before the eyes of men the fact of to-day steadily to that standard, thereby making the great great, and the small small, which is the true way to astonish and to reform mankind.

All the chief orators of the world have been grave men, relying on this reality. One thought the philosophers of Demosthenes's own time found running through all his orations, — this namely, that "virtue secures its own success." "To

3*

stand on one's own feet" Heeren finds the key-note to the
discourses of Demosthenes, as of Chatham.

Eloquence, like every other art, rests on laws the most exact and determinate. It is the best speech of the best soul.
It may well stand as the exponent of all that is grand and
immortal in the mind. If it do not so become an instrument,
but aspires to be somewhat of itself, and to glitter for show,
it is false and weak. In its right exercise, it is an elastic,
unexhausted power, — who has sounded, who has estimated
it?— expanding with the expansion of our interests and affections. Its great masters, whilst they valued every help to its
attainment, and thought no pains too great which contributed
in any manner to further it; — resembling the Arabian war-
rior of fame, who wore seventeen weapons in his belt, and in
personal combat used them all occasionally; — yet subordinated all means; never permitted any talent — neither voice,
rhythm, poetic power, anecdote, sarcasm — to appear for
show; but were grave men, who preferred their integrity to
their talent, and esteemed that object for which they toiled,
whether the prosperity of their country, or the laws, or a ref-
ormation, or liberty of speech or of the press, or letters, or
morals, as above the whole world, and themselves also.

DOMESTIC LIFE.

DOMESTIC LIFE.

THE perfection of the providence for childhood is easily acknowledged. The care which covers the seed of the tree under tough husks and stony cases provides for the human plant the mother's breast and the father's house. The size of the nestler is comic, and its tiny beseeching weakness is compensated perfectly by the happy patronizing look of the mother, who is a sort of high reposing Providence toward it. Welcome to the parents the puny struggler, strong in his weakness, his little arms more irresistible than the soldier's, his lips touched with persuasion which Chatham and Pericles in manhood had not. His unaffected lamentations when he lifts up his voice on high, or, more beautiful, the sobbing child, — the face all liquid grief, as he tries to swallow his vexation, — soften all hearts to pity, and to mirthful and clamorous compassion. The small despot asks so little that all reason and all nature are on his side. His ignorance is more charming than all knowledge, and his little sins more bewitching than any virtue. His flesh is angels' flesh, all alive. "Infancy," said Coleridge, "presents body and spirit in unity: the body is all animated." All day, between his three or four sleeps, he coos like a pigeon-house, sputters and spurs, and puts on his faces of importance; and when he fasts, the little Pharisee fails not to sound his trumpet before him. By lamplight he delights in shadows on the wall; by daylight in yellow and scarlet. Carry him out of doors, — he is overpowered by the light and by the extent of natural objects, and is silent. Then presently begins his use of his fingers, and he studies power, the lesson of his race. First it appears in no great harm, in architectural tastes. Out of blocks, threadspools, cards, and checkers, he will build his pyramid with the gravity of Palladio. With an acoustic apparatus of whistle and rattle he explores the laws of sound. But chiefly, like his senior countrymen, the young American studies new and speedier modes of transportation. Mistrusting the cunning of his small legs, he wishes to ride on the necks and shoulders of all flesh. The small enchanter nothing can withstand, — no seniority of age, no gravity of character; uncles, aunts, grandsires, grandams, fall an easy prey: he conforms to nobody, all conform to him; all caper and make mouths, and babble, and chirrup to him. On the strongest shoulders he rides, and pulls the hair of laurelled heads.

"The childhood," says Milton, "shows the man, as morning shows the day." The child realizes to every man his own earliest remembrance, and so supplies a defect in our education, or enables us to live over the unconscious history with a sympathy so tender as to be almost personal experience.

Fast — almost too fast for the wistful curiosity of the parents, studious of the witchcraft of curls and dimples and broken words — the little talker grows to a boy. He walks daily among wonders: fire, light, darkness, the moon, the stars, the furniture of the house, the red tin horse, the domestics, who like rude foster-mothers befriend and feed him, the faces that claim his kisses, are all in turn absorbing; yet warm, cheerful, and with good appetite the little sovereign subdues them without knowing it; the new knowledge is taken up into the life of to-day and becomes the means of more. The blowing rose is a new event; the garden full of flowers is Eden over again to the small Adam; the rain, the ice, the frost, make epochs in his life. What a holiday is the first snow in which Twoshoes can be trusted abroad!

What art can paint or gild any object in afterlife with the glow which Nature gives to the first baubles of childhood! St. Peter's cannot have the magical power over us that the red and gold covers of our first picture-book possessed. How the imagination cleaves to the warm glories of that tinsel even now! What entertainments make every day bright and short for the fine freshman! The street is old as Nature; the persons all have their sacredness. His imaginative life dresses all things in their best. His fears adorn the dark parts with poetry. He has heard of wild horses and of bad boys, and with a pleasing terror he watches at his gate for the passing of those varieties of each species. The first ride into the country, the first bath in running water, the first time the skates are put on, the first game out of doors in moonlight, the books of

the nursery, are new chapters of joy. The "Arabian Nights'
Entertainments," the "Seven Champions of Christendom,"
"Robinson Crusoe," and the "Pilgrim's Progress,"— what
mines of thought and emotion, what a wardrobe to dress the
whole world withal, are in this encyclopædia of young thinking! And so by beautiful traits, which, without art, yet seem
the masterpiece of wisdom, provoking the love that watches
and educates him, the little pilgrim prosecutes the journey
through nature which he has thus gayly begun. He grows up
the ornament and joy of the house, which rings to his glee, to
rosy boyhood.

The household is the home of the man, as well as of the
child. The events that occur therein are more near and affecting to us than those which are sought in senates and
academies. Domestic events are certainly our affair. What
are called public events may or may not be ours. If a man
wishes to acquaint himself with the real history of the world,
with the spirit of the age, he must not go first to the state-
house or the court-room. The subtle spirit of life must be
sought in facts nearer. It is what is done and suffered in the
house, in the constitution, in the temperament, in the personal
history, that has the profoundest interest for us. Fact is better than fiction, if only we could get pure fact. Do you think
any rhetoric or any romance would get your ear from the wise
gypsy who could tell straight on the real fortunes of the man;
who could reconcile your moral character and your natural
history; who could explain your misfortunes, your fevers, your
debts, your temperament, your habits of thought, your tastes,
and, in every explanation, not sever you from the whole, but
unite you to it? Is it not plain that not in senates, or courts,
or chambers of commerce, but in the dwelling-house must the
true character and hope of the time be consulted? These
facts are, to be sure, harder to read. It is easier to count the
census, or compute the square extent of a territory, to criticise
its polity, books, art, than to come to the persons and dwellings of men, and read their character and hope in their way of
life. Yet we are always hovering round this better divination.
In one form or another, we are always returning to it. The
physiognomy and phrenology of to-day are rash and mechanical systems enough, but they rest on everlasting foundations.
We are sure that the sacred form of man is not seen in these
whimsical, pitiful, and sinister masks (masks which we wear
and which we meet), these bloated and shrivelled bodies, bald

heads, bead eyes, short winds, puny and precarious healths, and early deaths. We live ruins amidst ruins. The great facts are the near ones. The account of the body is to be sought in the mind. The history of your fortunes is written first in your life.

Let us come, then, out of the public square, and enter the domestic precinct. Let us go to the sitting-room, the table-talk, and the expenditure of our contemporaries. An increased consciousness of the soul, you say, characterizes the period. Let us see if it has not only arranged the atoms at the circumference, but the atoms at the core. Does the household obey an idea? Do you see the man,—his form, genius, and aspiration,—in his economy? Is that translucent, thorough-lighted? There should be nothing confounding and conventional in economy, but the genius and love of the man so conspicuously marked in all his estate, that the eye that knew him should read his character in his property, in his grounds, in his ornaments, in every expense. A man's money should not follow the direction of his neighbor's money, but should represent to him the things he would willingliest do with it. I am not one thing and my expenditure another. My expenditure is me. That our expenditure and our character are twain, is the vice of society.

We ask the price of many things in shops and stalls, but some things each man buys without hesitation, if it were only letters at the post-office, conveyance in carriages and boats, tools for his work, books that are written to his condition, etc. Let him never buy anything else than what he wants, never subscribe at others' instance, never give unwillingly. Thus a scholar is a literary foundation. All his expense is for Aristotle, Fabricius, Erasmus, and Petrarch. Do not ask him to help with his savings young drapers or grocers to stock their shops, or eager agents to lobby in legislatures, or join a company to build a factory or a fishing-craft. These things are also to be done, but not by such as he. How could such a book as Plato's Dialogues have come down, but for the sacred savings of scholars and their fantastic appropriation of them.

Another man is a mechanical genius, an inventor of looms, a builder of ships,—a ship-building foundation, and could achieve nothing if he should dissipate himself on books or on horses. Another is a farmer,—an agricultural foundation; another is a chemist,—and the same rule holds for all. We must not make believe with our money, but spend heartily, and buy *up* and not *down*.

I am afraid that, so considered, our houses will not be found to have unity, and to express the best thought. The household, the calling, the friendships, of the citizens are not homogeneous. His house ought to show us his honest opinion of what makes his well-being when he rests among his kindred, and forgets all affectation, compilance, and even exertion of will. He brings home whatever commodities and ornaments have for years allured his pursuit, and his character must be seen in them. But what idea predominates in our houses? Thrift first, then convenience and pleasure. Take off all the roofs, from street to street, and we shall seldom find the temple of any higher god than Prudence. The progress of domestic living has been in cleanliness, in ventilation, in health, in decorum, in countless means and arts of comfort, in the concentration of all the utilities of every clime in each house. They are arranged for low benefits. The houses of the rich are confectioners' shops, where we get sweetmeats and wine ; the houses of the poor are imitations of these to the extent of their ability. With these ends housekeeping is not beautiful; it cheers and raises neither the husband, the wife, nor the child ; neither the host, nor the guest; it oppresses women. A house kept to the end of prudence is laborious without joy; a house kept to the end of display is impossible to all but a few women, and their success is dearly bought.

If we look at this matter curiously, it becomes dangerous. We need all the force of an idea to lift this load; for the wealth and multiplication of conveniences embarrass us, especially in northern climates. The shortest enumeration of our wants in this rugged climate appalls us by the multitude of things not easy to be done. And if you look at the multitude of particulars, one would say : Good housekeeping is impossible ; order is too precious a thing to dwell with men and women. See, in families where there is both substance and taste, at what expense any favorite punctuality is maintained. If the children, for example, are considered, dressed, dieted, attended, kept in proper company, schooled, and at home fostered by the parents, — then does the hospitality of the house suffer ; friends are less carefully bestowed, the daily table less catered. If the hours of meals are punctual, the apartments are slovenly. If the linens and hangings are clean and fine, and the furniture good, the yard, the garden, the

E

fences, are neglected. If all are well attended, then must the
master and mistress be studious of particulars at the cost of
their own accomplishments and growth, — or persons are
treated as things.

The difficulties to be overcome must be freely admitted ;
they are many and great. Nor are they to be disposed of by
any criticism or amendment of particulars taken one at a
time, but only by the arrangement of the household to a
higher end than those to which our dwellings are usually built
and furnished. And is there any calamity more grave, or
that more invokes the best good-will to remove it, than this ?
—• to go from chamber to chamber, and see no beauty ; to
find in the housemates no aim ; to hear an endless chatter
and blast ; to be compelled to criticise ; to hear only to dissent and to be disgusted ; to find no invitation to what is
good in us, and no receptacle for what is wise ; — this is a
great price to pay for sweet bread and warm lodging, — being
defrauded of affinity, of repose, of genial culture, and the in-
most presence of beauty.

It is a sufficient accusation of our ways of living, and certainly ought to open our ear to every good-minded reformer,
that our idea of domestic well-being now needs wealth to execute it. Give me the means, says the wife, and your house
shall not annoy your taste nor waste your time. On hearing
this, we understand how these Means have come to be so
omnipotent on earth. And indeed the love of wealth seems
to grow chiefly out of the root of the love of the beautiful.
The desire of gold is not for gold. It is not the love of much
wheat and wool and household-stuff. It is the means of freedom
and benefit. We scorn shifts ; we desire the elegance of
munificence ; we desire at least to put no stint or limit on
our parents, relatives, guests, or dependents ; we desire to
play the benefactor and the prince with our townsmen, with
the stranger at the gate, with the bard, or the beauty, with
the man or woman of worth, who alights at our door. How
can we do this, if the wants of each day imprison us in lucrative labors, and constrain us to a continual vigilance lest we
be betrayed into expense ?

Give us wealth, and the home shall exist. But that is a very
imperfect and inglorious solution of the problem, and therefore no solution. " *Give us wealth.*" You ask too much.
Few have wealth ; but all must have a home. Men are not
born rich ; and in getting wealth, the man is generally sacri-

ficed, and often is sacrificed without acquiring wealth at last.
Besides, that cannot be the right answer; — there are objections to wealth. Wealth is a shift. The wise man angles
with himself only, and with no meaner bait. Our whole use
of wealth needs revision and reform. Generosity does not
consist in giving money or money's worth. These so-called
goods are only the shadow of good. To give money to a sufferer
is only a come-off. It is only a postponement of the real
payment, a bribe paid for silence, — a credit-system in which
a paper promise to pay answers for the time instead of liqui-
dation. We owe to man higher succors than food and fire.
We owe to man man. If he is sick, is unable, is mean-spirited
and odious, it is because there is so much of his nature which
is unlawfully withholden from him. He should be visited in
this his prison with rebuke to the evil demons, with manly en-
couragement, with no mean-spirited offer of condolence because
you have not money, or mean offer of money as the utmost
benefit, but by your heroism, your purity, and your faith.
You are to bring with you that spirit which is understanding,
health and self-help. To offer him money in lieu of these is
to do him the same wrong as when the bridegroom offers his
betrothed virgin a sum of money to release him from his engage-
ments. The great depend on their heart, not on their purse.
Genius and virtue, like diamonds, are best plain-set, — set in
lead, set in poverty. The greatest man in history was the
poorest. How was it with the captains and sages of Greece
and Rome, with Socrates, with Epaminondas? Aristides was
made general receiver of Greece, to collect the tribute which
each state was to furnish against the barbarian. "Poor,"
says Plutarch, "when he set about it, poorer when he had
finished it." How was it with Æmilius and Cato? What
kind of house was kept by Paul and John, — by Milton and
Marvell, — by Samuel Johnson, — by Samuel Adams in Boston, and Jean Paul Richter at Baireuth?

I think it plain that this voice of communities and ages,
"Give us wealth, and the good household shall exist," is
vicious, and leaves the whole difficulty untouched. It is better,
certainly, in this form, "Give us your labor, and the household begins." I see now how serious labor, the labor of all
and every day, is to be avoided ; and many things betoken a
revolution of opinion and practice in regard to manual labor
that may go far to aid our practical inquiry. Another age
may divide the manual labor of the world more equally on all

the members of society, and so make the labors of a few hours
avail to the wants and add to the vigor of the man.   But the
reform that applies itself to the household must not be partial.   It must correct the whole system of our social living.
It must come with plain living and high thinking; it must
break up caste, and put domestic service on another foundation.   It must come in connection with a true acceptance by
each man of his vocation, — not chosen by his parents or
friends, but by his genius, with earnestness and love.

Nor is this redress so hopeless as it seems.   Certainly, if
we begin by reforming particulars of our present system, correcting a few evils and letting the rest stand, we shall soon
give up in despair.   For our social forms are very far from
truth and equity.   But the way to set the axe at the root of
the tree, is to raise our aim.   Let us understand, then, that a
house should bear witness in all its economy that human culture is the end to which it is built and garnished.   It stands
there under the sun and moon to ends analogous and not less
noble than theirs.   It is not for festivity, it is not for sleep:
but the pine and the oak shall gladly descend from the mountains to uphold the roof of men as faithful and necessary as
themselves; to be the shelter always open to good and true
persons; — a hall which shines with sincerity, brows ever
tranquil, and a demeanor impossible to disconcert; whose in-
mates know what they want; who do not ask your house how
theirs should be kept.   They have aims: they cannot pause
for trifles.   The diet of the house does not create its order,
but knowledge, character, action, absorb so much life and yield
so much entertainment that the refectory has ceased to be so
curiously studied.   With a change of aim has followed a
change of the whole scale by which men and things were wont
to be measured.   Wealth and poverty are seen for what they
are.   It begins to be seen that the poor are only they who
feel poor, and poverty consists in feeling poor.   The rich, as
we reckon them, and among them the very rich, in a true
scale would be found very indigent and ragged.   The great
make us feel, first of all, the indifference of circumstances.
They call into activity the higher perceptions, and subdue the
low habits of comfort and luxury; but the higher perceptions
find their objects everywhere: only the low habits need
palaces and banquets.

Let a man, then, say, My house is here in the county, for
the culture of the county; — an eating-house and sleeping-

house for travellers it shall be, but it shall be much more. I
pray you, O excellent wife, not to cumber yourself and me to
get a rich dinner for this man or this woman who has alighted
at our gate, nor a bedchamber made ready at too great a cost.
These things, if they are curious in, they can get for a dollar
at any village. But let this stranger, if he will, in your looks,
in your accent and behavior, read your heart and earnestness,
your thought and will, which he cannot buy at any price, in
any village or city, and which he may well travel fifty miles,
and dine sparely and sleep hard, in order to behold. Certainly,
let the board be spread and let the bed be dressed for the
traveller; but let not the emphasis of hospitality lie in these
things. Honor to the house where they are simple to the
verge of hardship, so that there the intellect is awake and
reads the laws of the universe, the soul worships truth and
love, honor and courtesy flow into all deeds.

There was never a country in the world which could so
easily exhibit this heroism as ours; never any where the
State has made such efficient provision for popular education,
where intellectual entertainment is so within reach of youthful
ambition. The poor man's son is educated. There is many a
humble house in every city, in every town, where talent and
taste, and sometimes genius, dwell with poverty and labor.
Who has not seen, and who can see unmoved, under a low
roof, the eager, blushing boys discharging as they can their
household chores, and hastening into the sitting-room to the
study of to-morrow's merciless lesson, yet stealing time to
read one chapter more of the novel hardly smuggled into the
tolerance of father and mother, — atoning for the same by
some pages of Plutarch or Goldsmith; the warm sympathy
with which they kindle each other in school-yard, or in barn
or wood-shed, with scraps of poetry or song, with phrases of
the last oration, or mimicry of the orator; the youthful criticism, on Sunday, of the sermons; the school declamation
faithfully rehearsed at home, sometimes to the fatigue, sometimes to the admiration of sisters; the first solitary joys of
literary vanity, when the translation or the theme has been
completed, sitting alone near the top of the house; the cautious comparison of the attractive advertisement of the arrival
of Macready, Booth, or Kemble, or of the discourse of a well-
known speaker, with the expense of the entertainment; the
affectionate delight with which they greet the return of each
one after the early separations which school or business re-

quire; the foresight with which, during such absences, they
hive the honey which opportunity offers, for the ear and imagination of the others; and the unrestrained glee with which
they disburden themselves of their early mental treasures
when the holidays bring them again together? What is the
hoop that holds them stanch? It is the iron band of poverty,
of necessity, of austerity, which, excluding them from the sensual enjoyments which make other boys too early old, has
directed their activity in safe and right channels, and made
them, despite themselves, reverers of the grand, the beautiful,
and the good. Ah! short-sighted students of books, of Nature,
and of man! too happy, could they know their advantages.
They pine for freedom from that mild parental yoke; they
sigh for fine clothes, for rides, for the theatre, and premature
freedom and dissipation, which others possess. Woe to them,
if their wishes were crowned! The angels that dwell with
them, and are weaving laurels of life for their youthful brows,
are Toil, and Want, and Truth, and Mutual Faith.

In many parts of true economy a cheering lesson may be
learned from the mode of life and manners of the later Romans,
as described to us in the letters of the younger Pliny. Nor
can I resist the temptation of quoting so trite an instance as
the noble housekeeping of Lord Falkland in Clarendon : "His
house being within little more than ten miles from Oxford, he
contracted familiarity and friendship with the most polite and
accurate men of that University, who found such an immense-
ness of wit, and such a solidity of judgment in him, so infinite
a fancy, bound in by a most logical ratiocination, such a vast
knowledge that he was not ignorant in any thing, yet such an
excessive humility, as if he had known nothing, that they frequently resorted and dwelt with him, as in a college situated
in a purer air; so that his house was a university in a less
volume, whither they came, not so much for repose as study,
and to examine and refine those grosser propositions which
laziness and consent made current in vulgar conversation."

I honor that man whose ambition it is, not to win laurels in
the state or the army, not to be a jurist or a naturalist, not
to be a poet or a commander, but to be a master of living
well, and to administer the offices of master or servant, of
husband, father, and friend. But it requires as much breadth
of power for this as for those other functions, — as much, or
more, — and the reason for the failure is the same. I think
the vice of our housekeeping is, that it does not hold man

sacred. The vice of government, the vice of education, the vice of religion, is one with that of private life.

In the old fables, we used to read of a cloak brought from fairy-land as a gift for the fairest and purest in Prince Arthur's court. It was to be her prize whom it would fit. Every one was eager to try it on, but it would fit nobody: for one it was a world too wide, for the next it dragged on the ground, and for the third it shrunk to a scarf. They, of course, said that the devil was in the mantle, for really the truth was in the mantle, and was exposing the ugliness which each would fain conceal. All drew back with terror from the garment. The innocent Genelas alone could wear it. In like manner, every man is provided in his thought with a measure of man which he applies to every passenger. Unhappily, not one in many thousands comes up to the stature and proportions of the model. Neither does the measurer himself, neither do the people in the street; neither do the select individuals whom he admires, — the heroes of the race. When he inspects them critically, he discovers that their aims are low, that they are too quickly satisfied. He observes the swiftness with which life culminates, and the humility of the expectations of the greatest part of men. To each occurs, soon after the age of puberty, some event, or society, or way of living, which becomes the crisis of life, and the chief fact in their history. In woman, it is love and marriage (which is more reasonable); and yet it is pitiful to date and measure all the facts and sequel of an unfolding life from such a youthful, and generally inconsiderate, period as the age of courtship and marriage. In men, it is their place of education, choice of an employment, settlement in a town, or removal to the East or to the West, or some other magnified trifle, which makes the meridian moment, and all the after years and actions only derive interest from their relation to that. Hence it comes that we soon catch the trick of each man's conversation, and, knowing his two or three main facts, anticipate what he thinks of each new topic that rises. It is scarcely less perceivable in educated men, so called, than in the uneducated. I have seen finely endowed men at college festivals, ten, twenty years after they had left the halls, returning, as it seemed, the same boys who went away. The same jokes pleased, the same straws tickled; the manhood and offices they brought thither at this return seemed mere ornamental masks: underneath they were boys yet. We never come to be citizens of the world, but are still villagers, who think that every thing in their petty town is a little superior to the same thing anywhere else. In each the circumstance signalized differs, but in each it is made the coals of an ever-burning egotism. In one, it was his going to sea; in a second, the difficulties he combated in going to college; in a third, his journey to the West, or his voyage to Canton; in a fourth, his coming out of the Quaker Society; in a fifth, his new diet and regimen; in a sixth, his coming forth from the abolition organizations; and in a seventh, his going into them. It is a life of toys and trinkets. We are too easily pleased.

I think this sad result appears in the manners. The men we see in each other do not give us the image and likeness of man. The men we see are whipped through the world; they are harried, wrinkled, anxious; they all seem the hacks of some invisible riders. How seldom do we behold tranquillity! We have never yet seen a man. We do not know the majestic manners that belong to him, which appease and exalt the beholder. There are no divine persons with us, and the multitude do not hasten to be divine. And yet we hold fast, all our lives long, a faith in a better life, in better men, in clean and noble relations, notwithstanding our total inexperience of a true society. Certainly, this was not the intention of nature, to produce, with all this immense expenditure of means and power, so cheap and humble a result. The aspirations in the heart after the good and true teach us better, — nay, the men themselves suggest a better life.

Every individual nature has its own beauty. One is struck in every company, at every fireside, with the riches of nature, when he hears so many new tones, all musical, sees in each person original manners, which have a proper and peculiar charm, and reads new expressions of face. He perceives that nature has laid for each the foundations of a divine building, if the soul will build thereon. There is no face, no form, which one cannot in fancy associate with great power of intellect or with generosity of soul. In our experience, to be sure, beauty is not, as it ought to be, the dower of man and of woman as invariably as sensation. Beauty is, even in the beautiful, occasional, — or, as one has said, culminating and perfect only a single moment, before which it is unripe, and after which it is on the wane. But beauty is never quite absent from our eyes. Every face, every figure, suggests its own right and sound estate. Our friends are not their own highest form.

But let the hearts they have agitated witness what power has lurked in the traits of these structures of clay that pass and repass us! The secret power of form over the imagination and affections transcends all our philosophy. The first glance we meet may satisfy us that matter is the vehicle of higher powers than its own, and that no laws of line or surface can ever account for the inexhaustible expressiveness of form. We see heads that turn on the pivot of the spine, — no more; and we see heads that seem to turn on a pivot as deep as the axle of the world, — so slow, and lazily, and great, they move. We see on the lip of our companion, the presence or absence of the great masters of thought and poetry to his mind. We read in his brow, on meeting him after many years, that he is where we left him, or that he has made great strides.

Whilst thus nature and the hints we draw from man suggest a true and lofty life, a household equal to the beauty and grandeur of this world, especially we learn the same lesson from those best relations to individual men which the heart is always prompting us to form. Happy will that house be in which the relations are formed from character, after the highest, and not after the lowest order; the house in which character marries, and not confusion and a miscellany of unavowable motives. Then shall marriage be a covenant to secure to either party the sweetness and honor of being a calm, continuing, inevitable benefactor to the other. Yes, and the sufficient reply to the sceptic who doubts the competence of man to elevate and to be elevated is in that desire and power to stand in joyful and ennobling intercourse with individuals, which makes the faith and the practice of all reasonable men.

The ornament of a house is the friends who frequent it. There is no event greater in life than the appearance of new persons about our hearth, except it be the progress of the character which draws them. It has been finely added by Landor to his definition of the *great man*, "It is he who can call together the most select company when it pleases him." A verse of the old Greek Menander remains, which runs in translation : —

> "Not on the store of sprightly wine,
> Nor plenty of delicious meats,
> Though generous Nature did design
> To court us with perpetual treats, —
> 'T is not on these we for content depend,
> So much as on the shadow of a friend."

It is the happiness which, where it is truly known, post-pones all other satisfactions, and makes politics and commerce and churches cheap. For we figure to ourselves, — do we not? — that when men shall meet as they should, as states meet, — each a benefactor, a shower of falling stars, so rich with deeds, with thoughts, with so much accomplishment, — it shall be the festival of nature, which all things symbolize ; and perhaps Love is only the highest symbol of Friendship, as all other things seem symbols of love. In the progress of each man's character, his relations to the best men, which at first seem only the romances of youth, acquire a graver importance ; and he will have learned the lesson of life who is skilful in the ethics of friendship.

Beyond its primary ends of the conjugal, parental, and ami-cable relations, the household should cherish the beautiful arts and the sentiment of veneration.

1. Whatever brings the dweller into a finer life, what edu-cates his eye, or ear, or hand, whatever purifies and enlarges him, may well find place there. And yet let him not think that a property in beautiful objects is necessary to his appre-hension of them, and seek to turn his house into a museum. Rather let the noble practice of the Greeks find place in our society, and let the creations of the plastic arts be collected with care in galleries by the piety and taste of the people, and yielded as freely as the sunlight to all. Meantime, be it re-membered, we are artists ourselves, and competitors, each one, with Phidias and Raphael in the production of what is graceful or grand. [The fountain of beauty is the heart, and every generous thought illustrates the walls of your cham-ber.] Why should we owe our power of attracting our friends to pictures and vases, to cameos and architecture? Why should we convert ourselves into showmen and appendages to our fine houses and our works of art? If by love and nobleness we take up into ourselves the beauty we admire, we shall spend it again on all around us. The man, the woman, needs not the embellishment of canvas and marble, whose every act is a subject for the sculptor, and to whose eye the gods and nymphs never appear ancient ; for they know by heart the whole instinct of majesty.

I do not undervalue the fine instruction which statues and pictures give. But I think the public museum in each town will one day relieve the private house of this charge of owning

and exhibiting them. I go to Rome and see on the walls of
the Vatican the Transfiguration, painted by Raphael, reckoned
the first picture in the world ; or in the Sistine Chapel I see
the grand sibyls and prophets, painted in fresco by Michael
Angelo, — which have every day now for three hundred years
inflamed the imagination and exalted the piety of what vast
multitudes of men of all nations ! I wish to bring home to
my children and my friends copies of these admirable forms,
which I can find in the shops of the engravers ; but I do not
wish the vexation of owning them. I wish to find in my own
town a library and museum which is the property of the town,
where I can deposit this precious treasure, where I and my
children can see it from time to time, and where it has its
proper place among hundreds of such donations from other
citizens who have brought thither whatever articles they have
judged to be in their nature rather a public than a private
property.

A collection of this kind, the property of each town, would
dignify the town, and we should love and respect our neighbors more. Obviously, it would be easy for every town to
discharge this truly municipal duty. Every one of us would
gladly contribute his share ; and the more gladly, the more
considerable the institution had become.

2. Certainly, not aloof from this homage to beauty, but in
strict connection therewith, the house will come to be esteemed
a Sanctuary. The language of a ruder age has given to common law the maxim that every man's house is his castle : the
progress of truth will make every house a shrine. Will not
man one day open his eyes and see how dear he is to the soul
of Nature, — how near it is to him ? Will he not see, through
all he miscalls accident, that Law prevails for ever and ever ;
that his private being is a part of it ; that its home is in his
own unsound heart ; that his economy, his labor, his good and
bad fortune, his health and manners, are all a curious and
exact demonstration in miniature of the genius of the Eternal
Providence ? When he perceives the Law, he ceases to despond. Whilst he sees it, every thought and act is raised, and
becomes an act of religion. Does the consecration of Sunday
confess the desecration of the entire week ? Does the consecration of the church confess the profanation of the house ?
Let us read the incantation backward. Let the man stand on
his feet. Let religion cease to be occasional ; and the pulses

of thought that go to the borders of the universe, let them proceed from the bosom of the Household.

These are the consolations, — these are the ends to which the household is instituted and the rooftree stands. If these are sought, and in any good degree attained, can the State, can commerce, can climate, can the labor of many for one, yield any thing better, or half as good? Beside these aims, Society is weak and the State an intrusion. I think that the heroism which at this day would make on us the impression of Epaminondas and Phocion must be that of a domestic conqueror. He who shall bravely and gracefully subdue this Gorgon of Convention and Fashion, and show men how to lead a clean, handsome, and heroic life amid the beggarly elements of our cities and villages ; whoso shall teach me how to eat my meat and take my repose, and deal with men, without any shame following, will restore the life of man to splendor, and make his own name dear to all history.

FARMING.

FARMING.

THE glory of the farmer is that, in the division of labors, it is his part to create. All trade rests at last on his primitive activity. He stands close to nature; he obtains from the earth the bread and the meat. The food which was not, he causes to be. The first farmer was the first man, and all historic nobility rests on possession and use of land. Men do not like hard work, but every man has an exceptional respect for tillage, and a feeling that this is the original calling of his race, and that he himself is only excused from it by some circumstance which made him delegate it for a time to other hands. If he have not some skill which recommends him to the farmer, some product for which the farmer will give him corn, he must himself return into his due place among the planters. And the profession has in all eyes its ancient charm, as standing nearest to God, the first cause.

Then the beauty of nature, the tranquillity and innocence of the countryman, his independence, and his pleasing arts, — the care of bees, of poultry, of sheep, of cows, the dairy, the care of hay, of fruits, of orchards, and forests, and the reaction of these on the workman, in giving him a strength and plain dignity, like the face and manners of nature, all men acknowledge. All men keep the farm in reserve as an asylum where, in case of mischance, to hide their poverty, — or a solitude, if they do not succeed in society. And who knows how many glances of remorse are turned this way from the bankrupts of trade, from mortified pleaders in courts and senates, or from the victims of idleness and pleasure? Poisoned by town life and town vices, the sufferer resolves: "Well, my children, whom I have injured, shall go back to the land, to be recruited and cured by that which should have been my nursery, and now shall be their hospital."

The farmer's office is precise and important, but you must not try to paint him in rose-color; you cannot make pretty compliments to fate and gravitation, whose minister he is. He represents the necessities. It is the beauty of the great economy of the world that makes his comeliness. He bends to the order of the seasons, the weather, the soils and crops, as the sails of a ship bend to the wind. He represents continuous hard labor, year in, year out, and small gains. He is a slow person, timed to nature, and not to city watches. He takes the pace of seasons, plants, and chemistry. Nature never hurries: atom by atom, little by little, she achieves her work. The lesson one learns in fishing, yachting, hunting, or planting, is the manners of Nature; patience with the delays of wind and sun, delays of the seasons, bad weather, excess or lack of water, — patience with the slowness of our feet, with the parsimony of our strength, with the largeness of sea and land we must traverse, &c. The farmer times himself to Nature, and acquires that livelong patience which belongs to her. Slow, narrow man, his rule is, that the earth shall feed and clothe him; and he must wait for his crop to grow. His entertainments, his liberties, and his spending must be on a farmer's scale, and not on a merchant's. It were as false for farmers to use a wholesale and massy expense, as for states to use a minute economy. But if thus pinched on one side, he has compensatory advantages. He is permanent, clings to his land as the rocks do. In the town where I live, farms remain in the same families for seven and eight generations; and most of the first settlers (in 1635), should they reappear on the farms to-day, would find their own blood and names still in possession. And the like fact holds in the surrounding towns.

This hard work will always be done by one kind of man; not by scheming speculators, nor by soldiers, nor professors, nor readers of Tennyson; but by men of endurance, — deep-chested, long-winded, tough, slow and sure, and timely. The farmer has a great health, and the appetite of health, and means to his end : he has broad lands for his home, wood to burn great fires, plenty of plain food; his milk, at least, is un-watered; and for sleep, he has cheaper and better and more of it than citizens.

He has grave trusts confided to him. In the great household of Nature, the farmer stands at the door of the bread-room, and weighs to each his loaf. It is for him to say whether men shall marry or not. Early marriages and the number of births are indissolubly connected with abundance of food ; or, as Burke said, "Man breeds at the mouth." Then he is the Board of Quarantine. The farmer is a hoarded capital of health, as the farm is the capital of wealth ; and it is from him that the health and power, moral and intellectual, of the cities came. The city is always recruited from the country. The men in cities who are the centres of energy, the driving-wheels of trade, politics, or practical arts, and the women of beauty and genius, are the children or grandchildren of farmers, and are spending the energies which their fathers' hardy, silent life accumulated in frosty furrows, in poverty, necessity, and darkness.

He is the continuous benefactor. He who digs a well, constructs a stone fountain, plants a grove of trees by the roadside, plants an orchard, builds a durable house, reclaims a swamp, or so much as puts a stone seat by the wayside, makes the land so far lovely and desirable, makes a fortune which he cannot carry away with him, but which is useful to his country long afterwards. The man that works at home helps society at large with somewhat more of certainty than he who devotes himself to charities. If it be true that, not by votes of political parties, but by the eternal laws of political economy, slaves are driven out of a slave State as fast as it is surrounded by free States, then the true abolitionist is the farmer, who, heedless of laws and constitutions, stands all day in the field, investing his labor in the land, and making a product with which no forced labor can compete.

We commonly say that the rich man can speak the truth, can afford honesty, can afford independence of opinion and action ; — and that is the theory of nobility. But it is the rich man in the true sense, that is to say, not the man of large income and large expenditure, but solely the man whose outlay is less than his income, and is steadily kept so.

In English factories, the boy that watches the loom, to tie the thread when the wheel stops to indicate that a thread is broken, is called a *minder*. And in this great factory of our Copernican globe, shifting its slides ; rotating its constellations, times, and tides ; bringing now the day of planting, then of watering, then of weeding, then of reaping, then of curing and storing, — the farmer is the *minder*. His machine is of colossal proportions, — the diameter of the water-wheel, the arms of the levers, the power of the battery, are out of

all mechanic measure ; — and it takes him long to understand
its parts and its working.   This pump never "sucks;" these
screws are never loose; this machine is never out of gear;
the vat and piston, wheels and tires, never wear out, but are
self-repairing.

Who are the farmer's servants?   Not the Irish, nor the
coolies, but Geology and Chemistry, the quarry of the air, the
water of the brook, the lightning of the cloud, the castings
of the worm, the plough of the frost.   Long before he was
born, the sun of ages decomposed the rocks, mellowed his
land, soaked it with light and heat, covered it with vegetable
film, then with forests, and accumulated the sphagnum whose
decays made the peat of his meadow.

Science has shown the great circles in which nature works;
the manner in which marine plants balance the marine animals, as the land plants supply the oxygen which the animals
consume, and the animals the carbon which the plants absorb.
These activities are incessant.   Nature works on a method of
all for each and each for all.   The strain that is made on one
point bears on every arch and foundation of the structure.
There is a perfect solidarity.   You cannot detach an atom
from its holdings, or strip off from it the electricity, gravitation, chemic affinity, or the relation to light and heat, and
leave the atom bare.   No, it brings with it its universal
ties.

Nature, like a cautious testator, ties up her estate so as not
to bestow it all on one generation, but has a forelooking tenderness and equal regard to the next and the next, and the
fourth, and the fortieth age.

There lie the inexhaustible magazines.   The eternal rocks,
as we call them, have held their oxygen or lime undiminished,
entire, as it was.   No particle of oxygen can rust or wear, but
has the same energy as on the first morning.   The good rocks,
those patient waiters, say to him : "We have the sacred power
as we received it.   We have not failed of our trust, and now
— when in our immense day the hour is at last struck — take
the gas we have hoarded ; mingle it with water ; and let it be
free to grow in plants and animals, and obey the thought of
man."

The earth works for him ; the earth is a machine which
yields almost gratuitous service to every application of intellect.   Every plant is a manufacturer of soil.   In the stomach
of the plant development begins.   The tree can draw on the

whole air, the whole earth, on all the rolling main. The
plant is all suction-pipe, — imbibing from the ground by its
root, from the air by its leaves, with all its might.

The air works for him. The atmosphere, a sharp solvent,
drinks the essence and spirit of every solid on the globe, — a
menstruum which melts the mountains into it. Air is matter
subdued by heat. As the sea is the grand receptacle of all
rivers, so the air is the receptacle from which all things spring,
and into which they all return. The invisible and creeping
air takes form and solid mass. Our senses are sceptics, and
believe only the impression of the moment, and do not believe the chemical fact that these huge mountain-chains are
made up of gases and rolling wind. But Nature is as subtle
as she is strong. She turns her capital day by day; deals
never with dead, but ever with quick subjects. All things are
flowing, even those that seem immovable. The adamant is
always passing into smoke. The plants imbibe the materials
which they want from the air and the ground. They burn,
that is, exhale and decompose their own bodies into the air
and earth again. The animal burns, or undergoes the like
perpetual consumption. The earth burns, — the mountains
burn and decompose, — slower, but incessantly. It is almost
inevitable to push the generalization up into higher parts of
nature, rank over rank into sentient beings. Nations burn
with internal fire of thought and affection, which wastes while
it works. We shall find finer combustion and finer fuel. Intellect is a fire: rash and pitiless it melts this wonderful
bone-house which is called man. Genius even, as it is the greatest good, is the greatest harm. Whilst all thus burns, — the
universe in a blaze kindled from the torch of the sun, — it
needs a perpetual tempering, a phlegm, a sleep, atmospheres
of azote, deluges of water, to check the fury of the con-
flagration; a hoarding to check the spending; a centripetence equal to the centrifugence; and this is invariably
supplied.

The railroad dirt cars are good excavators; but there is no
porter like Gravitation, who will bring down any weights
which man cannot carry, and if he wants aid, knows where to
find his fellow-laborers. Water works in masses, and sets its
irresistible shoulder to your mills or your ships, or transports
vast boulders of rock in its iceberg a thousand miles. But
its far greater power depends on its talent of becoming little,
and entering the smallest holes and pores. By this agency,

carrying in solution elements needful to every plant, the vegetable world exists.

But as I said, we must not paint the farmer in rose-color.
Whilst these grand energies have wrought for him, and made
his task possible, he is habitually engaged in small economies,
and is taught the power that lurks in petty things.   Great is
the force of a few simple arrangements; for instance, the
powers of a fence.   On the prairie you wander a hundred
miles and hardly find a stick or a stone.   At rare intervals, a
thin oak opening has been spared, and every such section has
been long occupied.   But the farmer manages to procure wood
from far, puts up a rail fence, and at once the seeds sprout
and the oaks rise.   It was only browsing and fire which had
kept them down.   Plant fruit-trees by the roadside, and their
fruit will never be allowed to ripen.   Draw a pine fence about
them, and for fifty years they mature for the owner their delicate fruit.   There is a great deal of enchantment in a chestnut rail or picketed pine boards.

Nature suggests every economical expedient somewhere on
a great scale.   Set out a pine-tree, and it dies in the first
year, or lives a poor spindle.   But Nature drops a pine-cone
in Mariposa, and it lives fifteen centuries, grows three or four
hundred feet high, and thirty in diameter, — grows in a grove
of giants, like a colonnade of Thebes.   Ask the tree how it
was done.   It did not grow on a ridge, but in a basin, where
it found deep soil, cold enough and dry enough for the pine;
defended itself from the sun by growing in groves, and from
the wind by the walls of the mountain.   The roots that shot
deepest, and the stems of happiest exposure, drew the nourishment from the rest, until the less thrifty perished and man-
ured the soil for the stronger, and the mammoth Sequoias rose
to their enormous proportions.   The traveller who saw them
remembered his orchard at home, where every year, in the
destroying wind, his forlorn trees pined like suffering virtue.
In September, when the pears hang heaviest, and are taking
from the sun their gay colors, comes usually a gusty day
which shakes the whole garden, and throws down the heaviest
fruit in bruised heaps.   The planter took the hint of the Sequoias, built a high wall, or — better — surrounded the orchard with a nursery of birches and evergreens.   Thus he
had the mountain basin in miniature; and his pears grew to
the size of melons, and the vines beneath them ran an eighth
of a mile.   But this shelter creates a new climate.   The wall

that keeps off the strong wind keeps off the cold wind. The
high wall reflecting the heat back on the soil gives that acre a
quadruple share of sunshine,

> " Enclosing in the garden square
> A dead and standing pool of air,"

and makes a little Cuba within it, whilst all without is Labrador.

The chemist comes to his aid every year by following out
some new hint drawn from nature, and now affirms that this
dreary space occupied by the farmer is needless : he will con-
centrate his kitchen garden into a box of one or two rods
square, will take the roots into his laboratory ; the vines and
stalks and stems may go sprawling about in the fields outside, he will attend to the roots in his tub, gorge them with
food that is good for them. The smaller his garden, the better he can feed it, and the larger the crop. As he nursed his
Thanksgiving turkeys on bread and milk, so he will pamper
his peaches and grapes on the viands they like best. If they
have an appetite for potash, or salt, or iron, or ground bones,
or even now and then for a dead hog, he will indulge them.
They keep the secret well, and never tell on your table whence
they drew their sunset complexion or their delicate flavors.

See what the farmer accomplishes by a cartload of tiles ; he
alters the climate by letting off water which kept the land
cold through constant evaporation, and allows the warm rain
to bring down into the roots the temperature of the air and
of the surface-soil ; and he deepens the soil, since the discharge of this standing water allows the roots of his plants to
penetrate below the surface to the subsoil, and accelerates the
ripening of the crop. The town of Concord is one of the oldest towns in this country, far on now in its third century.
The selectmen have once in every five years perambulated the
boundaries, and yet, in this very year, a large quantity of land
has been discovered and added to the town without a murmur
of complaint from any quarter. By drainage we went down
to a subsoil we did not know, and have found there is a Concord under old Concord, which we are now getting the best
crops from ; a Middlesex under Middlesex ; and, in fine, that
Massachusetts has a basement story more valuable, and that
promises to pay a better rent, than all the superstructure.
But these tiles have acquired by association a new interest.
These tiles are political economists, confuters of Malthus and
Ricardo ; they are so many Young Americans announcing a
better era, — more bread. They drain the land, make it

sweet and friable; have made English Chat Moss a garden, and will now do as much for the Dismal Swamp. But beyond this benefit, they are the text of better opinions and better auguries for mankind.

There has been a nightmare bred in England of indigestion and spleen among landlords and loom-lords, namely, the dogma that men breed too fast for the powers of the soil; that men multiply in a .geometrical ratio, whilst corn only in an arithmetical; and hence that, the more prosperous we are, the faster we approach these frightful limits; nay, the plight of every new generation is worse than of the foregoing, because the first comers take up the best lands; the next, the second best; and each succeeding. wave of population is driven to poorer, so that the land is ever yielding less returns to enlarging hosts of eaters. Henry Carey of Philadelphia replied: 'Not so, Mr. Malthus, but just the opposite of so is the fact.'

The first planter, the savage, without helpers, without tools, looking chiefly to safety from his enemy, — man or beast, — takes poor land. The better lands are loaded with timber, which he cannot clear; they need drainage, which he cannot attempt. He cannot plough, or fell trees, or drain the rich swamp. He is a poor creature; he scratches with a sharp stick, lives in a cave or a hutch, has no road but the trail of the moose or bear; he lives on their flesh when he can kill one, on roots and fruits when he cannot. He falls, and is lame; he coughs, he has a stitch in his side, he has a fever and chills: when he is hungry, he cannot always kill and eat a bear, — chances of war, — sometimes the bear eats him. 'T is long before he digs or plants at all, and then only a patch. Later he learns that his planting is better than hunting; that the earth works faster for him than he can work for himself, — works for him when he is asleep, when it rains, when heat overcomes him. The sunstroke which knocks him down brings his corn up. As his family thrive, and other planters come up around him, he begins to fell trees, and clear good land; and when, by and by, there is more skill, and tools and roads, the new generations are strong enough to open the lowlands, where the wash of mountains has accumulated the best soil, which yield a hundred-fold the former crops. The last lands are the best lands. It needs science and great numbers to cultivate the best lands, and in the best manner. Thus true political economy is not mean, but liberal, and on the pattern

of the sun and sky. Population increases in the ratio of morality : credit exists in the ratio of morality.

Meantime we cannot enumerate the incidents and agents of
the farm without reverting to their influence on the farmer.
He carries out this cumulative preparation of means to their
last effect. This crust of soil which ages have refined he refines again for the feeding of a civil and instructed people.
The great elements with which he deals cannot leave him unaffected, or unconscious of his ministry ; but their influence
somewhat resembles that which the same Nature has on the
child, — of subduing and silencing him. We see the farmer
with pleasure and respect, when we think what powers and
utilities are so meekly worn. He knows every secret of labor :
he changes the face of the landscape. Put him on a new
planet, and he would know where to begin ; yet there is no
arrogance in his bearing, but a perfect gentleness. The farmer stands well on the world. Plain in manners as in dress,
he would not shine in palaces ; he is absolutely unknown and
inadmissible therein ; living or dying, he never shall be heard
of in them ; yet the drawing-room heroes put down beside him
would shrivel in his presence,— he solid and unexpressive,
they expressed to gold-leaf. But he stands well on the world,
— as Adam did, as an Indian does, as Homer's heroes, Agamemnon or Achilles, do. He is a person whom a poet of any
clime — Milton, Firdusi, or Cervantes — would appreciate as
being really a piece of the old Nature, comparable to sun and
moon, rainbow and flood ; because he is, as all natural persons
are, representative of Nature as much as these.

That uncorrupted behavior which we admire in animals and
in young children belongs to him, to the hunter, the sailor —
the man who lives in the presence of Nature. Cities force
growth, and make men talkative and entertaining, but they
make them artificial. What possesses interest for us is the
naturel of each, his constitutional excellence. This is forever
a surprise, engaging and lovely ; we cannot be satiated with
knowing it, and about it ; and it is this which the conversation with Nature cherishes and guards.

WORKS AND DAYS.

WORKS AND DAYS.

OUR nineteenth century is the age of tools. They grow out of our structure. "Man is the metre of all things," said Aristotle ; " the hand is the instrument of instruments, and the mind is the form of forms." The human body is the magazine of inventions, the patent-office, where are the models from which every hint was taken. All the tools and engines on earth are only extensions of its limbs and senses. One definition of man is " an intelligence served by organs." Machines can only second, not supply, his unaided senses. The body is a metre. The eye appreciates finer differences than art can expose. The apprentice clings to his foot-rule, a practised mechanic will measure by his thumb and his arm with equal precision ; and a good surveyor will pace sixteen rods more accurately than another man can measure them by tape. The sympathy of eye and hand by which an Indian or a practised slinger hits his mark with a stone, or a wood-chopper or a carpenter swings his axe to a hair line on his log, are examples ; and there is no sense or organ which is not capable of exquisite performance.

Men love to wonder, and that is the seed of our science ; and such is the mechanical determination of our age, and so recent are our best contrivances, that use has not dulled our joy and pride in them ; and we pity our fathers for dying before steam and galvanism, sulphuric ether and ocean telegraphs, photograph and spectroscope arrived, as cheated out of half their human estate. These arts open great gates of a future, promising to make the world plastic and to lift human life out of its beggary to a godlike ease and power.

Our century, to be sure, had inherited a tolerable apparatus. We had the compass, the printing-press, watches, the spiral spring, the barometer, the telescope. Yet so many inventions have been added, that life seems almost made over new ; and as Leibnitz said of Newton, "that if he reckoned all that had been done by mathematicians from the beginning of the world down to Newton, and what had been done by him, his would be the better half," so one might say that the inventions of the last fifty years counterpoise those of the fifty centuries before them.   For the vast production and manifold application of iron is new ; and our common and indispensable utensils of house and farm are new ; the sewing-machine, the power-loom, the McCormick reaper, the mowing-machines, gas-light, lucifer matches, and the immense productions of the laboratory, are new in this century, and one franc's worth of coal does the work of a laborer for twenty days.

Why need I speak of steam, the enemy of space and time, with its enormous strength and delicate applicability, which is made in hospitals to bring a bowl of gruel to a sick man's bed, and can twist beams of iron like candy-braids, and vies with the forces which upheaved and doubled over the geologic strata?   Steam is an apt scholar and a strong-shouldered fellow, but it has not yet done all its work.   It already walks about the field like a man, and will do anything required of it. It irrigates crops, and drags away a mountain.   It must sew our shirts, it must drive our gigs ; taught by Mr. Babbage, it must calculate interest and logarithms.   Lord Chancellor Thurlow thought it might be made to draw bills and answers in chancery.   If that were satire, it is yet coming to render many higher services of a mechanico-intellectual kind, and will leave the satire short of the fact.

How excellent are the mechanical aids we have applied to the human body, as in dentistry, in vaccination, in the rhinoplastic treatment ; in the beautiful aid of ether, like a finer sleep ; and in the boldest promiser of all,— the transfusion of the blood,— which, in Paris, it was claimed, enables a man to change his blood as often as his linen !

What of this dapper caoutchouc and gutta-percha, which make water-pipes and stomach-pumps, belting for mill-wheels, and diving bells, and rain-proof coats for all climates, which teach us to defy the wet, and put every man on a footing with the beaver and the crocodile ?   What of the grand tools with which we engineer, like kobolds and enchanters,— tunnelling Alps, canalling the American Isthmus, piercing the Arabian desert ?   In Massachusetts, we fight the sea successfully with beach-grass and broom,— and the blowing sand-barrens with pine plantations. The soil of Holland, once the most populous in Europe, is below the level of the sea. Egypt, where no rain fell for three thousand years, now, it is said, thanks Mehemet Ali's irrigations and planted forests for late-returning showers. The old Hebrew king said, "He makes the wrath of man to praise him." And there is no argument of theism better than the grandeur of ends brought about by paltry means. The chain of western railroads from Chicago to the Pacific has planted cities and civilization in less time than it costs to bring an orchard into bearing.

What shall we say of the ocean telegraph, that extension of the eye and ear, whose sudden performance astonished mankind as if the intellect were taking the brute earth itself into training, and shooting the first thrills of life and thought through the unwilling brain?

There does not seem any limit to these new informations of the same Spirit that made the elements at first, and now, through man, works them. Art and power will go on as they have done,— will make day out of night, time out of space, and space out of time.

Invention breeds invention. No sooner is the electric telegraph devised, than gutta-percha, the very material it requires, is found. The aeronaut is provided with gun-cotton, the very fuel he wants for his balloon. When commerce is vastly enlarged, California and Australia expose the gold it needs. When Europe is over populated, America and Australia crave to be peopled; and so, throughout, every chance is timed, as if Nature, who made the lock, knew where to find the key. ◦

Another result of our arts is the new intercourse which is surprising us with new solutions of the embarrassing political problems. The intercourse is not new, but the scale is new. Our selfishness would have held slaves, or would have excluded from a quarter of the planet all that are not born on the soil of that quarter. Our politics are disgusting; but what can they help or hinder when from time to time the primal instincts are impressed on masses of mankind, when the nations are in exodus and flux? Nature loves to cross her stocks,— and German, Chinese, Turk, Russ, and Kanaka were putting out to sea, and intermarrying race with race; and commerce took the hint, and ships were built capacious enough to carry the people of a county.

This thousand-handed art has introduced a new element into

the state. The science of power is forced to remember the power of science. Civilization mounts and climbs. Malthus, when he stated that the mouths went on multiplying geometrically, and the food only arithmetically, forgot to say that the human mind was also a factor in political economy, and that the augmenting wants of society would be met by an augmenting power of invention.

Yes, we have a pretty artillery of tools now in our social arrangements : we ride four times as fast as our fathers did ; travel, grind, weave, forge, plant, till, and excavate better. We have new shoes, gloves, glasses, and gimlets ; we have the calculus ; we have the newspaper, which does its best to make every square acre of land and sea give an account of itself at your breakfast-table ; we have money, and paper money ; we have language,— the finest tool of all, and nearest to the mind. Much will have more. Man flatters himself that his command over nature must increase. Things begin to obey him. We are to have the balloon yet, and the next war will be fought in the air. We may yet find a rose-water that will wash the negro white. He sees the skull of the English race changing from its Saxon type under the exigencies of American life.

Tantalus, who in old times was seen vainly trying to quench his thirst with a flowing stream, which ebbed whenever he approached it, has been seen again lately. He is in Paris, in New York, in Boston. He is now in great spirits ; thinks he shall reach it yet ; thinks he shall bottle the wave. It is, however, getting a little doubtful. Things have an ugly look still. No matter how many centuries of culture have preceded, the new man always finds himself standing on the brink of chaos, always in a crisis. Can anybody remember when the times were not hard, and money not scarce ? Can anybody remember when sensible men, and the right sort of men, and the right sort of women, were plentiful ? Tantalus begins to think steam a delusion, and galvanism no better than it should be.

Many facts concur to show that we must look deeper for our salvation than to steam, photographs, balloons, or astronomy. These tools have some questionable properties. They are reagents. Machinery is aggressive. The weaver becomes a web, the machinist a machine. If you do not use the tools, they use you. All tools are in one sense edge-tools, and dangerous. A man builds a fine house ; and now he has a master and a task for life : he is to furnish, watch, show it, and keep it in repair, the rest of his days. A man has a reputation, and is no longer free, but must respect that. A man makes a picture or a book, and, if it succeeds, 't is often the worse for him. I saw a brave man the other day, hitherto as free as the hawk or the fox of the wilderness, constructing his cabinet of drawers for shells, eggs, minerals, and mounted birds. It was easy to see that he was amusing himself with making pretty links for his own limbs.

Then the political economist thinks " 't is doubtful if all the mechanical inventions that ever existed have lightened the day's toil of one human being." The machine unmakes the man. Now that the machine is so perfect, the engineer is nobody. Every new step in improving the engine restricts one more act of the engineer, — unteaches him. Once it took Archimedes ; now it only needs a fireman, and a boy to know the coppers, to pull up the handles or mind the water-tank. But when the engine breaks, they can do nothing.

What sickening details in the daily journals. I believe they have ceased to publish the " Newgate Calendar " and the " Pirate's Own Book " since the family newspapers, namely, the New York Tribune and the London Times, have quite superseded them in the freshness, as well as the horror, of their records of crime. Politics were never more corrupt and brutal ; and Trade, that pride and darling of our ocean, that educator of nations, that benefactor in spite of itself, ends in shameful defaulting, bubble, and bankruptcy all over the world. Of course, we resort to the enumeration of his arts and inventions as a measure of the worth of man. But if, with all his arts, he is a felon, we cannot assume the mechanical skill or chemical resources as the measure of worth. Let us try another gauge.

What have these arts done for the character, for the worth of mankind? Are men better? 'T is sometimes questioned whether morals have not declined as the arts have ascended. Here are great arts and little men. Here is greatness begotten of paltriness. We cannot trace the triumphs of civilization to such benefactors as we wish. The greatest meliorator of the world is selfish, huxtering Trade. Every victory over matter ought to recommend to man the worth of his nature. But now one wonders who did all this good. Look up the inventors. Each has his own knack ; his genius is in veins and spots. But the great, equal, symmetrical brain, fed from a great heart, you shall not find. Every one has more to hide than he has to show, or is lamed by his excellence. 'T is too plain that with the material power the moral progress has not kept pace. It appears that we have not made a judicious investment. Works and days were offered us, and we took works.

The new study of the Sanskrit has shown us the origin of the old names of God, — Dyaus, Deus, Zeus, Zeu pater, Jupiter, — names of the sun, still recognizable through the modifications of our vernacular words, importing that the Day is the Divine Power and Manifestation, and indicating that those ancient men, in their attempts to express the Supreme Power of the universe, called him the Day, and that this name was accepted by all the tribes.

Hesiod wrote a poem which he called " Works and Days," in which he marked the changes of the Greek year, instructing the husbandman at the rising of what constellation he might safely sow, when to reap, when to gather wood, when the sailor might launch his boat in security from storms, and what admonitions of the planets he must heed. It is full of economies for Grecian life, noting the proper age for marriage, the rules of household thrift, and of hospitality. The poem is full of piety as well as prudence, and is adapted to all meridians, by adding the ethics of works and of days. But he has not pushed his study of days into such inquiry and analysis as they invite.

A farmer said "he should like to have all the land that joined his own." Bonaparte, who had the same appetite, endeavored to make the Mediterranean a French lake. Czar Alexander was more expansive, and wished to call the Pacific *my ocean ;* and the Americans were obliged to resist his attempts to make it a close sea. But if he had the earth for his pasture, and the sea for his pond, he would be a pauper still. He only is rich who owns the day. There is no king, rich man, fairy, or demon who possesses such power as that. The days are ever divine as to the first Aryans. They are of the least pretension, and of the greatest capacity, of anything that exists. They come and go like muffled and veiled figures, sent from a distant friendly party ; but they say nothing ; and if we do not use the gifts they bring, they carry them as silently away.

How the day fits itself to the mind, winds itself round it like a fine drapery, clothing all its fancies ! Any holiday communicates to us its color. We wear its cockade and favors in our humor. Remember what boys think in the morning of " Election day," of the Fourth of July, of Thanksgiving, of

Christmas. The very stars in their courses wink to them of nuts and cakes, bonbons, presents, and fireworks. Cannot memory still descry the old school-house and its porch, somewhat hacked by jack-knives, where you spun tops and snapped marbles; and do you not recall that life was then calendared by moments, threw itself into nervous knots or glittering hours, even as now, and not spread itself abroad an equable felicity? In college terms, and in years that followed, the young graduate, when the Commencement anniversary returned, though he were in a swamp, would see a festive light, and find the air faintly echoing with plausive academic thunders. In solitude and in the country, what dignity distinguishes the holy time! The old Sabbath, or Seventh Day, white with the religions of unknown thousands of years, when this hallowed hour dawns out of the deep, — a clean page which the wise may inscribe with truth, whilst the savage scrawls it with fetishes, — the cathedral music of history breathes through it a psalm to our solitude.

So, in the common experience of the scholar, the weathers fit his moods. A thousand tunes the variable wind plays, a thousand spectacles it brings, and each is the frame or dwelling of a new spirit. I used formerly to choose my time with some nicety for each favorite book. One author is good for winter, and one for the dog-days. The scholar must look long for the right hour for Plato's Timæus. At last the elect morning arrives, the early dawn, — a few lights conspicuous in the heaven, as of a world just created and still becoming, — and in its wide leisures we dare open that book.

There are days when the great are near us, when there is no frown on their brow, no condescension even; when they take us by the hand, and we share their thought. There are days which are the carnival of the year. The angels assume flesh, and repeatedly become visible. The imagination of the gods is excited, and rushes on every side into forms. Yesterday not a bird peeped; the world was barren, peaked, and pining; to-day 't is inconceivably populous; creation swarms and meliorates.

The days are made on a loom whereof the warp and woof are past and future time. They are majestically dressed, as if every god brought a thread to the skyey web. 'T is pitiful the things by which we are rich or poor, — a matter of coins, coats, and carpets, a little more or less stone, or wood, or paint, the fashion of a cloak or hat; like the luck of naked

Indians, of whom one is proud in the possession of a glass bead or a red feather, and the rest miserable in the want of it. But the treasures which Nature spent itself to amass, — the secular, refined, composite anatomy of man, — which all strata go to form, which the prior races, from infusory and saurian, existed to ripen ; the surrounding plastic natures ; the earth with its foods ; the intellectual, temperamenting air ; the sea with its invitations ; the heaven deep with worlds ; and the answering brain and nervous structure replying to these ; the eye that looketh into the deeps, which again look back to the eye, — abyss to abyss ; — these, not like a glass bead, or the coins or carpets, are given immeasurably to all.

This miracle is hurled into every beggar's hands. The blue sky is a covering for a market, and for the cherubim and seraphim. The sky is the varnish or glory with which the Artist has washed the whole work, — the verge or confines of matter and spirit. Nature could no farther go. Could our happiest dream come to pass in solid fact, — could a power open our eyes to behold " millions of spiritual creatures walk the earth," — I believe I should find that mid-plain on which they moved floored beneath and arched above with the same web of blue depth which weaves itself over me now, as I trudge the streets on my affairs.

'T is singular that our rich English language should have no word to denote the face of the world. *Kinde* was the old English term, which, however, filled only half the range of our fine Latin word, with its delicate future tense, — *natura, about to be born,* or what German philosophy denotes as a *becoming.* But nothing expresses that power which seems to work for beauty alone. The Greek *Kosmos* did ; and therefore, with great propriety, Humboldt entitles his book, which recounts the last results of science, *Cosmos.*

Such are the days, — the earth is the cup, the sky is the cover, of the immense bounty of nature which is offered us for our daily aliment ; but what a force of *illusion* begins life with us, and attends us to the end ! We are coaxed, flattered, and duped, from morn to eve, from birth to death ; and where is the old eye that ever saw through the deception ? The Hindoos represent Maia, the illusory energy of Vishnu, as one of his principal attributes. As if, in this gale of warring elements, which life is, it was necessary to bind souls to human life as mariners in a tempest lash themselves to the mast and bulwarks of a ship, and Nature employed certain illusions as her ties and straps, — a rattle, a doll, an apple, for a child; skates, a river, a boat, a horse, a gun, for the growing boy; — and I will not begin to name those of the youth and adult, for they are numberless. Seldom and slowly the mask falls, and the pupil is permitted to see that all is one stuff, cooked and painted under many counterfeit appearances. Hume's doctrine was that the circumstances vary, the amount of happiness does not; that the beggar cracking fleas in the sunshine under a hedge, and the duke rolling by in his chariot, the girl equipped for her first ball, and the orator returning triumphant from the debate, had different means, but the same quantity of pleasant excitement.

This element of illusion lends all its force to hide the values of present time. Who is he that does not always find himself doing something less than his best task? "What are you doing?" "O, nothing; I have been doing thus, or I shall do so or so, but now I am only —" Ah! poor dupe, will you never slip out of the web of the master juggler, — never learn that, as soon as the irrecoverable years have woven their blue glory between to-day and us, these passing hours shall glitter and draw us, as the wildest romance and the homes of beauty and poetry? How difficult to deal erect with them! The events they bring, their trade, entertainments, and gossip, their urgent work, all throw dust in the eyes and distract attention. He is a strong man who can look them in the eye, see through this juggle, feel their identity, and keep his own; who can know surely that one will be like another to the end of the world, nor permit love, or death, or politics, or money, war, or pleasure, to draw him from his task.

The world is always equal to itself, and every man in moments of deeper thought is apprised that he is repeating the experiences of the people in the streets of Thebes or Byzantium. An everlasting Now reigns in nature, which hangs the same roses on our bushes which charmed the Roman and the Chaldæan in their hanging gardens. 'To what end, then,' he asks, 'should I study languages, and traverse countries, to learn so simple truths?'

History of ancient art, excavated cities, recovery of books and inscriptions, — yes, the works were beautiful, and the history worth knowing; and academies convene to settle the claims of the old schools. What journeys and measurements, — Niebuhr and Müller and Layard, — to identify the plain of Troy and Nimroud town! And your homage to Dante costs you so much sailing; and to ascertain the discoverers of America needs as much voyaging as the discovery cost. Poor child! that flexile clay of which these old brothers moulded their admirable symbols was not Persian, nor Memphian, nor Teutonic, nor local at all, but was common lime and silex and water, and sunlight, the heat of the blood, and the heaving of the lungs; it was that clay which thou heldest but now in thy foolish hands, and threwest away to go and seek in vain in sepulchres, mummy-pits, and old book-shops of Asia Minor, Egypt, and England. It was the deep to-day which all men scorn; the rich poverty, which men hate; the populous, all-loving solitude, which men quit for the tattle of towns. HE lurks, *he* hides, — *he* who is success, reality, joy, and power. One of the illusions is that the present hour is not the critical, decisive hour. Write it on your heart that every day is the best day in the year. No man has learned anything rightly, until he knows that every day is Doomsday. 'T is the old secret of the gods that they come in low disguises. 'T is the vulgar great who come dizened with gold and jewels. Real kings hide away their crowns in their wardrobes, and affect a plain and poor exterior. In the Norse legend of our ancestors, Odin dwells in a fisher's hut, and patches a boat. In the Hindoo legends, Hari dwells a peasant among peasants. In the Greek legend, Apollo lodges with the shepherds of Admetus; and Jove liked to rusticate among the poor Ethiopians. So, in our history, Jesus is born in a barn, and his twelve peers are fishermen. 'T is the very principle of science that Nature shows herself best in leasts; 't was the maxim of Aristotle and Lucretius; and, in modern times, of Swedenborg and of Hahnemann. The order of changes in the egg determines the age of fossil strata. So it was the rule of our poets, in the legends of fairy lore, that the fairies largest in power were the least in size. In the Christian graces, humility stands highest of all, in the form of the Madonna; and in life, this is the secret of the wise. We owe to genius always the same debt, of lifting the curtain from the common, and showing us that divinities are sitting disguised in the seeming gang of gypsies and pedlers. In daily life, what distinguishes the master is the using those materials he has, instead of looking about for what are more renowned, or what others have used well. "A general," said Bonaparte, "always has troops enough, if he only knows how to employ those he has, and bivouacs with them." Do not refuse the employment which the hour brings you, for one more ambitious. The highest heaven of wisdom is alike near from every point, and thou must find it, if at all, by methods native to thyself alone.

That work is ever the more pleasant to the imagination which is not now required. How wistfully, when we have promised to attend the working committee, we look at the distant hills and their seductions!

The use of history is to give value to the present hour and its duty. That is good which commends to me my country, my climate, my means and materials, my associates. I knew a man in a certain religious exaltation, who "thought it an honor to wash his own face." He seemed to me more sane than those who hold themselves cheap.

Zoölogists may deny that horse-hairs in the water change to worms; but I find that whatever is old corrupts, and the past turns to snakes. The reverence for the deeds of our ancestors is a treacherous sentiment. Their merit was not to reverence the old, but to honor the present moment; and we falsely make them excuses of the very habit which they hated and defied.

Another illusion is, that there is not time enough for our work. Yet we might reflect that though many creatures eat from one dish, each, according to its constitution, assimilates from the elements what belongs to it, whether time, or space, or light, or water, or food. A snake converts whatever prey the meadow yields him into snake; a fox into fox; and Peter and John are working up all existence into Peter and John. A poor Indian chief of the Six Nations of New York made a wiser reply than any philosopher, to some one complaining that he had not enough time. "Well," said Red Jacket, "I suppose you have all there is."

A third illusion haunts us, that a long duration, as a year, a decade, a century, is valuable. But an old French sentence says, "God works in moments," — "*En peu d'heure Dieu labeure.*" We ask for long life, but 't is deep life, or grand moments, that signify. Let the measure of time be spiritual, not mechanical. Life is unnecessarily long. Moments of insight, of fine personal relation, a smile, a glance, — what ample borrowers of eternity they are! Life culminates and concentrates; and Homer said, "The gods ever give to mortals their apportioned share of reason only on one day."

I am of the opinion of the poet Wordsworth, "that there is no real happiness in this life, but in intellect and virtue."

I am of the opinion of Pliny, "that, whilst we are musing on these things, we are adding to the length of our lives." I am of the opinion of Glauco, who said, "The measure of life, O Socrates, is, with the wise, the speaking and hearing such discourses as yours."

He only can enrich me who can recommend to me the space between sun and sun. 'T is the measure of a man, — his apprehension of a day. For we do not listen with the best regard to the verses of a man who is only a poet, nor to his problems, if he is only an algebraist; but if a man is at once acquainted with the geometric foundations of things and with their festal splendor, his poetry is exact and his arithmetic musical. And him I reckon the most learned scholar, not who can unearth for me the buried dynasties of Sesostris and Ptolemy, the Sothiac era, the Olympiads and consulships, but who can unfold the theory of this particular Wednesday. Can he uncover the ligaments concealed from all but piety, which attach the dull men and things we know to the First Cause? These passing fifteen minutes, men think, are time, not eternity; are low and subaltern, are but hope or memory, that is, the way *to* or the way *from* welfare, but not welfare. Can he show their tie? That interpreter shall guide us from a menial and eleemosynary existence into riches and stability. He dignifies the place where he is. This mendicant America, this curious, peering, itinerant, imitative America, studious of Greece and Rome, of England and Germany, will take off its dusty shoes, will take off its glazed traveller's cap, and sit at home with repose and deep joy on its face. The world has no such landscape, the aeons of history no such hour, the future no equal second opportunity. Now let poets sing! now let arts unfold!

One more view remains. But life is good only when it is magical and musical, a perfect timing and consent, and when we do not anatomize it. You must treat the days respectfully, you must be a day yourself, and not interrogate it like a college professor. The world is enigmatical, — everything said, and everything known or done, — and must not be taken literally, but genially. We must be at the top of our condition to understand anything rightly. You must hear the bird's song without attempting to render it into nouns and verbs. Cannot we be a little abstemious and obedient? Cannot we let the morning be?

Everything in the universe goes by indirection. There are

no straight lines. I remember well the foreign scholar who made a week of my youth happy by his visit. "The savages in the islands," he said, "delight to play with the surf, coming in on the top of the rollers, then swimming out again, and repeat the delicious manœuvre for hours. Well, human life is made up of such transits. There can be no greatness without abandonment. But here your very astronomy is an espionage. I dare not go out of doors and see the moon and stars, but they seem to measure my tasks, to ask how many lines or pages are finished since I saw them last. Not so, as I told you, was it in Belleisle. The days at Belleisle were all different, and only joined by a perfect love of the same object. Just to fill the hour, — that is happiness. Fill my hour, ye gods, so that I shall not say, whilst I have done this, 'Behold, also, an hour of my life is gone,' — but rather, 'I have lived an hour.'"

We do not want factitious men, who can do any literary or professional feat, as, to write poems, or advocate a cause, or carry a measure for money ; or turn their ability indifferently in any particular direction by the strong effort of will. No, what has been best done in the world, — the works of genius, — cost nothing. There is no painful effort, but it is the spontaneous flowing of the thought. Shakspeare made his Hamlet as a bird weaves its nest. Poems have been written between sleeping and waking, irresponsibly. Fancy defines herself : —

> "Forms that men spy
> With the half-shut eye
> In the beams of the setting sun, am I."

The masters painted for joy, and knew not that virtue had gone out of them. They could not paint the like in cold blood. The masters of English lyric wrote their songs so. It was a fine efflorescence of fine powers ; as was said of the letters of the Frenchwomen, — "the charming accident of their more charming existence." Then the poet is never the poorer for his song. A song is no song unless the circumstance is free and fine. If the singer sing from a sense of duty or from seeing no way of escape, I had rather have none. Those only can sleep who do not care to sleep ; and those only write or speak best who do not too much respect the writing or the speaking.

The same rule holds in science. The savant is often an amateur. His performance is a memoir to the Academy on fish-worms, tadpoles, or spiders' legs; he observes as other academicians observe; he is on stilts at a microscope, and, — his memoir finished and read and printed, — he retreats into his routinary existence, which is quite separate from his scientific. But in Newton, science was as easy as breathing; he used the same wit to weigh the moon that he used to buckle his shoes; and all his life was simple, wise, and majestic. So was it in Archimedes, — always self-same, like the sky. In Linnæus, in Franklin, the like sweetness and equality, — no stilts, no tiptoe; — and their results are wholesome and memorable to all men.

In stripping time of its illusions, in seeking to find what is the heart of the day, we come to the quality of the moment, and drop the duration altogether. It is the depth at which we live, and not at all the surface extension, that imports. We pierce to the eternity, of which time is the flitting surface; and, really, the least acceleration of thought, and the least increase of power of thought, make life to seem and to be of vast duration. We call it time; but when that acceleration and that deepening take effect, it acquires another and a higher name.

There are people who do not need much experimenting; who, after years of activity, say, we knew all this before; who love at first sight and hate at first sight; discern the affinities and repulsions; who do not care so much for conditions as others, for they are always in one condition, and enjoy themselves; who dictate to others, and are not dictated to; who in their consciousness of deserving success constantly slight the ordinary means of attaining it; who have self-existence and self-help; who are suffered to be themselves in society; who are great in the present; who have no talents, or care not to have them, — being that which was before talent, and shall be after it, and of which talent seems only a tool; — this is character, the highest name at which philosophy has arrived.

'T is not important how the hero does this or this, but what he is. What he is will appear in every gesture and syllable. In this way the moment and the character are one.

'T is a fine fable for the advantage of character over talent, the Greek legend of the strife of Jove and Phœbus. Phœbus challenged the gods, and said, " Who will outshoot the far-darting Apollo? Zeus said " I will." Mars shook the lots in his helmet, and that of Apollo leaped out first. Apollo stretched his bow and shot his arrow into the extreme west.

Then Zeus arose, and with one stride cleared the whole distance, and said, " Where shall I shoot ? there is no space left." So the bowman's prize was adjudged to him who drew no bow.

And this is the progress of every earnest mind; from the works of man and the activity of the hands to a delight in the faculties which rule them; from a respect to the works to a wise wonder at this mystic element of time in which he is conditioned ; from local skills and the economy which reckons the amount of production *per* hour to the finer economy which respects the quality of what is done, and the right we have to the work, or the fidelity with which it flows from ourselves; then to the depth of thought it betrays, looking to its universality, or, that its roots are in eternity, not in time. Then it flows from character, that sublime health which values one moment as another, and makes us great in all conditions, and is the only definition we have of freedom and power.

BOOKS.

BOOKS.

IT is easy to accuse books, and bad ones are easily found; and the best are but records, and not the things recorded; and certainly there is dilettanteism enough, and books that are merely neutral and do nothing for us. In Plato's "Gorgias," Socrates says : " The shipmaster walks in a modest garb near the sea, after bringing his passengers from Ægina or from Pontus, not thinking he has done anything extraordinary, and certainly knowing that his passengers are the same, and in no respect better than when he took them on board." So is it with books, for the most part; they work no redemption in us. The bookseller might certainly know that his customers are in no respect better for the purchase and consumption of his wares. The volume is dear at a dollar, and, after reading to weariness the lettered backs, we leave the shop with a sigh, and learn, as I did, without surprise, of a surly bank director, that in bank parlors they estimate all stocks of this kind as rubbish.

But it is not less true that there are books which are of that importance in a man's private experience, as to verify for him the fables of Cornelius Agrippa, of Michael Scott, or of the old Orpheus of Thrace, — books which take rank in our life with parents and lovers and passionate experiences, so medicinal, so stringent, so revolutionary, so authoritative, — books which are the work and the proof of faculties so comprehensive, so nearly equal to the world which they paint, that, though one shuts them with meaner ones, he feels his exclusion from them to accuse his way of living.

Consider what you have in the smallest chosen library. A company of the wisest and wittiest men that could be picked out of all civil countries, in a thousand years, have set in best order the results of their learning and wisdom. The men themselves were hid and inaccessible, solitary, impatient of interruption, fenced by etiquette; but the thought which they did not uncover to their bosom friend is here written out in transparent words to us, the strangers of another age.

We owe to books those general benefits which come from high intellectual action. Thus, I think, we often owe to them the perception of immortality. They impart sympathetic activity to the moral power. Go with mean people, and you think life is mean. Then read Plutarch, and the world is a proud place, peopled with men of positive quality, with heroes and demigods standing around us, who will not let us sleep. Then they address the imagination: only poetry inspires poetry. They become the organic culture of the time. College education is the reading of certain books which the common sense of all scholars agrees will represent the science already accumulated. If you know that, — for instance in geometry, if you have read Euclid and Laplace, — your opinion has some value; if you do not know these, you are not entitled to give any opinion on the subject. Whenever any sceptic or bigot claims to be heard on the questions of intellect and morals, we ask if he is familiar with the books of Plato, where all his pert objections have once for all been disposed of. If not, he has no right to our time. Let him go and find himself answered there.

Meantime the colleges, whilst they provide us with libraries, furnish no professor of books; and, I think, no chair is so much wanted. In a library we are surrounded by many hundreds of dear friends, but they are imprisoned by an enchanter in these paper and leathern boxes; and though they know us, and have been waiting two, ten, or twenty centuries for us, — some of them, — and are eager to give us a sign, and unbosom themselves, it is the law of their limbo that they must not speak until spoken to; and as the enchanter has dressed them, like battalions of infantry, in coat and jacket of one cut, by the thousand and ten thousand, your chance of hitting on the right one is to be computed by the arithmetical rule of Permutation and Combination, — not a choice out of three caskets, but out of half a million caskets all alike. But it happens in our experience, that in this lottery there are at least fifty or a hundred blanks to a prize. It seems, then, as if some charitable soul, after losing a great deal of time among the false books, and alighting upon a few true ones which made him happy and wise, would do a right act in naming those which have been bridges or ships to carry him safely over dark morasses and barren oceans, into the heart of sacred cities, into palaces and temples. This would best be done by those great masters of books who from time to time appear, — the Fabricii, the Seldens, Magliabecchis, Scaligers, Miran- dolas, Bayles, Johnsons, whose eyes sweep the whole horizon of learning. But private readers, reading purely for love of the book, would serve us by leaving each the shortest note of what he found.

There are books ; and it is practicable to read them, because they are so few. We look over with a sigh the monumental libraries of Paris, of the Vatican, and the British Museum. In 1858, the number of printed books in the Imperial Library at Paris was estimated at eight hundred thousand volumes ; with an annual increase of twelve thousand volumes ; so that the number of printed books extant to-day may easily exceed a million. It is easy to count the number of pages which a diligent man can read in a day, and the number of years which human life in favorable circumstances allows to reading ; and to demonstrate, that, though he should read from dawn till dark, for sixty years, he must die in the first alcoves. But nothing can be more deceptive than this arithmetic, where none but a natural method is really pertinent. I visit occasionally the Cambridge Library, and I can seldom go there without renew- ing the conviction that the best of it all is already within the four walls of my study at home. The inspection of the cata- logue brings me continually back to the few standard writers who are on every private shelf ; and to these it can afford only the most slight and casual additions. The crowds and centu- ries of books are only commentary and elucidation, echoes and weakeners of these few great voices of Time.

The best rule of reading will be a method from nature, and not a mechanical one of hours and pages. It holds each stu- dent to a pursuit of his native aim, instead of a desultory mis- cellany. Let him read what is proper to him, and not waste his memory on a crowd of mediocrities. As whole nations have derived their culture from a single book, — as the Bible has been the literature as well as the religion of large portions of Europe, — as Hafiz was the eminent genius of the Persians, Confucius of the Chinese, Cervantes of the Spaniards ; so, per- haps, the human mind would be a gainer, if all the secondary writers were lost, — say, in England, all but Shakspeare, Mil- ton, and Bacon, — through the profounder study so drawn to those wonderful minds. With this pilot of his own genius, let the student read one, or let him read many, he will read advantageously. Dr. Johnson said : " Whilst you stand deliberating which book your son shall read first, another boy has read both : read anything five hours a day, and you will soon be learned."

Nature is much our friend in this matter. Nature is always clarifying her water and her wine. No filtration can be so perfect. She does the same thing by books as by her gases and plants. There is always a selection in writers, and then a selection from the selection. In the first place, all books that get fairly into the vital air of the world were written by the successful class, by the affirming and advancing class, who utter what tens of thousands feel though they cannot say. There has already been a scrutiny and choice from many hundreds of young pens, before the pamphlet or political chapter which you read in a fugitive journal comes to your eye. All these are young adventurers, who produce their performance to the wise ear of Time, who sits and weighs, and, ten years hence, out of a million of pages reprints one. Again it is judged, it is winnowed by all the winds of opinion, and what terrific selection has not passed on it before it can be reprinted after twenty years, — and reprinted after a century ! — it is as if Minos and Rhadamanthus had indorsed the writing. 'T is therefore an economy of time to read old and famed books. Nothing can be preserved which is not good ; and I know beforehand that Pindar, Martial, Terence, Galen, Kepler, Galileo, Bacon, Erasmus, More, will be superior to the average intellect. In contemporaries, it is not so easy to distinguish betwixt notoriety and fame.

Be sure, then, to read no mean books. Shun the spawn of the press on the gossip of the hour. Do not read what you shall learn, without asking, in the street and the train. Dr. Johnson said, " he always went into stately shops " ; and good travellers stop at the best hotels ; for, though they cost more, they do not cost much more, and there is the good company and the best information. In like manner, the scholar knows that the famed books contain, first and last, the best thoughts and facts. Now and then, by rarest luck, in some foolish Grub Street is the gem we want. But in the best circles is the best information. If you should transfer the amount of your reading day by day from the newspaper to the standard authors —— But who dare speak of such a thing ?

The three practical rules, then, which I have to offer, are, —
1. Never read any book that is not a year old. 2. Never
read any but famed books. 3. Never read any but what you
like ; or, in Shakspeare's phrase,

> " No profit goes where is no pleasure ta'en :
> In brief, sir, study what you most affect."

Montaigne says, " Books are a languid pleasure "; but I
find certain books vital and spermatic, not leaving the reader
what he was : he shuts the book a richer man. I would never
willingly read any others than such. And I will venture, at
the risk of inditing a list of old primers and grammars, to
count the few books which a superficial reader must thank-
fully use.

Of the old Greek books, I think there are five which we
cannot spare : 1. Homer, who in spite of Pope and all the
learned uproar of centuries, has really the true fire, and is
good for simple minds, is the true and adequate germ of
Greece, and occupies that place as history, which nothing can
supply. It holds through all literature that our best history
is still poetry. It is so in Hebrew, in Sanskrit, and in Greek.
English history is best known through Shakspeare ; how much
through Merlin, Robin Hood and the Scottish ballads ! — the
German, through the Nibelungenlied ; — the Spanish, through
the Cid. Of Homer, George Chapman's is the heroic translation, though the most literal prose version is the best of all.
2. Herodotus, whose history contains inestimable anecdotes,
which brought it with the learned into a sort of disesteem ;
but in these days, when it is found that what is most memorable of history is a few anecdotes, and that we need not be
alarmed though we should find it not dull, it is regaining
credit. 3. Æschylus, the grandest of the three tragedians,
who has given us under a thin veil the first plantation of
Europe. The "Prometheus" is a poem of the like dignity
and scope as the Book of Job, or the Norse Edda. 4. Of
Plato I hesitate to speak, lest there should be no end. You
find in him that which you have already found in Homer, now
ripened to thought, — the poet converted to a philosopher,
with loftier strains of musical wisdom than Homer reached ;
as if Homer were the youth, and Plato the finished man ;
yet with no less security of bold and perfect song, when he
cares to use it, and with some harp-strings fetched from a
higher heaven. He contains the future, as he came out of
the past. In Plato, you explore modern Europe in its causes

and seed, — all that in thought, which the history of Europe embodies or has yet to embody. The well-informed man finds himself anticipated. Plato is up with him too. Nothing has escaped him. Every new crop in the fertile harvest of reform, every fresh suggestion of modern humanity, is there. If the student wish to see both sides, and justice done to the man of the world, pitiless exposure of pedants, and the supremacy of truth and the religious sentiment, he shall be contented also. Why should not young men be educated on this book? It would suffice for the tuition of the race, — to test their understanding, and to express their reason. Here is that which is so attractive to all men, — the literature of aristocracy shall I call it? — the picture of the best persons, sentiments, and manners, by the first master, in the best times, — portraits of Pericles, Alcibiades, Crito, Prodicus, Protagoras, Anaxagoras, and Socrates, with the lovely background of the Athenian and suburban landscape. Or who can overestimate the images with which Plato has enriched the minds of men, and which pass like bullion in the currency of all nations? Read the "Phædo," the "Protagoras," the "Phædrus," the "Timæus," the "Republic," and the "Apology of Socrates." 5. Plutarch cannot be spared from the smallest library; first, because he is so readable, which is much; then, that he is medicinal and invigorating. The lives of Cimon, Lycurgus, Alexander, Demosthenes, Phocion, Marcellus, and the rest, are what history has of best. But this book has taken care of itself, and the opinion of the world is expressed in the innumerable cheap editions, which make it as accessible as a newspaper. But Plutarch's "Morals" is less known, and seldom reprinted. Yet such a reader as I am writing to can as ill spare it as the "Lives." He will read in it the essays "On the Dæmon of Socrates," "On Isis and Osiris," "On Progress in Virtue," "On Garrulity," "On Love," and thank anew the art of printing, and the cheerful domain of ancient thinking. Plutarch charms by the facility of his associations; so that it signifies little where you open his book, you find yourself at the Olympian tables. His memory is like the Isthmian Games, where all that was excellent in Greece was assembled, and you are stimulated and recruited by lyric verses, by philosophic sentiments, by the forms and behavior of heroes, by the worship of the gods, and by the passing of fillets, parsley and laurel wreaths, chariots, armor, sacred cups, and utensils of sacrifice. An inestimable trilogy of ancient social pictures are the three " Banquets " respectively of Plato, Xenophon, and Plutarch. Plutarch's has the least approach to historical accuracy ; but the meeting of the Seven Wise Masters is a charming portraiture of ancient manners and discourse, and is as clear as the voice of a fife, and entertaining as a French novel. Xenophon's delineation of Athenian manners is an accessory to Plato, and supplies traits of Socrates ; whilst Plato's has merits of every kind, — being a repertory of the wisdom of the ancients on the subject of love, — a picture of a feast of wits, not less descriptive than Aristophanes, — and, lastly, containing that ironical eulogy of Socrates which is the source from which all the portraits of that philosopher current in Europe have been drawn.

Of course a certain outline should be obtained of Greek history, in which the important moments and persons can be rightly set down ; but the shortest is the best, and if one lacks stomach for Mr. Grote's voluminous annals, the old slight and popular summary of Goldsmith or of Gillies will serve. The valuable part is the age of Pericles and the next generation. And here we must read the "Clouds" of Aristophanes, and what more of that master we gain appetite for, to learn our way in the streets of Athens, and to know the tyranny of Aristophanes, requiring more genius and sometimes not less cruelty than belonged to the official commanders. Aristophanes is now very accessible, with much valuable commentary, through the labors of Mitchell and Cartwright. An excellent popular book is J. A. St. John's " Ancient Greece "; the " Life and Letters " of Niebuhr, even more than his Lectures, furnish leading views ; and Winckelmann, a Greek born out of due time, has become essential to an intimate knowledge of the Attic genius. The secret of the recent histories in German and in English is the discovery, owed first to Wolff, and later to Boeckh, that the sincere Greek history of that period must be drawn from Demosthenes, especially from the business orations, and from the comic poets.

If we come down a little by natural steps from the master to the disciples, we have, six or seven centuries later, the Platonists, — who also cannot be skipped, — Plotinus, Porphyry, Proclus, Synesius, Jamblichus. Of Jamblichus the Emperor Julian said, " that he was posterior to Plato in time, not in genius." Of Plotinus, we have eulogies by Porphyry and Longinus, and the favor of the Emperor Gallienus, — indicating the respect he inspired among his contemporaries.

If any one who had read with interest the "Isis and Osiris" of Plutarch should then read a chapter called "Providence," by Synesius, translated into English by Thomas Taylor, he will find it one of the majestic remains of literature, and, like one walking in the noblest of temples, will conceive new gratitude to his fellow-men, and a new estimate of their nobility. The imaginative scholar will find few stimulants to his brain like these writers. He has entered the Elysian Fields ; and the grand and pleasing figures of gods and dæmons and dæmoniacal men, of the "azonic" and the "aquatic gods," dæmons with fulgid eyes, and all the rest of the Platonic rhetoric, exalted a little under the African sun, sail before his eyes. The acolyte has mounted the tripod over the cave at Delphi ; his heart dances, his sight is quickened. These guides speak of the gods with such depth and with such pictorial details, as if they had been bodily present at the Olympian feasts. The reader of these books makes new acquaintance with his own mind ; new regions of thought are opened. Jamblichus's "Life of Pythagoras" works more directly on the will than the others ; since Pythagoras was eminently a practical person, the founder of a school of ascetics and socialists, a planter of colonies, and nowise a man of abstract studies alone.

The respectable and sometimes excellent translations of Bohn's Library have done for literature what railroads have done for internal intercourse. I do not hesitate to read all the books I have named, and all good books, in translations. What is really best in any book is translatable,— any real insight or broad human sentiment. Nay, I observe that, in our Bible, and other books of lofty moral tone, it seems easy and inevitable to render the rhythm and music of the original into phrases of equal melody. The Italians have a fling at translators,— *i traditori traduttori ;* but I thank them. I rarely read any Latin, Greek, German, Italian, sometimes not a French book in the original, which I can procure in a good version. I like to be beholden to the great metropolitan English speech, the sea which receives tributaries from every region under heaven. I should as soon think of swimming across Charles River when I wish to go to Boston, as of reading all my books in originals, when I have them rendered for me in my mother-tongue.

For history there is great choice of ways to bring the student through early Rome. If he can read Livy, he has a good book ; but one of the short English compends, some

Goldsmith or Ferguson, should be used, that will place in the cycle the bright stars of Plutarch. The poet Horace is the eye of the Augustan age; Tacitus, the wisest of historians; and Martial will give him Roman manners,— and some very bad ones,— in the early days of the Empire : but Martial must be read, if read at all, in his own tongue. These will bring him to Gibbon, who will take him in charge, and convey him with abundant entertainment down — with notice of all remarkable objects on the way — through fourteen hundred years of time. He cannot spare Gibbon, with his vast reading, — with such wit and continuity of mind, that, though never profound, his book is one of the conveniences of civilization, like the new railroad from ocean to ocean,— and, I think, will be sure to send the reader to his "Memoirs of Himself," and the "Extracts from my Journal," and "Abstracts of my Readings," which will spur the laziest scholar to emulation of his prodigious performance.

Now having our idler safe down as far as the fall of Constantinople in 1453, he is in very good courses; for here are trusty hands waiting for him. The cardinal facts of European history are soon learned. There is Dante's poem, to open the Italian Republics of the Middle Age; Dante's "Vita Nuova," to explain Dante and Beatrice; and Boccaccio's "Life of Dante,"— a great man to describe a greater. To help us, perhaps a volume or two of M. Sismondi's "Italian Republics" will be as good as the entire sixteen. When we come to Michel Angelo, his Sonnets and Letters must be read, with his Life by Vasari, or, in our day, by Herman Grimm. For the Church, and the Feudal Institution, Mr. Hallam's "Middle Ages" will furnish, if superficial, yet readable and conceivable outlines.

The "Life of the Emperor Charles V.," by the useful Robertson, is still the key of the following age. Ximenes, Columbus, Loyola, Luther, Erasmus, Melanchthon, Francis I., Henry VIII., Elizabeth, and Henry IV. of France, are his contemporaries. It is a time of seeds and expansions, whereof our recent civilization is the fruit.

If now the relations of England to European affairs bring him to British ground, he is arrived at the very moment when modern history takes new proportions. He can look back for the legends and mythology to the "Younger Edda" and the "Heimskringla" of Snorro Sturleson, to Mallet's "Northern Antiquities," to Ellis's "Metrical Romances," to Asser's "Life

of Alfred" and Venerable Bede, and to the researches of Sharon
Turner and Palgrave.   Hume will serve him for an intelligent
guide, and in the Elizabethan era he is at the richest period of
the English mind, with the chief men of action and of thought
which that nation has produced, and with a pregnant future
before him.   Here he has Shakespeare, Spenser, Sidney,
Raleigh,   Bacon,   Chapman,   Jonson,   Ford,   Beaumont   and
Fletcher, Herbert, Donne, Herrick ; and Milton, Marvell, and
Dryden, not long after.

In reading history, he is to prefer the history of individuals.
He will not repent the time he gives to Bacon,— not if he read
the " Advancement of Learning," the " Essays," the " Novum
Organum," the " History of Henry VII.," and then all the
" Letters " (especially those to the Earl of Devonshire, explain-
ing the Essex business), and all but his "Apophthegms."

The task is aided by the strong mutual light which these
men shed on each other.   Thus, the works of Ben Jonson are
a sort of hoop to bind all these fine persons together, and to
the land to which they belong.   He has written verses to or
on all his notable contemporaries ; and what with so many
occasional poems, and the portrait sketches in his " Discoveries," and the gossiping record of his opinions in his conversations with Drummond of Hawthornden, he has really illustrated the England of his time, if not to the same extent, yet
much in the same way, as Walter Scott has celebrated the
persons and places of Scotland.   Walton, Chapman, Herrick,
and Sir Henry Wotton write also to the times.

Among the best books are certain *Autobiographies :* as, St.
Augustine's Confessions ; Benvenuto Cellini's Life ; Montaigne's Essays ; Lord Herbert of Cherbury's Memoirs ; Memoirs of the Cardinal de Retz ; Rousseau's Confessions ;
Linnæus's Diary ; Gibbon's, Hume's, Franklin's, Burns's, Al-
fieri's, Goethe's, and Haydon's Autobiographies.

Another class of books closely allied to these, and of like
interest, are those which may be called *Table-Talks :* of which
the best are Saadi's Gulistan ; Luther's Table-Talk ; Aubrey's
Lives ; Spence's Anecdotes ; Selden's Table-Talk ; Boswell's
Life of Johnson ; Eckermann's Conversations with Goethe ;
Coleridge's Table-Talk ; and Hazlitt's Life of Northcote.

There is a class whose value I should designate as *Favorites :*
such as Froissart's Chronicles ; Southey's Chronicle of the
Cid ; Cervantes ; Sully's Memoirs ; Rabelais ; Montaigne ;
Izaak Walton ; Evelyn ; Sir Thomas Browne ; Aubrey ; Sterne ;

Horace Walpole; Lord Clarendon; Dr. Johnson; Burke, shedding floods of light on his times; Lamb, Landor, and De Quincey; — a list, of course, that may easily be swelled, as dependent on individual caprice. Many men are as tender and irritable as lovers in reference to these predilections. Indeed, a man's library is a sort of harem, and I observe that tender readers have a great pudency in showing their books to a stranger.

The annals of bibliography afford many examples of the delirious extent to which book-fancying can go, when the legitimate delight in a book is transferred to a rare edition or to a manuscript. This mania reached its height about the beginning of the present century. For an autograph of Shakspeare one hundred and fifty-five guineas were given. In May, 1812, the library of the Duke of Roxburgh was sold. The sale lasted forty-two days, — we abridge the story from Dibdin, — and among the many curiosities was a copy of Boccaccio published by Valdarfer, at Venice, in 1471; the only perfect copy of this edition. Among the distinguished company which attended the sale were the Duke of Devonshire, Earl Spencer, and the Duke of Marlborough, then Marquis of Blandford. The bid stood at five hundred guineas. "A thousand guineas," said Earl Spencer: "And ten," added the Marquis. You might hear a pin drop. All eyes were bent on the bidders. Now they talked apart, now ate a biscuit, now made a bet, but without the least thought of yielding one to the other. But to pass over some details, — the contest proceeded until the Marquis said, "Two thousand pounds." The Earl Spencer bethought him like a prudent general of useless bloodshed and waste of powder, and had paused a quarter of a minute, when Lord Althorp with long steps came to his side, as if to bring his father a fresh lance to renew the fight. Father and son whispered together, and Earl Spencer exclaimed, "Two thousand two hundred and fifty pounds!" An electric shock went through the assembly. "And ten," quietly added the Marquis. There ended the strife. Ere Evans let the hammer fall he paused; the ivory instrument swept the air; the spectators stood dumb, when the hammer fell. The stroke of its fall sounded on the farthest shores of Italy. The tap of that hammer was heard in the libraries of Rome, Milan, and Venice. Boccaccio stirred in his sleep of five hundred years, and M. Van Praet groped in vain among the royal alcoves in Paris, to detect a copy of the famed Valdarfer Boccaccio.

Another class I distinguish by the term *Vocabularies*. Burton's "Anatomy of Melancholy" is a book of great learning.
To read it is like reading in a dictionary. 'T is an inventory
to remind us how many classes and species of facts exist, and,
in observing into what strange and multiplex by-ways learning
has strayed, to infer our opulence. Neither is a dictionary a
bad book to read. There is no cant in it, no excess of explanation, and it is full of suggestion, — the raw material of possible poems and histories. Nothing is wanting but a little
shuffling, sorting, ligature, and cartilage. Out of a hundred
examples, Cornelius Agrippa "On the Vanity of Arts and
Sciences" is a specimen of that scribatiousness which grew to
be the habit of the gluttonous readers of his time. Like the
modern Germans, they read a literature, while other mortals
read a few books. They read voraciously, and must disburden
themselves ; so they take any general topic, as, Melancholy,
or Praise of Science, or Praise of Folly, and write and quote
without method or end. Now and then out of that affluence
of their learning comes a fine sentence from Theophrastus, or
Seneca, or Boëthius, but no high method, no inspiring efflux.
But one cannot afford to read for a few sentences ; they are
good only as strings of suggestive words.

There is another class, more needful to the present age, because the currents of custom run now in another direction,
and leave us dry on this side ; — I mean the *Imaginative*. A
right metaphysics should do justice to the co-ordinate powers
of Imagination, Insight, Understanding, and Will. Poetry,
with its aids of Mythology and Romance, must be well allowed
for an imaginative creature. Men are ever lapsing into a beggarly habit, wherein everything that is not ciphering, that is,
which does not serve the tyrannical animal, is hustled out of
sight. Our orators and writers are of the same poverty, and,
in this rag-fair, neither the Imagination, the great awakening
power, nor the Morals, creative of genius and of men, are addressed. But though orator and poet be of this hungry party,
the capacities remain. We must have symbols. The child
asks you for a story, and is thankful for the poorest. It is
not poor to him, but radiant with meaning. The man asks
for a novel, — that is, asks leave for a few hours to be a poet,
and to paint things as they ought to be. The youth asks for
a poem. The very dunces wish to go to the theatre. What
private heavens can we not open, by yielding to all the suggestion of rich music ! We must have idolatries, mythologies,

— some swing and verge for the creative power lying coiled and cramped here, driving ardent natures to insanity and crime if it do not find vent. Without the great arts which speak to the sense of beauty, a man seems to me a poor, naked, shivering creature. These are his becoming draperies, which warm and adorn him. Whilst the prudential and economical tone of society starves the imagination, affronted Nature gets such indemnity as she may. The novel is that allowance and frolic the imagination finds. Everything else pins it down, and men flee for redress to Byron, Scott, Disraeli, Dumas, Sand, Balzac, Dickens, Thackeray, and Reade. Their education is neglected; but the circulating library and the theatre, as well as the trout-fishing, the Notch Mountains, the Adirondack country, the tour to Mont Blanc, to the White Hills, and the Ghauts, make such amends as they can.

The imagination infuses a certain volatility and intoxication. It has a flute which sets the atoms of our frame in a dance, like planets; and, once so liberated, the whole man reeling drunk to the music, they never quite subside to their old stony state. But what is the imagination? Only an arm or weapon of the interior energy; only the precursor of the reason. And books that treat the old pedantries of the world, our times, places, professions, customs, opinions, histories, with a certain freedom, and distribute things, not after the usages of America and Europe, but after the laws of right reason, and with as daring a freedom as we use in dreams, put us on our feet again, enable us to form an original judgment of our duties, and suggest new thoughts for to-morrow.

"Lucrezia Floriani," "Le Péché de M. Antoine," "Jeanne," and "Consuelo," of George Sand, are great steps from the novel of one termination, which we all read twenty years ago. Yet how far off from life and manners and motives the novel still is! Life lies about us dumb; the day, as we know it, has not yet found a tongue. These stories are to the plots of real life what the figures in "La Belle Assemblée," which represent the fashion of the month, are to portraits. But the novel will find the way to our interiors one day, and will not always be the novel of costume merely. I do not think it inoperative now. So much novel-reading cannot leave the young men and maidens untouched; and doubtless it gives some ideal dignity to the day. The young study noble behavior; and as the player in "Consuelo" insists that he and his colleagues on the boards have taught princes the fine etiquette and strokes of grace and dignity which they practise with so much effect in their villas and among their dependents, so I often see traces of the Scotch or the French novel in the courtesy and brilliancy of young midshipmen, collegians, and clerks. Indeed, when one observes how ill and ugly people make their loves and quarrels, 't is pity they should not read novels a little more, to import the fine generosities, and the clear, firm conduct which are as becoming in the unions and separations which love effects under shingle roofs as in palaces and among illustrious personages.

In novels the most serious questions are beginning to be discussed. What made the popularity of "Jane Eyre," but that a central question was answered in some sort? The question there answered in regard to a vicious marriage will always be treated according to the habit of the party. A person of commanding individualism will answer it as Rochester does, — as Cleopatra, as Milton, as George Sand do, — magnifying the exception into a rule, dwarfing the world into an exception. A person of less courage, that is, of less constitution, will answer as the heroine does, — giving way to fate, to conventionalism, to the actual state and doings of men and women.

For the most part, our novel-reading is a passion for results. We admire parks, and high-born beauties, and the homage of drawing-rooms, and parliaments. They make us sceptical by giving prominence to wealth and social position.

I remember when some peering eyes of boys discovered that the oranges hanging on the boughs of an orange-tree in a gay piazza were tied to the twigs by thread. I fear 't is so with the novelist's prosperities. Nature has a magic by which she fits the man to his fortunes, by making them the fruit of his character. But the novelist plucks this event here, and that fortune there, and ties them rashly to his figures, to tickle the fancy of his readers with a cloying success, or scare them with shocks of tragedy. And so, on the whole, 't is a juggle. We are cheated into laughter or wonder by feats which only oddly combine acts that we do every day. There is no new element, no power, no furtherance. 'T is only confectionery, not the raising of new corn. Great is the poverty of their inventions. *She was beautiful, and he fell in love.* Money, and killing, and the Wandering Jew, and persuading the lover that his mistress is betrothed to another,— these are the main-springs : new names, but no new qualities in the men and women. Hence the vain endeavor to keep any bit of this fairy gold, which has rolled like a brook through our hands. A thousand thoughts awoke; great rainbows seemed to span the sky,— a morning among the mountains; — but we close the book, and not a ray remains in the memory of evening. But this passion for romance, and this disappointment, show how much we need real elevations and pure poetry : that which shall show us, in morning and night, in stars and mountains, and in all the plight and circumstance of men, the analogons of our own thoughts, and a like impression made by a just book and by the face of Nature.

If our times are sterile in genius, we must cheer us with books of rich and believing men who had atmosphere and amplitude about them. Every good fable, every mythology, every biography from a religious age, every passage of love, and even philosophy and science, when they proceed from an intellectual integrity, and are not detached and critical, have the imaginative element. The Greek fables, the Persian history (Firdusi), the "Younger Edda" of the Scandinavians, the "Chronicle of the Cid," the poem of Dante, the Sonnets of Michel Angelo, the English drama of Shakspeare, Beaumont and Fletcher, and Ford, and even the prose of Bacon and Milton, — in our time, the Ode of Wordsworth, and the poems and the prose of Goethe, have this enlargement, and inspire hope and generous attempts.

There is no room left, — and yet I might as well not have begun as to leave out a class of books which are the best : I mean the Bibles of the world, or the sacred books of each nation, which express for each the supreme result of their experience. After the Hebrew and Greek Scriptures, which constitute the sacred books of Christendom, these are, the Desatir of the Persians, and the Zoroastrian Oracles; the Vedas and Laws of Menu; the Upanishads, the Vishnu Purana, the Bhagvat Geeta, of the Hindoos; the books of the Buddhists; the "Chinese Classics," of four books, containing the wisdom of Confucius and Mencius. Also such other books as have acquired a semi-canonical authority in the world, as expressing the highest sentiment and hope of nations. Such are the "Hermes Trismegistus," pretending to be Egyptian remains; the "Sentences" of Epictetus; of Marcus Antoninus; the "Vishnu Sarma" of the Hindoos; the "Gulistan" of Saadi; the "Imitation of Christ," of Thomas à Kempis; and the "Thoughts" of Pascal.

All these books are the majestic expressions of the universal conscience, and are more to our daily purpose than this year's almanac or this day's newspaper. But they are for the closet, and to be read on the bended knee. Their communications are not to be given or taken with the lips and the end of the tongue, but out of the glow of the cheek, and with the throbbing heart. Friendship should give and take, solitude and time brood and ripen, heroes absorb and enact them. They are not to be held by letters printed on a page, but are living characters translatable into every tongue and form of life. I read them on lichens and bark; I watch them on waves on the beach; they fly in birds, they creep in worms; I detect them in laughter and blushes, and eye-sparkles of men and women. These are Scriptures which the missionary might well carry over prairie, desert, and ocean, to Siberia, Japan, Timbuctoo. Yet he will find that the spirit which is in them journeys faster than he, and greets him on his arrival, — was there already long before him. The missionary must be carried by it, and find it there, or he goes in vain. Is there any geography in these things? We call them Asiatic, we call them primeval; but perhaps that is only optical; for Nature is always equal to herself, and there are as good eyes and ears now in the planet as ever were. Only these ejaculations of the soul are uttered one or a few a time, at long intervals, and it takes millenniums to make a Bible.

These are a few of the books which the old and the later times have yielded us, which will reward the time spent on them. In comparing the number of good books with the shortness of life, many might well be read by proxy, if we had good proxies; and it would be well for sincere young men to borrow a hint from the French Institute and the British Association, and, as they divide the whole body into sections, each of which sits upon and reports of certain matters confided to it, so let each scholar associate himself to such persons as he can rely on, in a literary club, in which each shall undertake a single work or series for which he is qualified. For example, how attractive is the whole literature of the "Roman de la Rose," the "Fabliaux," and the *gaie science* of the French Troubadours! Yet who in Boston has time for that? But one of our company shall undertake it, shall study and master it, and shall report on it, as under oath; shall give us the sincere result, as it lies in his mind, adding nothing, keeping nothing back. Another member, meantime, shall as honestly search, sift, and as truly report, on British mythology, the Round Table, the histories of Brut, Merlin, and Welsh poetry; a third on the Saxon Chronicles, Robert of Gloucester, and William of Malmesbury; a fourth, on Mysteries, Early Drama, "Gesta Romanorum," Collier, and Dyce, and the Camden Society. Each shall give us his grains of gold, after the washing; and every other shall then decide whether this is a book indispensable to him also.

CLUBS.

CLUBS.

WE are delicate machines, and require nice treatment to get from us the maximum of power and pleasure. We need tonics, but must have those that cost little or no reaction. The flame of life burns too fast in pure oxygen, and nature has tempered the air with nitrogen. So thought is the native air of the mind, yet pure it is a poison to our mixed constitution, and soon burns up the bone-house of man, unless tempered with affection and coarse practice in the material world. Varied foods, climates, beautiful objects, — and especially the alternation of a large variety of objects, — are the necessity of this exigent system of ours. But our tonics, our luxuries, are force-pumps which exhaust the strength they pretend to supply ; and of all the cordials known to us, the best, safest, and most exhilarating, with the least harm, is society ; and every healthy and efficient mind passes a large part of life in the company most easy to him.

We seek society with very different aims, and the staple of conversation is widely unlike in its circles. Sometimes it is facts, — running from those of daily necessity to the last results of science, — and has all degrees of importance ; sometimes it is love, and makes the balm of our early and of our latest days ; sometimes it is thought, as from a person who is a mind only ; sometimes a singing, as if the heart poured out all like a bird ; sometimes experience. With some men it is a debate ; at the approach of a dispute they neigh like horses. Unless there be an argument, they think nothing is doing. Some talkers excel in the precision with which they formulate their thoughts, so that you get from them somewhat to remember ; others lay criticism asleep by a charm. Especially women use words that are not words, — as steps in a dance are not steps, — but reproduce the genius of that they speak

of ; as the sound of some bells makes us think of the bell
merely, whilst the church-chimes in the distance bring the
church and its serious memories before us.   Opinions are accidental in people, — have a poverty-stricken air.   A man valu-
ing himself as the organ of this or that dogma is a dull
companion enough ; but opinion native to the speaker is sweet
and refreshing, and inseparable from his image.   Neither do
we by any means always go to people for conversation.   How
often to say nothing, — and yet must go ; as a child will long
for his companions, but among them plays by himself.   'T is
only presence which we want.   But one thing is certain, — at
some rate, intercourse we must have.   The experience of re-
tired men is positive, — that we lose our days and are barren
of thought for want of some person to talk with.   The understanding can no more empty itself by its own action than can
a deal box.

The clergyman walks from house to house all day all the
year to give people the comfort of good talk.   The physician
helps them mainly in the same way, by healthy talk giving a
right tone to the patient's mind.   The dinner, the walk, the
fireside, all have that for their main end.

See how Nature has secured the communication of knowledge.   'T is certain that money does not more burn in a boy's
pocket than a piece of news burns in our memory until we can
tell it.   And, in higher activity of mind, every new perception
is attended with a thrill of pleasure, and the imparting of it
to others is also attended with pleasure.   Thought is the child
of the intellect, and this child is conceived with joy and born
with joy.

Conversation is the laboratory and workshop of the student.
The affection or sympathy helps.   The wish to speak to the
want of another mind assists to clear your own.   A certain
truth possesses us, which we in all ways strive to utter.   Every
time we say a thing in conversation, we get a mechanical advantage in detaching it well and deliverly.   I prize the me-
chanics of conversation.   'T is pulley and lever and screw.
To fairly disengage the mass, and send it jingling down, a good
boulder, — a block of quartz and gold, to be worked up at
leisure in the useful arts of life, — is a wonderful relief.

What are the best days in memory ?   Those in which we
met a companion who was truly such.   How sweet those hours
when the day was not long enough to communicate and compare our intellectual jewels, — the favorite passages of each

book, the proud anecdotes of our heroes, the delicious verses
we had hoarded! What a motive had then our solitary days!
How the countenance of our friend still left some light after
he had gone! We remember the time when the best gift we
could ask of fortune was to fall in with a valuable companion
in a ship's cabin, or on a long journey in the old stage-coach,
where, each passenger being forced to know every other, and
other employments being out of the question, conversation
naturally flowed, people became rapidly acquainted, and, if
well adapted, more intimate in a day than if they had been
neighbors for years.

In youth, in the fury of curiosity and acquisition, the day
is too short for books and the crowd of thoughts, and we are
impatient of interruption. Later, when books tire, thought
has a more languid flow; and the days come when we are
alarmed, and say there are no thoughts. "What a barren-wit-
ted pate is mine!" the student says; "I will go and learn
whether I have lost my reason." He seeks intelligent persons, whether more wise or less wise than he, who give him
provocation, and at once and easily the old motion begins in
his brain : thoughts, fancies, humors, flow; the cloud lifts;
the horizon broadens; and the infinite opulence of things is
again shown him. But the right conditions must be observed.
Mainly he must have leave to be himself. Sancho Panza
blessed the man who invented sleep. So I prize the good invention whereby everybody is provided with somebody who is
glad to see him.

If men are less when together than they are alone, they are
also in some respects enlarged. They kindle each other; and
such is the power of suggestion, that each sprightly story calls
out more; and sometimes a fact that had long slept in the
recesses of memory hears the voice, is welcomed to daylight,
and proves of rare value. Every metaphysician must have observed, not only that no thought is alone, but that thoughts
commonly go in pairs; though the related thoughts first appeared in his mind at long distances of time. Things are in
pairs : a natural fact has only half its value, until a fact in
moral nature, its counterpart, is stated. Then they confirm
and adorn each other; a story is matched by another story.
And that may be the reason why, when a gentleman has told
a good thing, he immediately tells it again.

Nothing seems so cheap as the benefit of conversation :
nothing is more rare. 'T is wonderful how you are balked

and baffled.   There is plenty of intelligence, reading, curiosity ; but serious, happy discourse, avoiding personalities, dealing with results, is rare : and I seldom meet with a reading
and thoughtful person but he tells me, as if it were his exceptional mishap, that he has no companion.

Suppose such a one to go out exploring different circles in
search of this wise and genial counterpart, — he might in-
quire far and wide.   Conversation in society is found to be on
a platform so low as to exclude science, the saint, and the poet.
Amidst all the gay banter, sentiment cannot profane itself and
venture out.   The reply of old Isocrates comes so often to
mind, — " The things which are now seasonable I cannot say ;
and for the things which I can say it is not now the time."   Besides, who can resist the charm of talent ?   The lover of letters
loves power too.   Among the men of wit and learning, he could
not withhold his homage from the gayety, grasp of memory,
luck, splendor, and speed ; such exploits of discourse, such
feats of society !   What new powers, what mines of wealth !
But when he came home, his brave sequins were dry leaves.
He found either that the fact they had thus dizened and
adorned was of no value, or that he already knew all and more
than all they had told him.   He could not find that he was
helped by so much as one thought or principle, one solid fact,
one commanding impulse : great was the dazzle, but the gain
was small.   He uses his occasions ; he seeks the company of
those who have convivial talent.   But the moment they meet,
to be sure they begin to be something else than they were ;
they play pranks, dance jigs, run on each other, pun, tell
stories, try many fantastic tricks, under some superstition that
there must be excitement and elevation ; — and they kill conversation at once.   I know well the rusticity of the shy hermit.   No doubt he does not make allowance enough for men
of more active blood and habit.   But it is only on natural
ground that conversation can be rich.   It must not begin with
uproar and violence.   Let it keep the ground, let it feel the
connection with the battery.   Men must not be off their centres.

Some men love only to talk where they are masters.   They
like to go to school-girls, or to boys, or into the shops where
the sauntering people gladly lend an ear to any one.   On
these terms they give information, and please themselves by
sallies and chat which are admired by the idlers ; and the
talker is at his ease and jolly, for he can walk out without cere-

mony when he pleases. They go rarely to their equals, and then as for their own convenience simply, making too much haste to introduce and impart their new whim or discovery; listen badly, or do not listen to the comment or to the thought by which the company strive to repay them; rather, as soon as their own speech is done, they take their hats. Then there are the gladiators, to whom it is always a battle; 't is no matter on which side, they fight for victory; then the heady men, the egotists, the monotones, the steriles, and the impracticables.

It does not help that you find as good or a better man than yourself, if he is not timed and fitted to you. The greatest sufferers are often those who have the most to say, — men of a delicate sympathy, who are dumb in mixed company. Able people, if they do not know how to make allowance for them, paralyze them. One of those conceited prigs who value nature only as it feeds and exhibits them is equally a pest with the roysterers. There must be large reception as well as giving. How delightful after these disturbers is the radiant, playful wit of — one whom I need not name, — for in every society there is his representative. Good-nature is stronger than tomahawks. His conversation is all pictures: he can reproduce whatever he has seen; he tells the best story in the county, and is of such genial temper that he disposes all others irresistibly to good-humor and discourse. Diderot said of the Abbé Galiani: "He was a treasure in rainy days; and if the cabinet-makers made such things, everybody would have one in the country."

One lesson we learn early, — that, in spite of seeming differences, men are all of one pattern. We readily assume this with our mates, and are disappointed and angry if we find that we are premature, and that their watches are slower than ours. In fact, the only sin which we never forgive in each other is difference of opinion. We know beforehand that yonder man must think as we do. Has he not two hands, — two feet, — hair and nails? Does he not eat, — bleed, — laugh, — cry? His dissent from me is the veriest affectation. This conclusion is at once the logic of persecution and of love. And the ground of our indignation is our conviction that his dissent is some wilfulness he practises on himself. He checks the flow of his opinion as the cross cow holds up her milk. Yes, and we look into his eye, and see that he knows it and hides his eye from ours.

But to come a little nearer to my mark, I am to say that there may easily be obstacles in the way of finding the pure article we are in search of; but when we find it, it is worth the pursuit, for beside its comfort as medicine and cordial, once in the right company, new and vast values do not fail to appear. All that man can do for man is to be found in that market. There are great prizes in this game. Our fortunes in the world are as our mental equipment for this competition is. Yonder is a man who can answer the questions which I cannot. Is it so? Hence comes to me boundless curiosity to know his experiences and his wit. Hence competition for the stakes dearest to man. What is a match at whist, or draughts, or billiards, or chess, to a match of mother-wit, of knowledge, and of resources? However courteously we conceal it, it is social rank and spiritual power that are compared; whether in the parlor, the courts, the caucus, the senate, or the chamber of science, — which are only less or larger theatres for this competition.

He that can define, he that can answer a question so as to admit of no further answer, is the best man. This was the meaning of the story of the Sphinx. In the old time conundrums were sent from king to king by ambassadors. The seven wise masters at Periander's banquet spent their time in answering them. The life of Socrates is a propounding and a solution of these. So, in the hagiology of each nation, the lawgiver was in each case some man of eloquent tongue, whose sympathy brought him face to face with the extremes of society. Jesus, Menu, the first Buddhist, Mahomet, Zertusht, Pythagoras, are examples.

Jesus spent his life in discoursing with humble people on life and duty, in giving wise answers, showing that he saw at a larger angle of vision, and at least silencing those who were not generous enough to accept his thoughts. Luther spent his life so; and it is not his theologic works, — his "Commentary on the Galatians," and the rest, but his "Table-Talk," which is still read by men. Dr. Johnson was a man of no profound mind, — full of English limitations, English politics, English Church, Oxford philosophy; yet having a large heart, mother-wit, and good sense, which impatiently overleaped his customary bounds, his conversation as reported by Boswell has a lasting charm. Conversation is the vent of character as well as of thought; and Dr. Johnson impresses his company, not only by the point of the remark, but also, when the point fails, because *he* makes it. His obvious religion or superstition, his deep wish that they should think so or so, weighs with them, — so rare is depth of feeling, or a constitutional value for a thought or opinion, among the light-minded men and women who make up society ; and though they know that there is in the speaker a degree of short-coming, of insincerity, and of talking for victory, yet the existence of character, and habitual reverence for principles over talent or learning, is felt by the frivolous.

One of the best records of the great German master, who towered over all his contemporaries in the first thirty years of this century, is his conversations as recorded by Eckermann ; and the " Table-Talk " of Coleridge is one of the best remains of his genius.

In the Norse legends, the gods of Valhalla, when they meet the Jotuns, converse on the perilous terms that he who cannot answer the other's questions forfeits his own life. Odin comes to the threshold of the Jotun Waftrhudnir in disguise, calling himself Gangrader ; is invited into the hall, and told that he cannot go out thence unless he can answer every question Waftrhudnir shall put. Waftrhudnir asks him the name of the god of the sun, and of the god who brings the night ; what river separates the dwellings of the sons of the giants from those of the gods ; what plain lies between the gods and Surtur, their adversary, etc. ; all of which the disguised Odin answers satisfactorily. Then it is his turn to interrogate, and he is answered well for a time by the Jotun. At last he puts a question which none but himself could answer : " What did Odin whisper in the ear of his son Balder when Balder mounted the funeral pile ? " The startled giant replies : " None of the gods knows what in the old time THOU saidst in the ear of thy son : with death on my mouth have I spoken the fate-words of the generation of the Æsir ; with Odin contended I in wise words. Thou must ever the wisest be."

And still the gods and giants are so known, and still they play the same game in all the million mansions of heaven and of earth ; at all tables, clubs, and *tête-à-têtes*, the lawyers in the court-house, the senators in the capitol, the doctors in the academy, the wits in the hotel. Best is he who gives an answer that cannot be answered again. *Omnis definitio periculosa est*, and only wit has the secret. The same thing took place when Leibnitz came to visit Newton ; when Schiller came to Goethe ; when France, in the person of Madame de

Staël, visited Goethe and Schiller; when Hegel was the guest
of Victor Cousin in Paris; when Linnæus was the guest of
Jussieu.   It happened many years ago, that an American
chemist carried a letter of introduction to Dr. Dalton of Man-
chester, England, the author of the theory of atomic proportions, and was coolly enough received by the Doctor in the
laboratory where he was engaged.   Only Dr. Dalton scratched
a formula on a scrap of paper and pushed it towards the
guest, — "Had he seen that?"   The visitor scratched on another paper a formula describing some results of his own with
sulphuric acid, and pushed it across the table, — "Had he seen
that?"   The attention of the English chemist was instantly
arrested, and they became rapidly acquainted.   To answer a
question so as to admit of no reply, is the test of a man, — to
touch bottom every time.   Hyde, Earl of Rochester, asked
Lord-Keeper Guilford, "Do you not think I could understand
any business in England in a month?"   "Yes, my Lord,"
replied the other, "but I think you would understand it better in two months."   When Edward I. claimed to be acknowledged by the Scotch (1292) as lord paramount, the nobles of
Scotland replied, "No answer can be made while the throne
is vacant."   When Henry III. (1217) plead duress against his
people demanding confirmation and execution of the Charter,
the reply was: "If this were admitted, civil wars could never
close but by the extirpation of one of the contending parties."

What can you do with one of these sharp respondents?
What can you do with an eloquent man?   No rules of debate,
no contempt of court, no exclusions, no gag-laws can be contrived, that his first syllable will not set aside or overstep and
annul.   You can shut out the light, it may be; but can you
shut out gravitation?   You may condemn his book; but can
you fight against his thought?   That is always too nimble for
you, anticipates you, and breaks out victorious in some other
quarter.   Can you stop the motion of good sense?   What
can you do with Beaumarchais, who converts the censor whom
the court has appointed to stifle his play into an ardent advocate!   The court appoints another censor, who shall crush it
this time.   Beaumarchais persuades him to defend it.   The
court successively appoints three more severe inquisitors;
Beaumarchais converts them all into triumphant vindicators
of the play which is to bring in the Revolution.   Who can
stop the mouth of Luther, — of Newton? — of Franklin, —
of Mirabeau, — of Talleyrand?

These masters can make good their own place, and need no patron. Every variety of gift — science, religion, politics, letters, art, prudence, war, or love — has its vent and exchange in conversation. Conversation is the Olympic games whither every superior gift resorts to assert and approve itself, — and, of course, the inspirations of powerful and public men, with the rest. But it is not this class, — whom the splendor of their accomplishment almost inevitably guides into the vortex of ambition, makes them chancellors and commanders of council and of action, and makes them at last fatalists, — not these whom we now consider. We consider those who are interested in thoughts, their own and other men's, and who delight in comparing them, who think it the highest compliment they can pay a man, to deal with him as an intellect, to expose to him the grand and cheerful secrets perhaps never opened to their daily companions, to share with him the sphere of freedom and the simplicity of truth.

But the best conversation is rare. Society seems to have agreed to treat fictions as realities, and realities as fictions; and the simple lover of truth, especially if on very high grounds, — as a religious or intellectual seeker, — finds himself a stranger and alien.

It is possible that the best conversation is between two persons who can talk only to each other. Even Montesquieu confessed that, in conversation, if he perceived he was listened to by a third person, it seemed to him from that moment the whole question vanished from his mind. I have known persons of rare ability who were heavy company to good, social men who knew well enough how to draw out others of retiring habit; and, moreover, were heavy to intellectual men who ought to have known them. And does it never occur that we, perhaps, live with people too superior to be seen, — as there are musical notes too high for the scale of most ears? There are men who are great only to one or two companions of more opportunity, or more adapted.

It was to meet these wants that in all civil nations attempts have been made to organize conversation by bringing together cultivated people under the most favorable conditions. 'T is certain there was liberal and refined conversation in the Greek, in the Roman, and in the Middle Age. There was a time when in France a revolution occurred in domestic architecture; when the houses of the nobility, which, up to that time, had been constructed on feudal necessities, in a hollow square, —

the ground-floor being resigned to offices and stables, and the
floors above to rooms of state and to lodging-rooms, — were
rebuilt with new purpose. It was the Marchioness of Rambouillet who first got the horses out of and the scholars into
the palaces, having constructed her *hôtel* with a view to society,
with superb suites of drawing-rooms on the same floor, and
broke through the *morgue* of etiquette by inviting to her house
men of wit and learning as well as men of rank, and piqued
the emulation of Cardinal Richelieu to rival assemblies, and
so to the founding of the French Academy. The history of the
Hôtel Rambouillet and its brilliant circles makes an important
date in French civilization. And a history of clubs from early
antiquity, tracing the efforts to secure liberal and refined conversation, through the Greek and Roman to the Middle Age,
and thence down through French, English, and German memoirs, tracing the clubs and coteries in each country, would
be an important chapter in history. We know well the Mer-
maid Club, in London, of Shakespeare, Ben Jonson, Chapman,
Herrick, Selden, Beaumont and Fletcher; its "Rules" are
preserved, and many allusions to their suppers are found in
Jonson, Herrick, and in Aubrey. Anthony Wood has many
details of Harrington's Club. Dr. Bentley's Club held Newton,
Wren, Evelyn, and Locke; and we owe to Boswell our knowledge of the club of Dr. Johnson, Goldsmith, Burke, Gibbon,
Reynolds, Garrick, Beauclerk, and Percy. And we have records of the brilliant society that Edinburgh boasted in the
first decade of this century. Such societies are possible only
in great cities, and are the compensation which these can make
to their dwellers for depriving them of the free intercourse
with Nature. Every scholar is surrounded by wiser men than
he — if they cannot write as well. Cannot they meet and
exchange results to their mutual benefit and delight? It was
a pathetic experience when a genial and accomplished person
said to me, looking from his country home to the capital of
New England, "There is a town of two hundred thousand
people, and not a chair in it for me." If he were sure to find
at No. 2000 Tremont Street what scholars were abroad after
the morning studies were ended, Boston would shine as the
New Jerusalem to his eyes.

Now this want of adapted society is mutual. The man of
thought, the man of letters, the man of science, the adminis-
trator skilful in affairs, the man of manners and culture, whom
you so much wish to find, — each of these is wishing to be

found. Each wishes to open his thought, his knowledge, his social skill to the daylight in your company and affection, and to exchange his gifts for yours; and the first hint of a select and intelligent company is welcome.

But the club must be self-protecting, and obstacles arise at the outset. There are people who cannot well be cultivated, whom you must keep down and quiet if you can. There are those who have the instinct of a bat to fly against any lighted candle and put it out, — marplots and contradictors. There are those who go only to talk, and those who go only to hear : both are bad. A right rule for a club would be, — Admit no man whose presence excludes any one topic. It requires people who are not surprised and shocked, who do and let do, and let be, who sink trifles, and know solid values, and who take a great deal for granted.

It is always a practical difficulty with clubs to regulate the laws of election so as to exclude peremptorily every social nuisance. Nobody wishes bad manners. We must have loyalty and character. The poet Marvell was wont to say "that he would not drink wine with any one with whom he could not trust his life." But neither can we afford to be superfine. A man of irreproachable behavior and excellent sense preferred on his travels taking his chance at a hotel for company, to the charging himself with too many select letters of introduction. He confessed he liked low company. He said the fact was incontestable, that the society of gypsies was more attractive than that of bishops. The girl deserts the parlor for the kitchen; the boy, for the wharf. Tutors and parents cannot interest him like the uproarious conversation he finds in the market or the dock. I knew a scholar, of some experience in camps, who said that he liked, in a bar-room, to tell a few 'coon stories, and put himself on a good footing with the company; then he could be as silent as he chose. A scholar does not wish to be always pumping his brains : he wants gossips. The black-coats are good company only for black-coats; but when the manufacturers, merchants, and ship-masters meet, see how much they have to say, and how long the conversation lasts! They have come from many zones; they have traversed wide countries; they know each his own arts, and the cunning artisans of his craft; they have seen the best and the worst of men. Their knowledge contradicts the popular opinion and your own on many points. Things which you fancy wrong they know to be right and

profitable ; things which you reckon superstitious they know
to be true.   They have found virtue in the strangest homes ;
and in the rich store of their adventures are instances and
examples which you have been seeking in vain for years, and
which they suddenly and unwittingly offer you.

I remember a social experiment in this direction, wherein it
appeared that each of the members fancied he was in need of
society, but himself unpresentable.   On trial they all found
that they could be tolerated by, and could tolerate, each other.
Nay, the tendency to extreme self-respect which hesitated to
join in a club was running rapidly down to abject admiration
of each other, when the club was broken up by new combinations.

The use of the hospitality of the club hardly needs explanation.   Men are unbent and social at table ; and I remember it
was explained to me, in a Southern city, that it was impossible
to set any public charity on foot unless through a tavern dinner.   I do not think our metropolitan charities would plead
the same necessity ; but to a club met for conversation a sup-
per is a good basis, as it disarms all parties, and puts pedantry
and business to the door.   All are in good humor and at
leisure, which are the first conditions of discourse ; the ordinary reserves are thrown off, experienced men meet with the
freedom of boys, and, sooner or later, impart all that is singular in their experience.

The hospitalities of clubs are easily exaggerated.   No doubt
the suppers of wits and philosophers acquire much lustre by
time and renown.   Plutarch, Xenophon, and Plato, who have
celebrated each a banquet of their set, have given us next to
no data of the viands ; and it is to be believed that an indifferent tavern dinner in such society was more relished by the
convives than a much better one in worse company.   Herrick's
verses to Ben Jonson no doubt paint the fact : —

> " When we such clusters had
> As made us nobly wild, not mad ;
> And yet, each verse of thine
> Outdid the meat, outdid the frolic wine."

Such friends make the feast satisfying ; and I notice that it
was when things went prosperously, and the company was
full of honor, at the banquet of the Cid, that " the guests all
were joyful, and agreed in one thing, — that they had not
eaten better for three years."

I need only hint the value of the club for bringing masters

in their several arts to compare and expand their views, to come to an understanding on these points, and so that their united opinion shall have its just influence on public questions of education and politics. 'T is agreed that in the sections of the British Association more information is mutually and effectually communicated, in a few hours, than in many months of ordinary correspondence, and the printing and transmission of ponderous reports. We know that *l'homme de lettres* is a little wary, and not fond of giving away his seed-corn; but there is an infallible way to draw him out, namely, by having as good as he. If you have Tuscaroora and he Canada, he may exchange kernel for kernel. If his discretion is incurable, and he dare not speak of fairy gold, he will yet tell what new books he has found, what old ones recovered, what men write and read abroad. A principal purpose also is the hospitality of the club, as a means of receiving a worthy foreigner with mutual advantage.

Every man brings into society some partial thought and local culture. We need range and alternation of topics, and variety of minds. One likes in a companion a phlegm which it is a triumph to disturb, and, not less, to make in an old acquaintance unexpected discoveries of scope and power through the advantage of an inspiring subject. Wisdom is like electricity. There is no permanently wise man, but men capable of wisdom, who, being put into certain company, or other favorable conditions, become wise for a short time, as glasses rubbed acquire electric power for a while. But, while we look complacently at these obvious pleasures and values of good companions, I do not forget that Nature is always very much in earnest, and that her great gifts have something serious and stern. When we look for the highest benefits of conversation, the Spartan rule of one to one is usually enforced. Discourse, when it rises highest and searches deepest, when it lifts us into that mood out of which thoughts come that remain as stars in our firmament, is between two.

COURAGE.

COURAGE.

I OBSERVE that there are three qualities which conspicuously attract the wonder and reverence of mankind : —

1. Disinterestedness, as shown in indifference to the ordinary bribes and influences of conduct, — a purpose so sincere and generous that it cannot be tempted aside by any prospects of wealth or other private advantage. Self-love is, in almost all men, such an over-weight, that they are incredulous of a man's habitual preference of the general good to his own ; but when they see it proved by sacrifices of ease, wealth, rank, and of life itself, there is no limit to their admiration. This has made the power of the saints of the East and West, who have led the religion of great nations. Self-sacrifice is the real miracle out of which all the reported miracles grew. This makes the renown of the heroes of Greece and Rome, — of Socrates, Aristides, and Phocion ; of Quintus Curtius, Cato, and Regulus ; of Hatem Tai's hospitality ; of Chatham, whose scornful magnanimity gave him immense popularity ; of Washington, giving his service to the public without salary or reward.

2. Practical power. Men admire the man who can organize their wishes and thoughts in stone and wood and steel and brass, — the man who can build the boat, who has the impiety to make the rivers run the way he wants them, who can lead his telegraph through the ocean from shore to shore ; who, sitting in his closet, can lay out the plans of a campaign, — sea-war and land-war ; such that the best generals and admirals, when all is done, see that they must thank him for success ; the power of better combination and foresight, however exhibited, which, whether it only plays a game of chess, or whether, more loftily, a cunning mathematician, penetrating the cubic weights of stars, predicts the planet which eyes

had never seen; or whether, exploring the chemical elements whereof we and the world are made, and seeing their secret, Franklin draws off the lightning in his hand, suggesting that one day a wiser geology shall make the earthquake harmless and the volcano an agricultural resource. Or here is one who, seeing the wishes of men, knows how to come at their end; whispers to this friend, argues down that adversary, moulds society to his purpose, and looks at all men as wax for his hands, — takes command of them as the wind does of clouds, as the mother does of the child, or the man that knows more does of the man that knows less; and leads them in glad surprise to the very point where they would be : this man is followed with acclamation.

3. The third excellence is courage, the perfect will, which no terrors can shake, which is attracted by frowns or threats or hostile armies, nay, needs these to awaken and fan its reserved energies into a pure flame, and is never quite itself until the hazard is extreme; then it is serene and fertile, and all its powers play well. There is a Hercules, an Achilles, a Rustem, an Arthur, or a Cid in the mythology of every nation; and in authentic history, a Leonidas, a Scipio, a Cæsar, a Richard Cœur de Lion, a Cromwell, a Nelson, a Great Condé, a Bertrand du Guesclin, a Doge Dandolo, a Napoleon, a Massena, a Ney. 'T is said courage is common, but the immense esteem in which it is held proves it to be rare. Animal resistance, the instinct of the male animal when cornered, is no doubt common; but the pure article, courage with eyes, courage with conduct, self-possession at the cannon's mouth, cheerfulness in lonely adherence to the right, is the endowment of elevated characters. I need not show how much it is esteemed, for the people give it the first rank. They forgive everything to it. What an ado we make through two thousand years about Thermopylæ and Salamis! What a memory of Poitiers and Crecy, and Bunker Hill, and Washington's endurance! And any man who puts his life in peril in a cause which is esteemed becomes the darling of all men. The very nursery-books, the ballads which delight boys, the romances which delight men, the favorite topics of eloquence, the thunderous emphasis which orators give to every martial defiance and passage of arms, and which the people greet, may testify. How short a time since this whole nation rose every morning to read or to hear the traits of courage of its sons and brothers in the field, and was never weary of the theme! We

have had examples of men who, for showing effective courage on a single occasion, have become a favorite spectacle to nations, and must be brought in chariots to every mass meeting.

Men are so charmed with valor, that they have pleased themselves with being called lions, leopards, eagles, and dragons, from the animals contemporary with us in the geologic formations. But the animals have great advantage of us in precocity. Touch the snapping-turtle with a stick, and he seizes it with his teeth. Cut off his head, and the teeth will not let go the stick. Break the egg of the young, and the little embryo, before yet the eyes are open, bites fiercely ; these vivacious creatures contriving, — shall we say ? — not only to bite after they are dead, but also to bite before they are born.

But man begins life helpless. The babe is in paroxysms of fear the moment its nurse leaves it alone, and it comes so slowly to any power of self-protection, that mothers say the salvation of the life and health of a young child is a perpetual miracle. The terrors of the child are quite reasonable, and add to his loveliness ; for his utter ignorance and weakness, and his enchanting indignation on such a small basis of capital, compel every by-stander to take his part. Every moment, as long as he is awake, he studies the use of his eyes, ears, hands, and feet, learning how to meet and avoid his dangers, and thus every hour loses one terror more. But this education stops too soon. A large majority of men being bred in families, and beginning early to be occupied day by day with some routine of safe industry, never come to the rough experiences that make the Indian, the soldier, or the frontiersman self-subsistent and fearless. Hence the high price of courage indicates the general timidity. "Mankind," said Franklin, "are dastardly when they meet with opposition." In war even, generals are seldom found eager to give battle. Lord Wellington said, "Uniforms were often masks"; and again, "When my journal appears, many statues must come down." The Norse Sagas relate that when Bishop Magne reproved King Sigurd for his wicked divorce, the priest who attended the bishop, expecting every moment when the savage king would burst with rage and slay his superior, said "that he saw the sky no bigger than a calf-skin." And I remember when a pair of Irish girls, who had been run away with in a wagon by a skittish horse, said that, when he began to rear, they were so frightened that they could not see the horse.

Cowardice shuts the eyes till the sky is not larger than a calf-skin; shuts the eyes so that we cannot see the horse that is running away with us; worse, shuts the eyes of the mind and chills the heart. Fear is cruel and mean. The political reigns of terror have been reigns of madness and malignity, — a total perversion of opinion; society is upside down, and its best men are thought too bad to live. Then the protection which a house, a family, neighborhood and property, even the first accumulation of savings, gives, go in all times to generate this taint of the respectable classes. Voltaire said, "One of the chief misfortunes of honest people is that they are cowardly." Those political parties which gather-in the well-disposed portion of the community, — how infirm and ignoble! what white lips they have! always on the defensive, as if the lead were intrusted to the journals, often written in great part by women and boys, who, without strength, wish to keep up the appearance of strength. They can do the hurras, the placarding, the flags, — and the voting, if it is a fair day; but the aggressive attitude of men who will have right done, will no longer be bothered with burglars and ruffians in the streets, counterfeiters in public offices, and thieves on the bench; that part, the part of the leader and soul of the vigilance committee, must be taken by stout and sincere men who are really angry and determined. In ordinary, we have a snappish criticism which watches and contradicts the opposite party. We want the will which advances and dictates. When we get an advantage, as in Congress the other day, it is because our adversary has committed a fault, not that we have taken the initiative and given the law. Nature has made up her mind that what cannot defend itself shall not be defended. Complaining never so loud, and with never so much reason, is of no use. One heard much cant of peace-parties long ago in Kansas and elsewhere, that their strength lay in the greatness of their wrongs, and dissuading all resistance, as if to make this strength greater. But were their wrongs greater than the negro's? and what kind of strength did they ever give him? It was always invitation to the tyrant, and bred disgust in those who would protect the victim. What cannot stand must fall; and the measure of our sincerity, and therefore of the respect of men, is the amount of health and wealth we will hazard in the defence of our right. An old farmer, my neighbor across the fence, when I ask him if he is not going to town-meeting, says: "No; 'tis no use balloting, for

it will not stay; but what you do with the gun will stay so."
Nature has charged every one with his own defence as with
his own support, and the only title I can have to your help is
when I have manfully put forth all the means I possess to
keep me, and, being overborne by odds, the by-standers have
a natural wish to interfere and see fair play.

But with this pacific education, we have no readiness for bad
times. I am much mistaken if every man who went to the
army in the late war had not a lively curiosity to know how he
should behave in action. Tender, amiable boys, who had
never encountered any rougher play than a base-ball match or
a fishing excursion, were suddenly drawn up to face a bayonet
charge or capture a battery. Of course, they must each go
into that action with a certain despair. Each whispers to
himself: "My exertions must be of small account to the result; only will the benignant Heaven save me from disgracing
myself and my friends and my State. Die! O yes, 1 can well
die; but I cannot afford to misbehave; and I do not know how
I shall feel." So great a soldier as the old French Marshal
Montluc acknowledges that he has often trembled with fear,
and recovered courage when he had said a prayer for the occasion. I knew a young soldier who died in the early campaign, who confided to his sister that he had made up his
mind to volunteer for the war. "I have not," he said, "any
proper courage, but I shall never let any one find it out."
And he had accustomed himself always to go into whatever
place of danger, and do whatever he was afraid to do, setting
a dogged resolution to resist this natural infirmity. Coleridge
has preserved an anecdote of an officer in the British Navy,
who told him that when he, in his first boat expedition, a mid-
shipman in his fourteenth year, accompanied Sir Alexander
Ball, "as we were rowing up to the vessel we were to attack,
amid a discharge of musketry, I was overpowered with fear,
my knees shook and I was ready to faint away. Lieutenant
Ball seeing me, placed himself close beside me, took hold of my
hand and whispered, 'Courage, my dear boy! you will recover
in a minute or so; I was just the same when I first went out
in this way.' It was as if an angel spoke to me. From that moment I was as fearless and as forward as the oldest of the boat's
crew. But I dare not think what would have become of me,
if, at that moment, he had scoffed and exposed me."

Knowledge is the antidote to fear, — Knowledge, Use, and
Reason, with its higher aids. The child is as much in danger

from a staircase, or the fire-grate, or a bath-tub, or a cat, as the soldier from a cannon or an ambush. Each surmounts the fear as fast as he precisely understands the peril, and learns the means of resistance. Each is liable to panic, which is, exactly, the terror of ignorance surrendered to the imagination. Knowledge is the encourager, knowledge that takes fear out of the heart, knowledge and use, which is knowledge in practice. They can conquer who believe they can. It is he who has done the deed once who does not shrink from attempting it again. It is the groom who knows the jumping horse well who can safely ride him. It is the veteran soldier, who, seeing the flash of the cannon, can step aside from the path of the ball. Use makes a better soldier than the most urgent considerations of duty,— familiarity with danger enabling him to estimate the danger. He sees how much is the risk, and is not afflicted with imagination; knows practically Marshal Saxe's rule, that every soldier killed costs the enemy his weight in lead.

The sailor loses fear as fast as he acquires command of sails and spars and steam; the frontiersman, when he has a perfect rifle and has acquired a sure aim. To the sailor's experience every new circumstance suggests what he must do. The terrific chances which make the hours and the minutes long to the passenger, he whiles away by incessant application of expedients and repairs. To him a leak, a hurricane, or a waterspout is so much work,— no more. The hunter is not alarmed by bears, catamounts, or wolves, nor the grazier by his bull, nor the dog-breeder by his bloodhound, nor an Arab by the simoom, nor a farmer by a fire in the woods. The forest on fire looks discouraging enough to a citizen : the farmer is skilful to fight it. The neighbors run together; with pine boughs they can mop out the flame, and, by raking with the hoe a long but little trench, confine to a patch the fire which would easily spread over a hundred acres.

In short, courage consists in equality to the problem before us. The school-boy is daunted before his tutor by a question of arithmetic, because he does not yet command the simple steps of the solution which the boy beside him has mastered. These once seen, he is as cool as Archimedes, and cheerily proceeds a step farther. Courage is equality to the problem, in affairs, in science, in trade, in council, or in action ; consists in the conviction that the agents with whom you contend are not superior in strength or resources or spirit to you. The general must stimulate the mind of his soldiers to the perception that they are men, and the enemy is no more. Knowledge, yes; for the danger of dangers is illusion. The eye is easily daunted; and the drums, flags, shining helmets, beard, and mustache of the soldier have conquered you long before his sword or bayonet reaches you.

But we do not exhaust the subject in the slight analysis; we must not forget the variety of temperaments, each of which qualifies this power of resistance. It is observed that men with little imagination are less fearful; they wait till they feel pain, whilst others of more sensibility anticipate it, and suffer in the fear of the pang more acutely than in the pang. 'T is certain that the threat is sometimes more formidable than the stroke, and 't is possible that the beholders suffer more keenly than the victims. Bodily pain is superficial, seated usually in the skin and the extremities, for the sake of giving us warning to put us on our guard; not in the vitals, where the rupture that produces death is perhaps not felt, and the victim never knew what hurt him. Pain is superficial, and therefore fear is. The torments of martyrdoms are probably most keenly felt by the by-standers. The torments are illusory. The first suffering is the last suffering, the later hurts being lost on insensibility. Our affections and wishes for the external welfare of the hero tumultuously rush to expression in tears and outcries; but we, like him, subside into indifferency and defiance, when we perceive how short is the longest arm of malice, how serene is the sufferer.

It is plain that there is no separate essence called courage, no cup or cell in the brain, no vessel in the heart containing drops or atoms that make or give this virtue; but it is the right or healthy state of every man, when he is free to do that which is constitutional to him to do. It is directness,— the instant performing of that which he ought. The thoughtful man says, you differ from me in opinion and methods; but do you not see that I cannot think or act otherwise than I do? that my way of living is organic? And to be really strong we must adhere to our own means. On organic action all strength depends. Hear what women say of doing a task by sheer force of will: it costs them a fit of sickness. Plutarch relates that the Pythoness who tried to prophesy without command in the Temple at Delphi, though she performed the usual rites, and inhaled the air of the cavern standing on the tripod, fell into convulsions, and died. Undoubtedly there is a temperamental courage, a warlike blood, which loves a fight, does not feel itself except in a quarrel, as one sees in wasps, or ants, or cocks, or cats. The like vein appears in certain races of men and in individuals of every race. In every school there are certain fighting boys; in every society, the contradicting men; in every town, bravoes and bullies, better or worse dressed, fancy-men, patrons of the cock-pit and the ring. Courage is temperamental, scientific, ideal. Swedenborg has left this record of his king : " Charles XII., of Sweden did not know what that was which others called fear, nor what that spurious valor and daring that is excited by inebriating draughts, for he never tasted any liquid but pure water. Of him we may say, that he led a life more remote from death, and in fact lived more, than any other man." It was told of the Prince of Condé, "that there not being a more furious man in the world, danger in fight never disturbs him more than just to make him civil, and to command in words of great obligation to his officers and men, and without any the least disturbance to his judgment or spirit." Each has his own courage, as his own talent; but the courage of the tiger is one, and of the horse another. The dog that scorns to fight, will fight for his master. The llama that will carry a load if you caress him, will refuse food and die if he is scourged. The fury of onset is one, and of calm endurance another. There is a courage of the cabinet as well as a courage of the field; a courage of manners in private assemblies, and another in public assemblies; a courage which enables one man to speak masterly to a hostile company, whilst another man who can easily face a cannon's mouth dares not open his own.

There is a courage of a merchant in dealing with his trade, by which dangerous turns of affairs are met and prevailed over. Merchants recognize as much gallantry, well judged too, in the conduct of a wise and upright man of business, in difficult times, as soldiers in a soldier.

There is a courage in the treatment of every art by a master in architecture, in sculpture, in painting, or in poetry, each cheering the mind of the spectator or receiver as by true strokes of genius, which yet nowise implies the presence of physical valor in the artist. This is the courage of genius, in every kind. A certain quantity of power belongs to a certain quantity of faculty. The beautiful voice at church goes sounding on, and covers up in its volume, as in a cloak, all the defects of the choir. The singers, I observe, all yield to it, and so the fair singer indulges her instinct, and dares, and dares, because she knows she can.

It gives the cutting edge to every profession. The judge puts his mind to the tangle of contradictions in the case, squarely accosts the question, and, by not being afraid of it, by dealing with it as business which must be disposed of, he sees presently that common arithmetic and common methods apply to this affair. Perseverance strips it of all peculiarity, and ranges it on the same ground as other business. Morphy played a daring game in chess : the daring was only an illusion of the spectator, for the player sees his move to be well fortified and safe. You may see the same dealing in criticism ; a new book astonishes for a few days, takes itself out of common jurisdiction, and nobody knows what to say of it : but the scholar is not deceived. The old principles which books exist to express are more beautiful than any book ; and out of love of the reality he is an expert judge how far the book has approached it and where it has come short. In all applications 't is the same power, — the habit of reference to one's own mind, as the home of all truth and counsel, and which can easily dispose of any book because it can very well do without all books. When a confident man comes into a company magnifying this or that author he has freshly read, the company grow silent and ashamed of their ignorance. But I remember the old professor, whose searching mind engraved every word he spoke on the memory of the class, when we asked if he had read this or that shining novelty, " No, I have never read that book " ; instantly the book lost credit, and was not to be heard of again.

Every creature has a courage of his constitution fit for his duties : — Archimedes, the courage of a geometer to stick to his diagram, heedless of the siege and sack of the city ; and the Roman soldier his faculty to strike at Archimedes. . Each is strong, relying on his own, and each is betrayed when he seeks in himself the courage of others.

Captain John Brown, the hero of Kansas, said to me in conversation, that " for a settler in a new country, one good, believing, strong-minded man is worth a hundred, nay, a thousand men without character ; and that the right men will give a permanent direction to the fortunes of a state. As for the bullying drunkards, of which armies are usually made up, he thought cholera, small-pox, and consumption as valuable recruits." He held the belief that courage and chastity are

silent concerning themselves. He said, "As soon as I hear
one of my men say, 'Ah, let me only get my eye on such a
man, I'll bring him down,' I don't expect much aid in the
fight from that talker. 'T is the quiet, peaceable men, the
men of principle, that make the best soldiers."

> " 'T is still observed those men most valiant are
> Who are most modest ere they came to war."

True courage is not ostentatious; men who wish to inspire
terror seem thereby to confess themselves cowards. Why do
they rely on it, but because they know how potent it is with
themselves?

The true temper has genial influences. It makes a bond
of union between enemies. Governor Wise of Virginia, in
the record of his first interviews with his prisoner, appeared
to great advantage. If Governor Wise is a superior man, or
inasmuch as he is a superior man, he distinguishes John
Brown. As they confer, they understand each other swiftly;
each respects the other. If opportunity allowed, they would
prefer each other's society and desert their former companions. Enemies would become affectionate. Hector and
Achilles, Richard and Saladin, Wellington and Soult, General
Daumas and Abdel Kader, become aware that they are nearer
and more alike than any other two, and, if their nation and
circumstance did not keep them apart, would run into each
other's arms.

See too what good contagion belongs to it. Everywhere it
finds its own with magnetic affinity. Courage of the soldier
awakes the courage of woman. Florence Nightingale brings
lint and the blessing of her shadow. Heroic women offer
themselves as nurses of the brave veteran. The troop of Vir-
ginian infantry that had marched to guard the prison of John
Brown ask leave to pay their respects to the prisoner. Poetry
and eloquence catch the hint, and soar to a pitch unknown
before. Everything feels the new breath, except the old
doting, nigh-dead politicians, whose heart the trumpet of resurrection could not wake.

The charm of the best courages is that they are inventions,
inspirations, flashes of genius. The hero could not have done
the feat at another hour, in a lower mood. The best act of
the marvellous genius of Greece was its first act; not in the
statue or the Parthenon, but in the instinct, which, at Thermopylæ, held Asia at bay, kept Asia out of Europe, — Asia
with its antiquities and organic slavery, — from corrupting

the hope and new morning of the West. The statue, the architecture, were the later and inferior creation of the same genius. In view of this moment of history, we recognize a certain prophetic instinct better than wisdom. Napoleon said well, " My hand is immediately ·connected with my head "; but the *sacred* courage is connected with the heart. The head is a half, a fraction, until it is enlarged and inspired by the moral sentiment. For it is not the means on which we draw, as health or wealth, practical skill or dexterous talent, or multitudes of followers, that count, but the aims only. The aim reacts back on the means. A great aim aggrandizes the means. The meal and water that are the commissariat of the *forlorn hope* that stake ·their lives to defend the pass are sacred as the Holy Grail, or as if one had eyes to see in chemistry the fuel that is rushing to feed the sun.

There is a persuasion in the soul of man that he is here for cause, that he was put down in this place by the Creator to do the work for which he inspires him, that thus he is an overmatch for all antagonists that could combine against him. The pious Mrs. Hutchinson says of some passages in the defence of Nottingham against the Cavaliers, " It was a great instruction that the best and highest courages are beams of the Almighty." And whenever the religious sentiment is adequately affirmed, it must be with dazzling courage. As long as it is cowardly insinuated, as with the wish to succor some partial and temporary interest, or to make it affirm some pragmatical tenet which our parish church receives to-day, it is not imparted, and cannot inspire or create. For it is always new, leads and surprises, and practice never comes up with it. There are ever appearing in the world men who, almost as soon as they are born, take a bee-line to the rack of the inquisitor, the axe of the tyrant, like Jordano Bruno, Vanini, Huss, Paul, Jesus, and Socrates. Look at Fox's Lives of the Martyrs, Sewel's History of the Quakers, Southey's Book of the Church, at the folios of the Brothers Bollandi, who collected the lives of. twenty-five thousand martyrs, confessors, ascetics, and self-tormentors. There is much of fable, but a broad basis of fact. The tender skin does not shrink from bayonets, the timid woman is not scared by fagots ; the rack is not frightful, nor the rope ignominious. The poor Puritan, Antony Parsons, at the stake, tied straw on his head, when the fire approached him, and said, " This is God's hat." Sacred courage indicates that a man loves an idea better than all things in the world; that he is aiming neither at pelf nor comfort, but will venture all to put in act the invisible thought in his mind. He is everywhere a liberator, but of a freedom that is ideal; not seeking to have land or money or conveniences, but to have no other limitation than that which his own constitution imposes. He is free to speak truth; he is not free to lie. He wishes to break every yoke all over the world which hinders his brother from acting after his thought.

There are degrees of courage, and each step upward makes us acquainted with a higher virtue. Let us say then frankly that the education of the will is the object of our existence. Poverty, the prison, the rack, the fire, the hatred and execrations of our fellow-men, appear trials beyond the endurance of common humanity; but to the hero whose intellect is aggrandized by the soul, and so measures these penalties against the good which his thought surveys, these terrors vanish as darkness at sunrise.

We have little right in piping times of peace to pronounce on these rare heights of character; but there is no assurance of security. In the most private life, difficult duty is never far off. Therefore we must think with courage. Scholars and thinkers are prone to an effeminate habit, and shrink if a coarser shout comes up from the street, or a brutal act is recorded in the journals. The Medical College piles up in its museum its grim monsters of morbid anatomy, and there are melancholy sceptics with a taste for carrion who batten on the hideous facts in history, — persecutions, inquisitions, St. Bartholomew massacres, devilish lives, Nero, Cæsar, Borgia, Marat, Lopez, — men in whom every ray of humanity was extinguished, parricides, matricides, and whatever moral monsters. These are not cheerful facts, but they do not disturb a healthy mind; they require of us a patience as robust as the energy that attacks us, and an unresting exploration of final causes. Wolf, snake, and crocodile are not inharmonious in nature, but are made useful as checks, scavengers, and pioneers; and we must have a scope as large as Nature's to deal with beastlike men, detect what scullion function is assigned them, and foresee in the secular melioration of the planet how these will become unnecessary, and will die out.

He has not learned the lesson of life who does not every day surmount a fear. I do not wish to put myself or any man into a theatrical position, or urge him to ape the courage of his comrade. Have the courage not to adopt another's cour-

age. There is scope and cause and resistance enough for us
in our proper work and circumstance. And there is no creed
of an honest man, be he Christian, Turk, or Gentoo, which
does not equally preach it. If you have no faith in beneficent
power above you, but see only an adamantine fate coiling its
folds above nature and man, then reflect that the best use of
fate is to teach us courage, if only because baseness cannot
change the appointed event. If you accept your thoughts as
inspirations from the Supreme Intelligence, obey them when
they prescribe difficult duties, because they come only so long
as they are used ; or, if your scepticism reaches to the last
verge, and you have no confidence in any foreign mind, then
be brave, because there is one good opinion which must always
be of consequence to you, namely, your own.

———

I am permitted to enrich my chapter by adding an anecdote of pure courage from real life, as narrated in a ballad
by a lady to whom all the particulars of the fact are exactly
known.

GEORGE NIDIVER.

Men have done brave deeds,
    And bards have sung them well:
I of good George Nidiver
    Now the tale will tell.

In Californian mountains
    A hunter bold was he:
Keen his eye and sure his aim
    As any you should see.

A little Indian boy
    Followed him everywhere,
Eager to share the hunter's joy,
    The hunter's meal to share.

And when the bird or deer
    Fell by the hunter's skill,
The boy was always near
    To help with right good-will.

One day as through the cleft
    Between two mountains steep,
Shut in both right and left,
    Their questing way they keep,

They see two grizzly bears
  With hunger fierce and fell
Rush at them unawares
  Right down the narrow dell.

The boy turned round with screams,
  And ran with terror wild;
One of the pair of savage beasts
  Pursued the shrieking child.

The hunter raised his gun, —
  He knew *one* charge was all, —
And through the boy's pursuing foe
  He sent his only ball.

The other on George Nidiver
  Came on with dreadful pace:
The hunter stood unarmed,
  And met him face to face.

I say *unarmed* he stood.
  Against those frightful paws,
The rifle but, or club of wood,
  Could stand no more than straws.

George Nidiver stood still
  And looked him in the face;
The wild beast stopped amazed,
  Then came with slackening pace.

Still firm the hunter stood,
  Although his heart beat high;
Again the creature stopped,
  And gazed with wondering eye.

The hunter met his gaze,
  Nor yet an inch gave way;
The bear turned slowly round,
  And slowly moved away.

What thoughts were in his mind
  It would be hard to spell:
What thoughts were in George Nidiver
  I rather guess than tell.

But sure that rifle's aim,
  Swift choice of generous part,
Showed in its passing gleam
  The depths of a brave heart.

SUCCESS.

OUR American people cannot be taxed with slowness in performance or in praising their performance. The earth is shaken by our enginerics. We are feeling our youth and nerve and bone. We have the power of territory and of sea-coast, and know the use of these. We count our census, we read our growing valuations, we survey our map, which becomes old in a year or two. Our eyes run approvingly along the lengthened lines of railroad and telegraph. We have gone nearest to the Pole. We have discovered the Antarctic continent. We interfere in Central and South America, at Canton, and in Japan; we are adding to an already enormous territory. Our political constitution is the hope of the world, and we value ourselves on all these feats.

'T is the way of the world; 't is the law of youth, and of unfolding strength. Men are made each with some triumphant superiority, which, through some adaptation of fingers, or ear, or eye, or ciphering, or pugilistic or musical or literary craft, enriches the community with a new art; and not only we, but all men of European stock value these certificates. Giotto could draw a perfect circle; Erwin of Steinbach could build a minster; Olaf, king of Norway, could run round his galley on the blades of the oars of the rowers, when the ship was in motion; Ojeda could run out swiftly on a plank projecting from the top of a tower, turn round swiftly and come back; Evelyn writes from Rome: "Bernini, the Florentine sculptor, architect, painter, and poet, a little before my coming to Rome, gave a public opera, wherein he painted the scenes, cut the statues, invented the engines, composed the music, writ the comedy, and built the theatre."

"There is nothing in war," said Napoleon, "which I cannot do by my own hands. If there is nobody to make gunpowder, I can manufacture it. The gun-carriages I know how to con-

K

struct.   If it is necessary to make cannons at the forge, I can make them.   The details of working them in battle, if it is necessary to teach, I shall teach them.   In administration, it is I alone who have arranged the finances, as you know."

It is recorded of Linnæus, among many proofs of his beneficent skill, that when the timber in the ship-yards of Sweden was ruined by rot, Linnæus was desired by the government to find a remedy.   He studied the insects that infested the timber, and found that they laid their eggs in the logs within certain days in April, and he directed that during ten days at that season the logs should be immersed under water in the docks; which being done the timber was found to be uninjured.

Columbus at Veragua found plenty of gold ; but leaving the coast, the ship full of one hundred and fifty skilful seamen, — some of them old pilots, and with too much experience of their craft and treachery to him, — the wise admiral kept his private record of his homeward path.   And when he reached Spain, he told the King and Queen, "that they may ask all the pilots who came with him, where is Veragua.   Let them answer and say, if they know where Veragua lies.   I assert that they can give no other account than that they went to lands where there was abundance of gold, but they do not know the way to return thither, but would be obliged to go on a voyage of discovery as much as if they had never been there before.   There is a mode of reckoning," he proudly adds, "derived from astronomy, which is sure and safe to any who understands it."

Hippocrates in Greece knew how to stay the devouring plague which ravaged Athens in his time, and his skill died with him.   Dr. Benjamin Rush, in Philadelphia, carried that city heroically through the yellow fever of the year 1793. Leverrier carries the Copernican system in his head, and knew where to look for the new planet.   We have seen an American woman write a novel of which a million copies were sold in all languages, and which had one merit, of speaking to the universal heart, and was read with equal interest to three audiences, namely, in the parlor, in the kitchen, and in the nursery of every house.   We have seen women who could institute hospitals and schools in armies.   We have seen a woman who by pure song could melt the souls of whole populations.   And there is no limit to these varieties of talent.

These are arts to be thankful for, — each one as it is a new direction of human power.   We cannot choose but respect

them. Our civilization is made up of a million contributions
of this kind. For success, to be sure, we esteem it a test in
other people, since we do first in ourselves. We respect ourselves more if we have succeeded. Neither do we grudge to
each of these benefactors the praise or the profit which accrues
from his industry.

Here are already quite different degrees of moral merit in
these examples. I don't know but we and our race elsewhere
set a higher value on wealth, victory, and coarse superiority of
all kinds, than other men, — have less tranquillity of mind,
are less easily contented. The Saxon is taught from his infancy to wish to be first. The Norseman was a restless rider,
fighter, freebooter. The ancient Norse ballads describe him
as afflicted with this inextinguishable thirst of victory. The
mother says to her son : —

> "Success shall be in thy courser tall,
> Success in thyself, which is best of all,
> Success in thy hand, success in thy foot,
> In struggle with man, in battle with brute : —
> The holy God and Saint Drothin dear
> Shall never shut eyes on thy career;
>   Look out, look out, Svend Vonved ! "

These feats that we extol do not signify so much as we say.
These boasted arts are of very recent origin. They are local
conveniences, but do not really add to our stature. The greatest
men of the world have managed not to want them. Newton
was a great man, without telegraph, or gas, or steam-coach, or
rubber shoes, or lucifer-matches, or ether for his pain ; so was
Shakspeare, and Alfred, and Scipio, and Socrates. These are
local conveniences, but how easy to go now to parts of the
world where not only all these arts are wanting, but where they
are despised. The Arabian sheiks, the most dignified people
in the planet, do not want them ; yet have as much self-respect as the English, and are easily able to impress the French-
man or the American who visits them with the respect due to
a brave and sufficient man.

These feats have, to be sure, great difference of merit, and
some of them involve power of a high kind. But the public
values the invention more than the inventor does. The inventor knows there is much more and better where this came
from. The public sees in it a lucrative secret. Men see the
reward which the inventor enjoys, and they think, ' How shall
we win that?' Cause and effect are a little tedious ; how to
leap to the result by short or by false means? We are not

scrupulous. What we ask is victory, without regard to the cause; after the Rob Roy rule, after the Napoleon rule, to be the strongest to-day, — the way of the Talleyrands, — prudent people, whose watches go faster than their neighbors', and who detect the first moment of decline, and throw themselves on the instant on the winning side. I have heard that Nelson used to say, "Never mind the justice or the impudence, only let me succeed." Lord Brougham's single duty of counsel is, "to get the prisoner clear." Fuller says 't is a maxim of lawyers, "that a crown once worn clears all defects of the wearer thereof." *Rien ne réussit mieux que le succès.* And we Americans are tainted with this insanity, as our bankruptcies and our reckless politics may show. We are great by exclusion, grasping, and egotism. Our success takes from all what it gives to one. 'T is a haggard, malignant, careworn running for luck.

Egotism is a kind of buckram that gives momentary strength and concentration to men, and seems to be much used in nature for fabrics in which local and spasmodic energy is required. I could point to men in this country of indispensable importance to the carrying on of American life, of this humor, whom we could ill spare; any one of them would be a national loss. But it spoils conversation. They will not try conclusions with you. They are ever thrusting this pampered self between you and them. It is plain they have a long education to undergo to reach simplicity and plain-dealing, which are what a wise man mainly cares for in his companion. Nature knows how to convert evil to good; Nature utilizes misers, fanatics, show-men, egotists, to accomplish her ends; but we must not think better of the foible for that. The passion for sudden success is rude and puerile, just as war, cannons, and executions are used to clear the ground of bad, lumpish, irreclaimable savages, but always to the damage of the conquerors.

I hate this shallow Americanism which hopes to get rich by credit, to get knowledge by raps on midnight tables, to learn the economy of the mind by phrenology, or skill without study, or mastery without apprenticeship, or the sale of goods through pretending that they sell, or power through making believe you are powerful, or through a packed jury or caucus, bribery and "repeating" votes, or wealth by fraud. They think they have got it, but they have got something else, — a crime which calls for another crime, and another devil behind that; these are steps to suicide, infamy, and the harming of mankind. We countenance each other in this life of show, puffing, advertisement, and manufacture of public opinion; and excellence is lost sight of in the hunger for sudden performance and praise.

There was a wise man, an Italian artist, Michel Angelo, who writes thus of himself: "Meanwhile the Cardinal Ippolito, in whom all my best hopes were placed, being dead, I began to understand that the promises of this world are, for the most part, vain phantoms, and that to confide in one's self, and become something of worth and value, is the best and safest course." Now, though I am by no means sure that the reader will assent to all my propositions, yet I think we shall agree in my first rule for success, — that we shall drop the brag and the advertisement, and take Michel Angelo's course, "to confide in one's self, and be something of worth and value."

Each man has an aptitude born with him to do easily some feat impossible to any other. Do your work. I have to say this often, but nature says it oftener. 'T is clownish to insist on doing all with one's own hands, as if every man should build his own clumsy house, forge his hammer, and bake his dough; but he is to dare to do what he can do best; not help others as they would direct him, but as he knows his helpful power to be. To do otherwise is to neutralize all those extraordinary special talents distributed among men. Yet, whilst this self-truth is essential to the exhibition of the world and to the growth and glory of each mind, it is rare to find a man who believes his own thought or who speaks that which he was created to say. As nothing astonishes men so much as common sense and plain-dealing, so nothing is more rare in any man than an act of his own. Any work looks wonderful to him except that which he can do. We do not believe our own thought; we must serve somebody; we must quote somebody; we dote on the old and the distant; we are tickled by great names; we import the religion of other nations; we quote their opinions; we cite their laws. The gravest and learnedest courts in this country shudder to face a new question, and will wait months and years for a case to occur that can be tortured into a precedent, and thus throw on a bolder party the *onus* of an initiative. Thus we do not carry a counsel in our breasts, or do not know it; and because we cannot shake off from our shoes this dust of Europe and Asia, the world seems to be born old, society is under a spell, every man is a borrower and a mimic, life is theatrical, and literature a quotation ; and hence that depression of spirits, that furrow of care, said to mark every American brow.

Self-trust is the first secret of success, the belief that, if you are here, the authorities of the universe put you here, and for cause, or with some task strictly appointed you in your constitution, and so long as you work at that you are well and successful. It by no means consists in rushing prematurely to a showy feat that shall catch the eye and satisfy spectators. It is enough if you work in the right direction. So far from the performance being the real success, it is clear that the success was much earlier than that, namely, when all the feats that make our civility were the thoughts of good heads. The fame of each discovery rightly attaches to the mind that made the formula which contains all the details, and not to the manufacturers who now make their gain by it ; although the mob uniformly cheers the publisher, and not the inventor. It is the dulness of the multitude that they cannot see the house, in the ground-plan ; the working, in the model of the projector. Whilst it is a thought, though it were a new fuel, or a new food, or the creation of agriculture, it is cried down ; it is a chimera : but when it is a fact, and comes in the shape of eight per cent, ten per cent, a hundred per cent, they cry, ' It is the voice of God.' Horatio Greenough, the sculptor, said to me of Robert Fulton's visit to Paris : " Fulton knocked at the door of Napoleon with steam, and was rejected ; and Napoleon lived long enough to know that he had excluded a greater power than his own."

Is there no loving of knowledge, and of art, and of our design, for itself alone ? Cannot we please ourselves with performing our work, or gaining truth and power, without being praised for it ? I gain my point, I gain all points, if I can reach my companion with any statement which teaches him his own worth. The sum of wisdom is, that the time is never lost that is devoted to work. The good workman never says, ' There, that will do ' ; but, ' There, that is it : try it, and come again, it will last always.' If the artist, in whatever art, is well at work on his own design, it signifies little that he does not yet find orders or customers. I pronounce that young man happy who is content with having acquired the skill which he had aimed at, and waits willingly when the occasion of making it appreciated shall arrive, knowing well that it will not loiter. The time your rival spends in dressing up his work for effect, hastily and for the market, you spend in study and experiments towards real knowledge and efficiency. He has thereby sold his picture or machine, or won the prize, or got the appointment; but you have raised yourself into a higher school of art, and a few years will show the advantage of the real master over the short popularity of the showman. I know it is a nice point to discriminate this self-trust, which is the pledge of all mental vigor and performance, from the disease to which it is allied, — the exaggeration of the part which we can play; — yet they are two things. But it is sanity to know, that, over my talent or knack, and a million times better than any talent, is the central intelligence which subordinates and uses all talents; and it is only as a door into this, that any talent or the knowledge it gives is of value. He only who comes into this central intelligence, in which no egotism or exaggeration can be, comes into self-possession.

My next point is that, in the scale of powers, it is not talent but sensibility, which is best: talent confines, but the central life puts us in relation to all. How often it seems the chief good to be born with a cheerful temper, and well adjusted to the tone of the human race. Such a man feels himself in harmony, and conscious by his receptivity of an infinite strength. Like Alfred, " good fortune accompanies him like a gift of God." Feel yourself, and be not daunted by things. 'T is the fulness of man that runs over into objects, and makes his Bibles and Shakspeares and Homers so great. The joyful reader borrows of his own ideas to fill their faulty outline, and knows not that he borrows and gives.

There is something of poverty in our criticism. We assume that there are few great men, all the rest are little; that there is but one Homer, but one Shakspeare, one Newton, one Socrates. But the soul in her beaming hour does not acknowledge these usurpations. We should know how to praise Socrates, or Plato, or Saint John, without impoverishing us. In good hours we do not find Shakspeare or Homer over-great, — only to have been translators of the happy present, — and every man and woman divine possibilities. 'T is the good reader that makes the good book; a good head cannot read amiss: in every book he finds passages which seem confidences or asides hidden from all else and unmistakably meant for his ear.

The light by which we see in this world comes out from the soul of the observer. Wherever any noble sentiment dwelt, it made the faces and houses around to shine. Nay, the powers of this busy brain are miraculous and illimitable. Therein are the rules and formulas by which the whole empire of matter is worked. There is no prosperity, trade, art, city, or great material wealth of any kind, but if you trace it home, you will find it rooted in a thought of some individual man.

Is all life a surface affair? 'T is curious, but our difference of wit appears to be only a difference of impressionability, or power to appreciate faint, fainter, and infinitely faintest voices and visions. When the scholar or the writer has pumped his brain for thoughts and verses, and then comes abroad into nature, has he never found that there is a better poetry hinted in a boy's whistle of a tune, or in the piping of a sparrow, than in all his literary results? We call it health. What is so admirable as the health of youth?—with his long days because his eyes are good, and brisk circulations keep him warm in cold rooms, and he loves books that speak to the imagination; and he can read Plato, covered to his chin with a cloak in a cold upper chamber, though he should associate the Dialogues ever after with a woollen smell. 'T is the bane of life that natural effects are continually crowded out, and artificial arrangements substituted. We remember when, in early youth, the earth spoke and the heavens glowed; when an evening, any evening, grim and wintry, sleet and snow, was enough for us; the houses were in the air. Now it costs a rare combination of clouds and lights to overcome the common and mean. What is it we look for in the landscape, in sunsets and sunrises, in the sea and the firmament? what but a compensation for the cramp and pettiness of human performances? We bask in the day, and the mind finds somewhat as great as itself. In Nature, all is large, massive repose. Remember what befalls a city boy who goes for the first time into the October woods. He is suddenly initiated into a pomp and glory that brings to pass for him the dreams of romance. He is the king he dreamed he was; he walks through tents of gold, through bowers of crimson, porphyry, and topaz, pavilion on pavilion, garlanded with vines, flowers, and sunbeams, with incense and music, with so many hints to his astonished senses; the leaves twinkle and pique and flatter him, and his eye and step are tempted on by what hazy distances to happier solitudes. All this happiness he owes only to his finer perception. The owner of the wood-lot finds only a number of discolored trees, and says, 'They ought to come down;

they are n't growing any better; they should be cut and corded before spring.'

Wordsworth writes of the delights of the boy in Nature : —

" For never will come back the hour
Of splendor in the grass, of glory in the flower."

But I have just seen a man, well knowing what he spoke of, who told me that the verse was not true for him ; that his eyes opened as he grew older, and that every spring was more beautiful to him than the last.

We live among gods of our own creation. Does that deeptoned bell, which has shortened many a night of ill nerves, render to you nothing but acoustic vibrations ? Is the old church, which gave you the first lessons of religious life, or the village school, or the college where you first knew the dreams of fancy and joys of thought, only boards or brick and mortar ? Is the house in which you were born, or the house in which your dearest friend lived, only a piece of real estate whose value is covered by the Hartford insurance ? You walk on the beach and enjoy the animation of the picture. Scoop up a little water in the hollow of your palm, take up a handful of shore sand ; well, these are the elements. What is the beach but acres of sand ? what is the ocean but cubic miles of water ? a little more or less signifies nothing. No, it is that this brute matter is part of somewhat not brute. It is that the sand floor is held by spheral gravity, and bent to be a part of the round globe, under the optical sky, — part of the astonishing astronomy, and existing, at last, to moral ends and from moral causes.

The world is not made up to the eye of figures, that is, only half ; it is also made of color. How that element washes the universe with its enchanting waves ! The sculptor had ended his work, and behold a new world of dream-like glory. 'T is the last stroke of Nature ; beyond color she cannot go. In like manner, life is made up, not of knowledge only, but of love also. If thought is form, sentiment is color. It clothes the skeleton world with space, variety, and glow. The hues of sunset make life great ; so the affections make some little web of cottage and fireside populous, important, and filling the main space in our history.

The fundamental fact in our metaphysic constitution is the correspondence of man to the world, so that every change in that writes a record in the mind. The mind yields sympathetically to the tendencies or law which stream through

things, and make the order of nature ; and in the perfection
of this correspondence or expressiveness, the health and force
of man consist.   If we follow this hint into our intellectual
education, we shall find that it is not propositions, not new
dogmas and a logical exposition of the world, that are our first
need ; but to watch and tenderly cherish the intellectual and
moral sensibilities, those fountains of right thought, and woo
them to stay and make their home with us.   Whilst they
abide with us, we shall not think amiss.   Our perception far
outruns our talent.   We bring a welcome to the highest lessons of religion and of poetry out of all proportion beyond our
skill to teach.   And, further, the great hearing and sympathy
of men is more true and wise than their speaking is wont to
be.   A deep sympathy is what we require for any student of
the mind ; for the chief difference between man and man is a
difference of impressionability.   Aristotle, or Bacon, or Kant
propound some maxim which is the key-note of philosophy
thenceforward.   But I am more interested to know, that, when
at last they have hurled out their grand word, it is only some
familiar experience of every man in the street.   If it be not, it
will never be heard of again.

Ah ! if one could keep this sensibility, and live in the happy
sufficing present, and find the day and its cheap means con-
tenting, which only ask receptivity in you, and no strained
exertion and cankering ambition, overstimulating to be at the
head of your class and the head of society, and to have distinction and laurels and consumption !   We are not strong
by our power to penetrate, but by our relatedness.   The world
is enlarged for us, not by new objects, but by finding more
affinities and potencies in those we have.

This sensibility appears in the homage to beauty which
exalts the faculties of youth, in the power which form and
color exert upon the soul ; when we see eyes that are a compliment to the human race, features that explain the Phidian
sculpture.   Fontenelle said : " There are three things about
which I have curiosity, though I know nothing of them,—
music, poetry, and love."   The great doctors of this science
are the greatest men,— Dante, Petrarch, Michel Angelo, and
Shakspeare.   The wise Socrates treats this matter with a certain archness, yet with very marked expressions.   " I am
always," he says, "asserting that I happen to know, I may
say, nothing but a mere trifle relating to matters of love ; yet
in that kind of learning I lay claim to being more skilled than

any one man of the past or present time." They may well
speak in this uncertain manner of their knowledge, and in this
confident manner of their will, for the secret of it is hard to
detect, so deep it is; and yet genius is measured by its skill
in this science.

Who is he in youth or in maturity, or even in old age, who
does not like to hear of those sensibilities which turn curled
heads round at church, and send wonderful eye-beams across
assemblies, from one to one, never missing in the thickest
crowd. The keen statist reckons by tens and hundreds; the
genial man is interested in every slipper that comes into
the assembly. The passion, alike everywhere, creeps under
the snows of Scandinavia, under the fires of the equator, and
swims in the seas of Polynesia. Lofn is as puissant a divinity
in the Norse Edda as Camadeva in the red vault of India,
Eros in the Greek, or Cupid in the Latin heaven. And what
is specially true of love is, that it is a state of extreme impressionability; the lover has more senses and finer senses than
others; his eye and ear are telegraphs; he reads omens on
the flower, and cloud, and face, and form, and gesture, and
reads them aright. In his surprise at the sudden and entire
understanding that is between him and the beloved person, it
occurs to him that they might somehow meet independently
of time and place. How delicious the belief that he could
elude all guards, precautions, ceremonies, means, and delays,
and hold instant and sempiternal communication! In solitude, in banishment, the hope returned and the experiment
was eagerly tried. The supernal powers seem to take his part.
What was on his lips to say is uttered by his friend. When
he went abroad, he met, by wonderful casualties, the one person he sought. If in his walk he chanced to look back, his
friend was walking behind him. And it has happened that
the artist has often drawn in his pictures the face of the future
wife whom he had not yet seen.

But also in complacences, nowise so strict as this of the passion, the man of sensibility counts it a delight only to hear a
child's voice fully addressed to him, or to see the beautiful
manners of the youth of either sex. When the event is past
and remote, how insignificant the greatest compared with the
piquancy of the present! To-day at the school examination
the professor interrogates Sylvina in the history class about
Odoacer and Alaric. Sylvina can't remember, but suggests
that Odoacer was defeated; and the professor tartly replies,

"No, he defeated the Romans." But 't is plain to the visitor, that 't is of no importance at all about Odoacer, and 't is a great deal of importance about Sylvina; and if she says he was defeated, why he had better, a great deal, have been defeated, than give her a moment's annoy. Odoácer, if there was a particle of the gentleman in him, would have said, Let me be defeated a thousand times.

And as our tenderness for youth and beauty gives a new and just importance to their fresh and manifold claims, so the like sensibility gives welcome to all excellence, has eyes and hospitality for merit in corners. An Englishman of marked character and talent, who had brought with him hither one or two friends and a library of mystics, assured me that nobody and nothing of possible interest was left in England,— he had brought all that was alive away. I was forced to reply: "No, next door to you, probably, on the other side of the partition in the same house, was a greater man than any you had seen." Every man has a history worth knowing, if he could tell it, or if we could draw it from him. Character and wit have their own magnetism. Send a deep man into any town, and he will find another deep man there, unknown hitherto to his neighbors. That is the great happiness of life,— to add to our high acquaintances. The very law of averages might have assured you that there will be in every hundred heads, say ten or five good heads. Morals are generated as the atmosphere is. 'T is a secret, the genesis of either; but the springs of justice and courage do not fail any more than salt or sulphur springs.

The world is always opulent, the oracles are never silent; but the receiver must by a happy temperance be brought to that top of condition, that frolic' health, that he can easily take and give these fine communications. Health is the condition of wisdom, and the sign is cheerfulness,— an open and noble temper. There was never poet who had not the heart in the right place. The old trouveur, Pons Capdueil, wrote,—

> "Oft have I heard, and deem the witness true,
> Whom man delights in, God delights in too."

All beauty warms the heart, is a sign of health, prosperity, and the favor of God. Everything lasting and fit for men, the Divine power has marked with this stamp. What delights, what emancipates, not what scares and pains us, is wise and good in speech and in the arts. For, truly, the heart at the centre of the universe with every throb hurls the flood of happiness into every artery, vein, and veinlet, so that the whole system is inundated with the tides of joy. The plenty of the poorest place is too great : the harvest cannot be gathered. Every sound ends in music. The edge of every surface is tinged with prismatic rays.

One more trait of true success. The good mind chooses what is positive, what is advancing, — embraces the affirmative. Our system is one of poverty. 'T is presumed, as I said, there is but one Shakspeare, one Homer, one Jesus, — not that all are or shall be inspired. But we must begin by affirming. Truth and goodness subsist forevermore. It is true there is evil and good, night and day : but these are not equal. The day is great and final. The night is for the day, but the day is not for the night. What is this immortal demand for more, which belongs to our constitution? this enormous ideal? There is no such critic and beggar as this terrible Soul. No historical person begins to content us. We know the satisfactoriness of justice, the sufficiency of truth. We know the answer that leaves nothing to ask. We know the Spirit by its victorious tone. The searching tests to apply to every new pretender are amount and quality, — what does he add? and what is the state of mind he leaves me in? Your theory is unimportant ; but what new stock you can add to humanity, or how high you can carry life? A man is a man only as he makes life and nature happier to us.

I fear the popular notion of success stands in direct opposition in all points to the real and wholesome success. One adores public opinion, the other private opinion ; one fame, the other desert ; one feats, the other humility ; one lucre, the other love ; one monopoly, and the other hospitality of mind.

We may apply this affirmative law to letters, to manners, to art, to the decorations of our houses, etc. I do not find executions or tortures or lazar-houses, or grisly photographs of the field on the day after the battle, fit subjects for cabinet pictures. I think that some so-called "sacred subjects" must be treated with more genius than I have seen in the masters of Italian or Spanish art to be right pictures for houses and churches. Nature does not invite such exhibition. Nature lays the ground-plan of each creature accurately, — sternly fit for all his functions ; then veils it scrupulously. See how carefully she covers up the skeleton. The eye shall not see it : the sun shall not shine on it. She weaves her tissues and integuments of flesh and skin and hair and beautiful colors of

the day over it, and forces death down underground, and
makes haste to cover it up with leaves and vines, and wipes
carefully out every trace by new creation. Who and what are
you that would lay the ghastly anatomy bare?

Don't hang a dismal picture on the wall, and do not daub
with sables and glooms in your conversation. Don't be a
cynic and disconsolate preacher. Don't bewail and bemoan.
Omit the negative propositions. Nerve us with incessant
affirmatives. Don't waste yourself in rejection, nor bark
against the bad, but chant the beauty of the good. When
that is spoken which has a right to be spoken, the chatter and
the criticism will stop. Set down nothing that will not help
somebody;

> " For every gift of noble origin
> Is breathed upon by Hope's perpetual breath."

The affirmative of affirmatives is love. As much love, so
much perception. As caloric to matter, so is love to mind;
so it enlarges, and so it empowers it. Good-will makes insight, as one finds his way to the sea by embarking on a river.
I have seen scores of people who can silence me, but I seek
one who shall make me forget or overcome the frigidities and
imbecilities into which I fall. The painter Giotto, Vasari
tells us, renewed art, because he put more goodness into his
heads. To awake in man and to raise the sense of worth, to
educate his feeling and judgment so that he shall scorn himself for a bad action, that is the only aim.

'T is cheap and easy to destroy. There is not a joyful boy
or an innocent girl buoyant with fine purposes of duty, in all
the street full of eager and rosy faces, but a cynic can chill
and dishearten with a single word. Despondency comes readily
enough to the most sanguine. The cynic has only to follow
their hint with his bitter confirmation, and they check that
eager courageous pace and go home with heavier step and
premature age. They will themselves quickly enough give
the hint he wants to the cold wretch. Which of them has
not failed to please where they most wished it? or blundered
where they were most ambitious of success? or found themselves awkward or tedious or incapable of study, thought, or
heroism, and only hoped by good sense and fidelity to do what
they could and pass unblamed? And this witty malefactor
makes their little hope less with satire and scepticism, and
slackens the springs of endeavor. Yes, this is easy; but to
help the young soul, add energy, inspire hope, and blow the

coals into a useful flame ; to redeem defeat by new thought, by firm action, that is not easy, that is the work of divine men.)

We live on different planes or platforms. There is an external life, which is educated at school, taught to read, write, cipher, and trade ; taught to grasp all the boy can get, urging him to put himself forward, to make himself useful and agreeable in the world, to ride, run, argue, and contend, unfold his talents, shine, conquer and possess.

But the inner life sits at home, and does not learn to do things, nor value these feats at all. 'T is a quiet, wise perception. It loves truth, because it is itself real ; it loves right, it knows nothing else ; but it makes no progress ; was as wise in our first memory of it as now ; is just the same now in maturity and hereafter in age, it was in youth. We have grown to manhood and womanhood ; we have powers, connection, children, reputations, professions : this makes no account of them all. It lives in the great present ; it makes the present great. This tranquil, well-founded, wide-seeing soul is no express-rider, no attorney, no magistrate, it lies in the sun, and broods on the world. A person of this temper once said to a man of much activity, " I will pardon you that you do so much, and you me that I do nothing." And Euripides says that " Zeus hates busybodies and those who do too much."

OLD AGE.

I.

OLD AGE.

O N the anniversary of the Phi Beta Kappa Society at Cambridge, in 1861, the venerable President Quincy, senior member of the Society, as well as senior alumnus of the University, was received at the dinner with peculiar demonstrations of respect. He replied to these compliments in a speech, and, gracefully claiming the privileges of a literary society, entered at some length into an Apology for Old Age, and, aiding himself by notes in his hand, made a sort of running commentary on Cicero's chapter "De Senectute." The character of the speaker, the transparent good faith of his praise and blame, and the *naïveté* of his eager preference of Cicero's opinions to King David's, gave unusual interest to the College festival. It was a discourse full of dignity, honoring him who spoke and those who heard.

The speech led me to look over at home — an easy task — Cicero's famous essay, charming by its uniform rhetorical merit ; heroic with Stoical precepts ; with a Roman eye to the claims of the State ; happiest, perhaps, in his praise of life on the farm ; and rising at the conclusion to a lofty strain. But he does not exhaust the subject ; rather invites the attempt to add traits to the picture from our broader modern life.

Cicero makes no reference to the illusions which cling to the element of time, and in which Nature delights. Wellington, in speaking of military men, said, " What masks are these uniforms to hide cowards ! " I have often detected the like deception in the cloth shoe, wadded pelisse, wig, spectacles, and padded chair of Age. Nature lends herself to these illusions, and adds dim sight, deafness, cracked voice, snowy hair, short memory, and sleep. These also are masks, and all is not Age that wears them. Whilst we yet call ourselves young, and our mates are yet youths with even boyish remains, one good fellow in the set prematurely sports a gray or a bald head, which does not impose on us who know how innocent of sanctity or of Platonism he is, but does deceive his juniors and the public, who presently distinguish him with a most amusing respect : and this lets us into the secret, that the venerable forms that so awed our childhood were just such impostors. Nature is full of freaks, and now puts an old head on young shoulders, and then a young heart beating under fourscore winters.

For if the essence of age is not present, these signs, whether of Art or Nature, are counterfeit and ridiculous : and the essence of age is intellect. Wherever that appears, we call it old. If we look into the eyes of the youngest person, we sometimes discover that here is one who knows already what you would go about with much pains to teach him ; there is that in him which is the ancestor of all around him : which fact the Indian Vedas express when they say, " He that can discriminate is the father of his father." And in our old British legends of Arthur and the Round Table, his friend and counsellor, Merlin the Wise, is a babe found exposed in a basket by the river-side, and, though an infant of only a few days, speaks articulately to those who discover him, tells his name and history, and presently foretells the fate of the by-standers. Wherever there is power, there is age. Don't be deceived by dimples and curls. I tell you that babe is a thousand years old.

Time is, indeed, the theatre and seat of illusion : nothing is so ductile and elastic. The mind stretches an hour to a century, and dwarfs an age to an hour. Saadi found in a mosque at Damascus an old Persian of a hundred and fifty years who was dying, and was saying to himself, " I said, coming into the world by birth, ' I will enjoy myself for a few moments.' Alas ! at the variegated table of life I partook of a few mouthfuls, and the Fates said, ' *Enough !* ' " That which does not decay is so central and controlling in us, that, as long as one is alone by himself, he is not sensible of the inroads of time, which always begin at the surface-edges. If, on a winter day, you should stand within a bell-glass, the face and color of the afternoon clouds would not indicate whether it were June or January ; and if we did not find the reflection of ourselves in the eyes of the young people, we could not know that the century clock had struck seventy instead of

twenty. How many men habitually believe that each chance
passenger with whom they converse is of their own age, and
presently find it was his father, and not his brother, whom
they knew?

But not to press too hard on these deceits and illusions of
Nature, which are inseparable from our condition, and looking
at age under an aspect more conformed to the common sense,
if the question be the felicity of age, I fear the first popular
judgments will be unfavorable. From the point of sensuous
experience, seen from the streets and markets and the haunts
of pleasure and gain, the estimate of age is low, melancholy, ·
and sceptical. Frankly face the facts, and see the result.
Tobacco, coffee, alcohol, hashish, prussic acid, strychnine, are
weak dilutions : the surest poison is time. This cup, which
Nature puts to our lips, has a wonderful virtue, surpassing
that of any other draught. It opens the senses, adds power,
fills us with exalted dreams, which we call hope, love, ambition, science : especially, it creates a craving for larger draughts
of itself. But they who take the larger draughts are drunk
with it, lose their stature, strength, beauty, and senses, and
end in folly and delirium. We postpone our literary work
until we have more ripeness and skill to write, and we one
day discover that our literary talent was a youthful effervescence which we have now lost. We had a judge in Massachusetts who at sixty proposed to resign, alleging that he
perceived a certain decay in his faculties ; he was dissuaded by
his friends, on account of the public convenience at that
time. At seventy it was hinted to him that it was time to
retire ; but he now replied that he thought his judgment as
robust, and all his faculties as good as ever they were. But
besides the self-deception, the strong and hasty laborers of
the street do not work well with the chronic valetudinarian.
Youth is everywhere in place. Age, like woman, requires fit
surroundings. Age is comely in coaches, in churches, in chairs
of state, and ceremony, in council-chambers, in courts of justice, and historical societies. Age is becoming in the country.
But in the rush and uproar of Broadway, if you look into the
faces of the passengers, there is dejection or indignation in
the seniors, a certain concealed sense of injury, and the lip
made up with a heroic determination not to mind it. Few
envy the consideration enjoyed by the oldest inhabitant. We
do not count a man's years, until he has nothing else to count.
The vast inconvenience of animal immortality was told in the

fable of Tithonus. In short, the creed of the street is, Old Age is not disgraceful, but immensely disadvantageous. Life is well enough, but we shall all be glad to get out of it, and they will all be glad to have us.

This is odious on the face of it. Universal convictions are not to be shaken by the whimseys of overfed butchers and firemen, or by the sentimental fears of girls who would keep the infantile bloom on their cheeks. We know the value of experience. Life and art are cumulative; and he who has accomplished something in any department alone deserves to be heard on that subject. A man of great employments and excellent performance used to assure me that he did not think a man worth anything until he was sixty; although this smacks a little of the resolution of a certain "Young Men's Republican Club," that all men should be held eligible who were under seventy. But in all governments the councils of power were held by the old; and patricians or *patres*, senate or *senes*, *seigneurs* or seniors, *gerousia*, the senate of Sparta, the presbytery of the Church, and the like, all signify simply old men.

The cynical creed or lampoon of the market is refuted by the universal prayer for long life, which is the verdict of Nature, and justified by all history. We have, it is true, examples of an accelerated pace by which young men achieved grand works; as in the Macedonian Alexander, in Raffaelle, Shakspeare, Pascal, Burns, and Byron; but these are rare exceptions. Nature, in the main, vindicates her law. Skill to do comes of doing; knowledge comes by eyes always open, and working hands; and there is no knowledge that is not power. Béranger said, "Almost all the good workmen live long." And if the life be true and noble, we have quite another sort of seniors than the frowzy, timorous, peevish dotards who are falsely old, — namely, the men who fear no city, but by whom cities stand; who appearing in any street, the people empty their houses to gaze at and obey them: as at "My Cid, with the fleecy beard," in Toledo; or Bruce, as Barbour reports him; as blind old Dandolo, elected Doge at eighty-four years, storming Constantinople at ninety-four, and after the revolt again victorious, and elected at the age of ninety-six to the throne of the Eastern Empire, which he declined, and died Doge at ninety-seven. We still feel the force of Socrates, "whom well-advised the oracle pronounced wisest of men"; of Archimedes, holding Syracuse against the Romans by his wit, and himself better than all their nation ; of Michel Angelo, wearing the four crowns of architecture, sculpture, painting and poetry ; of Galileo, of whose blindness Castelli said, " The noblest eye is darkened that Nature ever made, — an eye that hath seen more than all that went before him, and hath opened the eyes of all that shall come after him " ; of Newton, who made an important discovery for every one of his eighty-five years ; of Bacon, who "took all knowledge to be his province " ; of Fontenelle, " that precious porcelain vase laid up in the centre of France to be guarded with the utmost care for a hundred years " ; of Franklin, Jefferson, and Adams, the wise and heroic statesmen ; of Washington, the perfect citizen ; of Wellington, the perfect soldier ; of Goethe, the all-knowing poet ; of Humboldt, the encyclopædia of science.

Under the general assertion of the well-being of age, we can easily count particular benefits of that condition. It has weathered the perilous capes and shoals in the sea whereon we sail, and the chief evil of life is taken away in removing the grounds of fear. The insurance of a ship expires as she enters the harbor at home. It were strange, if a man should turn his sixtieth year without a feeling of immense relief from the number of dangers he has escaped. When the old wife says, ' Take care of that tumor in your shoulder, perhaps it is cancerous,' — he replies, ' I am yielding to a surer decomposition.' The humorous thief who drank a pot of beer at the gallows blew off the froth because he had heard it was unhealthy : but it will not add a pang to the prisoner marched out to be shot, to assure him that the pain in his knee threatens mortification. When the pleuro-pneumonia of the cows raged, the butchers said, that, though the acute degree was novel, there never was a time when this disease did not occur among cattle. All men carry seeds of all distempers through life latent, and we die without developing them ; such is the affirmative force of the constitution ; but if you are enfeebled by any cause, some of these sleeping seeds start and open. Meantime, at every stage we lose a foe. At fifty years, 't is said, afflicted citizens lose their sick-headaches. I hope this *hegira* is not as movable a feast as that one I annually look for, when the horticulturists assure me that the rose-bugs in our gardens disappear on the tenth of July ; they stay a fortnight later in mine. But be it as it may with the sick-headache, — 't is certain that graver headaches and heart-aches are lulled once for all, as we come up with certain goals of time. The passions have answered their purpose : that slight but dread overweight, with which, in each instance, Nature secures the execution of her aim, drops off. To keep man in the planet, she impresses the terror of death. To perfect the commissariat, she implants in each a certain rapacity to get the supply, and a little oversupply, of his wants. To insure the existence of the race, she reinforces the sexual instinct, at the risk of disorder, grief, and pain. To secure strength, she plants cruel hunger and thirst, which so easily overdo their office, and invite disease. But these temporary stays and shifts for the protection of the young animal are shed as fast as they can be replaced by nobler resources. We live in youth amidst this rabble of passions, quite too tender, quite too hungry and irritable. Later, the interiors of mind and heart open, and supply grander motives. We learn the fatal compensations that wait on every act. Then, — one after another, — this riotous time-destroying crew disappear.

I count it another capital advantage of age, this, that a success more or less signifies nothing. Little by little, it has amassed such a fund of merit, that it can very well afford to go on its credit when it will. When I chanced to meet the poet Wordsworth, then sixty-three years old, he told me, "that he had just had a fall and lost a tooth, and, when his companions were much concerned for the mischance, he replied, that he was glad it had not happened forty years before." Well, Nature takes care that we shall not lose our organs forty years too soon. A lawyer argued a cause yesterday in the Supreme Court, and I was struck with a certain air of levity and defiance which vastly became him. Thirty years ago it was a serious concern to him whether his pleading was good and effective. Now it is of importance to his client, but of none to himself. It has been long already fixed what he can do and cannot do, and his reputation does not gain or suffer from one or a dozen new performances. If he should, on a new occasion, rise quite beyond his mark, and achieve somewhat great and extraordinary, that, of course, would instantly tell ; but he may go below his mark with impunity, and people will say, 'O, he had headache,' or, 'He lost his sleep for two nights.' What a lust of appearance, what a load of anxieties that once degraded him, he is thus rid of ! Every one is sensible of this cumulative advantage in living. All the good days behind him are sponsors, who speak for him when he is silent, pay for him when he has no money, introduce him where he has no letters, and work for him when he sleeps.

A third felicity of age is, that it has found expression. The youth suffers not only from ungratified desires, but from powers untried, and from a picture in his mind of a career which has, as yet no outward reality. He is tormented with the want of correspondence between things and thoughts. Michel Angelo's head is full of masculine and gigantic figures as gods walking, which make him savage until his furious chisel can render them into marble ; and of architectural dreams, until a hundred stone-masons can lay them in courses of travertine. There is the like tempest in every good head in which some great benefit for the world is planted. The throes continue until the child is born. Every faculty new to each man thus goads him and drives him out into doleful deserts, until it finds proper vent. All the functions of human duty irritate and lash him forward, bemoaning and chiding, until they are performed. He wants friends, employment, knowledge, power, house and land, wife and children, honor and fame ; he has religious wants, æsthetic wants, domestic, civil, humane wants. One by one, day after day, he learns to coin his wishes into facts. He has his calling, homestead, social connection, and personal power, and thus, at the end of fifty years, his soul is appeased by seeing some sort of correspondence between his wish and his possession. This makes the value of age, the satisfaction it slowly offers to every craving. He is serene who does not feel himself pinched and wronged, but whose condition, in particular and in general, allows the utterance of his mind. In old persons, when thus fully expressed, we often observe a fair, plump, perennial, waxen complexion, which indicates that all the ferment of earlier days has subsided into serenity of thought and behavior.

The compensations of Nature play in age as in youth. In a world so charged and sparkling with power, a man does not live long and actively without costly additions of experience, which, though not spoken, are recorded in his mind. What to the youth is only a guess or a hope, is in the veteran a digested statute. He beholds the feats of the juniors with complacency, but as one who, having long ago known these games, has refined them into results and morals. The Indian Red Jacket, when the young braves were boasting their deeds, said, " But the sixties have all the twenties and forties in them."

For a fourth benefit, age sets its house in order, and finishes

its works, which to every artist is a supreme pleasure. Youth
has an excess of sensibility, before which every object glitters
and attracts.   We leave one pursuit for another, and the
young man's year is a heap of beginnings.   At the end of a
twelvemonth he has nothing to show for it, — not one completed work.   But the time is not lost.   Our instincts drove
us to hive innumerable experiences, that are yet of no visible
value, and which we may keep for twice seven years before
they shall be wanted.   The best things are of secular growth.
The instinct of classifying marks the wise and healthy mind.
. Linnæus projects his system, and lays out his twenty-four
classes of plants, before yet he has found in Nature a single
plant to justify certain of his classes.   His seventh class has
not one.   In process of time, he finds with delight the little
white *Trientalis*, the only plant with seven petals and sometimes seven stamens, which constitutes a seventh class in conformity with his system.   The conchologist builds his cabinet
whilst as yet he has few shells.   He labels shelves for classes,
cells for species : all but a few are empty.   But every year
fills some blanks, and with accelerating speed as he becomes
knowing and known.   An old scholar finds keen delight in
verifying the impressive anecdotes and citations he has met
with in miscellaneous reading and hearing, in all the years of
youth.   We carry in memory important anecdotes, and have
lost all clue to the author from whom we had them.   We have
a heroic speech from Rome or Greece, but cannot fix it on the
man who said it.   We have an admirable line worthy of
Horace, ever and anon resounding in our mind's ear, but have
searched all probable and improbable books for it in vain.   We
consult the reading men : but, strangely enough, they who
know everything know not this.   But especially we have a
certain insulated thought, which haunts us, but remains insulated and barren.   Well, there is nothing for all this but
patience and time.   Time, yes, that is the finder, the unweari-
able explorer, not subject to casualties, omniscient at last.   The
day comes when the hidden author of our story is found ; when
the brave speech returns straight to the hero who said it ; when
the admirable verse finds the poet to whom it belongs ; and best
of all, when the lonely thought, which seemed so wise, yet half-
wise, half-thought, because it cast no light abroad, is suddenly
matched in our mind by its twin, by its sequence, or next
related analogy, which gives it instantly radiating power, and
justifies the superstitious instinct with which we have hoarded

it. We remember our old Greek Professor at Cambridge, an ancient bachelor, amid his folios, possessed by this hope of completing a task, with nothing to break his leisure after the three hours of his daily classes, yet ever restlessly stroking his leg, and assuring himself "he should retire from the University and read the authors." In Goethe's Romance, Makaria, the central figure for wisdom and influence, pleases herself with withdrawing into solitude to astronomy and epistolary correspondence. Goethe himself carried this completion of studies to the highest point. Many of his works hung on the easel from youth to age, and received a stroke in every month or year. A literary astrologer, he never applied himself to any task but at the happy moment when all the stars consented. Bentley thought himself likely to live till fourscore, — long enough to read everything that was worth reading, — "*Et tunc magna mei sub terris ibit imago.*" Much wider is spread the pleasure which old men take in completing their secular affairs, the inventor his inventions, the agriculturist his experiments, and all old men in finishing their houses, rounding their estates, clearing their titles, reducing tangled interests to order, reconciling enmities, and leaving all in the best posture for the future. It must be believed that there is a proportion between the designs of a man and the length of his life : there is a calendar of his years, so of his performances.

America is the country of young men, and too full of work hitherto for leisure and tranquillity ; yet we have had robust centenarians, and examples of dignity and wisdom. I have lately found in an old note-book a record of a visit to ex-President John Adams, in 1825, soon after the election of his son to the Presidency. It is but a sketch, and nothing important passed in the conversation ; but it reports a moment in the life of a heroic person, who, in extreme old age, appeared still erect and worthy of his fame.

————, *Feb.*, 1825. To-day, at Quincy, with my brother, by invitation of Mr. Adams's family. The old President sat in a large stuffed arm-chair, dressed in a blue coat, black small-clothes, white stockings ; a cotton cap covered his bald head. We made our compliment, told him he must let us join our congratulations to those of the nation on the happiness of his house. He thanked us, and said : "I am rejoiced, because the nation is happy. The time of gratulation

and congratulations is nearly over with me : I am astonished
that I have lived to see and know of this event. I have lived
now nearly a century; [he was ninety in the following October :] a long, harassed, and distracted life." I said, " The
world thinks a good deal of joy has been mixed with it." —
" The world does not know," he replied, " how much toil,
anxiety, and sorrow I have suffered." — I asked if Mr. Adams's
letter of acceptance had been read to him. — " Yes," he said,
and, added, " My son has more political prudence than any
man that I know who has existed in my time ; he never was
put off his guard : and I hope he will continue such ; but
what effect age may work in diminishing the power of his
mind, I do not know ; it has been very much on the stretch,
ever since he was born. He has always been laborious, child
and man, from infancy." — When Mr. J. Q. Adams's age was
mentioned, he said, " He is now fifty-eight, or will be in July ";
and remarked that " all the Presidents were of the same age :
General Washington was about fifty-eight, and I was about
fifty-eight, and Mr. Jefferson, and Mr. Madison, and Mr. Mon-
roe." — We inquired when he expected to see Mr. Adams. —
He said : " Never : Mr. Adams will not come to Quincy but
to my funeral. It would be a great satisfaction to me to see
him, but I don't wish him to come on my account." — He
spoke of Mr. Lechmere, whom he " well remembered to have
seen come down daily, at a great age, to walk in the old town-
house," — adding, " And I wish I could walk as well as he did.
He was Collector of the Customs for many years under the
Royal Government." — E. said : " I suppose, sir, you would
not have taken his place, even to walk as well as he." — " No,"
he replied, " that was not what I wanted." — He talked of
Whitefield, and " remembered when he was a Freshman in
College, to have come into town to the *Old South* church,
[I think,] to hear him, but could not get into the house ; — I
however, saw him," he said, " through a window, and distinctly
heard all. He had a voice such as I never heard before or
since. He cast it out so that you might hear it at the meeting-
house, [pointing towards the Quincy meeting-house,] and he
had the grace of a dancing-master, of an actor of plays. His
voice and manner helped him more than his sermons. I went
with Jonathan Sewall." — " And you were pleased with him,
sir ?" — " Pleased ! I was delighted beyond measure." — We
asked if at Whitefield's return the same popularity continued.
— " Not the same fury," he said, " not the same wild enthusi-

asm as before, but a greater esteem, as he became more known.
He did not terrify, but was admired."

We spent about an hour in his room. He speaks very distinctly for so old a man, enters bravely into long sentences,
which are interrupted by want of breath, but carries them invariably to a conclusion, without correcting a word.

He spoke of the new novels of Cooper, and "Peep at the
Pilgrims," and "Saratoga," with praise, and named with accuracy the characters in them. He likes to have a person
always reading to him, or company talking in his room, and is
better the next day after having visitors in his chamber from
morning to night.

He received a premature report of his son's election, on Sunday afternoon, without any excitement, and told the reporter
he had been hoaxed, for it was not yet time for any news to
arrive. The informer, something damped in his heart, insisted
on repairing to the meeting-house, and proclaimed it aloud to
the congregation, who were so overjoyed that they rose in
their seats and cheered thrice. The Reverend Mr. Whitney
dismissed them immediately.

When life has been well spent, age is a loss of what it can
well spare, — muscular strength, organic instincts, gross bulk,
and works that belong to these. But the central wisdom,
which was old in infancy, is young in fourscore years, and,
dropping off obstructions, leaves in happy subjects the mind
purified and wise. I have heard that whoever loves is in no
condition old. I have heard, that, whenever the name of man
is spoken, the doctrine of immortality is announced; it cleaves
to his constitution. The mode of it baffles our wit, and no
whisper comes to us from the other side. But the inference
from the working of intellect, hiving knowledge, hiving skill,
— at the end of life just ready to be born, — affirms the inspirations of affection and of the moral sentiment.

LETTERS

AND

SOCIAL AIMS.

POETRY AND IMAGINATION.

POETRY AND IMAGINATION.

THE perception of matter is made the common-sense, and
for cause. This was the cradle, this the go-cart, of the
human child. We must learn the homely laws of fire and
water; we must feed, wash, plant, build. These are ends of
necessity, and first in the order of nature. Poverty, frost,
famine, disease, debt, are the beadles and guardsmen that hold
us to common-sense. The intellect, yielded up to itself, cannot supersede this tyrannic necessity. The restraining grace
of common-sense is the mark of all the valid minds, — of
Æsop, Aristotle, Alfred, Luther, Shakspeare, Cervantes, Franklin, Napoleon. The common-sense which does not meddle
with the absolute, but takes things at their word, — things
as they appear, — believes in the existence of matter, not because we can touch it, or conceive of it, but because it agrees
with ourselves, and the universe does not jest with us, but is
in earnest, — is the house of health and life. In spite of all
the joys of poets and the joys of saints, the most imaginative
and abstracted person never makes, with impunity, the least
mistake in this particular, — never tries to kindle his oven
with water, nor carries a torch into a powder-mill, nor seizes
his wild charger by the tail. We should not pardon the
blunder in another, nor endure it in ourselves.

But whilst we deal with this as finality, early hints are
given that we are not to stay here; that we must be making
ready to go ; — a warning that this magnificent hotel and con-
veniency we call Nature is not final. First innuendoes, then
broad hints, then smart taps, are given, suggesting that nothing stands still in nature but death ; that the creation is on
wheels, in transit, always passing into something else, streaming into something higher ; that matter is not what it appears ;
— that chemistry can blow it all into gas. Faraday, the

most exact of natural philosophers, taught that when we
should arrive at the monads, or primordial elements (the supposed little cubes or prisms of which all matter was built up),
we should not find cubes, or prisms, or atoms, at all, but
spherules of force. It was whispered that the globes of the
universe were precipitates of something more subtle; nay,
somewhat was murmured in our ear that dwindled astronomy
into a toy; — that too was no finality; — only provisional, —
a makeshift; — that under chemistry was power and purpose:
power and purpose ride on matter to the last atom. It was
steeped in thought, — did everywhere express thought; that,
as great conquerors have burned their ships when once they
were landed on the wished-for shore, so the noble house of
Nature we inhabit has temporary uses, and we can afford to
leave it one day. The ends of all are moral, and therefore the
beginnings are such. Thin or solid, everything is in flight.
I believe this conviction makes the charm of chemistry, —
that we have the same avoirdupois matter in an alembic, without a vestige of the old form; and in animal transformation
not less, as in grub and fly, in egg and bird, in embryo and
man; everything undressing and stealing away from its old
into new form, and nothing fast but those invisible cords
which we call laws, on which all is strung. Then we see that
things wear different names and faces, but belong to one family; that the secret cords, or laws, show their well-known
virtue through every variety,— be it animal, or plant, or
planet,— and the interest is gradually transferred from the
forms to the lurking method.

This hint, however conveyed, upsets our politics, trade, customs, marriages, nay, the common-sense side of religion and
literature, which are all founded on low nature,— on the
clearest and most economical mode of administering the material world, considered as final. The admission, never so
covertly, that this is a makeshift, sets the dullest brain in ferment; — our little sir, from his first tottering steps,— as soon
as he can crow,— does not like to be practised upon, suspects
that some one is "doing" him,— and, at this alarm, everything is compromised; — gunpowder is laid under every man's
breakfast-table.

But whilst the man is startled by this closer inspection of
the laws of matter, his attention is called to the independent
action of the mind,— its strange suggestions and laws,— a
certain tyranny which springs up in his own thoughts, which

have an order, method, and beliefs of their own, very different from the order which this common-sense uses.

Suppose there were in the ocean certain strong currents which drove a ship, caught in them, with a force that no skill of sailing with the best wind, and no strength of oars, or sails, or steam, could make any head against, any more than against the current of Niagara : such currents — so tyrannical — exist in thoughts, those finest and subtilest of all waters,— that, as soon as once thought begins, it refuses to remember whose brain it belongs to,— what country, tradition, or religion,— and goes whirling off — swim we merrily — in a direction self-chosen, by law of thought, and not by law of kitchen clock or county committee. It has its own polarity. One of these vortices or self-directions of thought is the impulse to search resemblance, affinity, identity, in all its objects, and hence our science, from its rudest to its most refined theories.

The electric word pronounced by John Hunter a hundred years ago,— *arrested and progressive development,*— indicating the way upward from the invisible protoplasm to the highest organisms,— gave the poetic key to Natural Science,— of which the theories of Geoffroy St. Hilaire, of Oken, of Goethe, of Agassiz, and Owen, and Darwin, in zoölogy and botany, are the fruits,— a hint whose power is not yet exhausted, showing unity and perfect order in physics.

The hardest chemist, the severest analyzer, scornful of all but dryest fact, is forced to keep the poetic curve of nature, and his result is like a myth of Theocritus. All multiplicity rushes to be resolved into unity. Anatomy, osteology, exhibit arrested or progressive ascent in each kind ; the lower pointing to the higher forms, the higher to the highest, from the fluid in an elastic sack, from radiate, mollusk, articulate, vertebrate, — up to man ; as if the whole animal world were only a Hunterian museum to exhibit the genesis of mankind.

Identity of law, perfect order in physics, perfect parallelism between the laws of Nature and the laws of thought exist. In botany we have the like, the poetic perception of metamorphosis,— that the same vegetable point or eye which is the unit of the plant can be transformed at pleasure into every part, as bract, leaf, petal, stamen, pistil, or seed.

In geology, what a useful hint was given to the early inquirers on seeing in the possession of Professor Playfair a bough of a fossil tree which was perfect wood at one end, and perfect mineral coal at the other. Natural objects, if individually described, and out of connection, are not yet known, since they are really parts of a symmetrical universe, like words of a sentence ; and if their true order is found, the poet can read their divine significance orderly as in a Bible. Each animal or vegetable form remembers the next inferior, and predicts the next higher.

There is one animal, one plant, one matter, and one force. The laws of light and of heat translate each other ; — so do the laws of sound and of color ; and so galvanism, electricity, and magnetism are varied forms of the selfsame energy. While the student ponders this immense unity, he observes that all things in nature, the animals, the mountain, the river, the seasons, wood, iron, stone, vapor,— have a mysterious relation to his thoughts and his life ; their growths, decays, quality, and use so curiously resemble himself, in parts and in wholes, that he is compelled to speak by means of them. His words and his thoughts are framed by their help. Every noun is an image. Nature gives him, sometimes in a flattered likeness, sometimes in caricature, a copy of every humor and shade in his character and mind. The world is an immense picture-book of every passage in human life. Every object he beholds is the mask of a man.

> " The privates of man's heart
> They speken and sound in his ear
> As tho' they loud winds were ";

for the universe is full of their echoes.

Every correspondence we observe in mind and matter suggests a substance older and deeper than either of these old nobilities. We see the law gleaming through, like the sense of a half-translated ode of Hafiz. The poet who plays with it with most boldness best justifies himself,— is most profound and most devout. Passion adds eyes,— is a magnifying-glass. Sonnets of lovers are mad enough, but are valuable to the philosopher, as are prayers of saints, for their potent symbolism.

Science was false by being unpoetical. It assumed to explain a reptile or mollusk, and isolated it,— which is hunting for life in graveyards. Reptile or mollusk or man or angel only exists in system, in relation. The metaphysician, the poet, only sees each animal form as an inevitable step in the path of the creating mind. The Indian, the hunter, the boy with his pets, have sweeter knowledge of these than the savant. We use semblances of logic until experience puts us in possession of real logic. The poet knows the missing link by the joy it gives. The poet gives us the eminent experiences only,— a god stepping from peak to peak, nor planting his foot but on a mountain.

Science does not know its debt to imagination. Goethe did not believe that a great naturalist could exist without this faculty. He was himself conscious of its help, which made him a prophet among the doctors. From this vision he gave brave hints to the zoölogist, the botanist, and the optician.

Poetry.— The primary use of a fact is low : the secondary use, as it is a figure or illustration of my thought, is the real worth. First, the fact ; second its impression, or what I think of it. Hence Nature was called " a kind of adulterated reason." Seas, forests, metals, diamonds, and fossils interest the eye, but 't is only with some preparatory or predicting charm. Their value to the intellect appears only when I hear their meaning made plain in the spiritual truth they cover. The mind, penetrated with its sentiment or its thought, projects it outward on whatever it beholds. The lover sees reminders of his mistress in every beautiful object ; the saint, an argument for devotion in every natural process ; and the facility with which Nature lends itself to the thoughts of man, the aptness with which a river, a flower, a bird, fire, day, or night, can express his fortunes, is as if the world were only a disguised man, and, with a change of form, rendered to him all his experience. We cannot utter a sentence in sprightly conversation without a similitude. Note our incessant use of the word *like,*— like fire, like a rock, like thunder, like a bee, " like a year without a spring." Conversation is not permitted without tropes ; nothing but great weight in things can afford a quite literal speech. It is ever enlivened by inversion and trope. God himself does not speak prose, but communicates with us by hints, omens, inference, and dark resemblances in objects lying all around us.

Nothing so marks a man as imaginative expressions. A figurative statement arrests attention, and is remembered and repeated. How often has a phrase of this kind made a reputation. Pythagoras's Golden Sayings were such, and Socrates's, and Mirabeau's, and Burke's, and Bonaparte's. Genius thus makes the transfer from one part of Nature to a remote part, and betrays the rhymes and echoes that pole makes with pole. Imaginative minds cling to their images, and do not wish

them rashly rendered into prose reality, as children resent
your showing them that their doll Cinderella is nothing but
pine wood and rags ; and my young scholar does not wish
to know what the leopard, the wolf, or Lucia, signify in
Dante's Inferno, but prefers to keep their veils on.   Mark the
delight of an audience in an image.   When some familiar
truth or fact appears in a new dress, mounted as on a fine horse,
equipped with a grand pair of ballooning wings, we cannot
enough testify our surprise and pleasure.   It is like the new
virtue shown in some unprized old property, as when a boy
finds that his pocket-knife will attract steel filings and take
up a needle ; or when the old horse-block in the yard is found
to be a Torso Hercules of the Phidian age.   Vivacity of expression may indicate this high gift, even when the thought
is of no great scope, as when Michel Angelo, praising the
terra cottas, said, " If this earth were to become marble, woe to
the antiques ! "   A happy symbol is a sort of evidence that
your thought is just.   I had rather have a good symbol of
my thought, or a good analogy, than the suffrage of Kant or
Plato.   If you agree with me, or if Locke or Montesquieu
agree, I may yet be wrong ; but if the elm-tree thinks the
same thing, if running water, if burning coal, if crystals, if
alkalies, in their several fashions, say what I say, it must be
true.   Thus, a good symbol is the best argument, and is a
missionary to persuade thousands.   The Vedas, the Edda, the
Koran, are each remembered by their happiest figure.   There
is no more welcome gift to men than a new symbol.   That
satiates, transports, converts them.   They assimilate themselves to it, — deal with it in all ways, and it will last a hundred years.   Then comes a new genius, and brings another.
Thus the Greek mythology called the sea " the tear of Sa-
turn."   The return of the soul to God was described as " a
flask of water broken in the sea."   St. John gave us the Christian figure of " souls washed in the blood of Christ."   The
aged Michel Angelo indicates his perpetual study as in boyhood, — " I carry my satchel still."   Machiavel described the
papacy as " a stone inserted in the body of Italy to keep the
wound open."   To the Parliament debating how to tax
America, Burke exclaimed, " Shear the wolf."   Our Kentuckian
orator said of his dissent from his companion, " I showed him
the back of my hand."   And our proverb of the courteous
soldier reads : " An iron hand in a velvet glove."
This belief that the higher use of the material world is to

furnish us types or pictures to express the thoughts of the mind is carried to its logical extreme by the Hindoos, who, following Buddha, have made it the central doctrine of their religion, that what we call Nature, the external world, has no real existence, — is only phenomenal. Youth, age, property, condition, events, persons, — self, even, — are successive *maias* (deceptions) through which Vishnu mocks and instructs the soul. I think Hindoo books the best gymnastics for the mind, as showing treatment. All European libraries might almost be read without the swing of this gigantic arm being suspected. But these Orientals deal with worlds and pebbles freely.

For the value of a trope is that the hearer is one ; and indeed Nature itself is a vast trope, and all particular natures are tropes. As the bird alights on the bough, — then plunges into the air again, so the thoughts of God pause but for a moment in any form. All thinking is analogizing, and 't is the use of life to learn metonymy. The endless passing of one element into new forms, the incessant metamorphosis, explains the rank which the imagination holds in our catalogue of mental powers. The imagination is the reader of these forms. The poet accounts all productions and changes of Nature as the nouns of language, uses them representatively, too well pleased with their ulterior to value much their primary meaning. Every new object so seen gives a shock of agreeable surprise. The impressions on the imagination make the great days of life : the book, the landscape, or the personalty which did not stay on the surface of the eye or ear, but penetrated to the inward sense, agitates us, and is not forgotten. Walking, working, or talking, the sole question is how many strokes vibrate on this mystic string, — how many diameters are drawn quite through from matter to spirit ; for, whenever you enunciate a natural law, you discover that you have enunciated a law of the mind. Chemistry, geology, hydraulics, are secondary science. The atomic theory is only an interior process *produced*, as geometers say, or the effect of a foregone metaphysical theory. Swedenborg saw gravity to be only an external of the irresistible attractions of affection and faith. Mountains and oceans we think we understand : — yes, so long as they are contented to be such, and are safe with the geologist, — but when they are melted in Promethean alembics, and come out men, and then, melted again, come out words, without any abatement, but with an exaltation of power ! —

9ª

In poetry we say we require the miracle. The bee flies among the flowers, and gets mint and marjoram, and generates a new product, which is not mint and marjoram, but honey; the chemist mixes hydrogen and oxygen to yield a new product, which is not these, but water; and the poet listens to conversation, and beholds all objects in nature, to give back, not them, but a new and transcendent whole.

Poetry is the perpetual endeavor to express the spirit of the thing, to pass the brute body, and search the life and reason which causes it to exist; — to see that the object is always flowing away, whilst the spirit or necessity which causes it subsists. Its essential mark is that it betrays in every word instant activity of mind, shown in new uses of every fact and image, — in preternatural quickness or perception of relations. All its words are poems. It is a presence of mind that gives a miraculous command of all means of uttering the thought and feeling of the moment. The poet squanders on the hour an amount of life that would more than furnish the seventy years of the man that stands next him.

The term genius, when used with emphasis, implies imagination; use of symbols, figurative speech. A deep insight will always, like Nature, ultimate its thought in a thing. As soon as a man masters a principle, and sees his facts in relation to it, fields, waters, skies, offer to clothe his thoughts in images. Then all men understand him : Parthian, Mede, Chinese, Spaniard, and Indian hear their own tongue. For he can now find symbols of universal significance, which are readily rendered into any dialect; as a painter, a sculptor, a musician, can in their several ways express the same sentiment of anger, or love, or religion.

The thoughts are few; the forms many; the large vocabulary or many-colored coat of the indigent unity. The savans are chatty and vain, — but hold them hard to principle and definition, and they become mute and near-sighted. What is motion? what is beauty? what is matter? what is life? what is force? Push them hard, and they will not be loquacious. They will come to Plato, Proclus, and Swedenborg. The invisible and imponderable is the sole fact. "Why changes not the violet earth into musk?" What is the term of the ever-flowing metamorphosis? I do not know what are the stoppages, but I see that a devouring unity changes all into that which changes not.

The act of imagination is ever attended by pure delight.

It infuses a certain volatility and intoxication into all nature.
It has a flute which sets the atoms of our frame in a dance.
Our indeterminate size is a delicious secret which it reveals to
us. The mountains begin to dislimn, and float in the air. In
the presence and conversation of a true poet, teeming with
images to express his enlarging thought, his person, his form,
grows larger to our fascinated eyes. And thus begins that
deification which all nations have made of their heroes in
every kind, — saints, poets, lawgivers, and warriors.

Imagination. — Whilst common-sense looks at things or visible nature as real and final facts, poetry, or the imagination
which dictates it, is a second sight, looking through these, and
using them as types or words for thoughts which they signify.
Or is this belief a metaphysical whim of modern times, and
quite too refined? On the contrary, it is old as the human
mind. Our best definition of poetry is one of the oldest sentences, and claims to come down to us from the Chaldæan Zoroaster, who wrote it thus : " Poets are standing transporters,
whose employment consists in speaking to the Father and to
matter ; in producing apparent imitations of unapparent
natures, and inscribing things unapparent in the apparent
fabrication of the world " ; in other words, the world exists
for thought : it is to make appear things which hide :
mountains, crystals, plants, animals, are seen ; that which
makes them is not seen : these, then, are " apparent copies of
unapparent natures." Bacon expressed the same sense in his
definition, " Poetry accommodates the shows of things to the
desires of the mind " ; and Swedenborg, when he said, " There is
nothing existing in human thought, even though related to
the most mysterious tenet of faith, but has combined with it a
natural and sensuous image." And again : " Names, countries,
nations, and the like are not at all known to those who are in
heaven ; they have no idea of such things, but of the realities
signified thereby." A symbol always stimulates the intellect ;
therefore is poetry ever the best reading. The very design of
imagination is to domesticate us in another, in a celestial, nature.

This power is in the image because this power is in nature.
It so affects, because it so is. All that is wondrous in Swedenborg is not his invention, but his extraordinary perception ;
— that he was necessitated so to see. The world realizes the
mind. Better than images is seen through them. The selec-

tion of the image is no more arbitrary than the power and significance of the image. The selection must follow fate. Poetry, if perfected, is the only verity; is the speech of man after the real, and not after the apparent.

Or, shall we say that the imagination exists by sharing the ethereal currents? The poet contemplates the central identity, sees it undulate and roll this way and that, with divine flowings, through remotest things; and, following it, can detect essential resemblances in natures never before compared. He can class them so audaciously, because he is sensible of the sweep of the celestial stream, from which nothing is exempt. His own body is a fleeing apparition, — his personality as fugitive as the trope he employs. In certain hours we can almost pass our hand through our own body. I think the use or value of poetry to be the suggestion it affords of the flux or fugaciousness of the poet. The mind delights in measuring itself thus with matter, with history, and flouting both. A thought, any thought, pressed, followed, opened, dwarfs matter, custom, and all but itself. But this second sight does not necessarily impair the primary or common sense. Pindar and Dante, yes, and the gray and timeworn sentences of Zoroaster, may all be parsed, though we do not parse them. The poet has a logic, though it be subtile. He observes higher laws than he transgresses. "Poetry must first be good sense, though it is something better."

This union of first and second sight reads nature to the end of delight and of moral use. Men are imaginative, but not overpowered by it to the extent of confounding its suggestions with external facts. We live in both spheres, and must not mix them. Genius certifies its entire possession of its thought, by translating it into a fact which perfectly represents it, and is hereby education. Charles James Fox thought "Poetry the great refreshment of the human mind, — the only thing, after all; that men first found out they had minds, by making and tasting poetry."

Man runs about restless and in pain when his condition or the objects about him do not fully match his thought. He wishes to be rich, to be old, to be young, that things may obey him. In the ocean, in fire, in the sky, in the forest, he finds facts adequate and as large as he. As his thoughts are deeper than he can fathom, so also are these. 'T is easier to read Sanscrit, to decipher the arrowhead character, than to interpret these familiar sights. 'T is even much to name them.

Thus Thomson's "Seasons" and the best parts of many old and many new poets are simply enumerations by a person who felt the beauty of the common sights and sounds, without any attempt to draw a moral or affix a meaning.

The poet discovers that what men value as substances have a higher value as symbols; that Nature is the immense shadow of man. A man's action is only a picture-book of his creed. He does after what he believes. Your condition, your employment, is the fable of *you*. The world is thoroughly anthropomorphized, as if it had passed through the body and mind of man, and taken his mould and form. Indeed, good poetry is always personification, and heightens every species of force in nature by giving it a human volition. We are advertised that there is nothing to which he is not related; that everything is convertible into every other. The staff in this hand is the *radius vector* of the sun. The chemistry of this is the chemistry of that. Whatever one act we do, whatever one thing we learn, we are doing and learning all things, — marching in the direction of universal power. Every healthy mind is a true Alexander or Sesostris, building a universal monarchy.

The senses imprison us, and we help them with metres as limitary, with a pair of scales and a foot-rule, and a clock. How long it took to find out what a day was, or what this sun, that makes days! It cost thousands of years only to make the motion of the earth suspected. Slowly, by comparing thousands of observations, there dawned on some mind a theory of the sun, — and we found the astronomical fact. But the astronomy is in the mind: the senses affirm that the earth stands still and the sun moves. The senses collect the surface facts of matter. The intellect acts on these brute reports, and obtains from them results which are the essence or intellectual form of the experiences. It compares, distributes, generalizes, and uplifts them into its own sphere. It knows that these transfigured results are not the brute experiences, just as souls in heaven are not the red bodies they once animated. Many transfigurations have befallen them. The atoms of the body were once nebulæ, then rock, then loam, then corn, then chyme, then chyle, then blood; and now the beholding and co-energizing mind sees the same refining and ascent to the third, the seventh, or the tenth power of the daily accidents which the senses report, and which make the raw material of knowledge. It was sensation; when memory came, it was experience; when mind acted, it was knowledge; when mind acted on it as knowledge, it was thought.

This metonymy, or seeing the same sense in things so diverse, gives a pure pleasure. Every one of a million times we find a charm in the metamorphosis. It makes us dance and sing. All men are so far poets. When people tell me they do not relish poetry, and bring me Shelley, or Aikin's Poets, or I know not what volumes of rhymed English, to show that it has no charm, I am quite of their mind. But this dislike of the books only proves their liking of poetry. For they relish Æsop, — cannot forget him, or not use him; bring them Homer's Iliad, and they like that; or the Cid, and that rings well : read to them from Chaucer, and they reckon him an honest fellow. "Lear" and "Macbeth" and "Richard III." they know pretty well without guide. Give them Robin Hood's ballads, or "Griselda," or "Sir Andrew Barton," or "Sir Patrick Spens," or "Chevy Chase," or "Tam O'Shanter," and they like these well enough. They like to see statues; they like to name the stars; they like to talk and hear of Jove, Apollo, Minerva, Venus, and the Nine. See how tenacious we are of the old names. They like poetry without knowing it as such. They like to go to the theatre and be made to weep; to Faneuil Hall, and be taught by Otis, Webster, or Kossuth, or Phillips, what great hearts they have, what tears, what new possible enlargements to their narrow horizons. They like to see sunsets on the hills or on a lake shore. Now, a cow does not gaze at the rainbow, or show or affect any interest in the landscape, or a peacock, or the song of thrushes.

Nature is the true idealist. When she serves us best, when, on rare days, she speaks to the imagination, we feel that the huge heaven and earth are but a web drawn around us, that the light, skies, and mountains are but the painted vicissitudes of the soul. Who has heard our hymn in the churches without accepting the truth, —

> " As o'er our heads the seasons roll,
> And soothe with *change of bliss* the soul "?

Of course, when we describe man as poet, and credit him with the triumphs of the art, we speak of the potential or ideal man, — not found now in any one person. You must go through a city or a nation, and find one faculty here, one there, to build the true poet withal. Yet all men know the portrait when it is drawn, and it is part of religion to believe its possible incarnation.

He is the healthy, the wise, the fundamental, the manly man, seer of the secret; against all the appearance, he sees and reports the truth, namely, that the soul generates matter. And poetry is the only verity, — the expression of a sound mind speaking after the ideal, and not after the apparent. As a power, it is the perception of the symbolic character of things, and the treating them as representative : as a talent, it is a magnetic tenaciousness of an image, and by the treatment demonstrating that this pigment of thought is as palpable and objective to the poet as is the ground on which he stands, or the walls of houses about him. And this power appears in Dante and Shakspeare. In some individuals this insight, or second sight, has an extraordinary reach which compels our wonder, as in Behmen, Swedenborg, and William Blake, the painter.

William Blake, whose abnormal genius, Wordsworth said, interested him more than the conversation of Scott or of Byron, writes thus : " He who does not imagine in stronger and better lineaments, and in stronger and better light than his perishing mortal eye can see, does not imagine at all. The painter of this work asserts that all his imaginations appear to him infinitely more perfect and more minutely organized, than anything seen by his mortal eye. . . . . I assert for myself that I do not behold the outward creation, and that to me it would be a hindrance, and not action. I question not my corporeal eye any more than I would question a window concerning a sight. I look through it, and not with it."

'T is a problem of metaphysics to define the province of Fancy and Imagination. The words are often used, and the things confounded. Imagination respects the cause. It is the vision of an inspired soul reading arguments and affirmations in all nature of that which it is driven to say. But as soon as this soul is released a little from its passion, and at leisure plays with the resemblances and types for amusement and not for its moral end, we call its action Fancy. Lear, mad with his affliction, thinks every man who suffers must have the like cause with his own. " What, have his daughters brought him to this pass ? " But when, his attention being diverted, his mind rests from this thought, he becomes fanciful with Tom, playing with the superficial resemblances of objects. Bunyan, in pain for his soul, wrote " Pilgrim's Progress " ; Quarles, after he was quite cool, wrote " Emblems."

Imagination is central ; fancy, superficial. Fancy relates

to surface, in which a great part of life lies. The lover is rightly said to fancy the hair, eyes, complexion of the maid. Fancy is a wilful, imagination a spontaneous act ; fancy, a play as with dolls and puppets which we choose to call men and women ; imagination, a perception and affirming of a real relation between a thought and some material fact. Fancy amuses ; imagination expands and exalts us. Imagination uses an organic classification. Fancy joins by accidental resemblance, surprises and amuses the idle, but is silent in the presence of great passion and action. Fancy aggregates ; imagination animates. Fancy is related to color ; imagination, to form. Fancy paints ; imagination sculptures.

Veracity. — I do not wish, therefore, to find that my poet is not partaker of the feast he spreads, or that he would kindle or amuse me with that which does not kindle or amuse him. He must believe in his poetry. Homer, Milton, Hafiz, Herbert, Swedenborg, Wordsworth, are heartily enamored of their sweet thoughts. Moreover, they know that this correspondence of things to thoughts is far deeper than they can penetrate, — defying adequate expression ; that it is elemental, or in the core of things. Veracity, therefore, is that which we require in poets, — that they shall say how it was with them, and not what might be said. And the fault of our popular poetry is that it is not sincere.

" What news ? " asks man of man everywhere. The only teller of news is the poet. When he sings, the world listens with the assurance that now a secret of God is to be spoken. The right poetic mood is or makes a more complete sensibility, — piercing the outward fact to the meaning of the fact ; shows a sharper insight : and the perception creates the strong expression of it, as the man who sees his way walks in it.

'T is a rule in eloquence, that the moment the orator loses command of his audience, the audience commands him. So, in poetry, the master rushes to deliver his thought, and the words and images fly to him to express it ; whilst colder moods are forced to respect the ways of saying it, and insinuate, or, as it were, muffle the fact, to suit the poverty or caprice of their expression, so that they only hint the matter, or allude to it, being unable to fuse and mould their words and images to fluid obedience. See how Shakspeare grapples at once with the main problem of the tragedy, as in " Lear " and " Macbeth," and the opening of " The Merchant of Venice."

All writings must be in a degree exoteric, written to a human *should* or *would*, instead of to the fatal *is :* this holds even of the bravest and sincerest writers. Every writer is a skater, and must go partly where he would, and partly where the skates carry him ; or a sailor, who can only land where sails can be blown. And yet it is to be added, that high poetry exceeds the fact, or nature itself, just as skates allow the good skater far more grace than his best walking would show, or sails more than riding. The poet writes from a real experience, the amateur feigns one. Of course, one draws the bow with his fingers, and the other with the strength of his body ; one speaks with his lips, and the other with a chest voice. Talent amuses, but if your verse has not a necessary and autobiographic basis, though under whatever gay poetic veils, it shall not waste my time.

For poetry is faith. To the poet the world is virgin soil : all is practicable ; the men are ready for virtue ; it is always time to do right. He is a true re-commencer, or Adam in the garden again. He affirms the applicability of the ideal law to this moment and the present knot of affairs. Parties, lawyers, and men of the world will invariably dispute such an application as romantic and dangerous : they admit the general truth, but they and their affair always constitute a case in bar of the statute. Free-trade, they concede, is very well as a principle, but it is never quite the time for its adoption without prejudicing actual interests. Chastity, they admit, is very well, — but then think of Mirabeau's passion and temperament ! — Eternal laws are very well, which admit no violation, — but so extreme were the times and manners of mankind, that you must admit miracles, — for the times constituted a case. Of course, we know what you say, that legends are found in all tribes, — but this legend is different. And so, throughout, the poet affirms the laws ; prose busies itself with exceptions, — with the local and individual.

I require that the poem should impress me, so that after I have shut the book, it shall recall me to itself, or that passages should. And inestimable is the criticism of memory as a corrective to first impressions. We are dazzled at first by new words and brilliancy of color, which occupy the fancy and deceive the judgment. But all this is easily forgotten. Later, the thought, the happy image which expressed it, and which was a true experience of the poet, recurs to mind, and sends me back in search of the book. And I wish that the

N

poet should foresee this habit of readers, and omit all but the important passages. Shakspeare is made up of important passages, like Damascus steel made up of old nails. Homer has his own, —

"One omen is good, to die for one's country" ;

and again, —

"They heal their griefs, for curable are the hearts of the noble."

Write, that I may know you. Style betrays you, as your eyes do. We detect at once by it whether the writer has a firm grasp on his fact or thought, — exists at the moment for that alone, or whether he has one eye apologizing, deprecatory, turned on his reader. In proportion always to his possession of his thought is his defiance of his readers. There is no choice of words for him who clearly sees the truth. That provides him with the best word.

Great design belongs to a poem, and is better than any skill of execution, — but how rare! I find it in the poems of Wordsworth, — "Laodamia," and the "Ode to Dion," and the plan of "The Recluse." We want design, and do not forgive the bards if they have only the art of enamelling. We want an architect, and they bring us an upholsterer.

If your subject do not appear to you the flower of the world at this moment, you have not rightly chosen it. No matter what it is, grand or gay, national or private, if it has a natural prominence to you, work away until you come to the heart of it : then it will, though it were a sparrow or a spider-web, as fully represent the central law, and draw all tragic or joyful illustration, as if it were the book of Genesis or the book of Doom. The subject — we must so often say it — is indifferent. Any word, every word in language, every circumstance, becomes poetic in the hands of a higher thought.

The test or measure of poetic genius is the power to read the poetry of affairs, — to fuse the circumstance of to-day; not to use Scott's antique superstitions, or Shakspeare's, but to convert those of the nineteenth century, and of the existing nations, into universal symbols. 'T is easy to repaint the mythology of the Greeks, or of the Catholic church, the feudal castle, the crusade, the martyrdoms of mediæval Europe ; but to point out where the same creative force is now working in our own houses and public assemblies, to convert the vivid energies acting at this hour, in New York and Chicago and San Francisco, into universal symbols, requires a subtile and commanding thought. 'T is boyish in Swedenborg to cumber himself with the dead scurf of Hebrew antiquity, as if the Divine creative energy had fainted in his own century. American life storms about us daily, and is slow to find a tongue. This contemporary insight is transubstantiation, the conversion of daily bread into the holiest symbols; and every man would be a poet, if his intellectual digestion were perfect. The test of the poet is the power to take the passing day, with its news, its cares, its fears, as he shares them, and hold it up to a divine reason, till he sees it to have a purpose and beauty, and to be related to astronomy and history, and the eternal order of the world. Then the dry twig blossoms in his hand. He is calmed and elevated.

The use of "occasional poems" is to give leave to originality. Every one delights in the felicity frequently shown in our drawing-rooms. In a game-party or picnic poem each writer is released from the solemn rhythmic traditions which alarm and suffocate his fancy, and the result is that one of the partners offers a poem in a new style that hints at a new literature. Yet the writer holds it cheap, and could do the like all day. On the stage, the farce is commonly far better given than the tragedy, as the stock actors understand the farce, and do not understand the tragedy. The writer in the parlor has more presence of mind, more wit and fancy, more play of thought, on the incidents that occur at table, or about the house, than in the politics of Germany or Rome. Many of the fine poems of Herrick, Jonson, and their contemporaries had this casual origin.

I know there is entertainment and room for talent in the artist's selection of ancient or remote subjects; as when the poet goes to India, or to Rome, or Persia, for his fable. But I believe nobody knows better than he, that herein he consults his ease, rather than his strength or his desire. He is very well convinced that the great moments of life are those in which his own house, his own body, the tritest and nearest ways and words and things, have been illuminated into prophets and teachers. What else is it to be a poet? What are his garland and singing robes? What but a sensibility so keen that the scent of an elder-blow, or the timber-yard and corporation works of a nest of pismires is event enough for him, — all emblems and personal appeals to him. His wreath and robe is to do what he enjoys; emancipation from other men's questions, and glad study of his own; escape from the gossip and routine of society, and the allowed right and practice of making better. He does not give his hand, but in sign of giving his heart; he is not affable with all, but silent, uncommitted, or in love, as his heart leads him. There is no subject that does not belong to him, — politics, economy, manufactures, and stock-brokerage, as much as sunsets and souls; only, these things, placed in their true order, are poetry; displaced, or put in kitchen order, they are unpoetic. Malthus is the right organ of the English proprietors; but we shall never understand political economy, until Burns or Béranger or some poet shall teach it in songs, and he will not teach Malthusianism.

Poetry is the *gai science*. The trait and test of the poet is that he builds, adds, and affirms. The critic destroys: the poet says nothing but what helps somebody; let others be distracted with cares, he is exempt. All their pleasures are tinged with pain. All his pains are edged with pleasure. The gladness he imparts he shares. As one of the old Minnesingers sung, —

> " Oft have I heard, and now believe it true,
>   Whom man delights in, God delights in too."

Poetry is the consolation of mortal men. They live cabined, cribbed, confined, in a narrow and trivial lot, — in wants, pains, anxieties, and superstitions, in profligate politics, in personal animosities, in mean employments, — and victims of these; and the nobler powers untried, unknown. A poet comes, who lifts the veil; gives them glimpses of the laws of the universe; shows them the circumstance as illusion; shows that nature is only a language to express the laws, which are grand and beautiful, — and lets them, by his songs, into some of the realities. Socrates; the Indian teachers of the Maia; the Bibles of the nations; Shakspeare, Milton, Hafiz, Ossian, the Welsh Bards, — these all deal with nature and history as means and symbols, and not as ends. With such guides they begin to see that what they had called pictures are realities, and the mean life is pictures. And this is achieved by words; for it is a few oracles spoken by perceiving men that are the texts on which religions and states are founded. And this perception has at once its moral sequence. Ben Jonson said, " The principal end of poetry is to inform men in the just reason of living."

Creation. — But there is a third step which poetry takes, and which seems higher than the others, namely, creation, or ideas taking forms of their own, — when the poet invents the fable, and invents the language which his heroes speak. He reads in the word or action of the man its yet untold results. His inspiration is power to carry out and complete the metamorphosis, which, in the imperfect kinds, arrested for ages, — in the perfecter, proceeds rapidly in the same individual. For poetry is science, and the poet a truer logician. Men in the courts or in the street think themselves logical, and the poet whimsical. Do they think there is chance or wilfulness in what he sees and tells? To be sure, we demand of him what he demands of himself, — veracity, first of all. But with that, he is the lawgiver, as being an exact reporter of the essential law. He knows that he did not make his thought, — no, his thought made him, and made the sun and the stars. Is the solar system good art and architecture? the same wise achievement is in the human brain also, can you only wile it from interference and marring. We cannot look at works of art but they teach us how near man is to creating. Michel Angelo is largely filled with the Creator that made and makes men. How much of the original craft remains in him, and he a mortal man! In him and the like perfecter brains the instinct is resistless, knows the right way, is melodious, and at all points divine. The reason we set so high a value on any poetry, — as often on a line or a phrase as on a poem, — is, that it is a new work of Nature, as a man is. It must be as new as foam and as old as the rock. But a new verse comes once in a hundred years; therefore Pindar, Hafiz, Dante, speak so proudly of what seems to the clown a jingle.

The writer, like the priest, must be exempted from secular labor. His work needs a frolic health; he must be at the top of his condition. In that prosperity he is sometimes caught up into a perception of means and materials, of feats and fine arts, of fairy machineries and funds of power hitherto utterly unknown to him, whereby he can transfer his visions to mortal canvas, or reduce them into iambic or trochaic, into lyric or heroic rhyme. These successes are not less admirable and astonishing to the poet than they are to his audience. He has seen something which all the mathematics and the best industry could never bring him unto. Now at this rare elevation above his usual sphere, he has come into new circulations. the marrow of the world is in his bones, the opulence of forms begins to pour into his intellect, and he is permitted to dip his brush into the old paint-pot with which birds, flowers, the human cheek, the living rock, the broad landscape, the ocean, and the eternal sky were painted.

These fine fruits of judgment, poesy, and sentiment, when once their hour is struck, and the world is ripe for them, know as well as coarser. how to feed and replenish themselves, and maintain their stock alive, and multiply; for roses and violets renew their race like oaks, and flights of painted moths are as old as the Alleghanies. The balance of the world is kept, and dewdrop and haze and the pencil of light are as long-lived as chaos and darkness.

Our science is always abreast of our self-knowledge. Poetry begins, or all becomes poetry, when we look from the centre outward, and are using all as if the mind made it. That only can we see which we are, and which we make. The weaver sees gingham; the broker sees the stock-list; the politician, the ward and county votes; the poet sees the horizon, and the shores of matter lying on the sky, the interaction of the elements,—the large effect of laws which correspond to the inward laws which he knows, and so are but a kind of extension of himself. "The attractions are proportional to the destinies." Events or things are only the fulfilment of the prediction of the faculties. Better men saw heavens and earths; saw noble instruments of noble souls. We see railroads, mills, and banks, and we pity the poverty of these dreaming Buddhists. There was as much creative force then as now, but it made globes, and astronomic heavens, instead of broadcloth and wine-glasses.

The poet is enamored of thoughts and laws. These know their way, and, guided by them, he is ascending from an interest in visible things to an interest in that which they signify, and from the part of a spectator to the part of a maker. And as everything streams and advances, as every faculty and every desire is procreant, and every perception is a destiny, there is no limit to his hope. "Anything, child, that the mind covets, from the milk of a cocoa to the throne of the three worlds, thou mayest obtain, by keeping the law of thy members and the law of thy mind." It suggests that there is higher poetry than we write or read.

Rightly, poetry is organic. We cannot know things by words and writing, but only by taking a central position in the universe, and living in its forms. We sink to rise.

> "None any work can frame,
> Unless himself become the same."

All the parts and forms of nature are the expression or production of divine faculties, and the same are in us. And the fascination of genius for us is this awful nearness to Nature's creations.

I have heard that the Germans think the creator of Trim and Uncle Toby, though he never wrote a verse, a greater poet than Cowper, and that Goldsmith's title to the name is not from his "Deserted Village," but derived from the "Vicar of Wakefield." Better examples are Shakspeare's Ariel, his Caliban, and his fairies in the "Midsummer Night's Dream." Barthold Niebuhr said well, "There is little merit in inventing a happy idea, or attractive situation, so long as it is only the author's voice which we hear. As a being whom we have called into life by magic arts, as soon as it has received existence acts independently of the master's impulse, so the poet creates his persons, and then watches and relates what they do and say. Such creation is poetry, in the literal sense of the term, and its possibility is an unfathomable enigma. The gushing fulness of speech belongs to the poet, and it flows from the lips of each of his magic beings in the thoughts and words peculiar to its nature." *

This force of representation so plants his figures before him that he treats them as real; talks to them as if they were bodily there; puts words in their mouth such as they should have spoken, and is affected by them as by persons. Vast is the difference between writing clean verses for magazines, and creating these new persons and situations,— new language with emphasis and reality. The humor of Falstaff, the terror of Macbeth, have each their swarm of fit thoughts and images, as if Shakspeare had known and reported the men, instead of inventing them at his desk. This power appears not only in the outline or portrait of his actors, but also in the bearing and behavior and style of each individual. Ben Jonson told Drummond "that Sidney did not keep a decorum in making every one speak as well as himself."

This reminds me that we all have one key to this miracle of the poet, and the dunce has experiences that may explain Shakspeare to him,— one key, namely, dreams. In dreams we are true poets; we create the persons of the drama; we give them appropriate figures, faces, costume; they are perfect in their organs, attitude, manners; moreover, they speak after their own characters, not ours; they speak to us, and we listen with surprise to what they say. Indeed, I

* Niebuhr, Letters, etc., Vol. III. p. 196.

doubt if the best poet has yet written any five-act play that can compare in thoroughness of invention with this unwritten play in fifty acts, composed by the dullest snorer on the floor of the watch-house.

Melody, Rhyme, Form.— Music and rhyme are among the earliest pleasures of the child, and, in the history of literature, poetry precedes prose. Every one may see, as he rides on the highway through an uninteresting landscape, how a little water instantly relieves the monotony : no matter what objects are near it,— a gray rock, a grass-patch, an alder-bush, or a stake, — they become beautiful by being reflected. It is rhyme to the eye, and explains the charm of rhyme to the ear. Shadows please us as still finer rhymes. Architecture gives the like pleasure by the repetition of equal parts in a colonnade, in a row of windows, or in wings ; gardens, by the symmetric contrasts of the beds and walks. In society, you have this figure in a bridal company, where a choir of white-robed maidens give the charm of living statues ; in a funeral procession, where all wear black ; in a regiment of soldiers in uniform.

The universality of this taste is proved by our habit of casting our facts into rhyme to remember them better, as so many proverbs may show. Who would hold the order of the almanac so fast but for the ding-dong,

> "Thirty days hath September," etc. ;

or of the Zodiac, but for

> "The Ram, the Bull, the heavenly Twins," etc. ?

We are lovers of rhyme and return, period and musical reflection. The babe is lulled to sleep by the nurse's song. Sailors can work better for their *yo-heave-o*. Soldiers can march better and fight better for the drum and trumpet. Metre begins with pulse-beat, and the length of lines in songs and poems is determined by the inhalation and exhalation of the lungs. If you hum or whistle the rhythm of the common English metres,— of the decasyllabic quatrain, or the octosyllabic with alternate sexisyllabic, or other rhythms, you can easily believe these metres to be organic, derived from the human pulse, and to be therefore not proper to one nation, but to mankind. I think you will also find a charm heroic, plaintive, pathetic, in these cadences, and be at once set on searching for the words that can rightly fill these vacant beats. Young

people like rhyme, drum-beat, tune, things in pairs and alter-
natives ; and, in higher degrees, we know the instant power of
music upon our temperaments to change our mood, and give
us its own : and human passion, seizing these constitutional
tunes, aims to fill them with appropriate words, or marry music
to thought, believing, as we believe of all marriage, that
matches are made in heaven, and that for every thought its
proper melody or rhyme exists, though the odds are immense
against our finding it, and only genius can rightly say the banns.

Another form of rhyme is iterations of phrase, as the record
of the death of Sisera : —

"At her feet he bowed, he fell, he lay down : at her feet he
bowed, he fell : where he bowed, there he fell down dead."

The fact is made conspicuous, nay, colossal, by this simple
rhetoric.

"They shall perish, but thou shalt endure : yea, all of them shall
wax old like a garment ; as a vesture shalt thou change them, and
they shall be changed : but thou art the same, and thy years shall
have no end."

Milton delights in these iterations : —

"Though fallen on evil days,
On evil days though fallen, and evil tongues."

"Was I deceived, or did a sable cloud
Turn forth its silver lining on the night ?
I did not err, there does a sable cloud
Turn forth its silver lining on the night."
Comus.

"A little onward lend thy guiding hand,
To these dark steps a little farther on."
Samson.

So in our songs and ballads the refrain skilfully used, and
deriving some novelty or better sense in each of many
verses : —

"Busk thee, busk thee, my bonny bonny bride,
Busk thee, busk thee, my winsome marrow."
HAMILTON.

Of course rhyme soars and refines with the growth of the
mind. The boy liked the drum, the people liked an overpowering jewsharp tune. Later they like to transfer that rhyme
to life, and to detect a melody as prompt and perfect in their
daily affairs. Omen and coincidence show the rhythmical
structure of man ; hence the taste for signs, sortilege, prophecy and fulfilment, anniversaries, etc. By and by, when they

apprehend real rhymes, namely, the correspondence of parts in
nature,— acid and alkali, body and mind, man and maid,
character and history, action and reaction,— they do not longer value rattles and ding-dongs, or barbaric word-jingle.   Astronomy, Botany, Chemistry, Hydraulics, and the elemental
forces have their own periods and returns, their own grand
strains of harmony not less exact, up to the primeval apothegm
" that there is nothing on earth which is not in the heavens in
a heavenly form, and nothing in the heavens which is not on
the earth in an earthly form."   They furnish the poet with
grander pairs and alternations, and will require an equal expansion in his metres.

There is under the seeming poverty of metres an infinite
variety, as every artist knows.   A right ode (however nearly
it may adopt conventional metre, as the Spenserian, or the
heroic blank-verse, or one of the fixed lyric meters) will by
any sprightliness be at once lifted out of conventionality,
and will modify the metre.   Every good poem that I know I
recall by its rhythm also.   Rhyme is a pretty good measure
of the latitude and opulence of a writer.   If unskilful, he is at
once detected by the poverty of his chimes.   A small, well-
worn, sprucely brushed vocabulary serves him.   Now try
Spenser, Marlow, Chapman, and see how wide they fly for
weapons, and how rich and lavish their profusion.   In their
rhythm is no manufacture, but a vortex, or musical tornado,
which falling on words and the experience of a learned mind,
whirls these materials into the same grand order as planets
and moons obey, and seasons, and monsoons.

There are also prose poets.   Thomas Taylor, the Platonist,
for instance, is really a better man of imagination, a better
poet, or perhaps I should say a better feeder to a poet, than
any man between Milton and Wordsworth.   Thomas Moore
had the magnanimity to say, " If Burke and Bacon were not
poets (measured lines not being necessary to constitute one),
he did not know what poetry meant."   And every good reader
will easily recall expressions or passages in works of pure
science, which have given him the same pleasure which he
seeks in professed poets.   Richard Owen, the eminent paleon-
tologist, said : —

" All hitherto observed causes of extirpation point either to continuous slowly operating geologic changes, or to no greater sudden
cause than the, so to speak, spectral appearance of mankind on a
limited tract of land not before inhabited."

St. Augustine complains to God of his friends offering him the books of the philosophers : —

" And these were the dishes in which they brought to me, being hungry, the Sun and the Moon instead of Thee."

It would not be easy to refuse to Sir Thomas Browne's " Fragment on Mummies " the claim of poetry : —

" Of their living habitations they made little account, conceiving of them but as *hospitia*, or inns, while they adorned the sepulchres of the dead, and, planting thereon lasting bases, defied the crumbling touches of time, and the misty vaporousness of oblivion. Yet all were but Babel vanities. Time sadly overcometh all things, and is now dominant, and sitteth upon a Sphinx, and looketh unto Memphis and old Thebes, while his sister Oblivion reclineth semisomnous on a pyramid, gloriously triumphing, making puzzles of Titanian erections, and turning old glories into dreams. History sinketh beneath her cloud. The traveller as he paceth through those deserts asketh of her, Who builded them ? and she mumbleth something, but what it is he heareth not."

Rhyme, being a kind of music, shares this advantage with music, that it has a privilege of speaking truth which all Philistia is unable to challenge. Music is the poor man's Parnassus. With the first note of the flute or horn, or the first strain of a song, we quit the world of common-sense, and launch on the sea of ideas and emotions : we pour contempt on the prose you so magnify ; yet the sturdiest Philistine is silent. The like allowance is the prescriptive right of poetry. You shall not speak ideal truth in prose uncontradicted : you may in verse. The best thoughts run into the best words ; imaginative and affectionate thoughts into music and metre. We ask for food and fire, we talk of our work, our tools, and material necessities in prose, that is, without any elevation or aim at beauty ; but when we rise into the world of thought, and think of these things only for what they signify, speech refines into order and harmony. I know what you say of mediæval barbarism and sleigh-bell rhyme, but we have not done with music, no, nor with rhyme, nor must console ourselves with prose poets so long as boys whistle and girls sing.

Let Poetry then pass, if it will, into music and rhyme. That is the form which itself puts on. We do not enclose watches in wooden, but in crystal cases, and rhyme is the transparent frame that allows almost the pure architecture of thought to become visible to the mental eye. Substance is much, but so are mode and form much. The poet, like a delighted boy, brings you heaps of rainbow bubbles, opaline, air-borne, spherical as the world, instead of a few drops of soap and water. Victor Hugo says well, "An idea steeped in verse becomes suddenly more incisive and more brilliant : the iron becomes steel." Lord Bacon, we are told, "loved not to see poesy go on other feet than poetical dactyls and spondees"; and Ben Jonson said, "that Donne, for not keeping of accent, deserved hanging."

Poetry being an attempt to express, not the common-sense, as the avoirdupois of the hero, or his structure in feet and inches, but the beauty and soul in his aspect as it shines to fancy and feeling, — and so of all other objects in nature, — runs into fable, personifies every fact : — "the clouds clapped their hands," — "the hills skipped," — "the sky spoke." This is the substance, and this treatment always attempts a metrical grace. Outside of the nursery the beginning of literature is the prayers of a people, and they are always hymns, poetic, — the mind allowing itself range, and therewith is ever a corresponding freedom in the style which becomes lyrical. The prayers of nations are rhythmic, — have iterations and alliterations, like the marriage-service and burial-service in our liturgies.

Poetry will never be a simple means, as when history or philosophy is rhymed, or laureate odes on state occasions are written. Itself must be its own end, or it is nothing. The difference between poetry and stock-poetry is this, that in the latter the rhythm is given, and the sense adapted to it ; while in the former the sense dictates the rhythm. I might even say that the rhyme is there in the theme, thought, and image themselves. Ask the fact for the form. For a verse is not a vehicle to carry a sentence as a jewel is carried in a case : the verse must be alive, and inseparable from its contents, as the soul of man inspires and directs the body ; and we measure the inspiration by the music. In reading prose, I am sensitive as soon as a sentence drags ; but in poetry as soon as one word drags. Ever as the thought mounts, the expression mounts. 'T is cumulative also ; the poem is made up of lines each of which filled the ear of the poet in its turn, so that mere synthesis produces a work quite superhuman.

Indeed, the masters sometimes rise above themselves to strains which charm their readers, and which neither any competitor could outdo, nor the bard himself again equal. Try this strain of Beaumont and Fletcher : —

" Hence, all ye vain delights,
As short as are the nights
In which you spend your folly!
There 's naught in this life sweet,
If men were wise to see 't,
But only melancholy.
Oh! sweetest melancholy!
Welcome, folded arms and fixed eyes,
A sigh that piercing mortifies,
A look that's fastened to the ground,
A tongue chained up, without a sound;
Fountain-heads and pathless groves,
Places which pale Passion loves,
Midnight walks, when all the fowls
Are warmly housed, save bats and owls;
A midnight bell, a passing groan,
These are the sounds we feed upon,
Then stretch our bones in a still, gloomy valley.
Nothing 's so dainty sweet as lovely melancholy."

Keats disclosed by certain lines in his "Hyperion" this inward skill; and Coleridge showed at least his love and appetency for it. It appears in Ben Jonson's songs, including certainly "The faery beam upon you," etc., Waller's "Go, lovely rose!" Herbert's "Virtue" and "Easter," and Lovelace's lines "To Althea" and "To Lucasta," and Collins's "Ode to Evening," all but the last verse, which is academical. Perhaps this dainty style of poetry is not producible to-day, any more than a right Gothic cathedral. It belonged to a time and taste which is not in the world.

As the imagination is not a talent of some men, but is the health of every man, so also is this joy of musical expression. I know the pride of mathematicians and materialists, but they cannot conceal from me their capital want. The critic, the philosopher, is a failed poet. Gray avows "that he thinks even a bad verse as good a thing or better than the best observation that was ever made on it." I honor the naturalist; I honor the geometer, but he has before him higher power and happiness than he knows. Yet we will leave to the masters their own forms. Newton may be permitted to call Terence a play-book, and to wonder at the frivolous taste for rhymers; he only predicts, one would say, a grander poetry: he only shows that he is not yet reached; that the poetry which satisfies more youthful souls is not such to a mind like his, accustomed to grander harmonics; — this being a child's whistle to his ear; that the music must rise to a loftier strain, up to Handel, up to Beethoven, up to the thorough-bass of the sea-shore, up to the largeness of astronomy: at last that great heart will hear in the music beats like its own : the waves of melody will wash and float him also, and set him into concert and harmony.

Bards and Trouveurs. — The metallic force of primitive words makes the superiority of the remains of the rude ages. It costs the early bard little talent to chant more impressively than the later, more cultivated poets.   His advantage is that his words are things, each the lucky sound which described the fact, and we listen to him as we do to the Indian, or the hunter, or miner, each of whom represents his facts as accurately as the cry of the wolf or the eagle tells of the forest or the air they inhabit.   The original force, the direct smell of the earth or the sea, is in these ancient poems, the Sagas of the North, the Nibelungen Lied, the songs and ballads of the English and Scotch.

I find or fancy more true poetry, the love of the vast and the ideal, in the Welsh and bardic fragments of Taliessin and his successors than in many volumes of British Classics.   An intrepid magniloquence appears in all the bards, as : —

> " The whole ocean flamed as one wound."
> *King Regner Lodbook.*

> " God himself cannot procure good for the wicked."
> *Welsh Triad.*

A favorable specimen is Taliessin's "Invocation of the Wind " at the door of Castle Teganwy.

> " Discover thou what it is, —
> The strong creature from before the flood,
> Without flesh, without bone, without head, without feet,
> It will neither be younger nor older than at the beginning;
> It has no fear, nor the rude wants of created things.
> Great God! how the sea whitens when it comes!
> It is in the field, it is in the wood,
> Without hand, without foot,
> Without age, without season,
> It is always of the same age with the ages of ages,
> And of equal breadth with the surface of the earth.
> It was not born, it sees not,
> And is not seen ; it does not come when desired ;
> It has no form, it bears no burden,
> For it is void of sin.
> It makes no perturbation in the place where God wills it,
> On the sea, on the land."

In one of his poems he asks : —

> " Is there but one course to the wind ?
> But one to the water of the sea ?
> Is there but one spark in the fire of boundless energy ? "

He says of his hero, Cunedda, —

"He will assimilate, he will agree with the deep and the shallow."

To another, —

"When I lapse to a sinful word,
May neither you nor others hear."

Of an enemy, —

" The caldron of the sea was bordered round by his land, but it would not boil the food of a coward."

To an exile on an island he says, —

" The heavy blue chain of the sea didst thou, O just man, endure."

Another bard in like tone says, —

" I am possessed of songs such as no son of man can repeat; one of them is called the 'Helper'; it will help thee at thy need in sickness, grief, and all adversities. I know a song which I need only to sing when men have loaded me with bonds : when I sing it, my chains fall in pieces and I walk forth at liberty."

The Norsemen have no less faith in poetry and its power, when they describe it thus : —

" Odin spoke everything in rhyme. He and his temple-gods were called song-smiths. He could make his enemies in battle blind or deaf, and their weapons so blunt that they could no more cut than a willow-twig. Odin taught these arts in runes or songs, which are called incantations." *

The Crusades brought out the genius of France, in the twelfth century, when Pierre d'Auvergne said, —

" I will sing a new song which resounds in my breast : never was a song good or beautiful which resembled any other."

And Pons de Capdeuil declares, —

" Since the air renews itself and softens, so must my heart renew itself, and what buds in it buds and grows outside of it."

There is in every poem a height which attracts more than other parts, and is best remembered. Thus, in " Morte d'Arthur," I remember nothing so well as Sir Gawain's parley with Merlin in his wonderful prison : —

* Heimskringla, Vol. I. p. 221.

" After the disappearance of Merlin from King Arthur's court he was seriously missed, and many knights set out in search of him. Among others was Sir Gawain, who pursued his search till it was time to return to the court. He came into the forest of Broceliande, lamenting as he went along. Presently, he heard the voice of one groaning on his right hand; looking that way, he could see nothing save a kind of smoke which seemed like air, and through which he could not pass; and this impediment made him so wrathful that it deprived him of speech. Presently he heard a voice which said, ' Gawain, Gawain, be not out of heart, for everything which must happen will come to pass.' And when he heard the voice which thus called him by his right name, he replied, ' Who can this be who hath spoken to me ?' ' How,' said the voice, ' Sir Gawain, know you me not ? You were wont to know me well, but thus things are interwoven and thus the proverb says true, " Leave the court and the court will leave you." So is it with me. Whilst I served King Arthur, I was well known by you and by other barons, but because I have left the court, I am known no longer, and put in forgetfulness, which I ought not to be if faith reigned in the world.' When Sir Gawain heard the voice which spoke to him thus, he thought it was Merlin, and he answered, ' Sir, certes I ought to know you well, for many times I have heard your words. I pray you appear before me so that I may be able to recognize you.' ' Ah, sir,' said Merlin, ' you will never see me more, and that grieves me, but I cannot remedy it, and when you shall have departed from this place, I shall nevermore speak to you nor to any other person, save only my mistress; for never other person will be able to discover this place for anything which may befall; neither shall I ever go out from hence, for in the world there is no such strong tower as this wherein I am confined; and it is neither of wood, nor of iron. nor of stone, but of air, without anything else ; and made by enchantment so strong, that it can never be demolished while the world lasts, neither can I go out, nor can any one come in, save she who hath enclosed me here, and who keeps me company when it pleaseth her : she cometh when she listeth, for her will is here.' ' How, Merlin, my good friend,' said Sir Gawain, ' are you restrained so strongly that you cannot deliver yourself nor make yourself visible unto me; how can this happen, seeing that you are the wisest man in the world ?' ' Rather,' said Merlin, ' the greatest fool ; for I well knew that all this would befall me, and I have been fool enough to love another more than myself, for I taught my mistress that whereby she hath imprisoned me in such manner that none can set me free.' ' Certes, Merlin,' replied Sir Gawain, ' of that I am right sorrowful, and so will King Arthur, my uncle, be, when he shall know it, as one who is making search after you throughout all countries.' ' Well,' said Merlin, ' it must be borne, for never will he see me, nor I him ; neither will any one speak with me again after you, it would be vain to attempt it ; for you yourself, when you have turned away, will never be able to find the place: but salute for me the king and the queen, and all the barons, and tell them of my condition. You will find the king at Carduel in Wales; and when you arrive there you will find there all the companions who departed with you, and who at this day will return. Now then go in the name of God, who will protect and save the King Arthur, and the realm of Logres, and you also, as the best knights who are in the world.' With that Sir Gawain departed joyful and sorrowful; joyful because of what Merlin had assured him should happen to him, and sorrowful that Merlin had thus been lost."

Morals. — We are sometimes apprised that there is a mental power and creation more excellent than anything which is commonly called philosophy and literature; that the high poets, — that Homer, Milton, Shakspeare, do not fully content us. How rarely they offer us the heavenly bread! The most they have done is to intoxicate us once and again with its taste. They have touched this heaven and retain afterwards some sparkle of it: they betray their belief that such discourse is possible. There is something — our brothers on this or that side of the sea do not know it or own it; the eminent scholars of England, historians and reviewers, romancers and poets included, might deny and blaspheme it — which is setting us and them aside and the whole world also, and planting itself. To true poetry we shall sit down as the result and justification of the age in which it appears, and think lightly of histories and statutes. None of your parlor or piano verse, — none of your carpet poets, who are content to amuse, will satisfy us. Power, new power, is the good which the soul seeks. The poetic gift we want, as the health and supremacy of man, — not rhymes and sonneteering, not bookmaking and bookselling; surely not cold spying and authorship.

Is not poetry the little chamber in the brain where is generated the explosive force which, by gentle shocks, sets in action the intellectual world? Bring us the bards who shall sing all our old ideas out of our heads, and new ones in; menmaking poets; poetry which, like the verses inscribed on Balder's columns in Breidablik, is capable of restoring the dead to life; — poetry like that verse of Saadi, which the angels testified "met the approbation of Allah in Heaven"; — poetry which finds its rhymes and cadences in the rhymes and iterations of nature, and is the gift to men of new images and symbols, each the ensign and oracle of an age; that shall

assimilate men to it, mould itself into religions and mythologies, and impart its quality to centuries; — poetry which
tastes the world and reports of it, upbuilding the world again
in the thought;

> " Not with tickling rhymes,
> But high and noble matter, such as flies
> From brains entranced, and filled with ecstasies."

Poetry must be affirmative. It is the piety of the intellect.
"Thus saith the Lord," should begin the song. The poet who
shall use nature as his hieroglyphic must have an adequate
message to convey thereby. Therefore, when we speak of the
Poet in any high sense, we are driven to such examples as
Zoroaster and Plato, St. John and Menu, with their moral
burdens. The Muse shall be the counterpart of Nature, and
equally rich. I find her not often in books. We know Nature,
and figure her exuberant, tranquil, magnificent in her fertility, coherent; so that every creation is omen of every other.
She is not proud of the sea, of the stars, of space or time, or
man or woman. All her kinds share the attributes of the
selectest extremes. But in current literature I do not find
her. Literature warps away from life, though at first it seems
to bind it. In the world of letters how few commanding
oracles! Homer did what he could, — Pindar, Æschylus, and
the Greek Gnomic poets and the tragedians. Dante was
faithful when not carried away by his fierce hatreds. But in
so many alcoves of English poetry I can count only nine or
ten authors who are still inspirers and lawgivers to their
race.

The supreme value of poetry is to educate us to a height
beyond itself, or which it rarely reaches; — the subduing mankind to order and virtue. He is the true Orpheus who writes
his ode, not with syllables, but men. "In poetry," said
Goethe, "only the really great and pure advances us, and this
exists as a second nature, either elevating us to itself, or re-
jecting us." The poet must let Humanity sit with the Muse
in his head, as the charioteer sits with the hero in the Iliad.
"Show me," said Sarona in the novel, "one wicked man who
has written poetry, and I will show you where his poetry is
not poetry; or rather, I will show you in his poetry no poetry
at all." *

I have heard that there is a hope which precedes and must
precede all science of the visible or the invisible world; and

* Miss Shepard's "Counterparts," Vol. I. p. 67.

that science is the realization of that hope in either region. I count the genius of Swedenborg and Wordsworth as the agents of a reform in philosophy, the bringing poetry back to nature, — to the marrying of nature and mind, undoing the old divorce in which poetry had been famished and false, and nature had been suspected and pagan. The philosophy which a nation receives, rules its religion, poetry, politics, arts, trades, and whole history. A good poem — say Shakspeare's "Macbeth," or "Hamlet," or the "Tempest" — goes about the world offering itself to reasonable men, who read it with joy and carry it to their reasonable neighbors. Thus it draws to it the wise and generous souls, confirming their secret thoughts, and, through their sympathy, really publishing itself. It affects the characters of its readers by formulating their opinions and feelings, and inevitably prompting their daily action. If they build ships, they write "Ariel" or "Prospero" or "Ophelia" on the ship's stern, and impart a tenderness and mystery to matters of fact. The ballad and romance work on the hearts of boys, who recite the rhymes to their hoops or their skates if alone, and these heroic songs or lines are remembered and determine many practical choices which they make later. Do you think Burns has had no influence on the life of men and women in Scotland, — has opened no eyes and ears to the face of nature and the dignity of man and the charm and excellence of woman?

We are a little civil, it must be owned, to Homer and Æschylus, to Dante and Shakspeare, and give them the benefit of the largest interpretation. We must be a little strict also, and ask whether, if we sit down at home, and do not go to Hamlet, Hamlet will come to us? whether we shall find our tragedy written in his, — our hopes, wants, pains, disgraces, described to the life, — and the way opened to the paradise which ever in the best hour beckons us? But our overpraise and idealization of famous masters is not in its origin a poor Boswellism, but an impatience of mediocrity. The praise we now give to our heroes we shall unsay when we make larger demands. How fast we outgrow the books of the nursery, — then those that satisfied our youth. What we once admired as poetry has long since come to be a sound of tin pans; and many of our later books we have outgrown. Perhaps Homer and Milton will be tin pans yet. Better not to be easily pleased. The poet should rejoice if he has taught us to despise his song; if he has so moved us as to lift us, — to open the eye of the intellect to see farther and better.

In proportion as a man's life comes into union with truth, his thoughts approach to a parallelism with the currents of natural laws, so that he easily expresses his meaning by nat-ural symbols, or uses the ecstatic or poetic speech. By succes-sive states of mind all the facts of nature are for the first time interpreted. In proportion as his life departs from this sim-plicity, he uses circumlocution, — by many words hoping to suggest what he cannot say. Vexatious to find poets, who are by excellence the thinking and feeling of the world, deficient in truth of intellect and of affection. Then is conscience un-faithful, and thought unwise. To know the merit of Shak-speare, read "Faust." I find "Faust" a little too modern and intelligible. We can find such a fabric at several mills, though a little inferior. "Faust" abounds in the disagree-able. The vice is prurient, learned, Parisian. In the pres-ence of Jove, Priapus may be allowed as an offset, but here he is an equal hero. The egotism, the wit, is calculated. The book is undeniably written by a master, and stands unhappily related to the whole modern world; but it is a very disagree-able chapter of literature, and accuses the author as well as the times. Shakspeare could, no doubt, have been disagree-able, had he less genius, and if ugliness had attracted him. In short, our English nature and genius has made us the worst critics of Goethe,

> " We, who speak the tongue
> That Shakspeare spake, the faith and morals hold
> Which Milton held."

It is not style or rhymes, or a new image more or less, that imports, but sanity; that life should not be mean; that life should be an image in every part beautiful; that the old for-gotten splendors of the universe should glow again for us; — that we should lose our wit, but gain our reason. And when life is true to the poles of nature, the streams of truth will roll through us in song.

Transcendency. — In a cotillon some persons dance and others await their turn when the music and the figure come to them. In the dance of God there is not one of the chorus but can and will begin to spin, monumental as he now looks, whenever the music and figure reach his place and duty. O celestial Bacchus! drive them mad, — this multitude of vaga-bonds, hungry for eloquence, hungry for poetry, starving for symbols, perishing for want of electricity to vitalize this too much pasture, and in the long delay indemnifying themselves with the false wine of alcohol, of politics, or of money.

Every man may be, and at some time a man is, lifted to a platform whence he looks beyond sense to moral and spiritual truth; and in that mood deals sovereignly with matter, and strings worlds like beads upon his thought. The success with which this is done can alone determine how genuine is the inspiration. (The poet is rare because he must be exquisitely vital and sympathetic, and, at the same time, immovably centred.) In good society, nay, among the angels in heaven, is not everything spoken in fine parable, and not so servilely as it befell to the sense? All is symbolized. Facts are not foreign, as they seem, but related. Wait a little and we see the return of the remote hyperbolic curve. The solid men complain that the idealist leaves out the fundamental facts; the poet complains that the solid men leave out the sky. To every plant there are two powers; one shoots down as rootlet, and one upward as tree. You must have eyes of science to see in the seed its nodes; you must have the vivacity of the poet to perceive in the thought its futurities. (The poet is representative, — whole man, diamond-merchant, symbolizer, emancipator; in him the world projects a scribe's hand and writes the adequate genesis.) The nature of things is flowing, a metamorphosis. The free spirit sympathizes not only with the actual form, but with the power or possible forms; but for obvious municipal or parietal uses, God has given us a bias or a rest on to-day's forms. Hence the shudder of joy with which in each clear moment we recognize the metamorphosis, because it is always a conquest, a surprise from the heart of things. One would say of the force in the works of nature, all depends on the battery. If it give one shock, we shall get to the fish form, and stop; if two shocks, to the bird; if three, to the quadruped; if four, to the man. Power of generalizing differences men. The number of successive saltations the nimble thought can make, measures the difference between the highest and lowest of mankind. The habit of saliency, of not pausing but going on, is a sort of importation or domestication of the Divine effort in a man. After the largest circle has been drawn, a larger can be drawn around it. The problem of the poet is to unite freedom with precision; to give the pleasure of color, and be not less the most powerful of sculptors. Music seems to you sufficient, or the subtle and delicate scent of lavender; but Dante was free imagination, — all

wings, — yet he wrote like Euclid.   And mark the equality of
Shakspeare to the comic, the tender and sweet, and to the
grand and terrible.   A little more or less skill in whistling is
of no account.   See those weary pentameter tales of Dryden
and others.   Turnpike is one thing and blue sky another.
Let the poet, of all men, stop with his inspiration.) The inexorable rule in the muses' court, *either inspiration or silence,*
compels the bard to report only his supreme moments.   It
teaches the enormous force of a few words, and in proportion
to the inspiration checks loquacity. ; Much that we call poetry
is but polite verse. \ The high poetry which shall thrill and
agitate mankind, restore youth and health, dissipate the
dreams under which men reel and stagger, and bring in the
new thoughts, the sanity and heroic aims of nations, is deeper
hid and longer postponed than was America or Australia, or
the finding of steam or of the galvanic battery.   We must not
conclude against poetry from the defects of poets.   They are,
in our experience, men of every degree of skill, — some of them
only once or twice receivers of an inspiration, and presently
falling back on a low life.   The drop of *ichor* that tingles in
their veins has not yet refined their blood, and cannot lift the
whole man to the digestion and function of ichor, — that is,
to godlike nature.   Time will be when ichor shall be their
blood, when what are now glimpses and aspirations shall be
the routine of the day.   Yet even partial ascents to poetry
and ideas are forerunners, and announce the dawn.   In the
mire of the sensual life, their religion, their poets, their admiration of heroes and benefactors, even their novel and newspaper, nay, their superstitions also, are hosts of ideals, — a
cordage of ropes that hold them up out of the slough.   Poetry
is inestimable as a lonely faith, a lonely protest in the uproar
of atheism.

But so many men are ill-born or ill-bred, — the brains are
so marred, so imperfectly formed, unheroically, — brains of
the sons of fallen men, — that the doctrine is imperfectly
received.   One man sees a spark or shimmer of the truth, and
reports it, and his saying becomes a legend or golden proverb
for ages, and other men report as much, but none wholly and
well. (Poems, — we have no poem.) Whenever that angel
shall be organized and appear on earth, the Iliad will be reckoned a poor ballad-grinding.   I doubt never the riches of
nature, the gifts of the future, the immense wealth of the
mind.   O yes, poets we shall have, mythology, symbols, reli-

gion, of our own. We, too, shall know how to take up all this industry and empire, this Western civilization, into thought, as easily as men did when arts were few; but not by holding it high, but by holding it low. The intellect uses and is not used, — uses London and Paris and Berlin, east and west, to its end. The only heart that can help us is one that draws, not from our society, but from itself, a counterpoise to society. What if we find partiality and meanness in us? The grandeur of our life exists in spite of us, — all over and under and within us, in what of us is inevitable and above our control. Men are facts as well as persons, and the involuntary part of their life so much as to fill the mind and leave them no countenance to say aught of what is so trivial as their selfish thinking and doing. Sooner or later that which is now life shall be poetry, and every fair and manly trait shall add a richer strain to the song.

SOCIAL AIMS.

SOCIAL AIMS.

MUCH ill-natured criticism has been directed on American manners. I do not think it is to be resented. Rather, if we are wise, we shall listen and mend. Our critics will then be our best friends, though they did not mean it. But in every sense the subject of manners has a constant interest to thoughtful persons. Who does not delight in fine manners? Their charm cannot be predicted or overstated. 'T is perpetual promise of more than can be fulfilled. It is music and sculpture and picture to many who do not pretend to appreciation of those arts. It is even true that grace is more beautiful than beauty. Yet how impossible to overcome the obstacle of an unlucky temperament, and acquire good manners, unless by living with the well-bred from the start; and this makes the value of wise forethought to give ourselves and our children as much as possible the habit of cultivated society.

'T is an inestimable hint that I owe to a few persons of fine manners, that they make behavior the very first sign of force, — behavior, and not performance, or talent, or, much less, wealth. Whilst almost everybody has a supplicating eye turned on events and things and other persons, a few natures are central and forever unfold, and these alone charm us. He whose word or deed you cannot predict, who answers you without any supplication in his eye, who draws his determination from within, and draws it instantly, — that man rules.

The staple figure in novels is the man of *aplomb*, who sits, among the young aspirants and desperates, quite sure and compact, and, never sharing their affections or debilities, hurls his word like a bullet when occasion requires, knows his way, and carries his points. They may scream or applaud, he is never engaged or heated. Napoleon is the type of this class in modern history; Byron's heroes in poetry. But we, for the most part, are all drawn into the *charivari;* we chide, lament, cavil, and recriminate.

I think Hans Andersen's story of the cobweb cloth woven so fine that it was invisible, — woven for the king's garment, — must mean manners, which do really clothe a princely nature. Such a one can well go in a blanket, if he would. In the gymnasium or on the sea-beach his superiority does not leave him. But he who has not this fine garment of behavior is studious of dress, and then not less of house and furniture and pictures and gardens, in all which he hopes to lie *perdu,* and not be exposed.

"Manners are stronger than laws." Their vast convenience I must always admire. The perfect defence and isolation which they effect makes an insuperable protection. Though the person so clothed wrestle with you, or swim with you, lodge in the same chamber, eat at the same table, he is yet a thousand miles off, and can at any moment finish with you. Manners seem to say, *You are you, and I am I.* In the most delicate natures, fine temperament and culture build this impassable wall. Balzac finely said : "Kings themselves cannot force the exquisite politeness of distance to capitulate, hid behind its shield of bronze."

Nature values manners. See how she has prepared for them. Who teaches manners of majesty, of frankness, of grace, of humility, — who but the adoring aunts and cousins that surround a young child? The babe meets such courting and flattery as only kings receive when adult ; and, trying experiments, and at perfect leisure with these posture-masters and flatterers all day, he throws himself into all the attitudes that correspond to theirs. Are they humble? he is composed. Are they eager? he is nonchalant. Are they encroaching? he is dignified and inexorable. And this scene is daily repeated in hovels as well as in high houses.

Nature is the best posture-master. An awkward man is graceful when asleep, or when hard at work, or agreeably amused. The attitudes of children are gentle, persuasive, royal, in their games and in their house-talk and in the street, before they have learned to cringe. 'T is impossible but thought disposes the limbs and the walk, and is masterly or secondary. No art can contravene it, or conceal it. Give me a thought, and my hands and legs and voice and face will all go right. And we are awkward for want of thought. The inspiration is scanty, and does not arrive at the extremities.

It is a commonplace of romances to show the ungainly manners of the pedant who has lived too long in college. Intellectual men pass for vulgar, and are timid and heavy with the elegant. But, if the elegant are also intellectual, instantly the hesitating scholar is inspired, transformed, and exhibits the best style of manners. An intellectual man, though of feeble spirit, is instantly reinforced by being put into the company of scholars, and, to the surprise of everybody, becomes a lawgiver. We think a man unable and desponding. It is only that he is misplaced. Put him with new companions, and they will find in him excellent qualities, unsuspected accomplishments, and the joy of life. 'T is a great point in a gallery, how you hang pictures; and not less in society, how you seat your party. The circumstance of circumstance is timing and placing. When a man meets his accurate mate, society begins, and life is delicious.

What happiness they give, — what ties they form! Whilst one man by his manners pins me to the wall, with another I walk among the stars. One man can, by his voice, lead the cheer of a regiment; another will have no following. Nature made us all intelligent of these signs, for our safety and our happiness. Whilst certain faces are illumined with intelligence, decorated with invitation, others are marked with warnings : certain voices are hoarse and truculent ; sometimes they even bark. There is the same difference between heavy and genial manners as between the perceptions of octogenarians and those of young girls who see everything in the twinkle of an eye.

Manners are the revealers of secrets, the betrayers of any disproportion or want of symmetry in mind and character. It is the law of our constitution that every change in our experience instantly indicates itself on our countenance and carriage, as the lapse of time tells itself on the face of a clock. We may be too obtuse to read it, but the record is there. Some men may be too obtuse to read it, but some men are not obtuse and do read it. In Borrow's "Lavengro," the gypsy instantly detects, by his companion's face and behavior, that some good fortune has befallen him, and that he has money. We say, in these days, that credit is to be abolished in trade : is it ? When a stranger comes to buy goods of you, do you not look in his face and answer according to what you read there ? Credit is to be abolished ? Can't you abolish faces and character, of which credit is the reflection ? As long as

men are born babes they will live on credit for the first fourteen or eighteen years of their life. Every innocent man has
in his countenance a promise to pay, and hence credit. Less
credit will there be? You are mistaken. There will always
be more and more. Character *must* be trusted ; and, just in
proportion to the morality of a people, will be the expansion
of the credit system.

There is even a little rule of prudence for the young experi-
menter which Dr. Franklin omitted to set down, yet which the
youth may find useful,— Do not go to ask your debtor the
payment of a debt on the day when you have no other resource. He will learn by your air and tone how it is with
you, and will treat you as a beggar. But work and starve a
little longer. Wait till your affairs go better, and you have
other means at hand ; you will then ask in a different tone,
and he will treat your claim with entire respect.

Now, we all wish to be graceful, and do justice to ourselves
by our manners ; but youth in America is wont to be poor and
hurried, not at ease, or not in society where high behavior
could be taught. But the sentiment of honor and the wish to
serve make all our pains superfluous. Life is not so short but
that there is always time enough for courtesy. Self-command
is the main elegance. "Keep cool, and you command everybody," said St. Just ; and the wily old Talleyrand would still
say, *Surtout, messieurs, pas de zèle,*—"Above all, gentlemen,
no heat."

Why have you statues in your hall, but to teach you
that, when the door-bell rings, you shall sit like them. "Eat
at your table as you would eat at the table of the king," said
Confucius. It is an excellent custom of the Quakers, if only
for a school of manners,— the silent prayer before meals. It
has the effect to stop mirth, and introduce a moment of reflection. After the pause all resume their usual intercourse from
a vantage-ground. What a check to the violent manners
which sometimes come to the table,— of wrath, and whining,
and heat in trifles !

'T is a rule of manners to avoid exaggeration. A lady loses
as soon as she admires too easily and too much. In man or
woman, the face and the person lose power when they are on
the strain to express admiration. A man makes his inferiors
his superiors by heat. Why need you, who are not a gossip,
talk as a gossip, and tell eagerly what the neighbors or the
journals say? State your opinion without apology. The at-

titude is the main point, assuring your companion that, come
good news or come bad, you remain in good heart and good
mind, which is the best news you can possibly communicate.
Self-control is the rule. You have in you there a noisy, sensual savage which you are to keep down, and turn all his
strength to beauty. For example, what a seneschal and de-
tective is laughter! It seems to require several generations of
education to train a squeaking or a shouting habit out of a
man. Sometimes, when in almost all expressions the Choctaw
and the slave have been worked out of him, a coarse nature
still betrays itself in his contemptible squeals of joy. It is
necessary for the purification of drawing-rooms, that these entertaining explosions should be under strict control. Lord
Chesterfield had early made this discovery, for he says, " I
am sure that since I had the use of my reason, no human
being has ever heard me laugh." I know that there go
two to this game, and, in the presence of certain formidable
wits, savage nature must sometimes rush out in some disorder.

To pass to an allied topic, one word or two in regard to
dress, in which our civilization instantly shows itself. No
nation is dressed with more good sense than ours. And everybody sees certain moral benefit in it. When the young European emigrant, after a summer's labor, puts on for the first
time a new coat, he puts on much more. His good and
becoming clothes put him on thinking that he must behave
like people who are so dressed ; and silently and steadily his
behavior mends. But quite another class of our own youth, I
should remind, of dress in general, that some people need it,
and others need it not. Thus a king or a general does not
need a fine coat, and a commanding person may save himself
all solicitude on that point. There are always slovens in State
Street or Wall Street, who are not less considered. If a man
have manners and talent he may dress roughly and carelessly.
It is only when mind and character slumber that the dress
can be seen. If the intellect were always awake, and every
noble sentiment, the man might go in huckaback or mats,
and his dress would be admired and imitated. Remember
George Herbert's maxim, " This coat with my discretion will be
brave." If, however, a man has not firm nerves, and has keen
sensibility, it is perhaps a wise economy to go to a good shop
and dress himself irreproachably. He can then dismiss all care
from his mind, and may easily find that performance an addi-

tion of confidence, a fortification that turns the scale in social encounters, and allows him to go gayly into conversations where else he had been dry and embarrassed. I am not ignorant,— I have heard with admiring submission the experience of the lady who declared "that the sense of being perfectly well-dressed gives a feeling of inward tranquillity which religion is powerless to bestow."

Thus much for manners: but we are not content with pantomime; we say, this is only for the eyes. We want real relations of the mind and the heart; we want friendship; we want knowledge; we want virtue; a more inward existence to read the history of each other. Welfare requires one or two companions of intelligence, probity, and grace, to wear out life with,— persons with whom we can speak a few reasonable words every day, by whom we can measure ourselves, and who shall hold us fast to good sense and virtue; and these we are always in search of. He must be inestimable to us to whom we can say what we cannot say to ourselves. Yet now and then we say things to our mates, or hear things from them, which seem to put it out of the power of the parties to be strangers again. "Either death or a friend," is a Persian proverb. I suppose I give the experience of many when I give my own. A few times in my life it has happened to me to meet persons of so good a nature and so good breeding, that every topic was open and discussed without possibility of offence,— persons who could not be shocked. One of my friends said in speaking of certain associates, "There is not one of them but I can offend at any moment." But to the company I am now considering, were no terrors, no vulgarity. All topics were broached,— life, love, marriage, sex, hatred, suicide, magic, theism, art, poetry, religion, myself, thyself, all selves, and whatever else, with a security and vivacity which belonged to the nobility of the parties and to their brave truth. The life of these persons was conducted in the same calm and affirmative manner as their discourse. Life with them was an experiment continually varied, full of results, full of grandeur, and by no means the hot and hurried business which passes in the world. The delight in good company, in pure, brilliant, social atmosphere; the incomparable satisfaction of a society in which everything can be safely said, in which every member returns a true echo, in which a wise freedom, an ideal republic of sense, simplicity, knowledge, and thorough good-meaning abide, — doubles the value of life.

It is this that justifies to each the jealousy with which the doors are kept. Do not look sourly at the set or the club which does not choose you. Every highly organized person knows the value of the social barriers, since the best society has often been spoiled to him by the intrusion of bad companions. He of all men would keep the right of choice sacred, and feel that the exclusions are in the interest of the admissions, though they happen at this moment to thwart his wishes.

The hunger for company is keen, but it must be discriminating, and must be economized. 'T is a defect in our manners that they have not yet reached the prescribing a limit to visits. That every well-dressed lady or gentleman should be at liberty to exceed ten minutes in his or her call on serious people, shows a civilization still rude. A universal etiquette should fix an iron limit after which a moment should not be allowed without explicit leave granted on request of either the giver or receiver of the visit. There is inconvenience in such strictness, but vast inconvenience in the want of it. To trespass on a public servant is to trespass on a nation's time. Yet presidents of the United States are afflicted by rude Western and Southern gossips (I hope it is only by them) until the gossip's immeasurable legs are tired of sitting; then he strides out and the nation is relieved.

It is very certain that sincere and happy conversation doubles our powers; that, in the effort to unfold our thought to a friend, we make it clearer to ourselves, and surround it with illustrations that help and delight us. It may happen that each hears from the other a better wisdom than any one else will ever hear from either. But these ties are taken care of by Providence to each of us. A wise man once said to me that "all whom he knew, met" : — meaning that he need not take pains to introduce the persons whom he valued to each other : they were sure to be drawn together as by gravitation. The soul of a man must be the servant of another. The true friend must have an attraction to whatever virtue is in us. Our chief want in life, — is it not somebody who can make us do what we can? And we are easily great with the loved and honored associate. We come out of our eggshell existence and see the great dome arching over us; see the zenith above and the nadir under us.

Speech is power : speech is to persuade, to convert, to compel. It is to bring another out of his bad sense into your good sense. You are to be missionary and carrier of all that is good and noble. Virtues speak to virtues, vices to vices, — each to their own kind in the people with whom we deal. If you are suspiciously and dryly on your guard, so is he or she. If you rise to frankness and generosity, they will respect it now or later.

In this art of conversation, Woman, if not the queen and victor, is the lawgiver. If every one recalled his experiences, he might find the best in the speech of superior women, — which was better than song, and carried ingenuity, character, wise counsel, and affection, as easily as the wit with which it was adorned. They are not only wise themselves, they make us wise. No one can be a master in conversation who has not learned much from women; their presence and inspiration are essential to its success. Steele said of his mistress, that "to have loved her was a liberal education." Shenstone gave no bad account of this influence in his description of the French woman : "There is a quality in which no woman in the world can compete with her, — it is the power of intellectual irritation. She will draw wit out of a fool. She strikes with such address the chords of self-love, that she gives unexpected vigor and agility to fancy, and electrifies a body that appeared non-electric." Coleridge esteems cultivated women as the depositaries and guardians of "English undefiled"; and Luther commends that accomplishment of "pure German speech" of his wife.

Madame de Staël, by the unanimous consent of all who knew her, was the most extraordinary converser that was known in her time, and it was a time full of eminent men and women; she knew all distinguished persons in letters or society, in England, Germany, and Italy, as well as in France, though she said, with characteristic nationality, "Conversation, like talent, exists only in France." Madame de Staël valued nothing but conversation. When they showed her the beautiful Lake Leman, she exclaimed, "O for the gutter of the Rue de Bac!" the street in Paris in which her house stood. And she said one day, seriously, to M. Molé, "If it were not for respect to human opinions, I would not open my window to see the Bay of Naples for the first time, whilst I would go five hundred leagues to talk with a man of genius whom I had not seen." Ste. Beuve tells us of the privileged circle at Coppet, that, after making an excursion one day, the party returned in two coaches from Chambéry to Aix, on the way to Coppet. The first coach had many rueful accidents to re-

late, — a terrific thunder-storm, shocking roads, and danger
and gloom to the whole company. The party in the second
coach, on arriving, heard this story with surprise ; — of thunder-storm, of steeps, of mud, of danger, they knew nothing ;
no, they had forgotten earth, and breathed a purer air : such
a conversation between Madame de Staël and Madame Réca-
mier and Benjamin Constant and Schlegel ! they were all in
a state of delight. The intoxication of the conversation had
made them insensible to all notice of weather or rough roads.
Madame de Tessé said, " If I were Queen, I should command
Madame de Staël to talk to me every day." Conversation
fills all gaps, supplies all deficiencies. What a good trait is
that recorded of Madame de Maintenon, that, during dinner,
the servant slipped to her side, " Please, madame, one anecdote more, for there is no roast to-day."

Politics, war, party, luxury, avarice, fashion, are all asses
with loaded panniers to serve the kitchen of Intellect, the
king. There is nothing that does not pass into lever or
weapon.

And yet there are trials enough of nerve and character,
brave choices enough of taking the part of truth and of the
oppressed against the oppressor, in privatest circles. A right
speech is not well to be distinguished from action. Courage
to ask questions ; courage to expose our ignorance. The
great gain is, not to shine, not to conquer your companion, —
then you learn nothing but conceit, — but to find a companion who knows what you do not ; to tilt with him and be
overthrown, horse and foot, with utter destruction of all
your logic and learning. There is a defeat that is useful.
Then you can see the real and the counterfeit, and will never
accept the counterfeit again. You will adopt the art of war
that has defeated you. You will ride to battle horsed on the
very logic which you found irresistible. You will accept the
fertile truth, instead of the solemn customary lie.

Let nature bear the expense. The attitude, the tone, is
all. Let our eyes not look away, but meet. Let us not look
east and west for materials of conversation, but rest in presence and unity. A just feeling will fast enough supply fuel
for discourse, if speaking be more grateful than silence.
When people come to see us, we foolishly prattle, lest we be
inhospitable. But things said for conversation are chalk eggs.
Don't *say* things. What you *are* stands over you the while,
and thunders so that I cannot hear what you say to the

contrary. A lady of my acquaintance said, " I don't care so much for what they say as I do for what makes them say it."

The main point is to throw yourself on the truth, and say with Newton, "There's no contending against facts." When Molyneux fancied that the observations of the nutation of the earth's axis destroyed Newton's theory of gravitation, he tried to break it softly to Sir Isaac, who only answered, " It may be so ; there 's no arguing against facts and experiments."

But there are people who cannot be cultivated, — people on whom speech makes no impression, — swainish, morose people, who must be kept down and quieted as you would those who are a little tipsy ; others, who are not only swainish, but are prompt to take oath that swainishness is the only culture ; and though their odd wit may have some salt for you, your friends would not relish it. Bolt these out. And I have seen a man of genius who made me think that if other men were like him co-operation were impossible. Must we always talk for victory, and never once for truth, for comfort, and joy ? Here is centrality and penetration, strong understanding, and the higher gifts, the insight of the real, or from the real, and the moral rectitude which belongs to it : but all this and all his resources of wit and invention are lost to me in every experiment that I make to hold intercourse with his mind ; always some weary, captious paradox to fight you with, and the time and temper wasted. And beware of jokes ; too much temperance cannot be used : inestimable for sauce, but corrupting for food : we go away hollow and ashamed. As soon as the company give in to this enjoyment, we shall have no Olympus. True wit never made us laugh. Mahomet seems to have borrowed by anticipation of several centuries a leaf from the mind of Swedenborg, when he wrote in the Koran : —

" On the day of resurrection, those who have indulged in ridicule will be called to the door of Paradise, and have it shut in their faces when they reach it. Again, on their turning back, they will be called to another door, and again, on reaching it, will see it closed against them ; and so on, *ad infinitum*, without end."

Shun the negative side. Never worry people with your contritions, nor with dismal views of politics or society. Never name sickness ; even if you could trust yourself on that perilous topic, beware of unmuzzling a valetudinarian, who will soon give you your fill of it.

The law of the table is Beauty, — a respect to the common soul of all the guests. Everything is unseasonable which is private to two or three or any portion of the company. Tact never violates for a moment this law; never intrudes the orders of the house, the vices of the absent, or a tariff of expenses, or professional privacies; as we say, we never "talk shop" before company. Lovers abstain from caresses, and haters from insults, whilst they sit in one parlor with common friends.

Stay at home in your mind. Don't recite other people's opinions. See how it lies there in you; and if there is no counsel, offer none. What we want is, not your activity or interference with your mind, but your content to be a vehicle of the simple truth. The way to have large occasional views, as in a political or social crisis, is to have large habitual views. When men consult you, it is not that they wish you to stand tiptoe, and pump your brains, but to apply your habitual view, your wisdom, to the present question, forbearing all pedantries, and the very name of argument; for in good conversation parties don't speak to the words, but to the meanings of each other.

Manners first, then conversation. Later, we see that, as life was not in manners, so it is not in talk. Manners are external; talk is occasional: these require certain material conditions, human labor for food, clothes, house, tools, and, in short, plenty and ease, — since only so can certain finer and finest powers appear and expand. In a whole nation of Hottentots there shall not be one valuable man, — valuable out of his tribe. In every million of Europeans or of Americans there shall be thousands who would be valuable on any spot on the globe.

The consideration the rich possess in all societies is not without meaning or right. It is the approval given by the human understanding to the act of creating value by knowledge and labor. It is the sense of every human being, that man should have this dominion of nature, should arm himself with tools, and force the elements to drudge for him and give him power. Every one must seek to secure his independence; but he need not be rich. The old Confucius in China admitted the benefit, but stated the limitation: "If the search for riches were sure to be successful, though I should become a groom with whip in hand to get them, I will do so. As the search may not be successful, I will follow after that which I love." There is in America a general conviction in the minds of all mature men, that every young man of good faculty and good habits can by perseverance attain to an adequate estate ; if he have a turn for business, and a quick eye for the opportunities which are always offering for investment, he can come to wealth, and in such good season as to enjoy as well as transmit it.

Every human society wants to be officered by a best class, who shall be masters instructed in all the great arts of life ; shall be wise, temperate, brave, public men, adorned with dignity and accomplishments. Every country wishes this, and each has taken its own method to secure such service to the state. In Europe, ancient and modern, it has been attempted to secure the existence of a superior class by hereditary nobility, with estates transmitted by primogeniture and entail. But in the last age, this system has been on its trial and the verdict of mankind is pretty nearly pronounced. That method secured permanence of families, firmness of customs, a certain external culture and good taste ; gratified the ear with preserving historic names : but the heroic father did not surely have heroic sons, and still less surely heroic grandsons ; wealth and ease corrupted the race.

In America, the necessity of clearing the forest, laying out town and street, and building every house and barn and fence, then church and town-house, exhausted such means as the Pilgrims brought, and made the whole population poor ; and the like necessity is still found in each new settlement in the Territories. These needs gave their character to the public debates in every village and State. I have been often impressed at our country town-meetings with the accumulated virility, in each village, of five or six or eight or ten men, who speak so well, and so easily handle the affairs of the town. I often hear the business of a little town (with which I am most familiar) discussed with a clearness and thoroughness, and with a generosity, too, that would have satisfied me had it been in one of the larger capitals. I am sure each one of my readers has a parallel experience. And every one knows that in every town or city is always to be found a certain number of public-spirited men, who perform, unpaid, a great amount of hard work in the interest of the churches, of schools, of public grounds, works of taste and refinement. And as in civil duties, so in social power and duties. Our gentlemen of the old school, that is, of the school of Washington, Adams,

and Hamilton, were bred after English types, and that style
of breeding furnished fine examples in the last generation; but,
though some of us have seen such, I doubt they are all gone.
But nature is not poorer to-day. With all our haste, and slip-
shod ways, and flippant self-assertion, I have seen examples of
new grace and power in address that honor the country. It
was my fortune not long ago, with my eyes directed on this
subject, to fall in with an American to be proud of. I said
never was such force, good meaning, good sense, good action,
combined with such domestic lovely behavior, such modesty
and persistent preference for others. Wherever he moved he
was the benefactor. It is of course that he should ride well,
shoot well, sail well, keep house well, administer affairs well,
but he was the best talker, also, in the company : what with
a perpetual practical wisdom, with an eye always to the working
of the thing, what with the multitude and distinction of his
facts (and one detected continually that he had a hand in
everything that has been done), and in the temperance with
which he parried all offence, and opened the eyes of the person he talked with without contradicting him. Yet I said to
myself, How little this man suspects, with his sympathy for
men and his respect for lettered and scientific people, that he
is not likely, in any company, to meet a man superior to himself. And I think this is a good country, that can bear such
a creature as he is.

The young men in America at this moment take little
thought of what men in England are thinking or doing. That
is the point which decides the welfare of a people ; *which way
does it look ?* If to any other people, it is not well with them.
If occupied in its own affairs and thoughts and men, with a
heat which excludes almost the notice of any other people, —
as the Jews, the Greeks, the Persians, the Romans, the Arabi-
ans, the French, the English, at their best times have done, —
they are sublime ; and we know that in this abstraction they
are executing excellent work. Amidst the calamities which
war has brought on our country this one benefit has accrued,
— that our eyes are withdrawn from England, withdrawn from
France, and look homeward. We have come to feel that "by
ourselves our safety must be bought"; to know the vast resources of the continent, the good-will that is in the people,
their conviction of the great moral advantages of freedom,
social equality, education, and religious culture, and their
determination to hold these fast, and, by them, to hold fast

the country and penetrate every square mile of it with this American civilization.

The consolation and happy moment of life, atoning for all short-comings, is sentiment; a flame of affection or delight in the heart, burning up suddenly for its object, — as the love of the mother for her child; of the child for its mate; of the youth for his friend; of the scholar for his pursuit; of the boy for sea-life, or for painting, or in the passion for his country; or in the tender-hearted philanthropist to spend and be spent for some romantic charity, as Howard for the prisoner, or John Brown for the slave. No matter what the object is, so it be good, this flame of desire makes life sweet and tolerable. It reinforces the heart that feels it, makes all its acts and words gracious and interesting. Now society in towns is infested by persons who, seeing that the sentiments please, counterfeit the expression of them. These we call sentimentalists, — talkers who mistake the description for the thing, saying for having. They have, they tell you, an intense love of nature; poetry, — O, they adore poetry, and roses, and the moon, and the cavalry regiment, and the governor; they love liberty, "dear liberty!" they worship virtue, "dear virtue!" Yes, they adopt whatever merit is in good repute, and almost make it hateful with their praise. The warmer their expressions, the colder we feel; we shiver with cold. A little experience acquaints us with the unconvertibility of the sentimentalist, the soul that is lost by mimicking soul. Cure the drunkard, heal the insane, mollify the homicide, civilize the Pawnee, but what lessons can be devised for the debauchee of sentiment? Was ever one converted? The innocence and ignorance of the patient is the first difficulty: he believes his disease is blooming health. A rough realist, or a phalanx of realists, would be prescribed; but that is like proposing to mend your bad road with diamonds. Then poverty, famine, war, imprisonment, might be tried. Another cure would be to fight fire with fire, to match a sentimentalist with a sentimentalist. I think each might begin to suspect that something was wrong.

Would we codify the laws that should reign in households, and whose daily transgression annoys and mortifies us, and degrades our household life — we must learn to adorn every day with sacrifices. Good manners are made up of petty sacrifices. Temperance, courage, love, are made up of the same jewels. Listen to every prompting of honor. "As soon as sacrifice becomes a duty and necessity to the man, I see no limit to the horizon which opens before me." *

Of course those people, and no others, interest us who believe in their thought, who are absorbed, if you please to say so, in their own dream. They only can give the key and leading to better society : those who delight in each other only because both delight in the eternal laws ; who forgive nothing to each other; who, by their joy and homage to these, are made incapable of conceit, which destroys almost all the fine wits. Any other affection between men than this geometric one of relation to the same thing, is a mere mush of materialism.

These are the bases of civil and polite society ; namely, manners, conversation, lucrative labor, and public action, whether political, or in the leading of social institutions. We have much to regret, much to mend, in our society ; but I believe that with all liberal and hopeful men there is a firm faith in the beneficent results which we really enjoy ; that intelligence, manly enterprise, good education, virtuous life, and elegant manners have been and are found here, and, we hope, in the next generation will still more abound.

* Ernest Renan.

11*

ELOQUENCE.

ELOQUENCE.

I DO not know any kind of history, except the event of a battle, to which people listen with more interest than to any anecdote of eloquence; and the wise think it better than a battle. It is a triumph of pure power, and it has a beautiful and prodigious surprise in it. For all can see and understand the means by which a battle is gained: they count the armies, they see the cannon, the musketry, the cavalry, and the character and advantages of the ground, so that the result is often predicted by the observer with great certainty before the charge is sounded. Not so in a court of law, or in a legislature. Who knows before the debate begins what the preparation, or what the means are of the combatants? The facts, the reasons, the logic, — above all, the flame of passion and the continuous energy of will which is presently to be let loose on this bench of judges, or on this miscellaneous assembly gathered from the streets, — are all invisible and unknown. Indeed, much power is to be exhibited which is not yet called into existence, but is to be suggested on the spot by the unexpected turn things may take, — at the appearance of new evidence, or by the exhibition of an unlooked-for bias in the judges, or in the audience. It is eminently the art which only flourishes in free countries. It is an old proverb, that "Every people has its prophet"; and every class of the people has. Our community runs through a long scale of mental power, from the highest refinement to the borders of savage ignorance and rudeness. There are not only the wants of the intellectual and learned and poetic men and women to be met, but also the vast interests of property, public and private, of mining, of manufactures, of trade, of railroads, etc. These must have their advocates of each improvement and each interest. Then the political questions, which agitate millions,

find or form a class of men by nature and habit fit to discuss
and deal with these measures, and make them intelligible and
acceptable to the electors. So of education, of art, of philan-
thropy.

Eloquence shows the power and possibility of man. There
is one of whom we took no note, but on a certain occasion it
appears that he has a secret virtue never suspected, — that he
can paint what has occurred, and what must occur, with such
clearness to a company, as if they saw it done before their
eyes. By leading their thought he leads their will, and can
make them do gladly what an hour ago they would not believe
that they could be led to do at all : he makes them glad or
angry or penitent at his pleasure ; of enemies makes friends,
and fills desponding men with hope and joy. After Sheridan's
speech in the trial of Warren Hastings, Mr. Pitt moved an
adjournment, that the House might recover from the overpowering effect of Sheridan's oratory. Then recall the delight
that sudden eloquence gives, — the surprise that the moment
is so rich. The orator is the physician. Whether he speaks
in the Capitol or on a cart, he is the benefactor that lifts men
above themselves, and creates a higher appetite than he satisfies. The orator is he whom every man is seeking when he
goes into the courts, into the conventions, into any popular
assembly — though often disappointed, yet never giving over
the hope. He finds himself perhaps in the Senate, when the
forest has cast out some wild, black-browed bantling to show
the same energy in the crowd of officials which he had learned
in driving cattle to the hills, or in scrambling through thickets
in a winter forest, or through the swamp and river for his
game. In the folds of his brow, in the majesty of his mien,
Nature has marked her son ; and in that artificial and perhaps
unworthy place and company shall remind you of the lessons
taught him in earlier days by the torrent in the gloom of the
pine-woods, when he was the companion of the mountain cattle, of jays and foxes, and a hunter of the bear. Or you may
find him in some lowly Bethel, by the seaside, where a hard-
featured, scarred, and wrinkled Methodist becomes the poet
of the sailor and the fisherman, whilst he pours out the abundant streams of his thought through a language all glittering
and fiery with imagination, — a man who never knew the
looking-glass or the critic, — a man whom college drill or pat-
ronage never made, and whom praise cannot spoil, — a man
who conquers his audience by infusing his soul into them, and

speaks by the right of being the person in the assembly who
has the most to say, and so makes all other speakers appear
little and cowardly before his face. For the time, his exceed-
ing life throws all other gifts into shade, — philosophy specu-
lating on its own breath, taste, learning, and all, — and yet
how every listener gladly consents to be nothing in his presence, and to share this surprising emanation, and be steeped
and ennobled in the new wine of this eloquence! It instructs
in the power of man over men; that a man is a mover; to
the extent of his being, a power; and, in contrast with the
efficiency he suggests, our actual life and society appears a
dormitory. Who can wonder at its influence on young and
ardent minds? Uncommon boys follow uncommon men; and
I think every one of us can remember when our first experiences made us for a time the victim and worshipper of the
first master of this art whom we happened to hear in the
court-house or in the caucus. We reckon the bar, the senate,
journalism, and the pulpit peaceful professions; but you cannot escape the demand for courage in these, and certainly
there is no true orator who is not a hero. His attitude in the
rostrum, on the platform, requires that he counterbalance his
auditory. He is challenger, and must answer all comers.
The orator must ever stand with forward foot, in the attitude
of advancing. His speech must be just ahead of the assembly, — ahead of the whole human race, — or it is superfluous.
His speech is not to be distinguished from action. It is the
electricity of action. It is action, as the general's word of
command, or chart of battle, is action. I must feel that the
speaker compromises himself to his auditory, comes for something, — it is a cry on the perilous edge of the fight, — or let
him be silent. You go to a town-meeting where the people
are called to some disagreeable duty, — such as, for example,
often occurred during the war, at the occasion of a new draft.
They come unwillingly: they have spent their money once or
twice very freely. They have sent their best men : the young
and ardent, those of a martial temper, went at the first draft,
or the second, and it is not easy to see who else can be spared,
or can be induced to go. The silence and coldness after the
meeting is opened, and the purpose of it stated, are not encouraging. When a good man rises in the cold and malicious
assembly, you think, Well, sir, it would be more prudent to
be silent; why not rest, sir, on your good record? Nobody
doubts your talent and power; but for the present business,

we know all about it, and are tired of being pushed into patriotism by people who stay at home. But he, taking no counsel of past things, but only of the inspiration of his to-day's feeling, surprises them with his tidings, with his better knowledge, his larger view, his steady gaze at the new and future event, whereof they had not thought, and they are interested, like so many children, and carried off out of all recollection of their malignant considerations, and he gains his victory by prophecy, where they expected repetition. He knew very well beforehand that they were looking behind and that he was looking ahead, and therefore it was wise to speak. Then the observer says, What a godsend is this manner of man to a town ! and he, what a faculty ! He is put together like a Waltham watch, or like a locomotive just finished at the Tredegar works.

No act indicates more universal health than eloquence. The special ingredients of this force are : clear perceptions ; memory ; power of statement ; logic ; imagination, or the skill to clothe your thought in natural images ; passion, which is the *heat ;* and then a grand will, which, when legitimate and abiding, we call *character,* the height of manhood. As soon as a man shows rare power of expression, like Chatham, Erskine, Patrick Henry, Webster, or Phillips, all the great interests, whether of state or of property, crowd to him to be their spokesman, so that he is at once a potentate, a ruler of men. A worthy gentleman, Mr. Alexander, listening to the debates of the General Assembly of the Scottish Kirk, in Edinburgh, and eager to speak to the questions, but utterly failing in his endeavors, — delighted with the talent shown by Dr. Hugh Blair, went to him, and offered him one thousand pounds sterling if he would teach him to speak with propriety in public. If the performance of the advocate reaches any high success, it is paid in England with dignities in the professions, and in the state with seats in the cabinet, earldoms, and woolsacks. And it is easy to see that the great and daily growing interests at stake in this country must pay proportional prices to their spokesmen and defenders. It does not surprise us, then, to learn from Plutarch what great sums were paid at Athens to the teachers of rhetoric ; and if the pupils got what they paid for, the lessons were cheap.

But this power which so fascinates and astonishes and commands is only the exaggeration of a talent which is universal. All men are competitors in this art. We have all attended meetings called for some object in which no one had before-hand any warm interest. Every speaker rose unwillingly, and even his speech was a bad excuse; but it is only the first plunge which is formidable, and deep interest or sympathy thaws the ice, loosens the tongue, and will carry the cold and fearful presently into self-possession, and possession of the audience. Go into an assembly well excited, some angry po-litical meeting on the eve of a crisis. Then it appears that eloquence is as natural as swimming, — an art which all men might learn, though so few do. It only needs that they should be once well pushed off into the water, overhead, without corks, and, after a mad struggle or two, they find their poise and the use of their arms, and henceforward they possess this new and wonderful element.

The most hard-fisted, disagreeably restless, thought-paralyz-ing companion sometimes turns out in a public assembly to be a fluent, various, and effective orator. Now you find what all that excess of power which so chafed and fretted you in a *tête-à-tête* with him was for. What is peculiar in it is a cer-tain creative heat, which a man attains to perhaps only once in his life. Those whom we admire — the great orators — have some *habit* of heat, and, moreover, a certain control of it, an art of husbanding it, — as if their hand was on the organ-stop, and could now use it temperately, and now let out all the length and breadth of the power. I remember that Jenny Lind, when in this country, complained of concert-rooms and town-halls, that they did not give her room enough to unroll her voice, and exulted in the opportunity given her in the great halls she found sometimes built over a railroad depot. And this is quite as true of the action of the mind itself, that a man of this talent sometimes finds himself cold and slow in private company, and perhaps a heavy companion; but give him a commanding occasion, and the inspiration of a great multitude, and he surprises by new and unlooked-for powers. Before, he was out of place, and unfitted as a cannon in a parlor. To be sure there are physical advantages, — some eminently leading to this art. I mentioned Jenny Lind's voice. A good voice has a charm in speech as in song; some-times of itself enchains attention, and indicates a rare sensi-bility, especially when trained to wield all its powers. The voice, like the face, betrays the nature and disposition, and soon indicates what is the range of the speaker's mind. Many people have no ear for music, but every one has an ear for

skilful reading. Every one of us has at some time been the
victim of a well-toned and cunning voice, and perhaps been
repelled once for all by a harsh, mechanical speaker. The
voice, indeed, is a delicate index of the state of mind. I have
heard an eminent preacher say, that he learns from the first
tones of his voice on a Sunday morning whether he is to have
a successful day. A singer cares little for the words of the
song; he will make any words glorious. I think the like rule
holds of the good reader. In the church I call him only a
good reader who can read sense and poetry into any hymn in
the hymn-book. Plutarch, in his enumeration of the ten Greek
orators, is careful to mention their excellent voices, and the
pains bestowed by some of them in training these. What
character, what infinite variety, belong to the voice! sometimes it is a flute, sometimes a trip-hammer; what range of
force! In moments of clearer thought or deeper sympathy,
the voice will attain a music and penetration which surprises
the speaker as much as the auditor; he also is a sharer of the
higher wind that blows over his strings. I believe that some
orators go to the assembly as to a closet where to find their
best thoughts. The Persian poet Saadi tells us that a person
with a disagreeable voice was reading the Koran aloud, when
a holy man, passing by, asked what was his monthly stipend.
He answered, "Nothing at all." "But why then do you take
so much trouble?" He replied, "I read for the sake of God."
The other rejoined, "For God's sake, do not read; for if you
read the Koran in this manner you will destroy the splendor
of Islamism." Then there are persons of natural fascination,
with certain frankness, winning manners, almost endearments
in their style; like Bouillon, who could almost persuade you
that a quartan ague was wholesome; like Louis XI. of France,
whom Commines praises for "the gift of managing all minds
by his accent and the caresses of his speech"; like Galiani,
Voltaire, Robert Burns, Barclay, Fox, and Henry Clay. What
must have been the discourse of St. Bernard, when mothers
hid their sons, wives their husbands, companions their friends,
lest they should be led by his eloquence to join the mon-
astery.

It is said that one of the best readers in his time was the
late President John Quincy Adams. I have heard that no
man could read the Bible with such powerful effect. I can
easily believe it, though I never heard him speak in public
until his fine voice was much broken by age. But the won-

ders he could achieve with that cracked and disobedient organ showed what power might have belonged to it in early manhood. If "indignation makes good verses," as Horace says, it is not less true that a good indignation makes an excellent speech. In the early years of this century, Mr. Adams, at that time a member of the United States Senate at Washington, was elected Professor of Rhetoric and Oratory in Harvard College. When he read his first lectures in 1806, not only the students heard him with delight, but the hall was crowded by the Professors and by unusual visitors. I remember when, long after, I entered college, hearing the story of the numbers of coaches in which his friends came from Boston to hear him. On his return in the winter to the Senate at Washington, he took such ground in the debates of the following session as to lose the sympathy of many of his constituents in Boston. When, on his return from Washington, he resumed his lectures in Cambridge, his class attended, but the coaches from Boston did not come, and, indeed, many of his political friends deserted him. In 1809 he was appointed Minister to Russia, and resigned his chair in the University. His last lecture, in taking leave of his class, contained some nervous allusions to the treatment he had received from his old friends, which showed how much it had stung him, and which made a profound impression on the class. Here is the concluding paragraph, which long resounded in Cambridge : —

"At no hour of your life will the love of letters ever oppress you as a burden, or fail you as a resource. In the vain and foolish exultation of the heart, which the brighter prospects of life will sometimes excite, the pensive portress of Science shall call you to the sober pleasures of her holy cell. In the mortifications of disappointment, her soothing voice shall whisper serenity and peace. In social converse with the mighty dead of ancient days, you will never smart under the galling sense of dependence upon the mighty living of the present age. And in your struggles with the world, should a crisis ever occur, when even friendship may deem it prudent to desert you, when even your country may seem ready to abandon herself and you, when priest and Levite shall come and look on you and pass by on the other side, seek refuge, my *unfailing* friends, and be assured you shall find it, in the friendship of Lælius and Scipio, in the patriotism of Cicero, Demosthenes, and Burke, as well as in the precepts and example of Him whose law is love, and who taught us to remember injuries only to forgive them."

The orator must command the whole scale of the language, from the most elegant to the most low and vile. Every one has felt how superior in force is the language of the street to that of the academy. The street must be one of his schools. Ought not the scholar to be able to convey his meaning in terms as short and strong as the porter or truck-man uses to convey his? And Lord Chesterfield thought "that without being instructed in the dialect of the *Halles* no man could be a complete master of French." The speech of the man in the street is invariably strong, nor can you mend it by making it what you call parliamentary. You say, "if he could only express himself"; but he does already bet-ter than any one can for him, — can always get the ear of an audience to the exclusion of everybody else. Well, this is an example in point. That something which each man was created to say and do, he only or he best can tell you, and has a right to supreme attention so far. The power of their speech is, that it is perfectly understood by all; and I believe it to be true, that when any orator at the bar or in the Senate rises in his thought, he descends in his language, — that is, when he rises to any height of thought or of passion he comes down to a language level with the ear of all his audience. It is the merit of John Brown and of Abraham Lincoln — one at Charlestown, one at Gettysburg — in the two best speci-mens of eloquence we have had in this country. And observe that all poetry is written in the oldest and simplest English words. Dr. Johnson said, "There is in every nation a style which never becomes obsolete, a certain mode of phraseology so consonant to the analogy and principles of its respective language as to remain settled and unaltered. This style is to be sought in the common intercourse of life among those who speak only to be understood, without ambition of elegance. The polite are always catching modish innovations, and the learned forsake the vulgar, when the vulgar is right; but there is a conversation above grossness and below refinement, where propriety resides."

But all these are the gymnastics, the education of elo-quence, and not itself. They cannot be too much considered and practised as preparation, but the powers are those I first named. If I should make the shortest list of the qualifica-tions of the orator, I should begin with *manliness;* and per-haps it means here presence of mind. Men differ so much in control of their faculties! You can find in many, and indeed in all, a certain fundamental equality. Fundamentally all feel alike and think alike, and at a great heat they can all express themselves with an almost equal force. But it costs a great heat to enable a heavy man to come up with those who have a quick sensibility. Thus we have all of us known men who lose their talents, their wit, their fancy, at any sudden call. Some men, on such pressure, collapse, and cannot rally. If they are to put a thing in proper shape, fit for the occasion and the audience, their mind is a blank. Something which any boy would tell with color and vivacity they can only stammer out with hard literalness, — say it in the very words they heard, and no other. This fault is very incident to men of study, — as if the more they had read the less they knew. Dr. Charles Chauncy was, a hundred years ago, a man of marked ability among the clergy of New England. But when once going to preach the Thursday lecture in Boston (which in those days people walked from Salem to hear), on going up the pulpit stairs he was informed that a little boy had fallen into Frog Pond on the Common, and was drowned, and the doctor was requested to improve the sad occasion. The doctor was much distressed, and in his prayer he hesitated, — he tried to make soft approaches, — he prayed for Harvard College, he prayed for the schools, he implored the Divine Being "to-to-to bless to them all the boy that was this morning drowned in Frog Pond." Now this is not want of talent or learning, but of manliness. The doctor, no doubt, shut up in his closet and his theology, had lost some natural relation to men, and quick application of his thought to the course of events. I should add what is told of him, — that he so disliked the "sensation" preaching of his time that he had once prayed that "he might never be eloquent"; and, it appears, his prayer was granted. On the other hand, it would be easy to point to many masters whose readiness is sure ; as the French say of Guizot, that "what Guizot learned this morning he has the air of having known from all eternity" This unmanliness is so common a result of our half-education, — teaching a youth Latin and metaphysics and history, and neglecting to give him the rough training of a boy, — allowing him to skulk from the games of ball and skates and coasting down the hills on his sled, and whatever else would lead him and keep him on even terms with boys, so that he can meet them as an equal, and lead in his turn, — that I wish his guardians to consider that they are thus preparing him to play a contemptible part when he is full-grown. In England they send the most delicate and protected child from his luxurious home to learn to rough it with boys in the public schools. A few bruises and scratches will do him no harm if he has thereby learned not to be afraid. It is this wise mixture of good drill in Latin grammar with good drill in cricket, boating, and wrestling, that is the boast of English education, and of high importance to the matter in hand.

Lord Ashley, in 1606, while the bill for regulating trials in cases of high treason was pending, attempting to utter a premeditated speech in Parliament in favor of that clause of the bill which allowed the prisoner the benefit of counsel, fell into such a disorder that he was not able to proceed ; but having recovered his spirits and the command of his faculties, he drew such an argument from his own confusion as more advantaged his cause than all the powers of eloquence could have done. " For," said he, " if I, who had no personal concern in the question, was so overpowered with my own apprehensions that I could not find words to express myself, what must be the case of one whose life depended on his own abilities to defend it ?" This happy turn did great service in promoting that excellent bill.

These are ascending stairs, — a good voice, winning manners, plain speech, chastened, however, by the schools into correctness ; but we must come to the main matter, of power of statement, — know your fact ; hug your fact. For the essential thing is heat, and heat comes of sincerity. Speak what you do know and believe, and are personally in it, and are answerable for every word. Eloquence is *the power to translate a truth into language perfectly intelligible to the person to whom you speak.* He who would convince the worthy Mr. Dunderhead of any truth which Dunderhead does not see, must be a master of his art. Declamation is common ; but such possession of thought as is here required, such practical chemistry as the conversion of a truth written in God's language into a truth in Dunderhead's language, is one of the most beautiful and cogent weapons that is forged in the shop of the Divine Artificer.

It was said of Robespierre's audience, that though they understood not the words, they understood a fury in the words, and caught the contagion.

This leads us to the high class, the men of character who bring an overpowering personality into court, and the cause they maintain borrows importance from an illustrious advocate. Absoluteness is required, and he must have it or simu-

late it. If the cause be unfashionable, he will make it
fashionable. 'T is the best man in the best training. If he
does not know your fact, he will show that it is not worth
the knowing. Indeed, as great generals do not fight many
battles, but conquer by tactics, so all eloquence is a war of
posts. What is said is the least part of the oration. It is
the attitude taken, the unmistakable sign, never so casually
given, in tone of voice, or manner, or word, that a greater
spirit speaks from you than is spoken to in him.

But I say, *provided your cause is really honest.* There is
always the previous question : How came you on that side ?
Your argument is ingenious, your language copious, your illustrations brilliant, but your major proposition palpably absurd. Will you establish a lie ? You are a very elegant
writer, but you can't write up what gravitates down.

An ingenious metaphysical writer, Dr. Stirling of Edinburgh, has noted that intellectual works in any department
breed each other by what he calls *zymosis,* i. e. fermentation ;
thus in the Elizabethan Age there was a dramatic *zymosis,*
when all the genius ran in that direction, until it culminated
in Shakspeare ; so in Germany we have seen a metaphysical
zymosis culminating in Kant, Schelling, Schleiermacher, Schopenhauer, Hegel, and so ending. To this we might add the
great eras not only of painters but of orators. The historian Paterculus says of Cicero, that only in Cicero's lifetime
was any great eloquence in Rome ; so it was said that no
member of either house of the British Parliament will be
ranked among the orators whom Lord North did not see, or
who did not see Lord North. But I should rather say that
when a great sentiment, as religion or liberty, makes itself
deeply felt in any age or country, then great orators appear.
As the Andes and Alleghanies indicate the line of the fissure
in the crust of the earth along which they were lifted, so the
great ideas that suddenly expand at some moment the mind
of mankind indicate themselves by orators.

If there ever was a country where eloquence was a power,
it is in the United States. Here is room for every degree of
it, on every one of its ascending stages, — that of useful
speech, in our commercial, manufacturing, railroad, and educational conventions ; that of political advice and persuasion
on the grandest theatre, reaching, as all good men trust, into
a vast future, and so compelling the best thought and noblest
administrative ability that the citizen can offer. And here

are the service of science, the demands of art, and the lessons of religion to be brought home to the instant practice of thirty millions of people. Is it not worth the ambition of every generous youth to train and arm his mind with all the resources of knowledge, of method, of grace, and of character, to serve such a constituency?

RESOURCES.

RESOURCES.

MEN are made up of potences. We are magnates in an iron globe. We have keys to all doors. We are all inventors, each sailing out on a voyage of discovery, guided each by a private chart, of which there is no duplicate. The world is all gates, all opportunities, strings of tension waiting to be struck; the earth sensitive as iodine to light; the most plastic and impressionable medium, alive to every touch, and, whether scarched by the plough of Adam, the sword of Cæsar, the boat of Columbus, the telescope of Galileo, or the survey-or's chain of Picard, or the submarine telegraph, to every one of these experiments it makes a gracious response. I am ben-efited by every observation of a victory of man over nature,— by seeing that wisdom is better than strength; by seeing that every healthy and resolute man is an organizer, a method coming into a confusion and drawing order out of it. We are touched and cheered by every such example. We like to see the inexhaustible riches of Nature, and the access of every soul to her magazines. These examples wake an infinite hope, and call every man to emulation. A low, hopeless spirit puts out the eyes; scepticism is slow suicide. A philosophy which sees only the worst; believes neither in virtue nor in genius; which says 't is all of no use, life is eating us up, 't is only question who shall be last devoured,— dispirits us; the sky shuts down before us. A Schopenhauer, with logic and learn-ing and wit, teaching pessimism,— teaching that this is the worst of all possible worlds, and inferring that sleep is better than waking, and death than sleep,— all the talent in the world cannot save him from being odious. But if, instead of these negatives, you give me affirmatives,— if you tell me that there is always life for the living; that what man has done man can do; that this world belongs to the energetic; that

there is always a way to everything desirable ; that every man
is provided, in the new bias of his faculty, with a key to nature,
and that man only rightly knows himself as far as he has ex-
perimented on things,— I am invigorated, put into genial and
working temper ; the horizon opens, and we are full of good-
will and gratitude to the Cause of Causes. I like the sentiment of the poor woman who, coming from a wretched garret
in an inland manufacturing town for the first time to the sea-
shore, gazing at the ocean, said " she was glad for once in her
life to see something which there was enough of."

Our Copernican globe is a great factory or shop of power,
with its rotating constellations, times, and tides. The
machine is of colossal size ; the diameter of the water-wheel,
the arms of the levers, and the volley of the battery, out of
all mechanic measure ; and it takes long to understand its
parts and its workings. This pump never sucks ; these screws
are never loose ; this machine is never out of gear. The vat,
the piston, the wheels and tires, never wear out, but are self-
repairing. Is there any load which water cannot lift ? If
there be, try steam ; or if not that, try electricity. Is there
any exhausting of these means ? Measure by barrels the
spending of the brook that runs through your field. Nothing
is great but the inexhaustible wealth of Nature. She shows
us only surfaces, but she is million fathoms deep. What
spaces ! what durations ! dealing with races as merely prepar-
ations of somewhat to follow ; or, in humanity, millions of
lives of men to collect the first observations on which our
astronomy is built ; millions of lives to add only sentiments
and guesses, which at last, gathered in by an ear of sensibility,
make the furniture of the poet. See how children build up a
language ; how every traveller, every laborer, every impatient
boss, who sharply shortens the phrase or the word to give his
order quicker, reducing it to the lowest possible terms,— and
there it must stay,— improves the national tongue. What
power does Nature not owe to her duration of amassing infin-
itesimals into cosmical forces !

The marked events in history, as the emigration of a colony
to a new and more delightful coast ; the building of a large
ship ; the discovery of the mariner's compass, which perhaps
the Phœnicians made ; the arrival among an old stationary
nation of a more instructed race, with new arts : each of these
events electrifies the tribe to which it befalls ; supplies the
tough barbarous sinew, and brings it into that state of sensi-

bility which makes the transition to civilization possible and sure. By his machines man can dive and remain under water like a shark; can fly like a hawk in the air; can see atoms like a gnat; can see the system of the universe like Uriel, the angel of the sun; can carry whatever loads a ton of coal can lift; can knock down cities with his fist of gunpowder; can recover the history of his race by the medals which the deluge, and every creature, civil or savage or brute, has involuntarily dropped of its existence; and divine the future possibility of the planet and its inhabitants by his perception of laws of nature. Ah! what a plastic little creature he is! so shifty, so adaptive! his body a chest of tools, and he making himself comfortable in every climate, in every condition.

Here in America are all the wealth of soil, of timber, of mines, and of the sea, put into the possession of a people who wield all these wonderful machines, have the secret of steam, of electricity, and have the power and habit of invention in their brain. We Americans have got suppled into the state of melioration. Life is always rapid here, but what acceleration to its pulse in ten years,— what in the four years of the war! We have seen the railroad and telegraph subdue our enormous geography; we have seen the snowy deserts on the northwest, seats of Esquimaux, become lands of promise. When our population, swarming west, had reached the boundary of arable land, as if to stimulate our energy, on the face of the sterile waste beyond, the land was suddenly in parts found covered with gold and silver, floored with coal. It was thought a fable, what Guthrie, a traveller in Persia, told us, that "in Taurida, in any piece of ground where springs of naphtha (or petroleum) obtain, by merely sticking an iron tube in the earth, and applying a light to the upper end, the mineral oil will burn till the tube is decomposed, or for a vast number of years." But we have found the Taurida in Pennsylvania and Ohio. If they have not the lamp of Aladdin, they have the Aladdin oil. Resources of America! why, one thinks of St. Simon's saying, "The Golden Age is not behind, but before you." Here is a man in the Garden of Eden; here the Genesis and the Exodus. We have seen slavery disappear like a painted scene in a theatre; we have seen the most healthful revolution in the politics of the nation,— the Constitution not only amended, but construed in a new spirit. We have seen China opened to European and American ambassadors and commerce; the like in Japan: our arts and produc-

tions begin to penetrate both.   As the walls of a modern house
are perforated with water-pipes, sound-pipes, gas-pipes, heat-
pipes, so geography and geology are yielding to man's convenience, and we begin to perforate and mould the old ball, as a
carpenter does with wood.   All is ductile and plastic.   We are
working the new Atlantic telegraph.   American energy is over-
riding every venerable maxim of political science.   America is
such a garden of plenty, such a magazine of power, that at her
shores all the common rules of political economy utterly fail.
Here is bread, and wealth, and power, and education for every
man who has the heart to use his opportunity.   The creation of
power had never any parallel.   It was thought that the immense production of gold would make gold cheap as pewter.
But the immense expansion of trade has wanted every ounce
of gold, and it has not lost its value.

See how nations of customers are formed.   The disgust of
California has not been able to drive nor kick the Chinaman
back to his home ; and now it turns out that he has sent home
to China American food and tools and luxuries, until he has
taught his people to use them, and a new market has grown
up for our commerce.   The emancipation has brought a whole
nation of negroes as customers to buy all the articles which
once their few masters bought, and every manufacturer and
producer in the North has an interest in protecting the negro
as the consumer of his wares.

The whole history of our civil war is rich in a thousand
anecdotes attesting the fertility of resource, the presence of
mind, the skilled labor of our people.   At Annapolis a regiment, hastening to join the army, found the locomotives
broken, the railroad destroyed, and no rails.   The commander
called for men in the ranks who could rebuild the road.   Many
men stepped forward, searched in the water, found the hidden
rails, laid the track, put the disabled engine together, and
continued their journey.   The world belongs to the energetic
man.   His will gives him new eyes.   He sees expedients and
means where we saw none.   The invalid sits shivering in
lamb's wool and furs ;   the woodsman knows how to make
warm garments out of cold and wet themselves.   The Indian,
the sailor, the hunter, only these know the power of the hands,
feet, teeth, eyes, and ears.   It is out of the obstacles to be
encountered that they make the means of destroying them.
The sailor by his boat and sail makes a ford out of deepest
waters.   The hunter, the soldier, rolls himself in his blanket,

and the falling snow, which he did not have to bring in his knapsack, is his eider-down, in which he sleeps warm till the morning. Nature herself gives the hint and the example, if we have wit to take it. See how Nature keeps the lakes warm by tucking them up under a blanket of ice, and the ground under a cloak of snow. The old forester is never far from shelter; no matter how remote from camp or city, he carries Bangor with him. A sudden shower cannot wet him, if he cares to be dry; he draws his boat ashore, turns it over in a twinkling against a clump of alders, with cat-briers, which keep up the lee-side, crawls under it, with his comrade, and lies there till the shower is over, happy in his stout roof. The boat is full of water, and resists all your strength to drag it ashore and empty it. The fisherman looks about him, puts a round stick of wood underneath, and it rolls as on wheels at once. Napoleon says, the Corsicans at the battle of Golo, not having had time to cut down the bridge, which was of stone, made use of the bodies of their dead to form an intrenchment. Malus, known for his discoveries in the polarization of light, was captain of a corps of engineers in Bonaparte's Egyptian campaign, which was heinously unprovided and exposed. "Wanting a picket to which to attach my horse," he says, "I tied him to my leg. I slept, and dreamed peaceably of the pleasures of Europe." M. Tissenet had learned among the Indians to understand their language, and, coming among a wild party of Illinois, he overheard them say that they would scalp him. He said to them, "Will you scalp me? Here is my scalp," and confounded them by lifting a little periwig he wore. He then explained to them that he was a great medicine-man, and that they did great wrong in wishing to harm him, who carried them all in his heart. So he opened his shirt a little and showed to each of the savages in turn the reflection of his own eyeball in a small pocket-mirror which he had hung next to his skin. He assured them that if they should provoke him he would burn up their rivers and their forests; and, taking from his portmanteau a small phial of white brandy, he poured it into a cup, and, lighting a straw at the fire in the wigwam, he kindled the brandy (which they believed to be water), and burned it up before their eyes. Then taking up a chip of dry pine, he drew a burning-glass from his pocket and set the chip on fire.

What a new face courage puts on everything! A determined man, by his very attitude and the tone of his voice, puts a stop to defeat, and begins to conquer. "For they can conquer who believe they can." Every one hears gladly that cheerful voice. He reveals to us the enormous power of one man over masses of men; that one man whose eye commands the end in view, and the means by which it can be attained, is not only better than ten men or a hundred men, but victor over all mankind who do not see the issue and the means. "When a man is once possessed with fear," said the old French Marshal Montluc, "and loses his judgment, as all men in a fright do, he knows not what he does. And it is the principal thing you are to beg at the hands of Almighty God, to preserve your understanding entire; for what danger soever there may be, there is still one way or other to get off, and perhaps to your honor. But when fear has once possessed you, God ye good even! You think you are flying towards the poop when you are running towards the prow, and for one enemy think you have ten before your eyes, as drunkards who see a thousand candles at once."

Against the terrors of the mob, which, intoxicated with passion, and once suffered to gain the ascendant, is diabolic and chaos come again, good sense has many arts of prevention and of relief. Disorganization it confronts with organization, with police, with military force. But in earlier stages of the disorder it applies milder and nobler remedies. The natural offset of terror is ridicule. And we have noted examples among our orators, who have on conspicuous occasions handled and controlled, and, best of all, converted a malignant mob, by superior manhood, and by a wit which disconcerted, and at last delighted the ringleaders. What can a poor truckman who is hired to groan and to hiss do, when the orator shakes him into convulsions of laughter so that he cannot throw his egg? If a good story will not answer, still milder remedies sometimes serve to disperse a mob. Try sending round the contribution-box. Mr. Marshall, the eminent manufacturer at Leeds, was to preside at a Free-Trade festival in that city; it was threatened that the operatives, who were in bad humor, would break up the meeting by a mob. Mr. Marshall was a man of peace; he had the pipes laid from the water-works of his mill, with a stopcock by his chair from which he could discharge a stream that would knock down an ox, and sat down very peacefully to his dinner, which was not disturbed.

See the dexterity of the good aunt in keeping the young people all the weary holiday busy and diverted without know-

ing it : the story, the pictures, the ballad, the game, the
cuckoo-clock, the stereoscope, the rabbits, the mino bird, the
pop-corn, and Christmas hemlock spurting in the fire. The
children never suspect how much design goes to it, and that
this unfailing fertility has been rehearsed a hundred times,
when the necessity came of finding for the little Asmodeus a
rope of sand to twist. She relies on the same principle that
makes the strength of Newton, — alternation of employment.
See how he refreshed himself, resting from the profound researches of the calculus by astronomy ; from astronomy by
optics ; from optics by chronology. 'T is a law of chemistry
that every gas is a vacuum to every other gas ; and when the
mind has exhausted its energies for one employment, it is still
fresh and capable of a different task. We have not a toy or
trinket for idle amusement, but somewhere it is the one thing
needful for solid instruction or to save the ship or army. In
the Mammoth Cave in Kentucky, the torches which each traveller carries make a dismal funeral procession, and serve no
purpose but to see the ground. When now and then the
vaulted roof rises high overhead, and hides all its possibilities
in lofty depths, 't is but gloom on gloom. But the guide
kindled a Roman candle, and held it here and there shooting
its fireballs successively into each crypt of the groined roof,
disclosing its starry splendor, and showing for the first time
what that plaything was good for.

Whether larger or less, these strokes and all exploits rest at
last on the wonderful structure of the mind. And we learn
that our doctrine of resources must be carried into higher
application, namely, to the intellectual sphere. But every
power in energy speedily arrives at its limits, and requires to
be husbanded ; the law of light, which Newton said proceeded
by " fits of easy reflection and transmission " ; the come-and-
go of the pendulum is the law of mind ; alternation of labors
is its rest. I should like to have the statistics of bold experimenting on the husbandry of mental power.

In England men of letters drink wine ; in Scotland, whiskey ;
in France, light wines ; in Germany, beer. In England everybody rides in the saddle ; in France the theatre and the ball
occupy the night. In this country we have not learned how
to repair the exhaustions of our climate. Is not the seaside
necessary in summer? Games, fishing, bowling, hunting, gymnastics, dancing, — are not these needful to you? The chapter
of pastimes is very long. There are better games than bil-

liards and whist. 'T was a pleasing trait in Goethe's romance, that Makaria retires from society "to astronomy and her correspondence."

I do not know that the treatise of Brillat-Savarin on the Physiology of Taste deserves its fame. I know its repute, and I have heard it called the France of France. But the subject is so large and exigent that a few particulars, and those the pleasures of the epicure, cannot satisfy. I know many men of taste whose single opinions and practice would interest much more. It should be extended to gardens and grounds, and mainly one thing should be illustrated : that life in the country wants all things on a low tone, — wants coarse clothes, old shoes, no fleet horse that a man cannot hold, but an old horse that will stand tied in a pasture half a day without risk, so allowing the picnic-party the full freedom of the woods. Natural history is, in the country, most attractive ; at once elegant, immortal, always opening new resorts. The first care of a man settling in the country should be to open the face of the earth to himself, by a little knowledge of nature, or a great deal, if he can, of birds, plants, rocks, astronomy ; in short, the art of taking a walk. This will draw the sting out of frost, dreariness out of November and March, and the drowsiness out of August. To know the trees is, as Spenser says of "the ash, for nothing ill." Shells, too ; how hungry I found myself, the other day, at Agassiz's Museum, for their names ! But the uses of the woods are many, and some of them for the scholar high and peremptory. When his task requires the wiping out from memory

> " all trivial fond records
> That youth and observation copied there,"

he must leave the house, the streets, and the club, and go to wooded uplands, to the clearing and the brook. Well for him if he can say with the old minstrel, "I know where to find a new song."

If I go into the woods in winter, and am shown the thirteen or fourteen species of willow that grow in Massachusetts, I learn that they quietly expand in the warmer days, or when nobody is looking at them, and, though insignificant enough in the general bareness of the forest, yet a great change takes place in them between fall and spring ; in the first relentings of March they hasten, and long before anything else is ready, these osiers hang out their joyful flowers in contrast to all the woods. You cannot tell when they do bud and blossom, these vivacious trees, so ancient, for they are almost the oldest of all. Among fossil remains, the willow and the pine appear with the ferns. They bend all day to every wind; the cart-wheel in the road may crush them; every passenger may strike off a twig with his cane; every boy cuts them for a whistle; the cow, the rabbit, the insect, bite the sweet and tender bark; yet, in spite of accident and enemy, their gentle persistency lives when the oak is shattered by storm, and grows in the night and snow and cold. When I see in these brave plants this vigor and immortality in weakness, I find a sudden relief and pleasure in observing the mighty law of vegetation, and I think it more grateful and health-giving than any news I am likely to find of man in the journals, and better than Washington politics.

It is easy to see that there is no limit to the chapter of Resources. I have not, in all these rambling sketches, gone beyond the beginning of my list. Resources of Man, — it is the inventory of the world, the roll of arts and sciences; it is the whole of memory, the whole of invention; it is all the power of passion, the majesty of virtue, and the omnipotence of will.

But the one fact that shines through all this plenitude of powers is, that, as is the receiver, so is the gift; that all these acquisitions are victories of the good brain and brave heart; that the world belongs to the energetic, belongs to the wise. It is in vain to make a paradise but for good men. The tropics are one vast garden; yet man is more miserably fed and conditioned there than in the cold and stingy zones. The healthy, the civil, the industrious, the learned, the moral race, — Nature herself only yields her secret to these. And the resources of America and its future will be immense only to wise and virtuous men.

THE COMIC.

THE COMIC.

A TASTE for fun is all but universal in our species, which is the only joker in nature. The rocks, the plants, the beasts, the birds, neither do anything ridiculous, nor betray a perception of anything absurd done in their presence. And as the lower nature does not jest, neither does the highest. The Reason pronounces its omniscient yea and nay, but meddles never with degrees or fractions; and it is in comparing fractions with essential integers or wholes that laughter begins.

Aristotle's definition of the ridiculous is, "what is out of time and place, without danger." If there be pain and danger, it becomes tragic; if not, comic. I confess, this definition, though by an admirable definer, does not satisfy me, does not say all we know.

The essence of all jokes, of all comedy, seems to be an honest or well-intended halfness; a non-performance of what is pretended to be performed, at the same time that one is giving loud pledges of performance. The balking of the intellect, the frustrated expectation, the break of continuity in the intellect, is comedy; and it announces itself physically in the pleasant spasms we call laughter.

With the trifling exception of the stratagems of a few beasts and birds, there is no seeming, no halfness in nature, until the appearance of man. Unconscious creatures do the whole will of wisdom. An oak or a chestnut undertakes no function it cannot execute; or if there be phenomena in botany which we call abortions, the abortion is also a function of nature, and assumes to the intellect the like completeness with the further function, to which in different circumstances it had attained. The same rule holds true of the animals. Their activity is marked by unerring good-sense. But man, through his access to Reason, is capable of the perception of a whole

and a part. Reason is the whole, and whatsoever is not that
is a part. The whole of nature is agreeable to the whole of
thought, or to the Reason ; but separate any part of nature,
and attempt to look at it as a whole by itself, and the feeling
of the ridiculous begins. The perpetual game of humor is to
look with considerate good-nature at every object in existence
aloof, as a man might look at a mouse, comparing it with the
eternal Whole ; enjoying the figure which each self-satisfied
particular creature cuts in the unrespecting All, and dismiss-
ing it with a benison. Separate any object, as a particular
bodily man, a horse, a turnip, a flour-barrel, an umbrella, from
the connection of things, and contemplate it alone, standing
there in absolute nature, it becomes at once comic ; no useful,
no respectable qualities can rescue it from the ludicrous. In
virtue of man's access to Reason or the Whole, the human form
is a pledge of wholeness, suggests to our imagination the perfection of truth or goodness, and exposes by contrast any halfness or imperfection. We have a primary association between
perfectness and this form. But the facts that occur when actual men enter do not make good this anticipation ; a discrepancy which is at once detected by the intellect, and the
outward sign is the muscular irritation of laughter.

Reason does not joke, and men of reason do not ; a prophet,
in whom the moral sentiment predominates, or a philosopher,
in whom the love of truth predominates, these do not joke,
but they bring the standard, the ideal whole, exposing all actual defect ; and hence, the best of all jokes is the sympathetic
contemplation of things by the understanding from the philosopher's point of view. There is no joke so true and deep in
actual life, as when some pure idealist goes up and down
among the institutions of society, attended by a man who
knows the world, and who, sympathizing with the philosopher's
scrutiny, sympathizes also with the confusion and indignation
of the detected skulking institutions. His perception of dis-
parity, his eye wandering perpetually from the rule to the
crooked, lying, thieving fact, makes the eyes run over with
laughter.

This is the radical joke of life and then of literature. The
presence of the ideal of right and of truth in all action makes
the yawning delinquencies of practice remorseful to the conscience, tragic to the interest, but droll to the intellect. The
activity of our sympathies may for a time hinder our perceiving the fact intellectually, and so deriving mirth from it ; but

all falsehoods, all vices seen at sufficient distance, seen from
the point where our moral sympathies do not interfere, become ludicrous. The comedy is in the intellect's perception
of discrepancy. And whilst the presence of the ideal discovers
the difference, the comedy is enhanced whenever that ideal is
embodied visibly in a man. Thus Falstaff, in Shakspeare, is a
character of the broadest comedy, giving himself unreservedly
to his senses, coolly ignoring the Reason, whilst he invokes its
name, pretending to patriotism and to parental virtues, not
with any intent to deceive, but only to make the fun perfect
by enjoying the confusion betwixt reason and the negation of
reason, — in other words, the rank rascaldom he is calling by
its name. Prince Hal stands by, as the acute understanding,
who sees the Right and sympathizes with it, and in the hey-
day of youth feels also the full attractions of pleasure, and is
thus eminently qualified to enjoy the joke. At the same time
he is to that degree under the Reason, that it does not amuse
him as much as it amuses another spectator.

If the essence of the comic be the contrast in the intellect
between the idea and the false performance, there is good
reason why we should be affected by the exposure. We have
no deeper interest than our integrity, and that we should be
made aware by joke and by stroke, of any lie we entertain.
Besides, a perception of the comic seems to be a balance-
wheel in our metaphysical structure. It appears to be an essential element in a fine character. Wherever the intellect
is constructive, it will be found. We feel the absence of it as a
defect in the noblest and most oracular soul. The perception
of the comic is a tie of sympathy with other men, a pledge of
sanity, and a protection from those perverse tendencies and
gloomy insanities in which fine intellects sometimes lose
themselves. A rogue alive to the ludicrous is still convertible. If that sense is lost, his fellow-men can do little for
him.

It is true the sensibility to the ludicrous may run into excess. Men celebrate their perception of halfness and a latent
lie by the peculiar explosions of laughter. So painfully sus-
ceptible are some men to these impressions, that if a man of
wit come into the room where they are, it seems to take them
out of themselves with violent convulsions of the face and
sides, and obstreperous roarings of the throat. How often
and with what unfeigned compassion we have seen such a
person receiving like a willing martyr the whispers into his

ear of a man of wit. The victim who has just received the discharge, if in a solemn company, has the air very much of a stout vessel which has just shipped a heavy sea; and though it does not split it, the poor bark is for the moment critically staggered. The peace of society and the decorum of tables seem to require that next to a notable wit should always be posted a phlegmatic bolt-upright man, able to stand without movement of muscle whole broadsides of this Greek fire. It is a true shaft of Apollo, and traverses the universe, and unless it encounter a mystic or a dumpish soul, goes everywhere heralded and harbingered by smiles and greetings. Wit makes its own welcome, and levels all distinctions. No dignity, no learning, no force of character, can make any stand against good wit. It is like ice, on which no beauty of form, no majesty of carriage, can plead any immunity, — they must walk gingerly, according to the laws of ice, or down they must go, dignity and all. " Dost thou think, because thou art virtuous, there shall be no more cakes and ale?" Plutarch happily expresses the value of the jest as a legitimate weapon of the philosopher. " Men cannot exercise their rhetoric unless they speak, but their philosophy even whilst they are silent or jest merrily; for as it is the highest degree of injustice not to be just and yet seem so, so it is the top of wisdom to philosophize yet not appear to do it, and in mirth to do the same with those that are serious and seem in earnest; for as in Euripides, the Bacchæ, though unprovided of iron weapons and unarmed, wounded their invaders with the boughs of trees, which they carried, thus the very jests and merry talk of true philosophers move those that are not altogether insensible, and unusually reform."

In all the parts of life, the occasion of laughter is some seeming, some keeping of the word to the ear and eye, whilst it is broken to the soul. Thus, as the religious sentiment is the most vital and sublime of all our sentiments, and capable of the most prodigious effects, so is it abhorrent to our whole nature, when, in the absence of the sentiment, the act or word or officer volunteers to stand in its stead. To the sympathies this is shocking, and occasions grief. But to the intellect the lack of the sentiment gives no pain; it compares incessantly the sublime idea with the bloated nothing which pretends to be it, and the sense of the disproportion is comedy. And as the religious sentiment is the most real and earnest thing in nature, being a mere rapture, and excluding, when it appears, all other considerations, the vitiating this is the greatest lie. Therefore, the oldest gibe of literature is the ridicule of false religion. This is the joke of jokes. In religion, the sentiment is all; the ritual or ceremony indifferent. But the inertia of men inclines them, when the sentiment sleeps, to imitate that thing it did; it goes through the ceremony omitting only the will, makes the mistake of the wig for the head, the clothes for the man. The older the mistake and the more overgrown the particular form is, the more ridiculous to the intellect. Captain John Smith, the discoverer of New England, was not wanting in humor. The Society in London which had contributed their means to convert the savages, hoping doubtless to see the Keokuks, Black Hawks, Roaring Thunders, and Tustanuggees of that day converted into church-wardens and deacons at least, pestered the gallant rover with frequent solicitations out of England touching the conversion of the Indians, and the enlargement of the Church. Smith, in his perplexity how to satisfy the Society, sent out a party into the swamp, caught an Indian, and sent him home in the first ship to London, telling the Society they might convert one themselves.

The satire reaches its climax when the actual Church is set in direct contradiction to the dictates of religious sentiment, as in the sketch of our Puritan politics in Hudibras : —

> " Our brethren of New England use
> Choice malefactors to excuse,
> And hang the guiltless in their stead,
> Of whom the churches have less need;
> As lately happened, in a town
> Where lived a cobbler, and but one,
> That out of doctrine could cut use,
> And mend men's lives as well as shoes.
> This precious brother having slain,
> In times of peace, an Indian,
> Not out of malice, but mere zeal
> (Because he was an infidel),
> The mighty Tottipottymoy
> Sent to our elders an envoy,
> Complaining loudly of the breach
> Of league held forth by Brother Patch,
> Against the articles in force
> Between both churches, his and ours,
> For which he craved the saints to render
> Into his hands, or hang the offender;
> But they, maturely having weighed
> They had no more but him o' th' trade
> (A man that served them in the double
> Capacity to teach and cobble),
> Resolved to spare him ; yet to do
> The Indian Hoghan Moghan too
> Impartial justice, in his stead did
> Hang an old weaver that was bedrid."

In science the jest at pedantry is analogous to that in religion which lies against superstition. A classification or no-
menclature used by the scholar only as a memorandum of
his last lesson in the laws of nature, and confessedly a makeshift, a bivouac for a night, and implying a march and a conquest to-morrow, becomes through indolence a barrack and a
prison, in which the man sits down immovably, and wishes to
detain others. The physiologist Camper humorously confesses the effect of his studies in dislocating his ordinary associations. "I have been employed," he says, "six months on
the *Cetacea;* I understand the osteology of the head of all
these monsters, and have made the combination with the
human head so well, that everybody now appears to me nar-
whale, porpoise, or marsouins. Women, the prettiest in society, and those whom I find less comely, they are all either
narwhales or porpoises to my eyes." I chanced the other
day to fall in with an odd illustration of the remark I had
heard, that the laws of disease are as beautiful as the laws
of health ; I was hastening to visit an old and honored friend,
who, I was informed, was in a dying condition, when I met
his physician, who accosted me in great spirits, with joy
sparkling in his eyes. "And how is my friend, the reverend
Doctor ?" I inquired. "O, I saw him this morning ; it is the
most correct apoplexy I have ever seen : face and hands livid,
breathing stertorous, all the symptoms perfect." And he
rubbed his hands with delight, for in the country we cannot
find every day a case that agrees with the diagnosis of the
books. I think there is malice in a very trifling story which
goes about, and which I should not take any notice of, did
I not suspect it to contain some satire upon my brothers of
the Natural History Society. It is of a boy who was learning his alphabet. "That letter is A," said the teacher; "A,"
drawled the boy. "That is B," said the teacher; "B,"
drawled the boy, and so on. "That is W," said the teacher.
"The devil !" exclaimed the boy, "is that W ?"

The pedantry of literature belongs to the same category.
In both cases there is a lie, when the mind, seizing a classification to help it to a sincerer knowledge of the fact, stops in
the classification ; or learning languages, and reading books,
to the end of a better acquaintance with man, stops in the
languages and books : in both the learner seems to be wise,
and is not.

The same falsehood, the same confusion of the sympathies

because a pretension is not made good, points the perpetual
satire against poverty, since, according to Latin poetry and
English doggerel,

> Poverty does nothing worse
> Than to make man ridiculous.

In this instance the halfness lies in the pretension of the
parties to some consideration on account of their condition.
If the man is not ashamed of his poverty, there is no joke.
The poorest man who stands on his manhood destroys the
jest. The poverty of the saint, of the rapt philosopher, of
the naked Indian, is not comic. The lie is in the surrender
of the man to his appearance; as if a man should neglect
himself and treat his shadow on the wall with marks of infinite respect. It affects us oddly, as to see things turned
upside down, or to see a man in a high wind run after his
hat, which is always droll. The relation of the parties is in-
verted, — hat being for the moment master, the by-standers
cheering the hat. The multiplication of artificial wants and
expenses in civilized life, and the exaggeration of all trifling
forms, present innumerable occasions for this discrepancy to
expose itself. Such is the story told of the painter Astley,
who, going out of Rome one day with a party for a ramble in
the Campagna, and the weather proving hot, refused to take
off his coat when his companions threw off theirs, but swel-
tered on; which, exciting remark, his comrades playfully
forced off his coat, and behold on the back of his waistcoat a
gay cascade was thundering down the rocks with foam and
rainbow, very refreshing in so sultry a day, — a picture of his
own, with which the poor painter had been fain to repair the
shortcomings of his wardrobe. The same astonishment of
the intellect at the disappearance of the man out of nature,
through some superstition of his house or equipage, as if
truth and virtue should be bowed out of creation by the
clothes they wore, is the secret of all the fun that circulates
concerning eminent fops and fashionists, and, in like manner,
of the gay Rameau of Diderot, who believes in nothing but
hunger, and that the sole end of art, virtue, and poetry is to
put something for mastication between the upper and lower
mandibles.

Alike in all these cases and in the instance of cowardice or
fear of any sort, from the loss of life to the loss of spoons, the
majesty of man is violated. He, whom all things should serve,
serves some one of his own tools. In fine pictures the head

sheds on the limbs the expression of the face. In Raphael's Angel driving Heliodorus from the Temple, the crest of the helmet is so remarkable, that but for the extraordinary energy of the face, it would draw the eye too much; but the countenance of the celestial messenger subordinates it, and we see it not. In poor pictures the limbs and trunk degrade the face. So among the women in the street: you shall see one whose bonnet and dress are one thing, and the lady herself quite another, wearing withal an expression of meek submission to her bonnet and dress; and another whose dress obeys and heightens the expression of her form.

More food for the comic is afforded whenever the personal appearance, the face, form, and manners, are subjects of thought with the man himself. No fashion is the best fashion for those matters which will take care of themselves. This is the butt of those jokes of the Paris drawing-rooms, which Napoleon reckoned so formidable, and which are copiously recounted in the French Mémoires. A lady of high rank, but of lean figure, had given the Countess Dulauloy the nickname of "Le Grenadier tricolore," in allusion to her tall figure, as well as to her republican opinions; the Countess retaliated by calling Madame "the Venus of the Père-la-Chaise," a compliment to her skeleton which did not fail to circulate. "Lord C," said the Countess of Gordon, "O, he is a perfect comb, all teeth and back." The Persians have a pleasant story of Tamerlane which relates to the same particulars: "Timur was an ugly man; he had a blind eye and a lame foot. One day when Chodscha was with him, Timur scratched his head, since the hour of the barber was come, and commanded that the barber should be called. Whilst he was shaven, the barber gave him a looking-glass in his hand. Timur saw himself in the mirror and found his face quite too ugly. Therefore he began to weep; Chodscha also set himself to weep, and so they wept for two hours. On this, some courtiers began to comfort Timur, and entertained him with strange stories in order to make him forget all about it. Timur ceased weeping, but Chodscha ceased not, but began now first to weep amain, and in good earnest. At last said Timur to Chodscha, 'Hearken! I have looked in the mirror, and seen myself ugly. Thereat I grieved, because, although I am Caliph, and have also much wealth, and many wives, yet still I am so ugly; therefore have I wept. But thou, why weepest thou without ceasing?' Chodscha answered, 'If thou hast only seen thy face once, and at once seeing hast not been able to contain thyself, but hast wept, what should we do,— we who see thy face every day and night? If we weep not, who should weep? Therefore have I wept.' Timur almost split his sides with laughing."

Politics also furnish the same mark for satire. What is nobler than the expansive sentiment of patriotism, which would find brothers in a whole nation? But when this enthusiasm is perceived to end in the very intelligible maxims of trade, so much for so much, the intellect feels again the half-man. Or what is fitter than that we should espouse and carry a principle against all opposition? But when the men appear who ask our votes as representatives of this ideal, we are sadly out of countenance.

But there is no end to this analysis. We do nothing that is not laughable whenever we quit our spontaneous sentiment. All our plans, managements, houses, poems, if compared with the wisdom and love which man represents, are equally imperfect and ridiculous. But we cannot afford to part with any advantages. We must learn by laughter, as well as by tears and terrors; explore the whole of nature,— the farce and buffoonery in the yard below, as well as the lessons of poets and philosophers upstairs, in the hall,— and get the rest and refreshment of the shaking of the sides. But the comic also has its own speedy limits. Mirth quickly becomes intemperate, and the man would soon die of inanition, as some persons have been tickled to death. The same scourge whips the joker and the enjoyer of the joke. When Carlini was convulsing Naples with laughter, a patient waited on a physician in that city, to obtain some remedy for excessive melancholy, which was rapidly consuming his life. The physician endeavored to cheer his spirits, and advised him to go to the theatre and see Carlini. He replied, "I am Carlini."

QUOTATION AND ORIGINALITY.

QUOTATION AND ORIGINALITY.

WHOEVER looks at the insect world, at flies, aphides, gnats, and innumerable parasites, and even at the infant mammals, must have remarked the extreme content they take in suction, which constitutes the main business of their life. If we go into a library or news-room, we see the same function on a higher plane, performed with like ardor, with equal impatience of interruption, indicating the sweetness of the act. In the highest civilization the book is still the highest delight. He who has once known its satisfactions is provided with a resource against calamity. Like Plato's disciple who has perceived a truth, "he is preserved from harm until another period." In every man's memory, with the hours when life culminated are usually associated certain books which met his views. Of a large and powerful class we might ask with confidence, What is the event they most desire? what gift? What but the book that shall come, which they have sought through all libraries, through all languages, that shall be to their mature eyes what many a tinsel-covered toy pamphlet was to their childhood, and shall speak to the imagination? Our high respect for a well-read man is praise enough of literature. If we encountered a man of rare intellect, we should ask him what books he read. We expect a great man to be a good reader; or in proportion to the spontaneous power should be the assimilating power. And though such are a more difficult and exacting class, they are not less eager. "He that borrows the aid of an equal understanding," said Burke, "doubles his own; he that uses that of a superior elevates his own to the stature of that he contemplates."

We prize books, and they prize them most who are themselves wise. Our debt to tradition through reading and conversation is so massive, our protest or private addition so rare and insignificant,— and this commonly on the ground of other reading or hearing,— that, in a large sense, one would say there is no pure originality. All minds quote. Old and new make the warp and woof of every moment. There is no thread that is not a twist of these two strands. By necessity, by proclivity, and by delight, we all quote. We quote not only books and proverbs, but arts, sciences, religion, customs, and laws; nay, we quote temples and houses, tables and chairs by imitation. The Patent-Office Commissioner knows that all machines in use have been invented and re-invented over and over; that the mariner's compass, the boat, the pendulum, glass, movable types, the kaleidoscope, the railway, the power-loom, etc., have been many times found and lost, from Egypt, China, and Pompeii down; and if we have arts which Rome wanted, so also Rome had arts which we have lost; that the invention of yesterday of making wood indestructible by means of vapor of coal-oil or paraffine was suggested by the Egyptian method which has preserved its mummy-cases four thousand years.

The highest statement of new philosophy complacently caps itself with some prophetic maxim from the oldest learning. There is something mortifying in this perpetual circle. This extreme economy argues a very small capital of invention. The stream of affection flows broad and strong; the practical activity is a river of supply; but the dearth of design accuses the penury of intellect. How few thoughts! In a hundred years, millions of men, and not a hundred lines of poetry, not a theory of philosophy that offers a solution of the great problems, not an art of education that fulfils the conditions. In this delay and vacancy of thought we must make the best amends we can by seeking the wisdom of others to fill the time.

If we confine ourselves to literature, 't is easy to see that the debt is immense to past thought. None escapes it. The originals are not original. There is imitation, model, and suggestion, to the very archangels, if we knew their history. The first book tyrannizes over the second. Read Tasso, and you think of Virgil; read Virgil, and you think of Homer; and Milton forces you to reflect how narrow are the limits of human invention. The "Paradise Lost" had never existed but for these precursors; and if we find in India or Arabia a book out of our horizon of thought and tradition, we are soon taught by new researches in its native country to discover its fore-goers, and its latent, but real connection with our own Bibles.

Read in Plato, and you shall find Christian dogmas, and not only so, but stumble on our evangelical phrases. Hegel pre-exists in Proclus, and, long before, in Heraclitus and Parmenides. Whoso knows Plutarch, Lucian, Rabelais, Montaigne, and Bayle will have a key to many supposed originalities. Rabelais is the source of many a proverb, story, and jest, derived from him into all modern languages; and if we knew Rabelais's reading, we should see the rill of the Rabelais river. Swedenborg, Behmen, Spinoza, will appear original to uninstructed and to thoughtless persons : their originality will disappear to such as are either well-read or thoughtful ; for scholars will recognize their dogmas as reappearing in men of a similar intellectual elevation throughout history. Albert, the " wonderful doctor," St. Buonaventura, the " seraphic doctor," Thomas Aquinas, the " angelic doctor " of the thirteenth century, whose books made the sufficient culture of these ages, Dante absorbed and he survives for us. " Renard the Fox," a German poem of the thirteenth century, was long supposed to be the original work, until Grimm found fragments of another original a century older. M. Le Grand showed that in the old Fabliaux were the originals of the tales of Molière, La Fontaine, Boccaccio, and of Voltaire.

Mythology is no man's work ; but, what we daily observe in regard to the *bon-mots* that circulate in society, — that every talker helps a story in repeating it, until, at last, from the slenderest filament of fact a good fable is constructed, — the same growth befalls mythology : the legend is tossed from believer to poet, from poet to believer, everybody adding a grace or dropping a fault or rounding the form, until it gets an ideal truth.

Religious literature, the psalms and liturgies of churches, are of course of this slow growth, — a fagot of selections gathered through ages, leaving the worse, and saving the better, until it is at last the work of the whole communion of worshippers. The Bible itself is like an old Cremona ; it has been played upon by the devotion of thousands of years, until every word and particle is public and tunable. And whatever undue reverence may have been claimed for it by the prestige of philonic inspiration, the stronger tendency we are describing is likely to undo. What divines had assumed as the distinctive revelations of Christianity, theologic criticism has matched by exact parallelisms from the Stoics and poets of Greece and Rome. Later, when Confucius and the Indian scriptures were made known, no claim to monopoly of ethical wisdom could be thought of; and the surprising results of the new researches into the history of Egypt have opened to us the deep debt of the churches of Rome and England to the Egyptian hierology.

The borrowing is often honest enough, and comes of magnanimity and stoutness. A great man quotes bravely, and will not draw on his invention when his memory serves him with a word as good. What he quotes, he fills with his own voice and humor, and the whole cyclopædia of his table-talk is presently believed to be his own. Thirty years ago, when Mr. Webster at the bar or in the Senate filled the eyes and minds of young men, you might often hear cited as Mr. Webster's three rules: first, never to do to-day what he could defer till to-morrow; secondly, never to do himself what he could make another do for him; and, thirdly, never to pay any debt to-day. Well, they are none the worse for being already told, in the last generation, of Sheridan; and we find in Grimm's *Mémoires* that Sheridan got them from the witty D'Argenson; who, no doubt, if we could consult him, could tell of whom he first heard them told. In our own college days we remember hearing other pieces of Mr. Webster's advice to students, — among others, this: that, when he opened a new book, he turned to the table of contents, took a pen, and sketched a sheet of matters and topics, — what he knew and what he thought, — before he read the book. But we find in Southey's "Commonplace Book" this said of the Earl of Strafford: "I learned one rule of him," says Sir G. Radcliffe, "which I think worthy to be remembered. When he met with a well-penned oration or tract upon any subject, he framed a speech upon the same argument, inventing and disposing what seemed fit to be said upon that subject, before he read the book; then, reading, compared his own with the author's, and noted his own defects and the author's art and fulness; whereby he drew all that ran in the author more strictly, and might better judge of his own wants to supply them." I remember to have heard Mr. Samuel Rogers, in London, relate, among other anecdotes of the Duke of Wellington, that a lady having expressed in his presence a passionate wish to witness a great victory, he replied: "Madam, there is nothing so dreadful as a great victory, — excepting a great defeat." But this speech is also D'Argenson's, and is reported by Grimm. So the sarcasm attributed to Lord Eldon upon Brougham, his predecessor on the woolsack, "What a wonderful versatile mind has Brougham! he knows politics, Greek, history, science; if he only knew a little of law, he would know a little of everything." You may find the original of this gibe in Grimm, who says that Louis XVI., going out of chapel after hearing a sermon from the Abbé Maury, said, "*Si l' Abbé nous avait parlé un peu de religion, il nous aurait parlé de tout.*" A pleasantry which ran through all the newspapers a few years since, taxing the eccentricities of a gifted family connection in New England, was only a theft of Lady Mary Wortley Montagu's *mot* of a hundred years ago, that "the world was made up of men and women and Herveys."

Many of the historical proverbs have a doubtful paternity. Columbus's egg is claimed for Brunelleschi. Rabelais's dying words, "I am going to see the great Perhaps" (*le grand Peut-être*), only repeats the "IF" inscribed on the portal of the temple at Delphi. Goethe's favorite phrase, "the open secret," translates Aristotle's answer to Alexander, "These books are published and not published." Madame de Staël's "Architecture is frozen music" is borrowed from Goethe's "dumb music," which is Vitruvius's rule, that "the architect must not only understand drawing, but music." Wordsworth's hero acting "on the plan which pleased his childish thought," is Schiller's "Tell him to reverence the dreams of his youth," and earlier, Bacon's "*Consilia juventutis plus divinitatis habent.*"

In romantic literature examples of this vamping abound. The fine verse in the old Scotch ballad of "The Drowned Lovers,"

> " Thou art roaring ower loud, Clyde water,
>   Thy streams are ower strang;
> Make me thy wrack when I come back,
>   But spare me when I gang."

is a translation of Martial's epigram on Hero and Leander, where the prayer of Leander is the same : —

> " Parcite dum propero, mergite dum redeo."

Hafiz furnished Burns with the song of "John Barleycorn," and furnished Moore with the original of the piece,

> " When in death I shall calm recline,
>   Oh, bear my heart to my mistress dear," etc.

There are many fables which, as they are found in every language, and betray no sign of being borrowed, are said to be agreeable to the human mind. Such are "The Seven

Sleepers," "Gyges's Ring," "The Travelling Cloak," "The Wandering Jew," "The Pied Piper," "Jack and his Beanstalk," the "Lady Diving in the Lake and Rising in the Cave," — whose omnipresence only indicates how easily a good story crosses all frontiers. The popular incident of Baron Munchausen, who hung his bugle up by the kitchen fire, and the frozen tune thawed out, is found in Greece in Plato's time. Antiphanes, one of Plato's friends, laughingly compared his writings to a city where the words froze in the air as soon as they were pronounced, and the next summer, when they were warmed and melted by the sun, the people heard what had been spoken in the winter. It is only within this century that England and America discovered that their nursery-tales were old German and Scandinavian stories; and now it appears that they came from India, and are the property of all the nations descended from the Aryan race, and have been warbled and babbled between nurses and children for unknown thousands of years.

If we observe the tenacity with which nations cling to their first types of costume, of architecture, of tools and methods in tillage, and of decoration, — if we learn how old are the patterns of our shawls, the capitals of our columns, the fret, the beads, and other ornaments on our walls, the alternate lotus-bud and leaf-stem of our iron fences, — we shall think very well of the first men, or ill of the latest.

Now shall we say that only the first men were well alive, and the existing generation is invalided and degenerate? Is all literature eavesdropping, and all art Chinese imitation? our life a custom, and our body borrowed, like a beggar's dinner, from a hundred charities? A more subtle and severe criticism might suggest that some dislocation has befallen the race; that men are off their centre; that multitudes of men do not live with Nature, but behold it as exiles. People go out to look at sunrises and sunsets who do not recognize their own quietly and happily, but know that it is foreign to them. As they do by books, so they *quote* the sunset and the star, and do not make them theirs. Worse yet, they live as foreigners in the world of truth, and quote thoughts, and thus disown them. Quotation confesses inferiority. In opening a new book we often discover, from the unguarded devotion with which the writer gives his motto or text, all we have to expect from him. If Lord Bacon appears already in the preface, I go and read the "Instauration" instead of the new book.

The mischief is quickly punished in general and in particular. Admirable mimics have nothing of their own. In every kind of parasite, when Nature has finished an aphis, a teredo, or a vampire bat,— an excellent sucking-pipe to tap another animal, or a mistletoe or dodder among plants, — the self-supplying organs wither and dwindle, as being superfluous. In common prudence there is an early limit to this leaning on an original. In literature quotation is good only when the writer whom I follow goes my way, and, being better mounted than I, gives me a cast, as we say ; but if I like the gay equipage so well as to go out of my road, I had better have gone afoot.

But it is necessary to remember there are certain considerations which go far to qualify a reproach too grave. This vast mental indebtedness has every variety that pecuniary debt has, — every variety of merit. The capitalist of either kind is as hungry to lend as the consumer to borrow ; and the transaction no more indicates intellectual turpitude in the borrower than the simple fact of debt involves bankruptcy. On the contrary, in far the greater number of cases the transaction is honorable to both. Can we not help ourselves as discreetly by the force of two in literature ? Certainly it only needs two well placed and well tempered for co-operation, to get somewhat far transcending any private enterprise ! Shall we converse as spies ? Our very abstaining to repeat and credit the fine remark of our friend is thievish. Each man of thought is surrounded by wiser men than he, if they cannot write as well. Cannot he and they combine ? Cannot they sink their jealousies in God's love, and call their poem Beaumont and Fletcher, or the Theban Phalanx's ? The city will for nine days or nine years make differences and sinister comparisons : there is a new and more excellent public that will bless the friends. Nay, it is an inevitable fruit of our social nature. The child quotes his father, and the man quotes his friend. Each man is a hero and an oracle to somebody, and to that person whatever he says has an enhanced value. Whatever we think and say is wonderfully better for our spirits and trust in another mouth. There is none so eminent and wise but he knows minds whose opinion confirms or qualifies his own : and men of extraordinary genius acquire an almost absolute ascendant over their nearest companions. The Comte de Crillon said one day to M. d'Allonville, with French vivacity, " If the universe and I professed one opinion, and M.

13*

Necker expressed a contrary one, I should be at once convinced that the universe and I were mistaken."

Original power is usually accompanied with assimilating power, and we value in Coleridge his excellent knowledge and quotations perhaps as much, possibly more, than his original suggestions. If an author give us just distinctions, inspiring lessons, or imaginative poetry, it is not so important to us whose they are. If we are fired and guided by these, we know him as a benefactor, and shall return to him as long as he serves us so well. We may like well to know what is Plato's and what is Montesquieu's or Goethe's part, and what thought was always dear to the writer himself; but the worth of the sentences consists in their radiancy and equal aptitude to all intelligence. They fit all our facts like a charm. We respect ourselves the more that we know them.

Next to the originator of a good sentence is the first quoter of it. Many will read the book before one thinks of quoting a passage. As soon as he has done this, that line will be quoted east and west. Then there are great ways of borrowing. Genius borrows nobly. When Shakspeare is charged with debts to his authors, Landor replies : " Yet he was more original than his originals. He breathed upon dead bodies and brought them into life." And we must thank Karl Ottfried Müller for the just remark, " Poesy, drawing within its circle all that is glorious and inspiring, gave itself but little concern as to where its flowers originally grew." So Voltaire usually imitated, but with such superiority that Dubuc said : " He is like the false Amphitryon ; although the stranger, it is always he who has the air of being master of the house." Wordsworth, as soon as he heard a good thing, caught it up, meditated upon it, and very soon reproduced it in his conversation and writing. If De Quincey said, " That is what I told you," he replied, " No : that is mine, — mine, and not yours." On the whole, we like the valor of it. 'T is on Marmontel's principle, " I pounce on what is mine, wherever I find it"; and on Bacon's broader rule, " I take all knowledge to be my province." It betrays the consciousness that the truth is the property of no individual, but is the treasure of all men. And inasmuch as any writer has ascended to a just view of man's condition, he has adopted this tone. In so far as the receiver's aim is on life, and not on literature, will be his indifference to the source. The nobler the truth or sentiment, the less imports the question of authorship. It never troubles the simple seeker from whom he derived such or such a sentiment. Whoever expresses to us a just thought makes ridiculous the pains of the critic who should tell him where such a word had been said before. "It is no more according to Plato than according to me." Truth is always present: it only needs to lift the iron lids of the mind's eye to read its oracles. But the moment there is the purpose of display, the fraud is exposed. In fact, it is as difficult to appropriate the thoughts of others, as it is to invent. Always some steep transition, some sudden alteration of temperature, of point or of view, betrays the foreign interpolation.

There is, besides, a new charm in such intellectual works as, passing through long time, have had a multitude of authors and improvers. We admire that poetry which no man wrote, — no poet less than the genius of humanity itself, — which is to be read in a mythology, in the effect of a fixed or national style of pictures, of sculptures, or drama, or cities, or sciences, on us. Such a poem also is language. Every word in the language has once been used happily. The ear, caught by that felicity, retains it, and it is used again and again, as if the charm belonged to the word, and not to the life of thought which so enforced it. These profane uses, of course, kill it, and it is avoided. But a quick wit can at any time reinforce it, and it comes into vogue again. Then people quote so differently: one finding only what is gaudy and popular; another, the heart of the author, the report of his select and happiest hour: and the reader sometimes giving more to the citation than he owes to it. Most of the classical citations you shall hear or read in the current journals or speeches were not drawn from the originals, but from previous quotations in English books; and you can easily pronounce, from the use and relevancy of the sentence, whether it had not done duty many times before, — whether your jewel was got from the mine or from an auctioneer. We are as much informed of a writer's genius by what he selects as by what he originates. We read the quotation with his eyes, and find a new and fervent sense; as a passage from one of the poets, well recited, borrows new interest from the rendering. As the journals say, "the italics are ours." The profit of books is according to the sensibility of the reader. The profoundest thought or passion sleeps as in a mine, until an equal mind and heart finds and publishes it. The passages of Shakspeare that we most prize were never quoted until within this century; and Milton's prose, and

Burke, even, have their best fame within it. Every one, too, remembers his friends by their favorite poetry or other reading.

Observe, also, that a writer appears to more advantage in the pages of another book than in his own. In his own, he waits as a candidate for your approbation ; in another's, he is a lawgiver.

Then another's thoughts have a certain advantage with us simply because they are another's. There is an illusion in a new phrase. A man hears a fine sentence out of Swedenborg, and wonders at the wisdom, and is very merry at heart that he has now got so fine a thing. Translate it out of the new words into his own usual phrase, and he will wonder again at his own simplicity, such tricks do fine words play with us.

'T is curious what new interest an old author acquires by official canonization in Tiraboschi, or Dr. Johnson, or Von Hammer-Purgstall, or Hallam, or other historian of literature. Their registration of his book, or citation of a passage, carries the sentimental value of a college diploma. Hallam, though never profound, is a fair mind, able to appreciate poetry, unless it becomes deep, being always blind and deaf to imaginative and analogy-loving souls, like the Platonists, like Giordano Bruno, like Donne, Herbert, Crashaw, and Vaughan'; and Hallam cites a sentence from Bacon or Sidney, and distinguishes a lyric of Edwards or Vaux, and straightway it commends itself to us as if it had received the Isthmian crown.

It is a familiar expedient of brilliant writers, and not less of witty talkers, the device of ascribing their own sentence to an imaginary person, in order to give it weight, — as Cicero, Cowley, Swift, Landor, and Carlyle have done. And Cardinal de Retz, at a critical moment in the Parliament of Paris, described himself in an extemporary Latin sentence, which he pretended to quote from a classic author, and which told admirably well. It is a curious reflex effect of this enhancement of our thought by citing it from another, that many men can write better under a mask than for themselves, — as Chatterton in archaic ballad, Le Sage in Spanish costume, Macpherson as " Ossian," — and, I doubt not, many a young barrister in chambers in London, who forges good thunder for the "Times," but never works as well under his own name. This is a sort of dramatizing talent ; as it is not rare to find great powers of recitation, without the least original eloquence, —

or people who copy drawings with admirable skill, but are incapable of any design.

In hours of high mental activity we sometimes do the book too much honor, reading out of it better things than the author wrote, — reading, as we say, between the lines. You have had the like experience in conversation : the wit was in what you heard, not in what the speakers said. Our best thought came from others. We heard in their words a deeper sense than the speakers put into them, and could express ourselves in other people's phrases to finer purpose than they knew. In Moore's Diary, Mr. Hallam is reported as mentioning at dinner one of his friends who had said, "I don't know how it is, a thing that falls flat from me seems quite an excellent joke when given at second-hand by Sheridan. I never like my own *bon-mots* until he adopts them." Dumont was exalted by being used by Mirabeau, by Bentham, and by Sir Philip Francis, who, again, was less than his own "Junius"; and James Hogg (except in his poems "Kilmeny" and "The Witch of Fife") is but a third-rate author, owing his fame to his effigy colossalized through the lens of John Wilson, — who, again, writes better under the domino of "Christopher North" than in his proper clothes. The bold theory of Delia Bacon, that Shakspeare's plays were written by a society of wits, — by Sir Walter Raleigh, Lord Bacon, and others around the Earl of Southampton, — had plainly for her the charm of the superior meaning they would acquire when read under this light ; this idea of the authorship controlling our appreciation of the works themselves. We once knew a man overjoyed at the notice of his pamphlet in a leading newspaper. What range he gave his imagination! Who could have written it? Was it not Colonel Carbine, or Senator Tonitrus, or, at the least, Professor Maximilian? Yes, he could detect in the style that fine Roman hand. How it seemed the very voice of the refined and discerning public, inviting merit at last to consent to fame, and come up and take place in the reserved and authentic chairs! He carried the journal with haste to the sympathizing Cousin Matilda, who is so proud of all we do. But what dismay, when the good Matilda, pleased with his pleasure, confessed she had written the criticism, and carried it with her own hands to the post-office! "Mr. Wordsworth," said Charles Lamb, "allow me to introduce to you my only admirer."

Swedenborg threw a formidable theory into the world, that

every soul existed in a society of souls, from which all its thoughts passed into it, as the blood of the mother circulates in her unborn child ; and he noticed that, when in his bed, — alternately sleeping and waking, — sleeping, he was surrounded by persons disputing and offering opinions on the one side and on the other side of a proposition ; waking, the like suggestions occurred for and against the proposition as his own thoughts ; sleeping again, he saw and heard the speakers as before : and this as often as he slept or waked. And if we expand the image, does it not look as if we men were thinking and talking out of an enormous antiquity, as if we stood, not in a coterie of prompters that filled a sitting-room, but in a circle of intelligences that reached through all thinkers, poets, inventors, and wits, men and women, English, German, Celt, Aryan, Ninevite, Copt, — back to the first geometer, bard, mason, carpenter, planter, shepherd, — back to the first negro, who, with more health or better perception, gave a shriller sound or name for the thing he saw and dealt with ? Our benefactors are as many as the children who invented speech, word by word. Language is a city, to the building of which every human being brought a stone ; yet he is no more to be credited with the grand result than the acaleph which adds a cell to the coral reef which is the basis of the continent.

Πάντα ρεῖ : all things are in flux. It is inevitable that you are indebted to the past. You are fed and formed by it. The old forest is decomposed for the composition of the new forest. The old animals have given their bodies to the earth to furnish through chemistry the forming race, and every individual is only a momentary fixation of what was yesterday another's, is to-day his, and will belong to a third to-morrow. So it is in thought. Our knowledge is the amassed thought and experience of innumerable minds : our language, our science, our religion, our opinions, our fancies we inherited. Our country, customs, laws, our ambitions, and our notions of fit and fair, — all these we never made ; we found them ready-made ; we but quote them. Goethe frankly said, "What would remain to me if this art of appropriation were derogatory to genius ? Every one of my writings has been furnished to me by a thousand different persons, a thousand things : wise and foolish have brought me, without suspecting it, the offering of their thoughts, faculties, and experience. My work is an aggregation of beings taken from the whole of nature ; it bears the name of Goethe."

But there remains the indefeasible persistency of the individual to be himself. One leaf, one blade of grass, one meridian, does not resemble another. Every mind is different; and the more it is unfolded, the more pronounced is that difference. He must draw the elements into him for food, and, if they be granite and silex, will prefer them cooked by sun and rain, by time and art, to his hand. But, however received, these elements pass into the substance of his constitution, will be assimilated, and tend always to form, not a partisan, but a possessor of truth. To all that can be said of the preponderance of the Past, the single word Genius is a sufficient reply. The divine resides in the new. The divine never quotes, but is, and creates. The profound apprehension of the Present is Genius, which makes the Past forgotten. Genius believes its faintest presentiment against the testimony of all history; for it knows that facts are not ultimates, but that a state of mind is the ancestor of everything. And what is Originality? It is being, being one's self, and reporting accurately what we see and are. Genius is, in the first instance, sensibility, the capacity of receiving just impressions from the external world, and the power of co-ordinating these after the laws of thought. It implies Will, or original force, for their right distribution and expression. If to this the sentiment of piety be added, if the thinker feels that the thought most strictly his own is not his own, and recognizes the perpetual suggestion of the Supreme Intellect, the oldest thoughts become new and fertile whilst he speaks them.

Originals never lose their value. There is always in them a style and weight of speech, which the immanence of the oracle bestowed, and which cannot be counterfeited. Hence the permanence of the high poets. Plato, Cicero, and Plutarch cite the poets in the manner in which Scripture is quoted in our churches. A phrase or a single word is adduced, with honoring emphasis, from Pindar, Hesiod, or Euripides, as precluding all argument, because thus had they said : importing that the bard spoke not his own, but the words of some god. True poets have always ascended to this lofty platform, and met this expectation. Shakspeare, Milton, Wordsworth, were very conscious of their responsibilities. When a man thinks happily, he finds no foot-track in the field he traverses. All spontaneous thought is irrespective of all else. Pindar uses this haughty defiance, as if it were impossible to find his sources : "There are many swift darts within my quiver, which have a voice for those with understanding; but to the crowd they need interpreters. He is gifted with genius who knoweth much by natural talent."

Our pleasure in seeing each mind take the subject to which it has a proper right is seen in mere fitness in time. He that comes second must needs quote him that comes first. The earliest describers of savage life, as Captain Cook's account of the Society Islands, or Alexander Henry's travels among our Indian tribes, have a charm of truth and just point of view. Landsmen and sailors freshly come from the most civilized countries, and with no false expectation, no sentimentality yet about wild life, healthily receive and report what they saw, — seeing what they must, and using no choice; and no man suspects the superior merit of the description, until Chateaubriand, or Moore, or Campbell, or Byron, or the artists arrive, and mix so much art with their picture that the incomparable advantage of the first narrative appears. For the same reason we dislike that the poet should choose an antique or far-fetched subject for his muse, as if he avowed want of insight. The great deal always with the nearest. Only as braveries of too prodigal power can we pardon it, when the life of genius is so redundant that out of petulance it flings its fire into some old mummy, and, lo! it walks and blushes again here in the street.

We cannot overstate our debt to the Past, but the moment has the supreme claim. The Past is for us; but the sole terms on which it can become ours are its subordination to the Present. Only an inventor knows how to borrow, and every man is or should be an inventor. We must not tamper with the organic motion of the soul. 'T is certain that thought has its own proper motion, and the hints which flash from it, the words overheard at unawares by the free mind, are trustworthy and fertile, when obeyed, and not perverted to low and selfish account. This vast memory is only raw material. The divine gift is ever the instant life, which receives and uses and creates, and can well bury the old in the omnipotency with which Nature decomposes all her harvest for recomposition.

PROGRESS OF CULTURE.

PROGRESS OF CULTURE.

ADDRESS READ BEFORE THE Φ B K SOCIETY AT CAMBRIDGE,
JULY 18, 1867.

WE meet to-day under happy omens to our ancient society, to the commonwealth of letters, to the country,
and to mankind. No good citizen but shares the wonderful
prosperity of the Federal Union. The heart still beats with the
public pulse of joy, that the country has withstood the rude
trial which threatened its existence, and thrills with the vast
augmentation of strength which it draws from this proof.
The storm which has been resisted is a crown of honor and a
pledge of strength to the ship. We may be well contented
with our fair inheritance. Was ever such coincidence of advantages in time and place as in America to-day? — the
fusion of races and religions; the hungry cry for men which
goes up from the wide continent; the answering facility of
immigration, permitting every wanderer to choose his climate
and government. Men come hither by nations. Science sur-
passes the old miracles of mythology, to fly with them over
the sea, and to send their messages under it. They come
from crowded, antiquated kingdoms to the easy sharing of our
simple forms. Land without price is offered to the settler,
cheap education to his children. The temper of our people
delights in this whirl of life. Who would live in the stone
age, or the bronze, or the iron, or the lacustrine? Who does
not prefer the age of steel, of gold, of coal, petroleum, cotton, steam, electricity, and the spectroscope?

> " Prisca juvent alios, ego me nunc denique natum
> Gratulor."

All this activity has added to the value of life, and to the
scope of the intellect. I will not say that American institutions have given a new enlargement to our idea of a finished
man, but they have added important features to the sketch.

Observe the marked ethical quality of the innovations urged or adopted. The new claim of woman to a political status is itself an honorable testimony to the civilization which has given her a civil status new in history. Now that, by the increased humanity of law she controls her property, she inevitably takes the next step to her share in power. The war gave us the abolition of slavery, the success of the Sanitary Commission and of the Freedmen's Bureau. Add to these the new scope of social science ; the abolition of capital punishment and of imprisonment for debt; the improvement of prisons ; the efforts for the suppression of intemperance ; the search for just rules affecting labor ; the co-operative societies ; the insurance of life and limb ; the free-trade league ; the improved almshouses ; the enlarged scale of charities to relieve local famine, or burned towns, or the suffering Greeks ; the incipient series of international congresses, — all, one may say, in a high degree revolutionary, — teaching nations the taking of government into their own hands, and superseding kings.

The spirit is new. A silent revolution has impelled, step by step, all this activity. A great many full-blown conceits have burst. The coxcomb goes to the wall. To his astonishment he has found that this country and this age belong to the most liberal persuasion ; that the day of ruling by scorn and sneers is past ; that good sense is now in power, and *that* resting on a vast constituency of intelligent labor, and, better yet, on perceptions less and less dim of laws the most sublime. Men are now to be astonished by seeing acts of good-nature, common civility, and Christian charity proposed by statesmen, and executed by justices of the peace, — by policemen and the constable. The fop is unable to cut the patriot in the street ; nay, he lies at his mercy in the ballot of the club.

Mark, too, the large resources of a statesman, of a socialist, of a scholar, in this age. When classes are exasperated against each other, the peace of the world is always kept by striking a new note. Instantly the units part, and form in a new order, and those who were opposed are now side by side. In this country the prodigious mass of work that must be done has either made new divisions of labor or created new professions. Consider, at this time, what variety of issues, of enterprises public and private, what genius of science, what of administration, what of practical skill, what masters, each in his several province, the railroad, the telegraph, the mines, the inland and marine explorations, the novel and powerful philanthropies, as well as agriculture, the foreign trade and the home trade (whose circuits in this country are as spacious as the foreign), manufactures, the very inventions, all on a national scale too, have evoked ! — all implying the appearance of gifted men, the rapid addition to our society of a class of true nobles, by which the self-respect of each town and State is enriched.

Take as a type the boundless freedom here in Massachusetts. People have in all countries been burned and stoned for saying things which are commonplaces at all our breakfast-tables. Every one who was in Italy twenty-five years ago will remember the caution with which his host or guest, in any house looked around him, if a political topic were broached. Here the tongue is free, and the hand ; and the freedom of action goes to the brink, if not over the brink, of license.

A controlling influence of the times has been the wide and successful study of Natural Science. Steffens said, " The religious opinions of men rest on their views of nature." Great strides have been made within the present century. Geology, astronomy, chemistry, optics, have yielded grand results. The correlation of forces and the polarization of light have carried us to sublime generalizations, — have affected an imaginative race like poetic inspirations. We have been taught to tread familiarly on giddy heights of thought, and to wont ourselves to daring conjectures. The narrow sectarian cannot read astronomy with impunity. The creeds of his church shrivel like dried leaves at the door of the observatory, and a new and healthful air regenerates the human mind, and imparts a sympathetic enlargement to its inventions and method. That cosmical west-wind which, meteorologists tell us, constitutes by the revolution of the globe, the upper current, is alone broad enough to carry to every city and suburb — to the farmer's house, the miner's shanty, and the fisher's boat — the inspirations of this new hope of mankind. Now, if any one say we have had enough of these boastful recitals, then I say, Happy is the land wherein benefits like these have grown trite and commonplace.

We confess that in America everything looks new and recent. Our towns are still rude, — the make-shifts of emigrants, — and the whole architecture tent-like, when compared with the monumental solidity of mediæval and primeval re-

mains in Europe and Asia. But geology has effaced these
distinctions.   Geology, a science of forty or fifty summers,
has had the effect to throw an air of novelty and mushroom
speed over entire history.   The oldest empires, — what we
called venerable antiquity, — now that we have true measures
of duration, show like creations of yesterday. 'T is yet quite
too early to draw sound conclusions.   The old six thousand
years of chronology become a kitchen clock, — no more a
measure of time than an hour-glass or an egg-glass, — since
the duration of geologic periods has come into view.   Geology itself is only chemistry with the element of time added ;
and the rocks of Nahant or the dikes of the White Hills disclose that the world is a crystal, and the soil of the valleys
and plains a continual decomposition and recomposition.
Nothing is old but the mind.

But I find not only this equality between new and old
countriès, as seen by the eye of science, but also a certain
equivalence of the ages of history ; and as the child is in his
playthings working incessantly at problems of natural philosophy, — working as hard and as successfully as Newton,
— so it were ignorance not to see that each nation and period
has done its full part to make up the result of existing civility.   We are all agreed that we have not on the instant
better men to show than Plutarch's heroes.   The world is
always equal to itself.   We cannot yet afford to drop Homer,
nor Æschylus, nor Plato, nor Aristotle, nor Archimedes.
Later, each European nation, after the breaking up of the
Roman Empire, had its romantic era, and the productions
of that era in each rose to about the same height.   Take
for an example in literature the *Romance of Arthur,* in Brit-
ain, or in the opposite province of Brittany ; the *Chansons
de Roland,* in France ; the Chronicle of the Cid, in Spain ;
the *Niebelungen Lied,* in Germany ; the Norse Sagas, in Scandinavia ; and, I may add, the Arabian Nights on the African coast.   But if these works still survive and multiply,
what shall we say of names more distant, or hidden through
their very superiority to their coevals, — names of men
who have left remains that certify a height of genius in
their several directions not since surpassed, and which men in
proportion to their wisdom still cherish, — as Zoroaster, Confucius, and the grand scriptures, only recently known to western nations, of the Indian Vedas, the Institutes of Menu, the
Puranas, the poems of the Mahabarat and the Ramayana ?

In modern Europe, the Middle Ages were called the Dark Ages. Who dares to call them so now? They are seen to be the feet on which we walk, the eyes with which we see. 'T is one of our triumphs to have reinstated them. Their Dante and Alfred and Wickliffe and Abelard and Bacon; their Magna Charta, decimal numbers, mariner's compass, gunpowder, glass, paper, and clocks; chemistry, algebra, astronomy; their Gothic architecture, their painting, — are the delight and tuition of ours. Six hundred years ago Roger Bacon explained the precession of the equinoxes, and the necessity of reform in the calendar; looking over how many horizons as far as into Liverpool and New York, he announced that machines can be constructed to drive ships more rapidly than a whole galley of rowers could do, nor would they need anything but a pilot to steer; carriages, to move with incredible speed, without aid of animals; and machines to fly into the air like birds. Even the races that we still call savage or semi-savage, and which preserve their arts from immemorial traditions, vindicate their faculty by the skill with which they make their yam-cloths, pipes, bows, boats, and carved war-clubs. The war-proa of the Malays in the Japanese waters struck Commodore Perry by its close resemblance to the yacht "America."

As we find thus a certain equivalence in the ages, there is also an equipollence of individual genius to the nation which it represents. It is a curious fact, that a certain enormity of culture makes a man invisible to his contemporaries. 'T is always hard to go beyond your public. If they are satisfied with cheap performance, you will not easily arrive at better. If they know what is good, and require it, you will aspire and burn until you achieve it. But, from time to time, in history, men are born a whole age too soon. The founders of nations, the wise men and inventors, who shine afterwards as their gods, were probably martyrs in their own time. All the transcendent writers and artists of the world, — 't is doubtful who they were, — they are lifted so fast into mythology, — Homer, Menu, Viasa, Dædalus, Hermes, Zoroaster, even Swedenborg and Shakspeare. The early names are too typical, — Homer, or *blind man;* Menu, or *man;* Viasa, *compiler;* Dædalus, *cunning;* Hermes, *interpreter;* and so on. Probably, the men were so great, so self-fed, that the recognition of them by others was not necessary to them. And every one has heard the remark (too often, I fear, politely made), that the philosopher was above his audience. I think I have seen two or three great men who, for that reason, were of no account among scholars.

But Jove is in his reserves. The truth, the hope of any time, must always be sought in the minorities. Michel Angelo was the conscience of Italy. We grow free with his name, and find it ornamental now ; but in his own days, his friends were few ; and you would need to hunt him in a conventicle with the Methodists of the era, namely, Savonarola, Vittoria Colonna, Contarini, Pole, Occhino, — superior souls, the religious of that day, drawn to each other, and under some cloud with the rest of the world, — reformers, the radicals of the hour, banded against the corruptions of Rome, and as lonely and as hated as Dante before them.

I find the single mind equipollent to a multitude of minds, say to a nation of minds, as a drop of water balances the sea ; and under this view the problem of culture assumes wonderful interest. ɣ Culture implies all which gives the mind possession of its own powers ; as languages to the critic, telescope to the astronomer. Culture alters the political status of an individual. It raises a rival royalty in a monarchy. 'T is king against king. It is ever the romance of history in all dynasties,— the co-presence of the revolutionary force in intellect. It creates a personal independence which the mona ch cannot look down, and to which he must often succumb. If a man know the laws of nature better than other men, his nation cannot spare him ; nor if he know the power of numbers, the secret of geometry, of algebra, on which the computations of astronomy, of navigation, of machinery, rest. If he can converse better than any other, he rules the minds of men wherever he goes ; if he has imagination, he intoxicates men. If he has wit, he tempers despotism by epigrams : a song, a satire, a sentence, has played its part in great events. Eloquence a hundred times has turned the scale of war and peace at will. The history of Greece is at one time reduced to two persons, — Philip, or the successor of Philip, on one side, and Demosthenes, a private citizen, on the other. If he has a military genius, like Belisarius, or administrative faculty, like Chatham or Bismarck, he is the king's king. If a theologian of deep convictions and strong understanding carries his country with him, like Luther, the state becomes Lutheran, in spite of the Emperor, as Thomas à Becket overpowered the English Henry. Wit has a great charter. Popes and kings and Councils of

Ten are very sharp with their censorships and inquisitions, but it is on dull people. Some Dante or Angelo, Rabelais, Hafiz, Cervantes, Erasmus, Béranger, Bettine von Arnim, or whatever genuine wit of the old inimitable class, is always allowed. Kings feel that this is that which they themselves represent ; this is no red-kerchiefed, red-shirted rebel, but loyalty, kingship. This is real kingship, and their own only titular. Even manners are a distinction, which, we sometimes see, are not to be overborne by rank or official power, or even by other eminent talents, since they too proceed from a certain deep innate perception of fit and fair.

It is too plain that a cultivated laborer is worth many untaught laborers ; that a scientific engineer, with instruments and steam, is worth many hundred men, many thousands ; that Archimedes or Napoleon is worth for labor a thousand thousands ; and that in every wise and genial soul we have England, Greece, Italy, walking, and can dispense with populations of *navvies*.

Literary history and all history is a record of the power of minorities, and of minorities of one. Every book is written with a constant secret reference to the few intelligent persons whom the writer believes to exist in the million. The artist has always the masters in his eye, though he affect to flout them. Michel Angelo is thinking of Da Vinci, and Raffaello is thinking of Michel Angelo. Tennyson would give his fame for a verdict in his favor from Wordsworth. Agassiz and Owen and Huxley affect to address the American and English people, but are really writing to each other. Everett dreamed of Webster. McKay, the ship-builder, thinks of George Steers ; and Steers, of Pook, the naval constructor. The names of the masters at the head of each department of science, art, or function are often little known to the world, but are always known to the adepts ; as Robert Brown in botany, and Gauss in mathematics. Often the master is a hidden man, but not to the true student ; invisible to all the rest, resplendent to him. All his own work and culture form the eye to see the master. In politics, mark the importance of minorities of one, as of Phocion, Cato, Lafayette, Arago. The importance of the one person who has the truth over nations who have it not, is because power obeys reality, and not appearance ; according to quality, and not quantity. How much more are men than nations ! the wise and good souls, the stoics in Greece and Rome, Socrates in Athens, and saints in Judæa,

Alfred the king, Shakspeare the poet, Newton the philosopher, the perceiver, and obeyer of truth, — than the foolish and sensual millions around them! so that wherever a true man appears, everything usually reckoned great dwarfs itself; he is the only great event, and it is easy to lift him into a mythological personage.

Then the next step in the series is the equivalence of the soul to nature. I said that one of the distinctions of our century has been the devotion of cultivated men to natural science. The benefits thence derived to the arts and to civilization are signal and immense. They are felt in navigation, in agriculture, in manufactures, in astronomy, in mining, and in war. But over all their utilities, I must hold their chief value to be metaphysical. The chief value is not the useful powers he obtained, but the test it has been of the scholar. He has accosted this immeasurable nature, and got clear answers. He understood what he read. He found agreement with himself. It taught him anew the reach of the human mind, and that it was citizen of the universe.

The first quality we know in matter is centrality, — we call it gravity, — which holds the universe together, which remains pure and indestructible in each mote, as in masses and planets, and from each atom rays out illimitable influence. To this material essence answers Truth, in the intellectual world, — Truth, whose centre is everywhere, and its circumference nowhere, whose existence we cannot disimagine, — the soundness and health of things, against which no blow can be struck but it recoils on the striker, — Truth, on whose side we always heartily are. And the first measure of a mind is its centrality, its capacity of truth, and its adhesion to it.

When the correlation of the sciences was announced by Oersted and his colleagues, it was no surprise; we were found already prepared for it. The fact stated accorded with the auguries or divinations of the human mind. Thus, if we should analyze Newton's discovery, we should say that if it had not been anticipated by him, it would not have been found. We are told that, in posting his books, after the French had measured on the earth a degree of the meridian, when he saw that his theoretic results were approximating that empirical one, his hand shook, the figures danced, and he was so agitated that he was forced to call in an assistant to finish the computation. Why agitated? — but because, when he saw, in the fall of an apple to the ground, the fall of the earth to the sun, of the sun and of all suns to the centre, that perception was accompanied by the spasm of delight by which the intellect greets a fact more immense still, a fact really universal, — holding in intellect as in matter, in morals as in intellect — that atom draws to atom throughout nature, and truth to truth throughout spirit? His law was only a particular of the more universal law of centrality. Every law in nature, as gravity, centripetence, repulsion, polarity, undulation, has a counterpart in the intellect. The laws above are sisters of the laws below. Shall we study the mathematics of the sphere, and not its causal essence also? Nature is a fable, whose moral blazes through it. There is no use in Copernicus, if the robust periodicity of the solar system does not show its equal perfection in the mental sphere, — the periodicity, the compensatory errors, the grand reactions. I shall never believe that centrifugence and centripetence balance, unless mind heats and meliorates, as well as the surface and soil of the globe.

On this power, this all-dissolving unity, the emphasis of heaven and earth is laid. Nature is brute but as this soul quickens it; Nature always the effect, mind the flowing cause. Nature, we find, is ever as is our sensibility; it is hostile to ignorance, — plastic, transparent, delightful, to knowledge. Mind carries the law; history is the slow and atomic unfolding. All things admit of this extended sense, and the universe at last is only prophetic, or, shall we say, symptomatic, of vaster interpretation and results. Nature an enormous system, but in mass and in particle curiously available to the humblest need of the little creature that walks on the earth! The immeasurableness of Nature is not more astounding than his power to gather all her omnipotence into a manageable rod or wedge, bringing it to a hair-point for the eye and hand of the philosopher.

Here stretches out of sight, out of conception even, this vast Nature, daunting, bewildering, but all penetrable, all self-similar, — an unbroken unity, — and the mind of man is a key to the whole. He finds that the universe, as Newton said, " was made at one cast "; the mass is like the atom, — the same chemistry, gravity, and conditions. The asteroids are the chips of an old star, and a meteoric stone is a chip of an asteroid. As language is in the alphabet, so is entire Nature — the play of all its laws — in one atom. The good wit finds the law from a single observation, — the law, and its limitations, and its correspondences, — as the farmer finds his

cattle by a footprint. "State the sun, and you state the
planets, and conversely."

Whilst its power is offered to his hand, its laws to his science, not less its beauty speaks to his taste, imagination, and
sentiment. Nature is sanative, refining, elevating. How
cunningly she hides every wrinkle of her inconceivable antiquity under roses, and violets, and morning dew! Every inch
of the mountains is scarred by unimaginable convulsions, yet
the new day is purple with the bloom of youth and love.
Look out into the July night, and see the broad belt of silver
flame which flashes up the half of heaven, fresh and delicate
as the bonfires of the meadow-flies. Yet the powers of numbers cannot compute its enormous age,— lasting as space and
time,— embosomed in time and space. And time and space,
— what are they? Our first problems, which we ponder all
our lives through, and leave where we found them; whose
outrunning immensity, the old Greeks believed, astonished the
gods themselves; of whose dizzy vastitudes all the worlds of
God are a mere dot on the margin; impossible to deny, impossible to believe. Yet the moral element in man counterpoises
this dismaying immensity, and bereaves it of terror. The
highest flight to which the muse of Horace ascended was in
that triplet of lines in which he described the souls which can
calmly confront the sublimity of nature : —

> "Hunc solem, et stellas, et decedentia certis
> Tempora momentis, sunt qui formidine nulla
> Imbuti spectant."

The sublime point of experience is the value of a sufficient
man. Cube this value by the meeting of two such, — of two
or more such,— who understand and support each other, and
you have organized victory. At any time, it only needs the
contemporaneous appearance of a few superior and attractive
men to give a new and noble turn to the public mind.

The benefactors we have indicated were exceptional men,
and great because exceptional. The question which the present age urges with increasing emphasis, day by day, is,
whether the high qualities which distinguish them can be imparted? The poet Wordsworth asked, "What one is, why
may not millions be?" Why not? Knowledge exists to be imparted. Curiosity is lying in wait for every secret. The in-
quisitiveness of the child to hear runs to meet the eagerness
of the parent to explain. The air does not rush to fill a
vacuum with such speed as the mind to catch the expected

fact. Every artist was first an amateur. The ear outgrows the tongue, is sooner ripe and perfect; but the tongue is always learning to say what the ear has taught it, and the hand obeys the same lesson.

There is anything but humiliation in the homage men pay to a great man; it is sympathy, love of the same things, effort to reach them,—the expression of their hope of what they shall become, when the obstructions of their mal-formation and mal-education shall be trained away. Great men shall not impoverish, but enrich us. Great men,—the age goes on their credit; but all the rest, when their wires are continued, and not cut, can do as signal things, and in new parts of nature. "No angel in his heart acknowledges any one superior to himself but the Lord alone." There is not a person here present to whom omens that should astonish have not predicted his future, have not uncovered his past. The dreams of the night supplement by their divination the imperfect experiments of the day. Every soliciting instinct is only a hint of a coming fact, as the air and water that hang invisibly around us hasten to become solid in the oak and the animal. But the recurrence to high sources is rare. In our daily intercourse, we go with the crowd, lend ourselves to low fears and hopes, become the victims of our own arts and implements, and disuse our resort to the Divine oracle. It is only in the sleep of the soul that we help ourselves by so many ingenious crutches and machineries. What is the use of telegraphs? What of newspapers? To know in each social crisis how men feel in Kansas, in California, the wise man waits for no mails, reads no telegrams. He asks his own heart. If they are made as he is, if they breathe the like air, eat of the same wheat, have wives and children, he knows that their joy or resentment rises to the same point as his own. ' The inviolate soul is in perpetual telegraphic communication with the Source of events, has earlier information, a private despatch, which relieves him of the terror which presses on the rest of the community.

⌣ The foundation of culture, as of character, is at last the moral sentiment. This is the fountain of power, preserves its eternal newness, draws its own rent out of every novelty in science. Science corrects the old creeds; sweeps away, with every new perception, our infantile catechisms; and necessitates a faith commensurate with the grander orbits and universal laws which it discloses. Yet it does not surprise the moral sentiment. That was older, and awaited expectant these larger insights.

The affections are the wings by which the intellect launches on the void, and is borne across it. Great love is the inventor and expander of the frozen powers, the feathers frozen to our sides. It was the conviction of Plato, of Van Helmont, of Pascal, of Swedenborg, that piety is an essential condition of science, that great thoughts come from the heart. It happens sometimes that poets do not believe their own poetry; they are so much the less poets. But great men are sincere. Great men are they who see that spiritual is stronger than any material force, that thoughts rule the world. No hope so bright but is the beginning of its own fulfilment. Every generalization shows the way to a larger. Men say, Ah! if a man could impart his talent, instead of his performance, what mountains of guineas would be paid! Yes, but in the measure of his absolute veracity he does impart it. When he does not play a part, does not wish to shine, when he talks to men with the unrestrained frankness which children use with each other, he communicates himself, and not his vanity. All vigor is contagious, and when we see creation we also begin to create. Depth of character, height of genius, can only find nourishment in this soil. The miracles of genius always rest on profound convictions which refuse to be analyzed. Enthusiasm is the leaping lightning, not to be measured by the horse-power of the understanding. Hope never spreads her golden wings but on unfathomable seas. The same law holds for the intellect as for the will. When the will is absolutely surrendered to the moral sentiment, that is virtue; when the wit is surrendered to intellectual truth, that is genius. Talent for talent's sake is a bauble and a show. Talent working with joy in the cause of universal truth lifts the possessor to new power as a benefactor. I know well to what assembly of educated, reflecting, successful, and powerful persons I speak. Yours is the part of those who have received much. It is an old legend of just men, *Noblesse oblige;* or, superior advantages bind you to larger generosity. Now I conceive that, in this economical world, where every drop and every crumb is husbanded, the transcendent powers of mind were not meant to be misused. The Divine Nature carries on its administration by good men. Here you are set down, scholars and idealists, as in a barbarous age; amidst insanity, to calm and guide it; amidst fools and blind, to see the right done; among violent proprietors, to check self-interest, stone-blind and stone-deaf, by considerations of humanity to the workman and to his child; amongst angry politicians swelling with self-esteem, pledged to parties, pledged to clients, you are to make valid the large considerations of equity and good sense; under bad governments, to force on them, by your persistence, good laws. Around that immovable persistency of yours, statesmen, legislatures, must revolve, denying you, but not less forced to obey.

We wish to put the ideal rules into practice, to offer liberty instead of chains, and see whether liberty will not disclose its proper checks; believing that a free press will prove safer than the censorship; to ordain free trade, and believe that it will not bankrupt us; universal suffrage, believing that it will not carry us to mobs, or back to kings again. I believe that the checks are as sure as the springs. It is thereby that men are great, and have great allies. And who are the allies? Rude opposition, apathy, slander, — even these. Difficulties exist to be surmounted. The great heart will no more complain of the obstructions that make success hard, than of the iron walls of the gun which hinder the shot from scattering. It was walled round with iron tube with that purpose, to give it irresistible force in one direction. A strenuous soul hates cheap successes. It is the ardor of the assailant that makes the vigor of the defender. The great are not tender at being obscure, despised, insulted. Such only feel themselves in adverse fortune. Strong men greet war, tempest, hard times, which search till they find resistance and bottom. They wish, as Pindar said, "to tread the floors of hell, with necessities as hard as iron." Periodicity, reaction, are laws of mind as well as of matter. Bad kings and governors help us, if only they are bad enough. In England, it was the game laws which exasperated the farmers to carry the Reform Bill. It was what we call *plantation manners* which drove peaceable, forgiving New England to emancipation without phrase. In the Rebellion, who were our best allies? Always the enemy. The community of scholars do not know their own power, and dishearten each other by tolerating political baseness in their members. Now, nobody doubts the power of manners, or that wherever high society exists, it is very well able to exclude pretenders. The intruder finds himself uncomfortable, and quickly departs to his own gang. It has been our misfortune that the politics of America have been often immoral. It has had the worst effect on character. We are a complaisant,

forgiving people, presuming, perhaps, on a feeling of strength.
But it is not by easy virtue, where the public is concerned,
that heroic results are obtained. We have suffered our young
men of ambition to play the game of politics and take the immoral side without loss of caste, — to come and go without
rebuke. But that kind of loose association does not leave a
man his own master. He cannot go from the good to the evil
at pleasure, and then back again to the good. There is a text
in Swedenborg, which tells in figure the plain truth. He saw
in vision the angels and the devils; but these two companies
stood not face to face and hand in hand, but foot to foot, —
these perpendicular up, and those perpendicular down.

Brothers, I draw new hope from the atmosphere we breathe
to-day, from the healthy sentiment of the American people,
and from the avowed aims and tendencies of the educated
class. The age has new convictions. We know that in certain historic periods there have been times of negation, — a
decay of thought, and a consequent national decline; that in
France, at one time, there was almost a repudiation of the
moral sentiment, in what is called, by distinction, society, —
not a believer within the Church, and almost not a theist out
of it. In England, the like spiritual disease affected the upper
class in the time of Charles II., and down into the reign of the
Georges. But it honorably distinguishes the educated class
here, that they believe in the succor which the heart yields to
the intellect, and draw greatness from its inspirations. And
when I say the educated class, I know what a benignant
breadth that word has, — new in the world — reaching millions instead of hundreds. And more, when I look around
me, and consider the sound material of which the cultivated
class here is made up, — what high personal worth, what love
of men, what hope, is joined with rich information and practical power, and that the most distinguished by genius and culture are in this class of benefactors, — I cannot distrust this
great knighthood of virtue, or doubt that the interests of science, of letters, of politics and humanity, are safe. I think
their hands are strong enough to hold up the Republic. I
read the promise of better times and of greater men.

PERSIAN POETRY.

14*

PERSIAN POETRY.

TO Baron von Hammer Purgstall, who died in Vienna in 1856, we owe our best knowledge of the Persians. He has translated into German, besides the "Divan" of Hafiz, specimens of two hundred poets, who wrote during a period of five and a half centuries, from A. D. 1050 to 1600. The seven masters of the Persian Parnassus — Firdousi, Enweri, Nisami, Dschelaleddin, Saadi, Hafiz, and Dschami — have ceased to be empty names ; and others, like Ferideddin Attar and Omar Chiam, promise to rise in Western estimation. That for which mainly books exist is communicated in these rich extracts. Many qualities go to make a good telescope, — as the largeness of the field, facility of sweeping the meridian, achromatic purity of lenses, and so forth, — but the one eminent value is the space-penetrating power ; and there are many virtues in books, — but the essential value is the adding of knowledge to our stock, by the record of new facts, and, better, by the record of intuitions, which distribute facts, and are the formulas which supersede all histories.

Oriental life and society, especially in the Southern nations, stand in violent contrast with the multitudinous detail, the secular stability, and the vast average of comfort of the Western nations. Life in the East is fierce, short, hazardous, and in extremes. Its elements are few and simple, not exhibiting the long range and undulation of European existence, but rapidly reaching the best and the worst. The rich feed on fruits and game, — the poor, on a watermelon's peel. All or nothing is the genius of Oriental life. Favor of the Sultan, or his displeasure, is a question of Fate. A war is undertaken for an epigram or a distich, as in Europe for a duchy. The prolific sun, and the sudden and rank plenty which his heat engenders, make subsistence easy. On the other side, the desert, the simoom, the mirage, the lion, and the plague endanger it, and life hangs on the contingency of a skin of water more or less. The very geography of old Persia showed these contrasts. "My father's empire," said Cyrus to Xenophon, "is so large, that people perish with cold, at one extremity, whilst they are suffocated with heat, at the other." The temperament of the people agrees with this life in extremes. Religion and poetry are all their civilization. The religion teaches an inexorable Destiny. It distinguishes only two days in each man's history, — his birthday, called *the Day of the Lot*, and the Day of Judgment. Courage and absolute submission to what is appointed him are his virtues.

The favor of the climate, making subsistence easy, and encouraging an outdoor life, allows to the Eastern nations a highly intellectual organization, — leaving out of view, at present, the genius of the Hindoos (more Oriental in every sense), whom no people have surpassed in the grandeur of their ethical statement. The Persians and the Arabs, with great leisure and few books, are exquisitely sensible to the pleasures of poetry. Layard has given some details of the effect which the *improvvisatori* produced on the children of the desert. "When the bard improvised an amatory ditty, the young chief's excitement was almost beyond control. The other Bedouins were scarcely less moved by these rude measures, which have the same kind of effect on the wild tribes of the Persian mountains. Such verses, chanted by their self-taught poets, or by the girls of their encampment, will drive warriors to the combat, fearless of death, or prove an ample reward, on their return from the dangers of the *ghazon*, or the fight. The excitement they produce exceeds that of the grape. He who would understand the influence of the Homeric ballads in the heroic ages should witness the effect which similar compositions have upon the wild nomads of the East." Elsewhere he adds, "Poetry and flowers are the wine and spirits of the Arab; a couplet is equal to a bottle, and a rose to a dram, without the evil effect of either."

The Persian Poetry rests on a mythology whose few legends are connected with the Jewish history, and the anterior traditions of the Pentateuch. The principal figure in the allusions of Eastern poetry is Solomon. Solomon had three talismans: first, the signet-ring, by which he commanded the spirits, on the stone of which was engraven the name of God; second, the glass, in which he saw the secrets of his enemies,

and the causes of all things, figured ; the third, the east-wind,
which was his horse. His counsellor was Simorg, king of
birds, the all-wise fowl, who had lived ever since the beginning of the world, and now lives alone on the highest summit
of Mount Kaf. No fowler has taken him, and none now living
has seen him. By him Solomon was taught the language of
birds, so that he heard secrets whenever he went into his
gardens. When Solomon travelled, his throne was placed on
a carpet of green silk, of a length and breadth sufficient for
all his army to stand upon, — men placing themselves on his
right hand, and the spirits on his left. When all were in
order, the east-wind, at his command, took up the carpet and
transported it, with all that were upon it, whither he pleased,
— the army of birds at the same time flying overhead, and
forming a canopy to shade them from the sun. It is related,
that, when the Queen of Sheba came to visit Solomon, he had
built, against her arrival, a palace, of which the floor or pave-
ment was of glass, laid over running water, in which fish were
swimming. The Queen of Sheba was deceived thereby, and
raised her robes, thinking she was to pass through the water.
On the occasion of Solomon's marriage, all the beasts, laden
with presents, appeared before his throne. Behind them all
came the ant with a blade of grass : Solomon did not despise
the gift of the ant. Asaph, the vizier, at a certain time, lost
the seal of Solomon, which one of the Dews, or evil spirits,
found, and, governing in the name of Solomon, deceived the
people.

Firdousi, the Persian Homer, has written in the *Shah Nameh*
the annals of the fabulous and heroic kings of the country : of
Karun (the Persian Crœsus), the immeasurably rich gold-
maker, who, with all his treasures, lies buried not far from the
Pyramids, in the sea which bears his name ; of Jamschid, the
binder of demons, whose reign lasted seven hundred years ; of
Kai Kaus, in whose palace, built by demons on Alberz, gold
and silver and precious stones were used so lavishly that, in
the brilliancy produced by their combined effect, night and
day appeared the same ; of Afrasiyab, strong as an elephant,
whose shadow extended for miles, whose heart was bounteous
as the ocean, and his hands like the clouds when rain falls
to gladden the earth. The crocodile in the rolling stream had
no safety from Afrasiyab. Yet when he came to fight against the
generals of Kaus, he was but an insect in the grasp of Rustem,
who seized him by the girdle, and dragged him from his horse.

Rustem felt such anger at the arrogance of the King of Mazinderau, that every hair on his body started up like a spear. The gripe of his hand cracked the sinews of an enemy.

These legends, — with Chiser, the fountain of life, Tuba, the tree of life, — the romances of the loves of Leila and Medschum, of Chosru and Schirin, and those of the nightingale for the rose, — pearl-diving, and the virtues of gems, — the cohol, a cosmetic by which pearls and eyebrows are indelibly stained black, — the bladder in which musk is brought, — the down of the lip, the mole on the cheek, the eyelash, — lilies, roses, tulips, and jasmines, — make the staple imagery of Persian odes.

The Persians have epics and tales, but, for the most part, they affect short poems and epigrams. Gnomic verses, rules of life conveyed in a lively image, especially in an image addressed to the eye, and contained in a single stanza, were always current in the East; and if the poem is long, it is only a string of unconnected verses. They use an inconsecutiveness quite alarming to Western logic, and the connection between the stanzas of their longer odes is much like that between the refrain of our old English ballads,

> "The sun shines fair on Carlisle wall,"

or

> "The rain it raineth every day,"

and the main story.

Take, as specimens of these gnomic verses, the following: —

> "The secret that should not be blown
> Not one of thy nation must know;
> You may padlock the gate of a town,
> But never the mouth of a foe."

Or this of Omar Chiam : —

> "On earth's wide thoroughfares below
> Two only men contented go:
> Who knows what 's right and what 's forbid,
> And he from whom is knowledge hid."

Here is a poem on a melon, by Adsched of Meru : —

> "Color, taste, and smell, smaragdus, sugar, and musk,—
> Amber for the tongue, for the eye a picture rare,—
> If you cut the fruit in slices, every slice a crescent fair,—
> If you leave it whole, the full harvest moon is there."

Hafiz is the prince of Persian poets, and in his extraordinary gifts adds to some of the attributes of Pindar, Anacreon,

Horace, and Burns, the insight of a mystic, that sometimes affords a deeper glance at Nature than belongs to either of these bards. He accosts all topics with an easy audacity. "He only," he says, "is fit for company, who knows how to prize earthly happiness at the value of a nightcap. Our father Adam sold Paradise for two kernels of wheat, then blame me not, if I hold it dear at one grapestone." He says to the Shah, "Thou who rulest after words and thoughts which no ear has heard and no mind has thought, abide firm until thy young destiny tears off his blue coat from the old graybeard of the sky." He says, —

> "I batter the wheel of heaven
> When it rolls not rightly by ;
> I am not one of the snivellers
> Who fall thereon and die."

The rapidity of his turns is always surprising us : —

> "See how the roses burn !
> Bring wine to quench the fire !
> Alas ! the flames come up with us,—
> We perish with desire."

After the manner of his nation, he abounds in pregnant sentences which might be engraved on a sword-blade and almost on a ring.

"In honor dies he to whom the great seems ever wonderful."

"Here is the sum, that, when one door opens, another shuts."

"On every side is an ambush laid by the robber-troops of circumstance ; hence it is that the horseman of life urges on his courser at headlong speed."

"The earth is a host who murders his guests."

"Good is what goes on the road of Nature. On the straight way the traveller never misses."

> "Alas ! till now I had not known
> My guide and Fortune's guide are one."

> "The understanding's copper coin
> Counts not with the gold of love."

> "'T is writ on Paradise's gate,
> 'Woe to the dupe that yields to Fate !'"

> "The world is a bride superbly dressed ; —
> Who weds her for dowry must pay his soul."

> "Loose the knots of the heart ; never think on thy fate :
> No Euclid has yet disentangled that snarl."

> "There resides in the grieving
> A poison to kill;
> Beware to go near them
> 'T is pestilent still."

Harems and wine-shops only give him a new ground of observation, whence to draw sometimes a deeper moral than regulated sober life affords,— and this is foreseen : —

> "I will be drunk and down with wine;
> Treasures we find in a ruined house."

Riot, he thinks, can snatch from the deeply hidden lot the veil that covers it : —

> "To be wise the dull brain so earnestly throbs,
> Bring bands of wine for the stupid head."

> "The Builder of heaven
> Hath sundered the earth,
> So that no footway
> Leads out of it forth.

> "On turnpikes of wonder
> Wine leads the mind forth,
> Straight, sidewise, and upward,
> West, southward, and north.

> "Stands the vault adamantine
> Until the Doomsday;
> The wine-cup shall ferry
> Thee o'er it away."

That hardihood and self-equality of every sound nature, which result from the feeling that the spirit in him is entire and as good as the world, which entitle the poet to speak with authority, and make him an object of interest, and his every phrase and syllable significant, are in Hafiz, and abundantly fortify and ennoble his tone.

His was the fluent mind in which every thought and feeling came readily to the lips. "Loose the knots of the heart," he says. We absorb elements enough, but have not leaves and lungs for healthy perspiration and growth. An air of sterility, of incompetence to their proper aims, belongs to many who have both experience and wisdom. But a large utterance, a river that makes its own shores, quick perception and corresponding expression, a constitution to which every morrow is a new day, which is equal to the needs of life, at once tender and bold, with great arteries, — this generosity of ebb and flow satisfies, and we should be willing to die when our time comes, having had our swing and gratification. The difference is not so much in the quality of men's thoughts as in the power of uttering them. What is pent and smouldered in the dumb actor is not pent in the poet, but passes over into new form, at once relief and creation.

The other merit of Hafiz is his intellectual liberty, which is a certificate of profound thought. We accept the religions and politics into which we fall; and it is only a few delicate spirits who are sufficient to see that the whole web of convention is the imbecility of those whom it entangles, — that the mind suffers no religion and no empire but its own. It indicates this respect to absolute truth by the use it makes of the symbols that are most stable and reverend, and therefore is always provoking the accusation of irreligion.

Hypocrisy is the perpetual butt of his arrows.

"Let us draw the cowl through the brook of wine."

He tells his mistress, that not the dervis, or the monk, but the lover, has in his heart the spirit which makes the ascetic and the saint; and certainly not their cowls and mummeries, but her glances, can impart to him the fire and virtue needful for such self-denial. Wrong shall not be wrong to Hafiz for the name's sake. A law or statute is to him what a fence is to a nimble school-boy, — a temptation for a jump. "We would do nothing but good, else would shame come to us on the day when the soul must hie hence; and should they then deny us Paradise, the Houris themselves would forsake that, and come out to us."

His complete intellectual emancipation he communicates to the reader. There is no example of such facility of allusion, such use of all materials. Nothing is too high, nothing too low, for his occasion. He fears nothing, he stops for nothing. Love is a leveller, and Allah becomes a groom, and heaven a closet, in his daring hymns to his mistress or to his cupbearer. This boundless charter is the right of genius.

We do not wish to strew sugar on bottled spiders, or try to make mystical divinity out of the song of Solomon, much less out of the erotic and bacchanalian songs of Hafiz. Hafiz himself is determined to defy all such hypocritical interpretation, and tears off his turban and throws it at the head of the meddling dervis, and throws his glass after the turban. But the love or the wine of Hafiz is not to be confounded with vulgar debauch. It is the spirit in which the song is written that imports, and not the topics. Hafiz praises wine, roses, maid-

ens, boys, birds, mornings, and music, to give vent to his immense hilarity and sympathy with every form of beauty and
joy ; and lays the emphasis on these to mark his scorn of
sanctimony and base prudence.   These are the natural topics
and language of his wit and perception.   But it is the play of
wit and the joy of song that he loves ; and if you mistake
him for a low rioter he turns short on you with verses which
express the poverty of sensual joys, and to ejaculate with
equal fire the most unpalatable affirmations of heroic sentiment and contempt for the world.   Sometimes it is a glance
from the height of thought, as thus : —

" Bring wine ; for, in the audience-hall of the soul's independence, what is sentinel or Sultan? what is the wise man or the
intoxicated ? "

And sometimes his feast, feasters, and world are only one
pebble more in the eternal vortex and revolution of Fate : —

" I am : what I am
My dust will be again."

A saint might lend an ear to the riotous fun of Falstaff ; for
it is not created to excite the animal appetites, but to vent
the joy of a supernal intelligence.   In all poetry Pindar's rule
holds, — συνετοῖς φωνεί, it speaks to the intelligent ; and Hafiz
is a poet for poets, whether he write, as sometimes, with a
parrot's, or, as at other times, with an eagle's quill.

Every song of Hafiz affords new proof of the unimportance
of your subject to success, provided only the treatment be
cordial.   In general, what is more tedious than dedications or
panegyrics addressed to grandees?   Yet in the " Divan " you
would not skip them, since his muse seldom supports him
better.

" What lovelier forms things wear,
Now that the Shah comes back ! "

And again : —

" Thy foes to hunt, thy enviers to strike down,
Poises Arcturus aloft morning and evening his spear."

It is told of Hafiz, that, when he had written a compliment to a handsome youth, —

" Take my heart in thy hand, O beautiful boy of Shiraz !
I would give for the mole on thy cheek Samarcand and Buchara ! "—

the verses came to the ears of Timour in his palace.   Timour
taxed Hafiz with treating disrespectfully his two cities, to raise

and adorn which he had conquered nations. Hafiz replied, "Alas, my lord, if I had not been so prodigal, I had not been so poor!

The Persians had a mode of establishing copyright the most secure of any contrivance with which we are acquainted. The law of the *ghaselle*, or shorter ode, requires that the poet insert his name in the last stanza. Almost every one of several hundreds of poems of Hafiz contains his name thus interwoven more or less closely with the subject of the piece. It is itself a test of skill, as this self-naming is not quite easy. We remember but two or three examples in English poetry : that of Chaucer, in the "House of Fame"; Jonson's epitaph on his son,—

> "Ben Jonson his best piece of poetry" ;

and Cowley's,—

> "The melancholy Cowley lay."

But it is easy to Hafiz. It gives him the opportunity of the most playful self-assertion, always gracefully, sometimes almost in the fun of Falstaff, sometimes with feminine delicacy. He tells us, "The angels in heaven were lately learning his last pieces." He says, "The fishes shed their pearls, out of desire and longing as soon as the ship of Hafiz swims the deep."

> "Out of the East, and out of the West, no man understands me;
> O, the happier I, who confide to none but the wind!
> This morning heard I how the lyre of the stars resounded,
> 'Sweeter tones have we heard from Hafiz!'"

Again,—

> "I heard the harp of the planet Venus, and it said in the early morning, 'I am the disciple of the sweet-voiced Hafiz!'"

And again,—

> "When Hafiz sings, the angels hearken, and Anaitis, the leader of the starry host, calls even the Messiah in heaven out to the dance."

> "No one has unvailed thoughts like Hafiz, since the locks of the Word-bride were first curled."

> "Only he despises the verse of Hafiz who is not himself by nature noble."

But we must try to give some of these poetic flourishes the metrical form which they seem to require : —

> "Fit for the Pleiads' azure chord
> The songs I sung, the pearls I bored."

Another : —

> " I have no hoarded treasure,
>   Yet have I rich content;
> The first from Allah to the Shah,
>   The last to Hafiz went."

Another : —

> " High heart, O Hafiz! though not thine
>   Fine gold and silver ore;
> More worth to thee the gift of song,
>   And the clear insight more."

Again : —

> " O Hafiz! speak not of thy need;
>   Are not these verses thine?
> Then all the poets are agreed,
>   No man can less repine."

He asserts his dignity as bard and inspired man of his people.   To the vizier returning from Mecca he says, —

" Boast not rashly, prince of pilgrims, of thy fortune.   Thou hast indeed seen the temple; but I, the Lord of the temple.   Nor has any man inhaled from the musk-bladder of the merchant, or from the musky morning-wind, that sweet air which I am permitted to breathe every hour of the day."

And with still more vigor in the following lines : —

> "Oft have I said, I say it once more,
> I, a wanderer, do not stray from myself.
> I am a kind of parrot; the mirror is holden to me;
> What the Eternal says, I stammering say again.
> Give me what you will; I eat thistles as roses,
> And according to my food I grow and I give.
> Scorn me not, but know I have the pearl,
> And am only seeking one to receive it."

And his claim has been admitted from the first.   The muleteers and camel-drivers, on their way through the desert, sing snatches of his songs, not so much for the thought, as for their joyful temper and tone ; and the cultivated Persians know his poems by heart.   Yet Hafiz does not appear to have set any great value on his songs, since his scholars collected them for the first time after his death. .
     In the following poem the soul is figured as the Phœnix alighting on Tuba, the tree of Life : —

> " My phœnix long ago secured
>   His nest in the sky-vault's cope;
> In the body's cage immured,
>   He was weary of life's hope.

"Round and round this heap of ashes
  Now flies the bird amain,
But in that odorous niche of heaven
  Nestles the bird again.

"Once flies he upward, he will perch
  On Tuba's golden bough;
His home is on that fruited arch
  Which cools the blest below.

"If over this world of ours
  His wings my phœnix spread,
How gracious falls on land and sea
  The soul-refreshing shade!

"Either world inhabits he
  Sees oft below him planets roll;
His body is all of air compact,
  Of Allah's love his soul."

Here is an ode which is said to be a favorite with all educated Persians : —

"Come! — the palace of heaven rests on aëry pillars; —
Come, and bring me wine; our days are wind.
I declare myself the slave of that masculine soul
Which ties and alliance on earth once forever renounces.
Told I thee yester-morn how the Iris of heaven
Brought to me in my cup a gospel of joy?
O high-flying falcon! the Tree of Life is thy perch;
This nook of grief fits thee ill for a nest.
Hearken! they call to thee down from the ramparts of heaven;
I cannot divine what holds thee here in a net.
I, too, have a counsel for thee; O, mark it and keep it,
Since I received the same from the Master above:
Seek not for faith or for truth in a world of light-minded girls;
A thousand suitors reckons this dangerous bride.
Cumber thee not for the world, and this my precept forget not,
'T is but a toy that a vagabond sweetheart has left us.
Accept whatever befalls; uncover thy brow from thy locks;
Never to me nor to thee was option imparted;
Neither endurance nor truth belongs to the laugh of the rose.
The loving nightingale mourns; — cause enow for mourning; —
Why envies the bird the streaming verses of Hafiz?
Know that a god bestowed on him eloquent speech."

The cedar, the cypress, the palm, the olive, and fig-tree, the birds that inhabit them, and the garden flowers, are never wanting in these musky verses, and are always named with effect. "The willows," he says, "bow themselves to every wind, out of shame for their unfruitfulness." We may open anywhere on a floral catalogue.

"By breath of beds of roses drawn,
  I found the grove in the morning pure,
In the concert of the nightingales
  My drunken brain to cure.

> " With unrelated glance
> 　　I looked the rose in the eye:
> The rose in the hour of gloaming
> 　　Flamed like a lamp hard-by.

> " She was of her beauty proud,
> 　　And prouder of her youth,
> The while unto her flaming heart
> 　　The bulbul gave his truth.

> " The sweet narcissus closed
> 　　Its eye, with passion pressed;
> The tulips out of envy burned
> 　　Moles in their scarlet breast.

> " The lilies white prolonged
> 　　Their sworded tongue to the smell;
> The clustering anemones
> 　　Their pretty secrets tell."

Presently we have,—

> " All day the rain
> Bathed the dark hyacinths in vain,
> The flood may pour from morn till night
> Nor wash the pretty Indians white."

And so onward, through many a page.

This picture of the first days of Spring, from Enweri, seems to belong to Hafiz : —

> " O'er the garden water goes the wind alone
> 　　To rasp and to polish the cheek of the wave;
> The fire is quenched on the dear hearthstone,
> 　　But it burns again on the tulips brave."

Friendship is a favorite topic of the Eastern poets, and they have matched on this head the absoluteness of Montaigne.

Hafiz says,—

" Thou learnest no secret until thou knowest friendship ; since to the unsound no heavenly knowledge enters."

Ibn Jemin writes thus : —

> " Whilst I disdain the populace,
> I find no peer in higher place.
> Friend is a word of royal tone,
> Friend is a poem all alone.
> Wisdom is like the elephant,
> Lofty and rare inhabitant :
> He dwells in deserts or in courts;
> With hucksters he has no resorts."

Dschami says,—

> "A friend is he, who, hunted as a foe,
>   So much the kindlier shows him than before;
> Throw stones at him, or ruder javelins throw,
>   He builds with stone and steel a firmer floor."

Of the amatory poetry of Hafiz we must be very sparing in our citations, though it forms the staple of the " Divan." He has run through the whole gamut of passion,— from the sacred to the borders, and over the borders, of the profane. The same confusion of high and low, the celerity of flight and allusion which our colder muses forbid, is habitual to him. From the plain text,—

> " The chemist of love
>   Will this perishing mould,
> Were it made out of mire,
>   Transmute into gold,"—

he proceeds to the celebration of his passion ; and nothing in his religious or in his scientific traditions is too sacred or too remote to afford a token of his mistress. The Moon thought she knew her own orbit well enough ; but when she saw the curve on Zuleika's cheek, she was at a loss : —

> " And since round lines are drawn
>   My darling's lips about,
> The very Moon looks puzzled on,
>   And hesitates in doubt
> If the sweet curve that rounds thy mouth
> Be not her true way to the South."

His ingenuity never sleeps : —

> " Ah, could I hide me in my song,
>   To kiss thy lips from which it flows! —

and plays in a thousand pretty courtesies : —

> " Fair fall thy soft heart!
>   A good work wilt thou do ?
> O, pray for the dead
>   Whom thine eyelashes slew! "

And what a nest has he found for his bonny bird to take up her abode in ! —

> " They strew in the path of kings and czars
>   Jewels and gems of price :
> But for thy head I will pluck down stars,
>   And pave thy way with eyes.
>
> " I have sought for thee a costlier dome
>   Than Mahmoud's palace high,
> And thou, returning,. find thy home
>   In the apple of Love's eye."

Then we have all degrees of passionate abandonment : —

> " I know this perilous love-lane
> No whither the traveller leads,
> Yet my fancy the sweet scent of
> Thy tangled tresses feeds.
>
> " In the midnight of thy locks,
> I renounce the day ;
> In the ring of thy rose-lips,"
> My heart forgets to pray."

And sometimes his love rises to a religious sentiment : —

> " Plunge in yon angry waves,
> Renouncing doubt and care ;
> The flowing of the seven broad seas
> Shall never wet thy hair.
>
> " Is Allah's face on thee
> Bending with love benign,
> And thou not less on Allah's eye
> O fairest ! turnest thine."

We add to these fragments of Hafiz a few specimens from other poets.

NISAMI.

> " While roses bloomed along the plain,
> The nightingale to the falcon said,
> ' Why, of all birds, must thou be dumb ?
> With closed mouth thou utterest,
> Though dying, no last word to man.
> Yet sitt'st thou on the hand of princes,
> And feedest on the grouse's breast,
> Whilst I, who hundred thousand jewels
> Squander in a single tone,
> Lo! I feed myself with worms,
> And my dwelling is the thorn.' —
> The falcon answered, ' Be all ear:
> I, experienced in affairs,
> See fifty things, say never one;
> But thee the people prizes not,
> Who, doing nothing, say'st a thousand.
> To me, appointed to the chase,
> The king's hand gives the grouse's breast;
> Whilst a chatterer like thee
> Must gnaw worms in the thorn.   Farewell!' "

The following passages exhibit the strong tendency of the Persian poets to contemplative and religious poetry and to allegory.

ENWERI.

BODY AND SOUL.

> " A painter in China once painted a hall ; —
> Such a web never hung on an emperor's wall ; —

One half from his brush with rich colors did run.
The other he touched with a beam of the sun ;
So that all which delighted the eye in one side,
The same, point for point, in the other replied.
"In thee, friend, that Tyrian chamber is found ;
Thine the star-pointing roof, and the base on the ground :
Is one half depicted with colors less bright ?
Beware that the counterpart blazes with light !"

IBN JEMIN.

"I read on the porch of a palace bold
  In a purple tablet letters cast, —
'A house though a million winters old,
  A house of earth comes down at last ;
Then quarry thy stones from the crystal All.
And build the dome that shall not fall.'"

"What need," cries the mystic Feisi, "of palaces and tapestry ? What need even of a bed ?

"The eternal Watcher who doth wake
  All night in the body's earthen chest,
Will of thine arms a pillow make,
  And a bolster of thy breast."

Ferideddin Attar wrote the "Bird Conversations," a mystical tale, in which the birds, coming together to choose their king, resolve on a pilgrimage to Mount Kaf, to pay their homage to the Simorg. From this poem, written five hundred years ago, we cite the following passage, as a proof of the identity of mysticism in all periods. The tone is quite modern. In the fable, the birds were soon weary of the length and difficulties of the way, and at last almost all gave out. Three only persevered, and arrived before the throne of the Simorg.

"The bird-soul was ashamed ;
  Their body was quite annihilated ;
They had cleaned themselves from the dust,
  And were by the light ensouled.
What was, and was not, — the Past, —
  Was wiped out from their breast.
The sun from near-by beamed
  Clearest light into their soul ;
The resplendence of the Simorg beamed
  As one back from all three.
They knew not, amazed, if they
  Were either this or that.
They saw themselves all as Simorg,
  Themselves in the eternal Simorg.
When to the Simorg up they looked,
  They beheld him among themselves ;
And when they looked on each other,
  They saw themselves in the Simorg.

A single look grouped the two parties,
The Simorg emerged, the Simorg vanished,
This in that, and that in this,
As the world has never heard.
So remained they, sunk in wonder,
Thoughtless in deepest thinking,
And quite unconscious of themselves.
Speechless prayed they to the Highest
To open this secret,
And to unlock *Thou* and *We*.
There came an answer without tongue. —
'The Highest is a sun mirror;
Who comes to Him sees himself therein,
Sees body and soul, and soul and body ;
When you came to the Simorg,
Three therein appeared to you,
And had fifty of you come,
So had you seen yourselves as many.
Him has none of us yet seen.
Ants see not the Pleiades.
Can the gnat grasp with his teeth
The body of the elephant ?
What you see is He not ;
What you hear is He not.
The valleys which you traverse,
The actions which you perform,
They lie under our treatment
And among our properties.
You as three birds are amazed,
Impatient, heartless, confused :
Far over you am I raised,
Since I am in act Simorg.
Ye blot out my highest being,
That ye may find yourselves on my throne;
Forever ye blot out yourselves,
As shadows in the sun. Farewell! ' ''

INSPIRATION.

INSPIRATION.

I T was Watt who told King George III. that he dealt in an
article of which kings were said to be fond, — Power. 'T is
certain that the one thing we wish to know is, where power is
to be bought. But we want a finer kind than that of commerce ; and every reasonable man would give any price of
house and land, and future provision, for condensation, concentration, and the recalling at will of high mental energy.
Our money is only a second best. We would jump to buy
power with it, that is, intellectual perception moving the will.
That is first best. But we don't know where the shop is. If
Watt knew, he forgot to tell us the number of the street.
There are times when the intellect is so active that everything seems to run to meet it. Its supplies are found without
much thought as to studies. Knowledge runs to the man,
and the man runs to knowledge. In spring, when the snow
melts, the maple-trees flow with sugar, and you cannot get
tubs fast enough ; but it is only for a few days. The hunter
on the prairie, at the right season, has no need of choosing his
ground ; east, west, by the river, by the timber, he is everywhere near his game. But the favorable conditions are rather
the exception than the rule.

The aboriginal man in geology, and in the dim lights of
Darwin's microscope, is not an engaging figure. We are very
glad that he ate his fishes and snails and marrow-bones out
of our sight and hearing, and that his doleful experiences were
got through with so very long ago. They combed his mane,
they pared his nails, cut off his tail, set him on end, sent him
to school, and made him pay taxes, before he could begin to
write his sad story for the compassion or the repudiation of
his descendants, who are all but unanimous to disown him.
We must take him as we find him, — pretty well on in his

education, and, in all *our* knowledge of him, an interesting creature, with a will, an invention, an imagination, a conscience, and an inextinguishable hope.

The Hunterian law of *arrested development* is not confined to vegetable and animal structure, but reaches the human intellect also. In the savage man, thought is infantile; and in the civilized, unequal, and ranging up and down a long scale. In the best races it is rare and imperfect. In happy moments it is reinforced, and carries out what were rude suggestions to larger scope, and to clear and grand conclusions. The poet cannot see a natural phenomenon which does not express to him a correspondent fact in his mental experience; he is made aware of a power to carry on and complete the metamorphosis of natural into spiritual facts. Everything which we hear for the first time was expected by the mind; the newest discovery was expected. In the mind we call this enlarged power Inspiration. I believe that nothing great and lasting can be done except by inspiration, by leaning on the secret augury. The man's insight and power are interrupted and occasional; he can see and do this or that cheap task at will, but it steads him not beyond. He is fain to make the ulterior step by mechanical means. It cannot so be done. That ulterior step is to be also by inspiration; if not through him, then by another man. Every real step is by what a poet called "lyrical glances," by lyrical facility, and never by main strength and ignorance. Years of mechanic toil will only seem to do it; it will not so be done.

Inspiration is like yeast. 'T is no matter in which of half a dozen ways you procure the infection; you can apply one or the other equally well to your purpose, and get your loaf of bread. And every earnest workman, in whatever kind, knows some favorable conditions for his task. When I wish to write on any topic, 't is of no consequence what kind of book or man gives me a hint or a motion, nor how far off that is from my topic.

Power is the first good. Rarey can tame a wild horse; but if he could give speed to a dull horse, were not that better? The toper finds, without asking, the road to the tavern, but the poet does not know the pitcher that holds his nectar. Every youth should know the way to prophecy as surely as the miller understands how to let on the water or the engineer the steam. A rush of thoughts is the only conceivable prosperity that can come to us. Fine clothes, equipages, villa, park, social consideration, cannot cover up real poverty and insignificance from my own eyes, or from others like mine.

Thoughts let us into realities. Neither miracle, nor magic, nor any religious tradition, not the immortality of the private soul, is incredible, after we have experienced an insight, a thought. I think it comes to some men but once in their life, sometimes a religious impulse, sometimes an intellectual insight. But what we want is consecutiveness. 'T is with us a flash of light, then a long darkness, then a flash again. The separation of our days by sleep almost destroys identity. Could we but turn these fugitive sparkles into an astronomy of Copernican worlds ! With most men, scarce a link of memory holds yesterday and to-day together. Their house and trade and families serve them as ropes to give a coarse continuity. But they have forgotten the thoughts of yesterday ; they say to-day what occurs to them, and something else to-morrow. This insecurity of possession, this quick ebb of power, — as if life were a thunder-storm wherein you can see by a flash the horizon, and then cannot see your hand, — tantalizes us. We cannot make the inspiration consecutive. A glimpse, a point of view that by its brightness excludes the purview, is granted, but no panorama. A fuller inspiration should cause the point to flow and become a line, should bend the line and complete the circle. To-day the electric machine will not work, no spark will pass ; then presently the world is all a cat's back, all sparkle and shock. Sometimes there is no sea-fire, and again the sea is aglow to the horizon. Sometimes the Æolian harp is dumb all day in the window, and again it is garrulous, and tells all the secrets of the world. In June the morning is noisy with birds ; in August they are already getting old and silent.

Hence arises the question, Are these moods in any degree within control? If we knew how to command them ! But where is the Franklin with kite or rod for this fluid ? — a Franklin who can draw off electricity from Jove himself, and convey it into the arts of life, inspire men, take them off their feet, withdraw them from the life of trifles and gain and comfort, and make the world transparent, so that they can read the symbols of nature ? What metaphysician has undertaken to enumerate the tonics of the torpid mind, the rules for the recovery of inspiration ? That is least within control which is best in them. Of the *modus* of inspiration we have no knowledge. But in the experience of meditative men there is a certain agreement as to the conditions of reception. Plato, in his seventh Epistle, notes that the perception is only accomplished by long familiarity with the objects of intellect, and a life according to the things themselves. "Then a light, as if leaping from a fire, will on a sudden be enkindled in the soul, and will then itself nourish itself."

He said again, "The man who is his own master knocks in vain at the doors of poetry." The artists must be sacrificed to their art. Like the bees, they must put their lives into the sting they give. What is a man good for without enthusiasm ? and what is enthusiasm but this daring of ruin for its object ? There are thoughts beyond the reaches of our souls ; we are not the less drawn to them. The moth flies into the flame of the lamp ; and Swedenborg must solve the problems that haunt him, though he be crazed or killed.

There is genius as well in virtue as in intellect. 'T is the doctrine of faith over works. The raptures of goodness are as old as history and new with this morning's sun. The legends of Arabia, Persia, and India are of the same complexion as the Christian. Socrates, Menu, Confucius, Zertusht, — we recognize in all of them this ardor to solve the hints of thought.

I hold that ecstasy will be found normal, or only an example on a higher plane of the same gentle gravitation by which stones fall and rivers run. Experience identifies. Shakspeare seems to you miraculous ; but the wonderful juxtapositions, parallelisms, transfers, which his genius affected were all to him locked together as links of a chain, and the mode precisely as conceivable and familiar to higher intelligence as the index-making of the literary hack. The result of the hack is inconceivable to the type-setter who waits for it.

We must prize our own youth. Later, we want heat to execute our plans : the good-will, the knowledge, the whole armory of means, are all present ; but a certain heat that once used not to fail refuses its office, and all is vain until this capricious fuel is supplied. It seems a semi-animal heat ; as if tea, or wine, or sea-air, or mountains, or a genial companion, or a new thought suggested in book or conversation, could fire the train, wake the fancy, and the clear perception. Pit-coal, — where to find it ? 'T is of no use that your engine is made like a watch, — that you are a good workman, and know how to drive it, if there is no coal. We are waiting until some tyrannous idea emerging out of heaven shall

seize and bereave us of this liberty with which we are
falling abroad. Well, we have the same hint or suggestion,
day by day. "I am not," says the man, "at the top of my
condition to-day, but the favorable hour will come when I
can command all my powers, and when that will be easy to do
which is at this moment impossible." See how the passions
augment our force, — anger, love, ambition ! sometimes sympathy, and the expectation of men. Garrick said, that on the
stage his great paroxysms surprised himself as much as his
audience. If this is true on this low plane, it is true on the
higher. Swedenborg's genius was the perception of the
doctrine "that the Lord flows into the spirits of angels and
of men"; and all poets have signalized their consciousness
of rare moments when they were superior to themselves, —
when a light, a freedom, a power came to them, which
lifted them to performances far better than they could reach
at other times ; so that a religious poet once told me that
"he valued his poems, not because they were his, but because
they were not." He thought the angels brought them to
him.

Jacob Behmen said : "Art has not wrote here, nor was
there any time to consider how to set it punctually down according to the right understanding of the letters, but all was
ordered according to the direction of the spirit, which often
went on haste, — so that the penman's hand, by reason he
was not accustomed to it, did often shake. And, though I
could have written in a more accurate, fair, and plain manner,
the burning fire often forced forward with speed, and the hand
and pen must hasten directly after it, for it comes and goes
as a sudden shower. In one quarter of an hour I saw and
knew more, than if I had been many years together at an
university."

The depth of the notes which we accidentally sound on the
strings of nature is out of all proportion to our taught and
ascertained faculty, and might teach us what strangers and
novices we are, vagabond in this universe of pure power, to
which we have only the smallest key. Herrick said : —

> " 'T is not every day that I
> Fitted am to prophesy;
> No, but when the spirit fills
> The fantastic panicles,
> Full of fire, then I write
> As the Goddess doth indite.
> Thus, enraged, my lines are hurled,
> Like the Sibyl's, through the world:

15*

> Look how next the holy fire
> Either slakes, or doth retire;
> So the fancy cools, — till when
> That brave spirit comes again."

Bonaparte said : " There is no man more pusillanimous than I, when I make a military plan. I magnify all the dangers and all the possible mischances. I am in an agitation utterly painful. That does not prevent me from appearing quite serene to the persons who surround me. I am like a woman with child, and when my resolution is taken, all is forgot, except whatever can make it succeed."

There are, to be sure, certain risks in this presentiment of the decisive perception, as in the use of ether or alcohol.

> " Great wits to madness nearly are allied ;
> Both serve to make our poverty our pride."

Aristotle said : " No great genius was ever without some mixture of madness, nor can anything grand or superior to the voice of common mortals be spoken except by the agitated soul." We might say of these memorable moments of life, that we were in them, not they in us. We found ourselves by happy fortune in an illuminated portion or meteorous zone, and passed out of it again, so aloof was it from any will of ours. " 'T is a principle of war," said Napoleon, " that when you can use the lightning, 't is better than cannon."

How many sources of inspiration can we count? As many as our affinities. But to a practical purpose we may reckon a few of these.

1. Health is the first muse, comprising the magical benefits of air, landscape, and bodily exercise on the mind. The Arabs say that " Allah does not count from life the days spent in the chase," that is, those are thrown in. Plato thought " exercise would almost cure a guilty conscience." Sydney Smith said : " You will never break down in a speech on the day when you have walked twelve miles."

I honor health as the first muse, and sleep as the condition of health. Sleep benefits mainly by the sound health it produces ; incidentally also by dreams, into whose farrago a divine lesson is sometimes slipped. Life is in short cycles or periods ; we are quickly tired, but we have rapid rallies. A man is spent by his work, starved, prostrate ; he will not lift his hand to save his life ; he can never think more. He sinks into deep sleep and wakes with renewed youth, with hope, courage, fertile in resources, and keen for daring adventure.

> " Sleep is like death, and after sleep
>   The world seems new begun ;
> White thoughts stand luminous and firm,
>   Like statues in the sun ;
> Refreshed from supersensuous founts,
> The soul to clearer vision mounts." *

A man must be able to escape from his cares and fears, as well as from hunger and want of sleep ; so that another Arabian proverb has its coarse truth : "When the belly is full, it says to the head, Sing, fellow !" The perfection of writing is when mind and body are both in key ; when the mind finds perfect obedience in the body. And wine, no doubt, and all fine food, as of delicate fruits, furnish some elemental wisdom. And the fire, too, as it burns in the chimney ; for I fancy that my logs, which have grown so long in sun and wind by Walden, are a kind of muses. So of all the particulars of health and exercise, and fit nutriment, and tonics. Some people will tell you there is a great deal of poetry and fine sentiment in a chest of tea.

2. The experience of writing letters is one of the keys to the *modus* of inspiration. When we have ceased for a long time to have any fulness of thoughts that once made a diary a joy as well as a necessity, and have come to believe that an image or a happy turn of expression is no longer at our command, in writing a letter to a friend we may find that we rise to thought and to a cordial power of expression that costs no effort, and it seems to us that this facility may be indefinitely applied and resumed. The wealth of the mind in this respect of seeing is like that of a looking-glass, which is never tired or worn by any multitude of objects which it reflects. You may carry it all round the world, it is ready and perfect as ever for new millions.

3. Another consideration, though it will not so much interest young men, will cheer the heart of older scholars, namely, that there is diurnal and secular rest. As there is this daily renovation of sensibility, so it sometimes, if rarely, happens that after a season of decay or eclipse, darkening months or years, the faculties revive to their fullest force. One of the best facts I know in metaphysical science is Niebuhr's joyful record that, after his genius for interpreting history had failed him for several years, this divination returned to him. As this rejoiced me, so does Herbert's poem "The

* Allingham.

Flower." His health had broken down early, he had lost
his muse, and in this poem he says : —

> " And now in age I bud again,
> After so many deaths I live and write ;
> I once more smell the dew and rain,
> And relish versing: O my only light,
>   It cannot be
>   That I am he
> On whom thy tempests fell all night."

His poem called " The Forerunners " also has supreme interest. I understand " The Harbingers " to refer to the signs
of age and decay which he detects in himself, not only in his constitution, but in his fancy and his facility and grace in writing
verse ; and he signalizes his delight in this skill, and his pain
that the Herricks, Lovelaces, and Marlows, or whoever else,
should use the like genius in language to sensual purpose, and
consoles himself that his own faith and the divine life in him
remain to him unchanged, unharmed.

4. The power of the will is sometimes sublime ; and what
is will for, if it cannot help us in emergencies ? Seneca says
of an almost fatal sickness that befell him, " The thought of
my father, who could not have sustained such a blow as my
death, restrained me ; I commanded myself to live." Goethe
said to Eckermann, " I work more easily when the barometer
is high than when it is low. Since I know this, I endeavor,
when the barometer is low, to counteract the injurious effect
by greater exertion, and my attempt is successful."

" To the persevering mortal the blessed immortals are
swift." Yes, for they know how to give you in one moment
the solution of the riddle you have pondered for months.
" Had I not lived with Mirabeau," says Dumont, " I never
should have known all that can be done in one day, or, rather,
in an interval of twelve hours. A day to him was of more
value than a week or a month to others. To-morrow to him
was not the same impostor as to most others."

5. Plutarch affirms that " souls are naturally endowed with
the faculty of prediction, and the chief cause that excites this
faculty and virtue is a certain temperature of air and winds."
My anchorite thought it " sad that atmospheric influences
should bring to our dust the communion of the soul with the
Infinite." But I am glad that the atmosphere should be an
excitant, glad to find the dull rock itself to be deluged with
Deity, — to be theist, Christian, poetic. The fine influences
of the morning few can explain, but all will admit. Goethe

acknowledges them in the poem in which he dislodges the nightingale from her place as Leader of the Muses.

MUSAGETES.

"Often in deep midnights
I called on the sweet muses.
No dawn shines,
And no day will appear:
But at the right hour
The lamp brings me pious light,
That it, instead of Aurora or Phœbus,
May enliven my quiet industry.
But they left me lying in sleep
Dull, and not to be enlivened,
And after every late morning
Followed unprofitable days.

"When now the Spring stirred,
I said to the nightingales:
 Dear nightingales, trill
Early, O, early before my lattice,
Wake me out of the deep sleep
Which mightily chains the young man.'
But the love-filled singers
Poured by night before my window
Their sweet melodies, —
Kept awake my dear soul,
Roused tender new longings
In my lately touched bosom,
And so the night passed,
And Aurora found me sleeping;
Yea, hardly did the sun wake me.
At last it has become summer.
And at the first glimpse of morning
The busy early fly stings me
Out of my sweet slumber.
Unmerciful she returns again:
When often the half-awake victim
Impatiently drives her off,
She calls hither the unscrupulous sisters,
And from my eyelids
Sweet sleep must depart.
Vigorous, I spring from my couch,
Seek the beloved Muses,
Find them in the beech grove,
Pleased to receive me;
And I thank the annoying Insect
For many a golden hour.
Stand, then, for me, ye tormenting creatures,
Highly praised by the poet
As the true Musagetes."

The French have a proverb to the effect that not the day only, but all things have their morning, — "*Il n'y a que le matin en toutes choses.*" And it is a primal rule to defend your

morning, to keep all its dews on, and with fine foresight to
relieve it from any jangle of affairs, even from the question,
Which task? I remember a capital prudence of old President
Quincy, who told me that he never went to bed at night until
he had laid out the studies for the next morning. I believe
that in our good days a well-ordered mind has a new thought
awaiting it every morning. And hence, eminently thoughtful
men, from the time of Pythagoras down, have insisted on an
hour of solitude every day to meet their own mind, and learn
what oracle it has to impart. If a new view of life or mind
gives us joy, so does new arrangement. I don't know but we
take as much delight in finding the right place for an old observation, as in a new thought.

6. Solitary converse with nature; for thence are ejaculated
sweet and dreadful words never uttered in libraries. Ah!
the spring days, the summer dawns, the October woods! I
confide that my reader knows these delicious secrets, has perhaps

> "Slighted Minerva's learned tongue,
> But leaped with joy when on the wind the shell of Clio rung."

Are you poetical, impatient of trade, tired of labor and affairs? Do you want Monadnoc, Agiocochook, — or Helvellyn,
or Plinlimmon, dear to English song, in your closet? Caerleon,
Provence, Ossian, and Cadwallon? Tie a couple of strings
across a board and set it in your window, and you have an
instrument which no artist's harp can rival. It needs no instructed ear; if you have sensibility, it admits you to sacred
interiors; it has the sadness of nature, yet, at the changes,
tones of triumph and festal notes ringing out all measures of
loftiness. "Did you never observe," says Gray, " 'While
rocking winds are piping loud,' that pause, as the gust is rec-
ollecting itself, and rising upon the ear in a shrill and plaintive
note like the swell of an Æolian harp? I do assure you there
is nothing in the world so like the voice of a spirit." Perhaps
you can recall a delight like it, which spoke to the eye, when
you have stood by a lake in the woods, in summer, and saw
where little flaws of wind whip spots or patches of still water
into fleets of ripples, so sudden, so slight, so spiritual, that it
was more like the rippling of the Aurora Borealis, at night,
than any spectacle of day.

7. But the solitude of nature is not so essential as solitude
of habit. I have found my advantage in going in summer to
a country inn, in winter to a city hotel, with a task which

would not prosper at home. I thus secured a more absolute seclusion ; for it is almost impossible for a housekeeper, who is in the country a small farmer, to exclude interruptions, and even necessary orders, though I bar out by system all I can, and resolutely omit, to my constant damage, all that can be omitted. At home, the day is cut into short strips. In the hotel, I have no hours to keep, no visits to make or receive, and I command an astronomic leisure. I forget rain, wind, cold, and heat. At home, I·remember in my library the wants of the farm, and have all too much sympathy. I envy the abstraction of some scholars I have known, who could sit on a curbstone in State Street, put up their back, and solve their problem. I have more womanly eyes. All the conditions must be right for my success, slight as that is. What untunes is as bad as what cripples or stuns me. Novelty, surprise, change of scene, refresh the artist, — "break up the tiresome old roof of heaven into new forms," as Hafiz said. The sea-shore, and the taste of two metals in contact, and our enlarged powers in the presence, or rather at the approach and at the departure of a friend, and the mixture of lie in truth, and the experience of poetic creativeness which is not found in staying at home, nor yet in travelling, but in transitions from one to the other, which must therefore be adroitly managed to present as much transitional surface as possible, — these are the types or conditions of this power. "A ride near the sea, a sail near the shore," said the ancient. So Montaigne travelled with his books, but did not read in them. "*La Nature aime les croisements*," says Fourier.

I know there is room for whims here ; but in regard to some apparent trifles there is great agreement as to their annoyance. And the machine with which we are dealing is of such an inconceivable delicacy that whims also must be respected. Fire must lend its aid. We not only want time, but warm time. George Sand says, "I have no enthusiasm for nature which the slightest chill will not instantly destroy." And I remember that Thoreau, with his robust will, yet found certain trifles disturbing the delicacy of that health which composition exacted, — namely, the slightest irregularity, even to the drinking too much water on the preceding day. Even a steel pen is a nuisance to some writers. Some of us may remember, years ago, in the English journals, the petition, signed by Carlyle, Browning, Tennyson, Dickens, and other writers in London, against the license of the organ-grinders, who infested the streets near their houses, to levy on them blackmail.

Certain localities, as mountain-tops, the sea-side, the shores of rivers and rapid brooks, natural parks of oak and pine, where the ground is smooth and unencumbered, are excitants of the muse. Every artist knows well some favorite retirement. And yet the experience of some good artists has taught them to prefer the smallest and plainest chamber, with one chair and table, and with no outlook, to these picturesque liberties. William Blake said, "Natural objects always did and do weaken, deaden, and obliterate imagination in me." And Sir Joshua Reynolds had no pleasure in Richmond ; he used to say "the human face was his landscape." These indulgences are to be used with great caution. Allston rarely left his studio by day. An old friend took him, one fine afternoon, a spacious circuit into the country, and he painted two or three pictures as the fruits of that drive. But he made it a rule not to go to the city on two consecutive days. One was rest ; more was lost time. The times of force must be well husbanded, and the wise student will remember the prudence of Sir Tristram in *Morte d'Arthur,* who, having received from the fairy an enchantment of six hours of growing strength every day, took care to fight in the hours when his strength increased ; since from noon to night his strength abated. What prudence, again, does every artist, every scholar, need in the security of his easel or his desk ! These must be remote from the work of the house, and from all knowledge of the feet that come and go therein. Allston, it is said, had two or three rooms in different parts of Boston, where he could not be found. For the delicate muses lose their head, if their attention is once diverted. Perhaps if you were successful abroad in talking and dealing with men, you would not come back to your book-shelf and your task. When the spirit chooses you for its scribe to publish some commandment, it makes you odious to men, and men odious to you, and you shall accept that loathesomeness with joy. The moth must fly to the lamp, and you must solve those questions though you die.

8. Conversation, which, when it is best, is a series of intoxications. Not Aristotle, not Kant or Hegel, but conversation, is the right metaphysical professor. This is the true school of philosophy, — this the college where you learn what thoughts are, what powers lurk in those fugitive gleams, and

what becomes of them; how they make history. A wise man goes to this game to play upon others, and to be played upon, and at least as curious to know what can be drawn from himself as what can be drawn from them. For, in discourse with a friend, our thought, hitherto wrapped in our consciousness, detaches itself, and allows itself to be seen as a thought, in a manner as new and entertaining to us as to our companions. For provocation of thought, we use ourselves and use each other. Some perceptions — I think the best — are granted to the single soul; they come from the depth, and go to the depth, and are the permanent and controlling ones. Others it takes two to find. We must be warmed by the fire of sympathy to be brought into the right conditions and angles of vision. Conversation; for intellectual activity is contagious. We are emulous. If the tone of the companion is higher than ours, we delight in rising to it. 'Tis a historic observation that a writer must find an audience up to his thought, or he will no longer care to impart it, but will sink to their level, or be silent. Homer said, "When two come together, one apprehends before the other"; but it is because one thought well that the other thinks better: and two men of good mind will excite each other's activity, each attempting still to cap the other's thought. In enlarged conversation we have suggestions that require new ways of living, new books, new men, new arts and sciences. By sympathy, each opens to the eloquence, and begins to see with the eyes of his mind. We were all lonely, thoughtless; and now a principle appears to all : we see new relations, many truths; every mind seizes them as they pass; each catches by the mane one of these strong coursers like horses of the prairie, and rides up and down in the world of the intellect. We live day by day under the illusion that it is the fact or event that imports, whilst really it is not that which signifies, but the use we put it to, or what we think of it. We esteem nations important, until we discover that a few individuals much more concern us; then, later, that it is not at last a few individuals, or any sacred heroes, but the lowliness, the outpouring, the large equality to truth, of a single mind, — as if in the narrow walls of a human heart the whole realm of truth, the world of morals, the tribunal by which the universe is judged, found room to exist.

9. New poetry; by which I mean chiefly, old poetry that is new to the reader. I have heard from persons who had

w

practice in rhyming, that it was sufficient to set them on
writing verses, to read any original poetry. What is best in
literature is the affirming, prophesying, spermatic words of
men-making poets. Only that is poetry which cleanses and
mans me.

Words used in a new sense, and figuratively, dart a delightful lustre ; and *every* word admits a new use, and hints ulterior meanings. We have not learned the law of the mind, —
cannot control and domesticate at will the high states of contemplation and continuous thought. Neither by sea nor by
land," said Pindar, "canst thou find the way to the Hyper-
boreans "; neither by idle wishing, nor by rule of three or
rule of thumb. Yet I find a mitigation or solace by providing
always a good book for my journeys, as Horace, or Martial or
Goethe, — some book which lifts me quite out of prosaic
surroundings, and from which I draw some lasting knowledge.
A Greek epigram out of the anthology, a verse of Herrick or
Lovelace, are in harmony both with sense and spirit.

You shall not read newspapers, nor politics, nor novels, nor
Montaigne, nor the newest French book. You may read
Plutarch, Plato, Plotinus, Hindoo mythology, and ethics.
You may read Chaucer, Shakspeare, Ben Jonson, Milton, —
and Milton's prose as his verse ; read Collins and Gray ; read
Hafiz and the Trouveurs ; nay, Welsh and British mythology
of Arthur, and (in your ear) Ossian ; fact-books, which all
geniuses prize as raw material, and as antidote to verbiage
and false poetry. Fact-books, if the facts be well and thoroughly told, are much more nearly allied to poetry than many
books are that are written in rhyme. Only our newest knowledge works as a source of inspiration and thought, as only the
outmost layer of *liber* on the tree. Books of natural science,
especially those written by the ancients, — geography, botany,
agriculture, explorations of the sea, of meteors, of astronomy,
— all the better if written without literary aim or ambition.
Every book is good to read which sets the reader in a working mood. The deep book, no matter how remote the subject,
helps us best.

Neither are these all the sources, nor can I name all. The
receptivity is rare. The occasions or predisposing circumstances I could never tabulate ; but now one, now another
landscape, form, color, or companion, or perhaps one kind of
sounding word or syllable, "strikes the electric chain with
which we are darkly bound," and it is impossible to detect

and wilfully repeat the fine conditions to which we have owed our happiest frames of mind. The day is good in which we have had the most perceptions. The analysis is the more difficult, because poppy-leaves are strewn when a generalization is made ; for I can never remember the circumstances to which I owe it, so as to repeat the experiment or put myself in the conditions.

> " 'T is the most difficult of tasks to keep
> Heights which the soul is competent to gain."

I value literary biography for the hints it furnishes from so many scholars, in so many countries, of what hygiene, what ascetic, what gymnastic, what social practices their experience suggested and approved. They are, for the most part, men who needed only a little wealth. Large estates, political relations, great hospitalities, would have been impediments to them. They are men whom a book could entertain, a new thought intoxicate, and hold them prisoners for years perhaps. Aubrey and Burton and Wood tell me incidents which I find not insignificant.

These are some hints towards what is in all education a chief necessity, the right government, or, shall I not say, the right obedience to the powers of the human soul. Itself is the dictator ; the mind itself the awful oracle. All our power, all our happiness, consists in our reception of its hints, which ever become clearer and grander as they are obeyed.

GREATNESS.

GREATNESS.

THERE is a prize which we are all aiming at, and the more power and goodness we have, so much more the energy of that aim. Every human being has a right to it, and in the pursuit we do not stand in each other's way. For it has a long scale of degrees, a wide variety of views, and every aspirant, by his success in the pursuit, does not hinder but helps his competitors. I might call it completeness, but that is later, — perhaps adjourned for ages. I prefer to call it Greatness. It is the fulfilment of a natural tendency in each man. It is a fruitful study. It is the best tonic to the young soul. And no man is unrelated; therefore we admire eminent men, not for themselves, but as representatives. It is very certain that we ought not to be, and shall not be contented with any goal we have reached. Our aim is no less than greatness; that which invites all, belongs to us all, — to which we are all sometimes untrue, cowardly, faithless, but of which we never quite despair, and which, in every sane moment, we resolve to make our own. It is also the only platform on which all men can meet. What anecdotes of any man do we wish to hear or read? Only the best. Certainly not those in which he was degraded to the level of dulness or vice, but those in which he rose above all competition by obeying a light that shone to him alone. This is the worthiest history of the world.

Greatness, — what is it? Is there not some injury to us, some insult in the word? What we commonly call greatness is only such in our barbarous or infant experience. 'T is not the soldier, not Alexander or Bonaparte or Count Moltke surely, who represent the highest force of mankind; not the strong hand, but wisdom and civility, the creation of laws, institutions, letters, and art. These we call by distinction the *humanities;* these, and not the strong arm and brave heart, which are also indispensable to their defence. For the scholars represent the intellect, by which man is man; the intellect and the moral sentiment, — which in the last analysis can never be separated. Who can doubt the potency of an individual mind, who sees the shock given to torpid races — torpid for ages — by Mahomet; a vibration propagated over Asia and Africa? What of Menu? what of Buddha? of Shakspeare? of Newton? of Franklin?

There are certain points of identity in which these masters agree. Self-respect is the early form in which greatness appears. The man in the tavern maintains his opinion, though the whole crowd takes the other side; we are at once drawn to him. The porter or truckman refuses a reward for finding your purse, or for pulling you drowning out of the river. Thereby, with the service, you have got a moral lift. You say of some new person, That man will go far, — for you see in his manners that the recognition of him by others is not necessary to him. And what a bitter-sweet sensation when we have gone to pour out our acknowledgment of a man's nobleness, and found him quite indifferent to our good opinion! They may well fear Fate who have any infirmity of habit or aim; but he who rests on what he is, has a destiny above destiny, and can make mouths at Fortune. If a man's centrality is incomprehensible to us, we may as well snub the sun. There is something in Archimedes or in Luther or Samuel Johnson that needs no protection. There is somewhat in the true scholar which he cannot be laughed out of, nor be terrified or bought off from. Stick to your own; don't inculpate yourself in the local, social, or national crime, but follow the path your genius traces like the galaxy of heaven, for you to walk in.

A sensible person will soon see the folly and wickedness of thinking to please. Sensible men are very rare. A sensible man does not brag, avoids introducing the names of his creditable companions, omits himself as habitually as another man obtrudes himself in the discourse, and is content with putting his fact or theme simply on its ground. You shall not tell me that your commercial house, your partners, or yourself are of importance; you shall not tell me that you have learned to know men; you shall make me feel that; your saying so unsays it. You shall not enumerate your brilliant acquaintances, nor tell me by their titles what books you have read. I am to infer that you keep good company by your better information and manners, and to infer your reading from the wealth and accuracy of your conversation.

Young men think that the manly character requires that they should go to California, or to India, or into the army. When they have learned that the parlor and the college and the counting-room demand as much courage as the sea or the camp, they will be willing to consult their own strength and education in their choice of place.

There are to each function and department of nature supplementary men : to geology, sinewy, out-of-doors men, with a taste for mountains and rocks, a quick eye for differences and for chemical changes. Give such, first, a course in chemistry, and then a geological survey. Others find a charm and a profession in the natural history of man and the mammalia, or related animals ; others in ornithology, or fishes, or insects ; others in plants ; others in the elements of which the whole world is made. These lately have stimulus to their study through the extraordinary revelations of the spectroscope that the sun and the planets are made in part or in whole of the same elements as the earth is. Then there is the boy who is born with a taste for the sea, and must go thither if he has to run away from his father's house to the forecastle ; another longs for travel in foreign lands ; another will be a lawyer ; another, an astronomer ; another, a painter, sculptor, architect, or engineer. · Thus there is not a piece of nature in any kind, but a man is born, who, as his genius opens, aims slower or faster to dedicate himself to that. Then there is the poet, the philosopher, the politician, the orator, the clergyman, the physician. 'T is gratifying to see this adaptation of man to the world, and to every part and particle of it.

Many readers remember that Sir Humphrey Davy said, when he was praised for his important discoveries, " My best discovery was Michael Faraday." In 1848 I had the privilege of hearing Professor Faraday deliver, in the Royal Institution in London, a lecture on what he called Diamagnetism, — by which he meant *cross-magnetism ;* and he showed us various experiments on certain gases, to prove that whilst, ordinarily, magnetism of steel is from north to south, in other substances, gases, it acts from east to west. And further experiments led him to the theory that every chemical substance would be found to have its own, and a different, polarity. I do not know how far his experiments and others have been pushed in this matter, but one fact is clear to me, that diamagnetism is a law of the *mind*, to the full extent of Faraday's idea ; namely, that every mind has a new compass, a new north, a new direction of its own, differencing its genius and aim from every other mind ; — as every man, with whatever family resemblances, has a new countenance, new manner, new voice, new thoughts, and new character. Whilst he shares with all mankind the gift of reason and the moral sentiment, there is a teaching for him from within, which is leading him in a new path, and, the more it is trusted, separates and signalizes him, while it makes him more important and necessary to society. We call this specialty the *bias* of each individual. And none of us will ever accomplish anything excellent or commanding except when he listens to this whisper which is heard by him alone. Swedenborg called it the *proprium*, — not a thought shared with others, but constitutional to the man. A point of education that I can never too much insist upon is this tenet, that every individual man has a bias which he must obey, and that it is only as he feels and obeys this that he rightly develops and attains his legitimate power in the world. It is his magnetic needle, which points always in one direction to his proper path, with more or less variation from any other man's. He is never happy nor strong until he finds it, keeps it ; learns to be at home with himself ; learns to watch the delicate hints and insights that come to him, and to have the entire assurance of his own mind. And in this self-respect, or hearkening to the privatest oracle, he consults his ease, I may say, or need never be at a loss. In morals this is conscience ; in intellect, genius ; in practice, talent ; — not to imitate or surpass a particular man in *his* way, but to bring out your own new way ; to each his own method, style, wit, eloquence. 'T is easy for a commander to command. Clinging to Nature, or to that province of nature which he knows, he makes no mistakes, but works after her laws and at her own pace, so that his doing, which is perfectly natural, appears miraculous to dull people. Montluc, the great Marshal of France, says of the Genoese admiral, Andrew Doria, " It seemed as if the sea stood in awe of this man." And a kindred genius, Nelson, said, " I feel that I am fitter to do the action than to describe it." Therefore I will say that another trait of greatness is facility.

This necessity of resting on the real, of speaking *your* private thought and experience few young men apprehend. Set

ten men to write their journal for one day, and nine of them
will leave out their thought, or proper result, — that is, their
net experience, — and lose themselves in misreporting the
supposed experience of other people. Indeed, I think it an
essential caution to young writers, that they shall not in their
discourse leave out the one thing which the discourse was
written to say. Let that belief which you hold alone have
free course. I have observed that in all public speaking, the
rule of the orator begins, not in the array of his facts, but
when his deep conviction and the right and necessity he feels
to convey that conviction to his audience, — when these shine
and burn in his address ; when the thought which he stands
for gives its own authority to him, — adds to him a grander
personality, gives him valor, breadth, and new intellectual power,
so that not he, but mankind, seems to speak through his lips.
There is a certain transfiguration ; all great orators have it,
and men who wish to be orators simulate it.

If we should ask ourselves what is this self-respect, — it
would carry us to the highest problems. It is our practical
perception of the Deity in man. It has its deep foundations
in religion. If you have ever known a good mind among the
Quakers, you will have found *that* is the element of their
faith. As they express it, it might be thus : " I do not pretend to any commandment or large revelation, but if at any
time I form some plan, propose a journey, or a course of conduct, I perhaps find a silent obstacle in my mind that I cannot account for. Very well, — I let it lie, thinking it may
pass away, but if it do not pass away, I yield to it, obey it.
You ask me to describe it. I cannot describe it. It is not
an oracle, nor an angel, nor a dream, nor a law ; it is too
simple to be described, it is but a grain of mustard-seed, but
such as it is, it is something which the contradiction of all
mankind could not shake, and which the consent of all mankind could not confirm."

You are rightly fond of certain books or men that you have
found to excite your reverence and emulation. But none of
these can compare with the greatness of that counsel which is
open to you in happy solitude. I mean that there is for you
the following of an inward leader, — a slow discrimination that
there is for each a Best Counsel which enjoins the fit word and
the fit act for every moment. And the path of each pursued
leads to greatness. How grateful to find in man or woman a
new emphasis of their own.

But if the first rule is to obey your native bias, to accept that work for which you were inwardly formed, the second rule is concentration, which doubles its force. Thus if you are a scholar, be that. The same laws hold for you as for the laborer. The shoemaker makes a good shoe because he makes nothing else. Let the student mind his own charge; sedulously wait every morning for the news concerning the structure of the world which the spirit will give him.

No way has been found for making heroism easy, even for the scholar. Labor, iron labor, is for him. The world was created as an audience for him; the atoms of which it is made are opportunities. Read the performance of Bentley, of Gibbon, of Cuvier, Geoffroy St. Hilaire, Laplace. "He can toil terribly," said Cecil of Sir Walter Raleigh. These few words sting and bite and lash us when we are frivolous. Let us get out of the way of their blows, by making them true of ourselves. There is so much to be done that we ought to begin quickly to bestir ourselves. This day-labor of ours, we confess, has hitherto a certain emblematic air, like the annual ploughing and sowing of the Emperor of China. Let us make it an honest sweat. Let the scholar measure his valor by his power to cope with intellectual giants. Leave others to count votes and calculate stocks. His courage is to weigh Plato, judge Laplace, know Newton, Faraday, judge of Darwin, criticize Kant and Swedenborg, and on all these arouse the central courage of insight. The scholar's courage should be as terrible as the Cid's, though it grow out of spiritual nature, not out of brawn. Nature when she adds difficulty adds brain.

With this respect to the bias of the individual mind, add, what is consistent with it, the most catholic receptivity for the genius of others. The day will come when no badge, uniform, or medal will be worn; when the eye, which carries in it planetary influences from all the stars, will indicate rank fast enough by exerting power. For it is true that the stratification of crusts in geology is not more precise than the degrees of rank in minds. A man will say: 'I am born to this position; I must take it, and neither you nor I can help or hinder me. Surely, then, I need not fret myself to guard my own dignity.' The great man loves the conversation or the book that convicts him, not that which soothes or flatters him He makes himself of no reputation; he conceals his learning, conceals his charity. For the highest wisdom does not concern itself with particular men, but with man enamored with the law and the Eternal Source. Say with Antoninus, "If the picture is good, who cares who made it? What matters it by whom the good is done, by yourself or another?" If it is the truth, what matters who said it? If it was right, what signifies who did it? All greatness is in degree, and there is more above than below. Where were your own intellect, if greater had not lived? And do you know what the right meaning of Fame is? 'T is that sympathy, rather that fine element by which the good become partners of the greatness of their superiors.

Extremes meet, and there is no better example than the haughtiness of humility. No aristocrat, no prince born to the purple, can begin to compare with the self-respect of the saint. Why is he so lowly, but that he knows that he can well afford it, resting on the largeness of God in him? I have read in an old book that Barcena, the Jesuit, confessed to another of his order that when the Devil appeared to him in his cell, one night, out of his profound humility he rose up to meet him, and prayed him to sit down on his chair, for he was more worthy to sit there than himself.

Shall I tell you the secret of the true scholar? It is this: Every man I meet is my master in some point, and in that I learn of him. The populace will say, with Horne Tooke, "If you would be powerful, pretend to be powerful." I prefer to say, with the old Hebrew prophet, "Seekest thou great things, seek them not;" or, what was said of the Spanish prince, "The more you took from him, the greater he appeared," *Plus on lui ôte, plus il est grand.*

Scintillations of greatness appear here and there in men of unequal character, and are by no means confined to the cultivated and so-called moral class. 'T is easy to draw traits from Napoleon, who was not generous nor just, but was intellectual, and knew the law of things. Napoleon commands our respect by his enormous self-trust, — the habit of seeing with his own eyes, never the surface, but to the heart of the matter, whether it was a road, a cannon, a character, an officer, or a king, — and by the speed and security of his action in the premises, always new. He has left a library of manuscripts, a multitude of sayings, every one of widest application. He was a man who always fell on his feet. When one of his favorite schemes missed, he had the faculty of taking up his genius, as he said, and of carrying it somewhere else.

"Whatever they may tell you, believe that one fights with cannon as with fists; when once the fire is begun, the least want of ammunition renders what you have done already use-less." | I find it easy to translate all his technics into all of mine, and his official advices are to me more literary and philosophical than the memoirs of the Academy. \ His advice to his brother, King Joseph of Spain, was : "I have only one counsel for you, — *Be Master.*" Depth of intellect relieves even the ink of crime with a fringe of light. We perhaps look on its crimes as experiments of a universal student; as he may read any book who reads all books, and as the English judge in old times, when learning was rare, forgave a culprit who could read and write. \ 'T is difficult to find greatness pure.) Well, I please myself with its diffusion, — to find a spark of true fire amid much corruption. It is some guaranty, I hope, for the health of the soul which has this generous blood. How many men, detested in contemporary hostile history, of whom, now that the mists have rolled away, we have learned to correct our old estimates, and to see them as, on the whole, instruments of great benefit. Diderot was no model, but unclean as the society in which he lived; yet was he the best-natured man in France, and would help any wretch at a pinch. His humanity knew no bounds. A poor scribbler who had written a lampoon against him, and wished to dedi-cate it to a pious Duc d'Orleans, came with it in his poverty to Diderot, and Diderot, pitying the creature, wrote the dedi-cation for him, and so raised five-and-twenty louis to save his famishing lampooner alive.

Meantime we hate snivelling. I do not wish you to sur-pass others in any narrow or professional or monkish way. We like the natural greatness of health and wild power. I confess that I am as much taken by it in boys, and sometimes in people not normal, nor educated, nor presentable, nor church-members, — even in persons open to the suspicion of irregular and immoral living, — in Bohemians, — as in more orderly examples. For we must remember that in the lives of soldiers, sailors, and men of large adventure, many of the stays and guards of our household life are wanting, and yet the opportunities and incentives to sublime daring and perform-ance are often close at hand. We must have some charity for the sense of the people which admires natural power, and will elect it over virtuous men who have less. It has this excuse, that natural is really allied to moral power, and may always be expected to approach it by its own instincts. Intellect at least is not stupid, and will see the force of morals over men, if it does not itself obey. Henry VII. of England was a wise king. When Gerald, Earl of Kildare, who was in rebellion against him, was brought to London, and examined before the Privy Council, one said, " All Ireland cannot govern this Earl." "Then let this Earl govern all Ireland," replied the King.

'T is noted of some scholars, like Swift, and Gibbon and Donne, that they pretended to vices which they had not, so much did they hate hypocrisy. William Blake, the artist, frankly says, "I never knew a bad man in whom there was not something very good." Bret Harte has pleased himself with noting and recording the sudden virtue blazing in the wild reprobates of the ranches and mines of California.

Men are ennobled by morals and by intellect; but those two elements know each other and always beckon to each other, until at last they meet in the man, if he is to be truly great. The man who sells you a lamp shows you that the flame of oil, which contented you before, casts a strong shade in the path of the petroleum which he lights behind it; and this again casts a shadow in the path of the electric light. So does intellect when brought into the presence of character; character puts out that light. Goethe, in his correspondence with his Grand Duke of Weimar, does not shine. We can see that the Prince had the advantage of the Olmypian genius. It is more plainly seen in the correspondence between Voltaire and Frederick of Prussia. Voltaire is brilliant, nimble, and various, but Frederick has the superior tone. But it is curious that Byron *writes down* to Scott; Scott writes up to him. The Greeks surpass all men till they face the Romans, when Roman character prevails over Greek genius. Whilst degrees of intellect interest only classes of men who pursue the same studies, as chemists or astronomers, mathematicians or linguists, and have no attraction for the crowd, there are always men who have a more catholic genius, are really great as men, and inspire universal enthusiasm. A great style of hero draws equally all classes, all the extremes of society, till we say the very dogs believe in him. We have had such examples in this country, in Daniel Webster, Henry Clay, and the seamen's preacher, Father Taylor; in England, Charles James Fox; in Scotland, Robert Burns; and in France, though it is less intelligible to us, Voltaire. Abraham Lincoln is perhaps the most remarkable example of this class that we have seen, — a man who was at home and welcome with the humblest, and with a spirit and a practical vein in the times of terror that commanded the admiration of the wisest. His heart was as great as the world, but there was no room in it to hold the memory of a wrong.

These may serve as local examples to indicate a magnetism which is probably known better and finer to each scholar in the little Olympus of his own favorites, and which makes him require geniality and humanity in his heroes. What are these but the promise and the preparation of a day when the air of the world shall be purified by nobler society; when the measure of greatness shall be usefulness in the highest sense, — greatness consisting in truth, reverence, and good-will ?

Life is made of illusions, and a very common one is the opinion you hear expressed in every village : ' O yes, if I lived in New York or Philadelphia, Cambridge or New Haven or Boston or Andover there might be fit society; but it happens that there are no fine young men, no superior women in my town.' You may hear this every day; but it is a shallow remark. Ah! have you yet to learn that the eye altering alters all; "that the world is an echo which returns to each of us what we say"? 'T is not examples of greatness, but sensibility to see them, that is wanting. The good botanist will find flowers between the street pavements, and any man filled with an idea or a purpose will find examples and illustrations and coadjutors wherever he goes. Wit is a magnet to find wit, and character to find character. Do you not know that people are as those with whom they converse? And if all or any are heavy to me, that fact accuses me. Why complain, as if a man's debt to his inferiors were not at least equal to his debt to his superiors? If men were equals, the waters would not move; but the difference of level which makes Niagara a cataract, makes eloquence, indignation, poetry, in him who finds there is much to communicate. With self-respect, then, there must be in the aspirant the strong fellow-feeling, the humanity, which makes men of all classes warm to him as their leader and representative.

We are thus forced to express our instinct of the truth, by exposing the failures of experience. The man whom we have not seen, in whom no regard of self degraded the adorer of the laws, — who by governing himself governed others ; sportive in manner, but inexorable in act; who sees longevity in his cause; whose aim is always distinct to him; who is suffered to be himself in society; who carries fate in his eye; — he it is whom we seek, encouraged in every good hour that here or hereafter he shall be found.

IMMORTALITY.

IMMORTALITY.

IN the year 626 of our era, when Edwin, the Anglo-Saxon king, was deliberating on receiving the Christian missionaries, one of his nobles said to him : " The present life of man, O King, compared with that space of time beyond, of which we have no certainty, reminds me of one of your winter feasts, where you sit with your generals and ministers. The hearth blazes in the middle and a grateful heat is spread around, while storms of rain and snow are raging without. Driven by the chilling tempest, a little sparrow enters at one door and flies delighted around us till it departs through the other. Whilst it stays in our mansion it feels not the winter storm ; but when this short moment of happiness has been enjoyed, it is forced again into the same dreary tempest from which it had escaped, and we behold it no more. Such is the life of man, and we are as ignorant of the state which preceded our present existence as of that which will follow it. Things being so I feel that if this new faith can give us more certainty, it deserves to be received."

In the first records of a nation in any degree thoughtful and cultivated, some belief in the life beyond life would of course be suggested. The Egyptian people furnish us the earliest details of an established civilization, and I read, in the second book of Herodotus, this memorable sentence : " The Egyptians are the first of mankind who have affirmed the immortality of the soul." Nor do I read it with less interest, that the historian connects it presently with the doctrine of metempsychosis ; for I know well that, where this belief once existed, it would necessarily take a base form for the savage and a pure form for the wise ; — so that I only look on the counterfeit as a proof that the genuine faith had been there. The credence of men, more than race or climate, makes their

manners and customs; and the history of religion may be read
in the forms of sepulture.   There never was a time when the
doctrine of a future life was not held.   Morals must be en-
joined, but among rude men moral judgments were rudely
figured under the forms of dogs and whips, or of an easier and
more plentiful life after death.   And as the savage could not
detach in his mind the life of the soul from the body, he took
great care for his body.   Thus the whole life of man in the
first ages was ponderously determined on death; and, as we
know, the polity of the Egyptians, the by-laws of towns, of
streets and houses, respected burial.   It made every man an
undertaker, and the priesthood a senate of sextons.   Every
palace was a door to a pyramid; a king or rich man was a
pyramidaire.   The labor of races was spent on the excavation
of catacombs.   The chief end of man being to be buried well,
the arts most in request were masonry and embalming, to
give imperishability to the corpse.

The Greek, with his perfect senses and perceptions, had
quite another philosophy.   He loved life and delighted in
beauty.   He set his wit and taste, like elastic gas, under these
mountains of stone, and lifted them.   He drove away the
embalmers; he built no more of those doleful mountainous
tombs.   He adorned death, brought wreaths of parsley and
laurel; made it bright with games of strength and skill, and
chariot-races.   He looked at death only as the distributor of
imperishable glory.   Nothing can excel the beauty of his
sarcophagus.   He carried his arts to Rome, and built his
beautiful tombs at Pompeii.   The poet Shelley says of these
delicately carved white marble cells, "they seem not so much
tombs, as voluptuous chambers for immortal spirits."   In the
same spirit the modern Greeks, in their songs, ask that they
may be buried where the sun can see them, and that a little
window may be cut in the sepulchre, from which the swallow
might be seen when it comes back in the spring.

Christianity brought a new wisdom.   But learning depends
on the learner.   No more truth can be conveyed than the
popular mind can bear; and the barbarians who received the
cross took the doctrine of the resurrection as the Egyptians
took it.   It was an affair of the body, and narrowed again
by the fury of sect; so that grounds were sprinkled with holy
water to receive only orthodox dust; and to keep the body
still more sacredly safe for resurrection, it was put into the
walls of the church: and the churches of Europe are really

sepulchres. I read at Melrose Abbey the inscription on the ruined gate : —

> " The Earth goes on the Earth glittering with gold ;
> The Earth goes to the Earth sooner than it should ;
> The Earth builds on the Earth castles and towers ;
> The Earth says to the Earth, All this is ours."

Meantime the true disciples saw through the letter the doctrine of eternity which dissolved the poor corpse and nature also, and gave grandeur to the passing hour. The most remarkable step in the religious history of recent ages is that made by the genius of Swedenborg, who described the moral faculties and affections of man, with the hard realism of an astronomer describing the suns and planets of our system, and explained his opinion of the history and destiny of souls in a narrative form, as of one who had gone in a trance into the society of other worlds. Swedenborg described an intelligible heaven, by continuing the like employments in the like circumstances as those we know, — men in societies, in houses, towns, trades, entertainments, — continuations of our earthly experience. We shall pass to the future existence as we enter into an agreeable dream. All nature will accompany us there. Milton anticipated the leading thought of Swedenborg, when he wrote, in " Paradise Lost," —

> " What if Earth
> Be but the shadow of Heaven, and things therein
> Each to the other like more than on earth is thought ? "

Swedenborg had a vast genius, and announced many things true and admirable, though always clothed in somewhat sad and Stygian colors. These truths, passing out of his system into general circulation, are now met with every day, qualifying the views and creeds of all churches, and of men of no church. And I think we are all aware of a revolution in opinion. Sixty years ago, the books read, the sermons and prayers heard, the habits of thought of religious persons, were all directed on death. All were under the shadow of Calvinism and of the Roman Catholic purgatory, and death was dreadful. The emphasis of all the good books given to young people was on death. We were all taught that we were born to die ; and over that, all the terrors that theology could gather from savage nations were added to increase the gloom. A great change has occurred. Death is seen as a natural event, and is met with firmness. A wise man in our time caused to be written on his tomb, " Think on living." That inscription describes a progress in opinion. Cease from this antedating of your experience. Sufficient to to-day are the duties of to-day. Don't waste life in doubts and fears ; spend yourself on the work before you, well assured that the right performance of this hour's duties will be the best preparation for the hours or ages that follow it.

> " The name of death was never terrible
> To him that knew to live."

A man of thought is willing to die, willing to live ; I suppose, because he has seen the thread on which the beads are strung, and perceived that it reaches up and down, existing quite independently of the present illusions. A man of affairs is afraid to die, is pestered with terrors, because he has not this vision, and is the victim of those who have moulded the religious doctrines into some neat and plausible system, as Calvinism, Romanism, or Swedenborgism, for household use. It is the fear of the young bird to trust its wings. The experiences of the soul will fast outgrow this alarm. The saying of Marcus Antoninus it were hard to mend : " It were well to die if there be gods, and sad to live if there be none." I think all sound minds rest on a certain preliminary conviction, namely, that if it be best that conscious personal life shall continue, it will continue ; if not best, then it will not : and we, if we saw the whole, should of course see that it was better so. Schiller said, " What is so universal as death, must be benefit." A friend of Michel Angelo saying to him that his constant labor for art must make him think of death with regret, " By no means," he said ; " for if life be a pleasure, yet since death also is sent by the hand of the same Master, neither should that displease us." Plutarch, in Greece, has a deep faith that the doctrine of the Divine Providence and that of the immortality of the soul rest on one and the same basis. Hear the opinion of Montesquieu : " If the immortality of the soul were an error, I should be sorry not to believe it. I avow that I am not so humble as the atheist ; I know not how they think, but for me, I do not wish to exchange the idea of immortality against that of the beatitude of one day. I delight in believing myself as immortal as God himself. Independently of revealed ideas, metaphysical ideas give me a vigorous hope of my eternal well-being, which I would never renounce." *

* Pensées Diverses, p. 223.

I was lately told of young children who feel a certain terror at the assurance of life without end. "What! will it never stop?" the child said; "what!—never die? *never*, never? It makes me feel so tired." And I have in mind the expression of an older believer, who once said to me, "The thought that this frail being is never to end is so overwhelming that my only shelter is God's presence." This disquietude only marks the transition. The healthy state of mind is the love of life. What is so good, let it endure.

I find that what is called great and powerful life, — the administration of large affairs, in commerce, in the courts, in the state, — is prone to develop narrow and special talent; but, unless combined with a certain contemplative turn, a taste for abstract truth, for the moral laws, — does not build up faith, or lead to content. There is a profound melancholy at the base of men of active and powerful talent, seldom suspected. Many years ago, there were two men in the United States Senate, both of whom are now dead. I have seen them both; one of them I personally knew. Both were men of distinction, and took an active part in the politics of their day and generation. They were men of intellect, and one of them, at a later period, gave to a friend this anecdote : He said that when he entered the Senate he became in a short time intimate with one of his colleagues, and, though attentive enough to the routine of public duty, they daily returned to each other, and spent much time in conversation on the immortality of the soul, and other intellectual questions, and cared for little else. When my friend at last left Congress, they parted, his colleague remaining there, and, as their homes were widely distant from each other, it chanced that he never met him again, until, twenty-five years afterwards, they saw each other, through open doors, at a distance, in a crowded reception at the President's house in Washington. Slowly they advanced towards each other, as they could, through the brilliant company, and at last met, — said nothing, but shook hands long and cordially. At last his friend said, "Any light, Albert?" "None," replied Albert. "Any light, Lewis?" "None," replied he. They looked in each other's eyes silently, gave one more shake each to the hand he held, and thus parted for the last time. Now I should say that the impulse which drew these minds to this inquiry through so many years was a better affirmative evidence than their failure to find a confirmation was negative. I ought to add that, though men of good minds, they were both pretty strong materialists in their daily aims and way of life. I admit that you shall find a good deal of scepticism in the streets and hotels and places of coarse amusement. But that is only to say that the practical faculties are faster developed than the spiritual. Where there is depravity there is a slaughter-house style of thinking. One argument of future life is the recoil of the mind in such company, — our pain at every sceptical statement. The sceptic affirms that the universe is a nest of boxes with nothing in the last box. All laughter at man is bitter, and puts us out of good activity. When Bonaparte insisted that the heart is one of the entrails; that it is the pit of the stomach that moves the world; — do we thank him for the gracious instruction? Our disgust is the protest of human nature against a lie.

The ground of hope is in the infinity of the world, which infinity reappears in every particle; the powers of all society in every individual, and of all mind in every mind. I know against all appearances that the universe can receive no detriment; that there is a remedy for every wrong and a satisfaction for every soul. Here is this wonderful thought. But whence came it? Who put it in the mind? It was not I, it was not you; it is elemental,— belongs to thought and virtue, and whenever we have either, we see the beams of this light. When the Master of the universe has points to carry in his government he impresses his will in the structure of minds.

But proceeding to the enumeration of the few simple elements of the natural faith, the first fact that strikes us is our delight in permanence. All great natures are lovers of stability and permanence, as the type of the Eternal. After science begins, belief of permanence must follow in a healthy mind. Things so attractive, designs so wise, the secret workman so transcendently skilful that it tasks successive generations of observers only to find out, part with part, the delicate contrivance and adjustment of a weed, of a moss, to its wants, growth, and perpetuation, all these adjustments becoming perfectly intelligible to our study, — and the contriver of it all forever hidden! To breathe, to sleep, is wonderful. But never to know the Cause, the Giver, and infer his character and will! Of what import this vacant sky, these puffing elements, these insignificant lives full of selfish loves and quarrels and ennui? Everything is prospective, and man is to live hereafter. That the world is for his education is the only sane solution of the enigma. And I think that the naturalist works not for himself, but for the believing mind, which turns his discoveries to revelations, receives them as private tokens of the grand good-will of the Creator.

The mind delights in immense time ; delights in rocks, in metals, in mountain-chains, and in the evidence of vast geologic periods which these give ; in the age of trees, say of the Sequoias, a few of which will span the whole history of mankind ; in the noble toughness and imperishableness of the palm-tree, which thrives under abuse ; delights in architecture, whose building lasts so long, — "a house," says Ruskin, "is not in its prime until it is five hundred years old," — and here are the Pyramids, which have as many thousands, and cromlechs and earth-mounds much older than these.

We delight in stability, and really are interested in nothing that ends. What lasts a century pleases us in comparison with what lasts an hour. But a century, when we have once made it familiar and compared it with a true antiquity, looks dwarfish and recent ; and it does not help the matter adding numbers, if we see that it has an end, which it will reach just as surely as the shortest. A candle a mile long or a hundred miles long does not help the imagination ; only a self-feeding fire, an inextinguishable lamp, like the sun and the star, that we have not yet found date and origin for. But the nebular theory threatens their duration also, bereaves them of this glory, and will make a shift to eke out a sort of eternity by succession, as plants and animals do.

And what are these delights in the vast and permanent and strong, but approximations and resemblances of what is entire and sufficing, creative and self-sustaining life ? For the Creator keeps his word with us. These long-lived or long-enduring objects are to us, as we see them, only symbols of somewhat in us far longer-lived. Our passions, our endeavors, have something ridiculous and mocking, if we come to so hasty an end. If not to *be*, how like the bells of a fool is the trump of fame ! Nature does not, like the Empress Anne of Russia, call together all the architectural genius of the Empire to build and finish and furnish a palace of snow, to melt again to water in the first thaw. Will you, with vast cost and pains, educate your children to be adepts in their several arts, and, as soon as they are ready to produce a masterpiece, call out a file of soldiers to shoot them down ? We must infer our destiny from the preparation. We are driven by instinct to hive innumerable experiences, which are of no visible value, and which we may revolve through many lives before we shall assimilate or exhaust them. Now there is nothing in nature capricious, or whimsical, or accidental, or unsupported. Nature never moves by jumps, but always in steady and supported advances. The implanting of a desire indicates that the gratification of that desire is in the constitution of the creature that feels it ; the wish for food, the wish for motion, the wish for sleep, for society, for knowledge, are not random whims, but grounded in the structure of the creature, and meant to be satisfied by food, by motion, by sleep, by society, by knowledge. If there is the desire to live, and in larger sphere, with more knowledge and power, it is because life and knowledge and power are good for us, and we are the natural depositaries of these gifts. The love of life is out of all proportion to the value set on a single day, and seems to indicate, like all our other experiences, a conviction of immense resources and possibilities proper to us, on which we have never drawn.

All the comfort I have found teaches me to confide that I shall not have less in times and places that I do not yet know. I have known admirable persons, without feeling that they exhaust the possibilities of virtue and talent. I have seen what glories of climate, of summer mornings and evenings, of midnight sky, — I have enjoyed the benefits of all this complex machinery of arts and civilization, and its results of comfort. The good Power can easily provide me millions more as good. Shall I hold on with both hands to every paltry possession ? All I have seen teaches me to trust the Creator for all I have not seen. Whatever it be which the great Providence prepares for us, it must be something large and generous, and in the great style of his works. The future must be up to the style of our faculties, — of memory, of hope, of imagination, of reason. I have a house, a closet which holds my books, a table, a garden, a field : are these, any or all, a reason for refusing the angel who beckons me away, — as if there were no room or skill elsewhere that could reproduce for me as my like or my enlarging wants may require? We wish to live for what is great, not for what is mean. I do not wish to live for the sake of my warm house, my orchard, or my pictures. I do not wish to live to wear out my boots.

As a hint of endless being, we may rank that novelty which perpetually attends life. The soul does not age with the body. On the borders of the grave, the wise man looks forward with equal elasticity of mind, or hope; and why not, after millions of years, on the verge of still newer existence? — for it is the nature of intelligent beings to be forever new to life. Most men are insolvent, or promise by their countenance and conversation and by their early endeavor much more than they ever perform, — suggesting a design still to be carried out; the man must have new motives, new companions, new condition, and another term. Franklin said, "Life is rather a state of embryo, a preparation for life. A man is not completely born until he has passed through death." Every really able man, in whatever direction he work, — a man of large affairs, an inventor, a statesman, an orator, a poet, a painter, — if you talk sincerely with him, considers his work, however much admired, as far short of what it should be. What is this Better, this flying Ideal, but the perpetual promise of his Creator?

The fable of the Wandering Jew is agreeable to men, because they want more time and land in which to execute their thoughts. But a higher poetic use must be made of the legend. Take us as we are, with our experience, and transfer us to a new planet, and let us digest for its inhabitants what we could of the wisdom of this. After we have found our depth there, and assimilated what we could of the new experience, transfer us to a new scene. In each transfer we shall have acquired, by seeing them at a distance, a new mastery of the old thoughts, in which we were too much immersed. In short, all our intellectual action, not promises, but bestows a feeling of absolute existence. We are taken out of time and breathe a purer air. I know not whence we draw the assurance of prolonged life, of a life which shoots that gulf we call death, and takes hold of what is real and abiding, by so many claims as from our intellectual history. Salt is a good preserver; cold is: but a truth cures the taint of mortality better, and "preserves from harm until another period." A sort of absoluteness attends all perception of truth, — no smell of age, no hint of corruption. It is self-sufficing, sound, entire.

Lord Bacon said: "Some of the philosophers who were least divine denied generally the immortality of the soul, yet came to this point, that whatsoever motions the spirit of man could act and perform without the organs of the body might remain after death, which were only those of the understanding, and not of the affections; so immortal and incorruptible a thing did knowledge seem to them to be." And Van Hel-

mont, the philosopher of Holland, drew his sufficient proof
purely from the action of the intellect. "It is my greatest
desire," he said, "that it might be granted unto atheists to
have tasted, at least but one only moment, what it is intellectually to understand ; whereby they may feel the immortality of the mind, as it were, by touching." A farmer, a
laborer, a mechanic, is driven by his work all day, but it ends
at night ; it has an end. But, as far as the mechanic or farmer
is also a scholar or thinker, his work has no end. That which
he has learned is that there is much more to be learned. The
wiser he is, he feels only the more his incompetence. "What
we know is a point to what we do not know." A thousand
years, — tenfold, a hundred-fold his faculties, would not suffice.
The demands of his task are such that it becomes omnipresent.
He studies in his walking, at his meals, in his amusements,
even in his sleep. Montesquieu said, "The love of study is in
us almost the only eternal passion. All the others quit us in
proportion as this miserable machine which holds them approaches its ruin." "Art is long," says the thinker, "and life
is short." He is but as a fly or a worm to this mountain, this
continent, which his thoughts inhabit. It is a perception that
comes by the activity of the intellect ; never to the lazy or
rusty mind. Courage comes naturally to those who have the
habit of facing labor and danger, and who therefore know the
power of their arms and bodies ; and courage or confidence in
the mind comes to those who know by use its wonderful forces
and inspirations and returns. Belief in its future is a reward
kept only for those who use it. "To me," said Goethe, "the
eternal existence of my soul is proved from my idea of activity.
If I work incessantly till my death, nature is bound to give
me another form of existence, when the present can no longer
sustain my spirit."

It is a proverb of the world that good-will makes intelligence, that goodness itself is an eye ; and the one doctrine in
which all religions agree, is that new light is added to the
mind in proportion as it uses that which it has. "He that
doeth the will of God abideth forever."

Ignorant people confound reverence for the intuitions with
egotism. There is no confusion in the things themselves.
Health of mind consists in the perception of law. Its dignity
consists in being under the law. Its goodness is the most generous extension of our private interests to the dignity and
generosity of ideas. Nothing seems to me so excellent as a

belief in the laws. It communicates nobleness, and, as it were, an asylum in temples to the loyal soul.

I confess that everything connected with our personality fails. Nature never spares the individual; we are always balked of a complete success: no prosperity is promised to our self-esteem. We have our indemnity only in the moral and intellectual reality to which we aspire. That is immortal, and we only through that.

The soul stipulates for no private good. That which is private I see not to be good. "If truth live, I live; if justice live, I live," said one of the old saints, "and these by any man's suffering are enlarged and enthroned."

The moral sentiment measures itself by sacrifice. It risks or ruins property, health, life itself, without hesitation, for its thought, and all men justify the man by their praise for this act. And Mahomet in the same mind declared, "Not dead but living ye are to account all those who are slain in the way of God."

On these grounds I think that wherever man ripens, this audacious belief presently appears, — in the savage, savagely; in the good, purely. As soon as thought is exercised, this belief is inevitable; as soon as virtue glows, this belief confirms itself. It is a kind of summary or completion of man. It cannot rest on a legend; it cannot be quoted from one to another; it must have the assurance of a man's faculties that they can fill a larger theatre and a longer term than nature here allows him. Goethe said: "It is to a thinking being quite impossible to think himself non-existent, ceasing to think and live; so far does every one carry in himself the proof of immortality, and quite spontaneously. But so soon as the man will be objective and go out of himself, so soon as he dogmatically will grasp a personal duration to bolster up in cockney fashion that inward assurance, he is lost in contradiction." The doctrine is not sentimental, but is grounded in the necessities and forces we possess. Nothing will hold but that which we must be and must do.

> " Man's heart the Almighty to the Future set
> By secret but inviolable springs."

The revelation that is true is written on the palms of the hands, the thought of our mind, the desire of our heart, or nowhere. My idea of heaven is that there is no melodrama in it at all; that it is wholly real. Here is the emphasis of

conscience and experience ; this is no speculation, but the most
practical of doctrines. Do you think that the eternal chain
of cause and effect which pervades nature, which threads the
globes as beads on a string, leaves this out of its circuit, —
leaves out this desire of God and men as a waif and a caprice,
altogether cheap and common, and falling without reason or
merit ?

We live by desire to live; we live by choice; by will, by
thought, by virtue, by the vivacity of the laws which we obey,
and obeying share their life, — or we die by sloth, by disobe-
dience, by losing hold of life, which ebbs out of us. But
whilst I find the signatures, the hints and suggestions, noble
and wholesome, — whilst I find that all the ways of virtuous
living lead upward and not downward, — yet it is not my duty
to prove to myself the immortality of the soul. That knowledge is hidden very cunningly. Perhaps the archangels cannot find the secret of their existence, as the eye cannot see
itself ; but, ending or endless, to live whilst I live.

There is a drawback to the value of all statements of the
doctrine ; and I think that one abstains from writing or printing on the immortality of the soul, because, when he comes to
the end of his statement, the hungry eyes that run through
it will close disappointed ; the listeners say, That is not here
which we desire, — and I shall be as much wronged by their
hasty conclusion, as they feel themselves wronged by my
omissions. I mean that I am a better believer, and all serious
souls are better believers, in the immortality that we can give
grounds for. The real evidence is too subtle, or is higher
than we can write down in propositions, and therefore Wordsworth's "Ode" is the best modern essay on the subject.

We cannot prove our faith by syllogisms. The argument
refuses to form in the mind. A conclusion, an inference, a
grand augury, is ever hovering; but attempt to ground it,
and the reasons are all vanishing and inadequate. You cannot make a written theory or demonstration of this as you
can an orrery of the Copernican astronomy. It must be
sacredly treated. Speak of the mount in the mount. Not
by literature or theology, but only by rare integrity, by a
man permeated and perfumed with airs of heaven, — with
manliest or womanliest enduring love, — can the vision be
clear to a use the most sublime. And hence the fact that in
the minds of men the testimony of a few inspired souls has
had such weight and penetration. You shall not say, " O my

bishop, O my pastor, is there any resurrection? What do you think? Did Dr. Channing believe that we should know each other? did Wesley? did Butler? did Fenelon?" What questions are these! Go read Milton, Shakspeare, or any truly ideal poet. Read Plato, or any seer of the interior realities. Read St. Augustine, Swedenborg, Immanuel Kant. Let any master simply recite to you the substantial laws of the intellect, and in the presence of the laws themselves you will never ask such primary-school questions.

Is immortality only an intellectual quality, or, shall I say, only an energy, there being no passive? He has it, and he alone, who gives life to all names, persons, things, where he comes. No religion, not the wildest mythology, dies for him; no art is lost. He vivifies what he touches. Future state is an illusion for the ever-present state. It is not length of life but depth of life. It is not duration, but a taking of the soul out of time, as all high action of the mind does: when we are living in the sentiments we ask no questions about time. The spiritual world takes place; — that which is always the same. But see how the sentiment is wise. Jesus explained nothing, but the influence of him took people out of time, and they felt eternal. A great integrity makes us immortal; an admiration, a deep love, a strong will, arms us above fear. It makes a day memorable. We say we lived years in that hour. It is strange that Jesus is esteemed by mankind the bringer of the doctrine of immortality. He is never once weak or sentimental; he is very abstemious of explanation, he never preaches the personal immortality; whilst Plato and Cicero had both allowed themselves to overstep the stern limits of the spirit, and gratify the people with that picture.

How ill agrees this majestical immortality of our religion with the frivolous population! Will you build magnificently for mice? Will you offer empires to such as cannot set a house or private affairs in order? Here are people who cannot dispose of a day; an hour hangs heavy on their hands; and will you offer them rolling ages without end? But this is the way we rise. Within every man's thought is a higher thought, — within the character he exhibits to-day, a higher character. The youth puts off the illusions of the child, the man puts off the ignorance and tumultuous passions of youth; proceeding thence puts off the egotism of manhood, and becomes at last a public and universal soul. He is rising to greater heights, but also rising to realities; the outer relations and circumstances dying out, he entering deeper into God, God into him, until the last garment of egotism falls, and he is with God, — shares the will and the immensity of the First Cause.

It is curious to find the selfsame feeling, that it is not immortality, but eternity, — not duration, but a state of abandonment to the Highest, and so the sharing of His perfection, — appearing in the farthest east and west. The human mind takes no account of geography, language, or legends, but in all utters the same instinct.

Yama, the Lord of Death, promised Nachiketas, the son of Gautama, to grant him three boons at his own choice. Nachiketas, knowing that his father Gautama was offended with him, said, "O Death! let Gautama be appeased in mind, and forget his anger against me : this I choose for the first boon." Yama said, "Through my favor, Gautama will remember thee with love as before." For the second boon, Nachiketas asks that the fire by which heaven is gained be made known to him ; which also Yama allows, and says, "Choose the third boon, O Nachiketas!" Nachiketas said, there is this inquiry. Some say the soul exists after the death of man ; others say it does not exist. This I should like to know, instructed by thee. Such is the third of the boons. Yama said, "For this question, it was inquired of old, even by the gods; for it is not easy to understand it. Subtle is its nature. Choose another boon, O Nachiketas! Do not compel me to this." Nachiketas said, "Even by the gods was it inquired. And as to what thou sayest, O Death, that it is not easy to understand it, there is no other speaker to be found like thee. There is no other boon like this." Yama said, "Choose sons and grandsons who may live a hundred years ; choose herds of cattle ; choose elephants and gold and horses ; choose the wide expanded earth, and live thyself as many years as thou listeth. Or, if thou knowest a boon like this, choose it, together with wealth and far-extending life. Be a king, O Nachiketas! On the wide earth I will make thee the enjoyer of all desires. All those desires that are difficult to gain in the world of mortals, all those ask thou at thy pleasure ; — those fair nymphs of heaven with their chariots, with their musical instruments ; for the like of them are not to be gained by men. I will give them to thee, but do not ask the question of the state of the soul after death." Nachiketas said, "All those enjoyments are of yesterday. With thee remain thy horses and elephants, with thee the dance and song. If we should obtain wealth, we live only as long as thou pleasest. The boon which I choose I have said." Yama said, "One thing is good, another is pleasant. Blessed is he who takes the good, but he who chooses the pleasant loses the object of man. But thou, considering the objects of desire, hast abandoned them. These two, ignorance (whose object is what is pleasant) and knowledge (whose object is what is good), are known to be far asunder, and to lead to different goals. Believing this world exists, and not the other, the careless youth is subject to my sway. That knowledge for which thou hast asked is not to be obtained by argument. I know worldly happiness is transient, for that firm one is not to be obtained by what is not firm. The wise, by means of the union of the intellect with the soul, thinking him whom it is hard to behold, leaves both grief and joy. Thee, O Nachiketas! I believe a house whose door is open to Brahma. Brahma the supreme, whoever knows him, obtains whatever he wishes. The soul is not born; it does not die; it was not produced from any one. Nor was any produced from it. Unborn, eternal, it is not slain, though the body is slain; subtler than what is subtle, greater than what is great, sitting it goes far, sleeping it goes everywhere. Thinking the soul as unbodily among bodies, firm among fleeting things, the wise man casts off all grief. The soul cannot be gained by knowledge, not by understanding, not by manifold science. It can be obtained by the soul by which it is desired. It reveals its own truths."

FORTUNE OF THE REPUBLIC.

FORTUNE OF THE REPUBLIC.

I T is a rule that holds in economy as well as in hydraulics, that you must have a source higher than your tap. The mills, the shops, the theatre and the caucus, the college and the church, have all found out this secret. The sailors sail by chronometers that do not lose two or three seconds in a year, ever since Newton explained to Parliament that the way to improve navigation was to get good watches, and to offer public premiums for a better time-keeper than any then in use. The manufacturers rely on turbines of hydraulic perfection; the carpet-mill, on mordants and dyes which exhaust the skill of the chemist; the calico print, on designers of genius who draw the wages of artists, not of artisans. Wedgewood, the eminent potter, bravely took the sculptor Flaxman to counsel, who said, "Send to Italy, search the museums for the forms of old Etruscan vases, urns, water-pots, domestic and sacrificial vessels of all kinds." They built great works and called their manufacturing village Etruria. Flaxman, with his Greek taste, selected and combined the loveliest forms, which were executed in English clay; sent boxes of these as gifts to every court of Europe, and formed the taste of the world. It was a renaissance of the breakfast table and china-closet. The brave manufacturers made their fortune. The jewellers imitated the revived models in silver and gold.

The theatre avails itself of the best talent of poet, of painter, and of amateur of taste, to make the *ensemble* of dramatic effect. The marine insurance office has its mathematical counsellor to settle averages; the life-assurance, its table of annuities. The wine merchant has his analyst and taster, the more exquisite the better. He has also, I fear, his debts to the chemist as well as to the vineyard.

Our modern wealth stands on a few staples, and the interest

nations took in our war was exasperated by the importance of the cotton trade. And what is cotton? One plant out of some two hundred thousand known to the botanist, vastly the larger part of which are reckoned weeds. And what is a weed? A plant whose virtues have not yet been discovered, — every one of the two hundred thousand probably yet to be of utility in the arts. As Bacchus of the vine, Ceres of the wheat, as Arkwright and Whitney were the demi-gods of cotton, so prolific Time will yet bring an inventor to every plant. There is not a property in nature but a mind is born to seek and find it. For it is not the plants or the animals, innumerable as they are, nor the whole magazine of material nature that can give the sum of power, but the infinite applicability of these things in the hands of thinking man, every new application being equivalent to a new material.

Our sleepy civilization, ever since Roger Bacon and Monk Schwartz invented gunpowder, has built its whole art of war, all fortification by land and sea, all drill and military education, on that one compound, — all is an extension of a gun-barrel, — and is very scornful about bows and arrows, and reckons Greeks and Romans and Middle Ages little better than Indians and bow-and-arrow times. As if the earth, water, gases, lightning and caloric had not a million energies, the discovery of any one of which could change the art of war again, and put an end to war by the exterminating forces man can apply.

Now, if this is true in all the useful and in the fine arts, that the direction must be drawn from a superior source or there will be no good work, does it hold less in our social and civil life?

In our popular politics you may note that each aspirant who rises above the crowd, however at first making his obedient apprenticeship in party tactics, if he have sagacity, soon learns that it is by no means by obeying the vulgar weathercock of his party, the resentments, the fears, and whims of it, that real power is gained, but that he must often face and resist the party, and abide by his resistance, and put them in fear; that the only title to their permanent respect, and to a larger following, is to see for himself what is the real public interest, and to stand for that; — that is a principle, and all the cheering and hissing of the crowd must by and by accommodate itself to it. Our times easily afford you very good examples.

The law of water and all fluids is true of wit. Prince Metternich said, "Revolutions begin in the best heads and run

steadily down to the populace." It is a very old observation ; not truer because Metternich said it, and not less true.
\ There have been revolutions which were not in the interest of feudalism and barbarism, but in that of society. And these are distinguished not by the numbers of the combatants nor the numbers of the slain, but by the motive. No interest now attaches to the wars of York and Lancaster, to the wars of German, French, and Spanish emperors, which were only dynastic wars, but to those in which a principle was involved. These are read with passionate interest and never lose their pathos by time. When the cannon is aimed by ideas, when men with religious convictions are behind it, when men die for what they live for, and the mainspring that works daily urges them to hazard all, then the cannon articulates its explosions with the voice of a man, then the rifle seconds the cannon and the fowling-piece the rifle, and the women make the cartridges, and all shoot at one mark ; then gods join in the combat ; then poets are born, and the better code of laws at last records the victory.

Now the culmination of these triumphs of humanity — and which did virtually include the extinction of slavery — is the planting of America.

At every moment some one country more than any other represents the sentiment and the future of mankind. None will doubt that America occupies this place in the opinion of nations, as is proved by the fact of the vast immigration into this country from all the nations of Western and Central Europe. And when the adventurers have planted themselves and looked about, they send back all the money they can spare to bring their friends.

Meantime they find this country just passing through a great crisis in its history, as necessary as lactation or dentition or puberty to the human individual. We are in these days settling for ourselves and our descendants questions which, as they shall be determined in one way or the other, will make the peace and prosperity or the calamity of the next ages. The questions of Education, of Society, of Labor, the direction of talent, of character, the nature and habits of the American, may well occupy us, and more the question of Religion.

The new conditions of mankind in America are really favorable to progress, the removal of absurd restrictions and antique inequalities. The mind is always better the more it is used, and here it is kept in practice. The humblest is daily chal-

17*

lenged to give his opinion on practical questions, and while civil and social freedom exists, nonsense even has a favorable effect. Cant is good to provoke common sense. The Catholic Church, the trance-mediums, the rebel paradoxes, exasperate the common sense. The wilder the paradox, the more sure is Punch to put it in the pillory.

The lodging the power in the people, as in republican forms, has the effect of holding things closer to common sense; for a court or an aristocracy, which must always be a small minority, can more easily run into follies than a republic, which has too many observers, — each with a vote in his hand, — to allow its head to be turned by any kind of nonsense : since hunger, thirst, cold, the cries of children, and debt are always holding the masses hard to the essential duties.

One hundred years ago the American people attempted to carry out the bill of political rights to an almost ideal perfection. They have made great strides in that direction since. They are now proceeding, instructed by their success, and by their many failures, to carry out, not the bill of rights, but the bill of human duties.

And look what revolution that attempt involves. Hitherto government has been that of the single person or of the aristocracy. In this country the attempt to resist these elements, it is asserted, must throw us into the government not quite of mobs, but in practice of an inferior class of professional politicians, who by means of newspapers and caucuses really thrust their unworthy minority into the place of the old aristocracy on the one side, and of the good, industrious, well-taught but unambitious population on the other, win the posts of power, and give their direction to affairs. Hence liberal congresses and legislatures ordain, to the surprise of the people, equivocal, interested, and vicious measures. The men themselves are suspected, and charged with lobbying and being lobbied. No measure is attempted for itself, but the opinion of the people is courted in the first place, and the measures are perfunctorily carried through as secondary. We do not choose our own candidate, no, nor any other man's first choice, — but only the available candidate, whom, perhaps, no man loves. We do not speak what we think, but grope after the practicable and available. Instead of character, there is a studious exclusion of character. The people are feared and flattered. They are not reprimanded. The country is governed in bar-rooms, and in the mind of bar-rooms. The low can best win the low, and each aspirant for power vies with his rival which can stoop lowest, and depart widest from himself.

The partisan on moral, even on religious questions, will choose a proven rogue who can answer the tests, over an honest, affectionate, noble gentleman ; the partisan ceasing to be a man that he may be a sectarian.

The spirit of our political economy is low and degrading. The precious metals are not so precious as they are esteemed. Man exists for his own sake, and not to add a laborer to the state. The spirit of our political action, for the most part, considers nothing less than the sacredness of man. Party sacrifices man to the measure.

We have seen the great party of property and education in the country drivelling and huckstering away, for views of party fear or advantage, every principle of humanity and the dearest hopes of mankind ; the trustees of power only energetic when mischief could be done, imbecile as corpses when evil was to be prevented.

Our great men succumb so far to the forms of the day as to peril their integrity for the sake of adding to the weight of their personal character the authority of office, or making a real government titular. Our politics are full of adventurers, who having by education and social innocence a good repute in the state, break away from the law of honesty and think they can afford to join the devil's party. 'T is odious, these offenders in high life. You rally to the support of old charities and the cause of literature, and there, to be sure, are these brazen faces. In this innocence you are puzzled how to meet them ; must shake hands with them under protest. We feel toward them as the minister about the Cape Cod farm, — in the old time when the minister was still invited, in the spring, to make a prayer for the blessing of a piece of land, — the good pastor being brought to the spot, stopped short : "No, this land does not want a prayer, this land wants manure."

> " 'T is virtue which they want, and, wanting it,
> Honor no garment to their backs can fit."

Parties keep the old names, but exhibit a surprising fugacity in creeping out of one snake-skin into another of equal ignominy and lubricity, and the grasshopper on the turret of Faneuil Hall gives a proper hint of the men below.

Everything yields. The very glaciers are viscous or relegate into conformity, and the stiffest patriots falter and compromise ; so that *will* cannot be depended on to save us.

How rare are acts of will! We are all living according to custom; we do as other people do, and shrink from an act of our own. Every such act makes a man famous, and we can all count the few cases, — half a dozen in our time, — when a public man ventured to act as he thought, without waiting for orders or for public opinion. John Quincy Adams was a man of an audacious independence that always kept the public curiosity alive in regard to what he might do. None could predict his word, and a whole congress could not gainsay it when it was spoken. General Jackson was a man of will, and his phrase on one memorable occasion, "I will take the responsibility," is a proverb ever since.

The American marches with a careless swagger to the height of power, very heedless of his own liberty, or of other people's, in his reckless confidence that he can have all he wants, risking all the prized charters of the human race, bought with battles and revolutions and religion, gambling them all away for a paltry selfish gain.

He sits secure in the possession of his vast domain, rich beyond all experience in resources, sees its inevitable force unlocking itself in elemental order day by day, year by year; looks from his coal-fields, his wheat-bearing prairie, his goldmines, to his two oceans on either side, and feels the security that there can be no famine in a country reaching through so many latitudes, no want that cannot be supplied, no danger from any excess of importation of art or learning into a country of such native strength, such immense digestive power.

In proportion to the personal ability of each man, he feels the invitation and career which the country opens to him. He is easily fed with wheat and game, with Ohio wine, but his brain is also pampered by finer draughts, by political power and by the power in the railroad board, in the mills, or the banks. This elevates his spirits, and gives, of course, an easy self-reliance that makes him self-willed and unscrupulous.

I think this levity is a reaction on the people from the extraordinary advantages and invitations of their condition. When we are most disturbed by their rash and immoral voting, it is not malignity, but recklessness. They are careless of politics, because they do not entertain the possibility of being seriously caught in meshes of legislation. They feel strong and irresistible. They believe that what they have enacted they can repeal if they do not like it. But one may run a risk once too often. They stay away from the polls, saying that one vote can do no good! Or they take another step, and say one vote can do no harm! and vote for something which they do not approve, because their party or set votes for it. Of course this puts them in the power of any party having a steady interest to promote, which does not conflict manifestly with the pecuniary interest of the voters.   But if they should come to be interested in themselves and in their career, they would no more stay away from the election than from their own counting-room or the house of their friend.

The people are right-minded enough on ethical questions, but they must pay their debts, and must have the means of living well, and not pinching.   So it is useless to rely on them to go to a meeting, or to give a vote, if any check from this must-have-the-money side arises.   If a customer looks grave at their newspaper, or damns their member of Congress, they take another newspaper, and vote for another man.   They must have money, for a certain style of living fast becomes necessary ; they must take wine at the hotel, first, for the look of it, and second, for the purpose of sending the bottle to two or three gentlemen at the table ; and presently, because they have got the taste, and do not feel that they have dined without it.

The record of the election now and then alarms people by the all but unanimous choice of a rogue and brawler.   But how was it done?   What lawless mob burst into the polls and threw in these hundreds of ballots in defiance of the magistrates?   This was done by the very men you know, — the mildest, most sensible, best-natured people.   The only account of this is, that they have been scared or warped into some association in their mind of the candidate with the interest of their trade or of their property.

Whilst each cabal urges its candidate, and at last brings, with cheers and street-demonstrations, men whose names are a knell to all hope of progress, the good and wise are hidden in their active retirements, and are quite out of question.

> " These we must join to wake, for these are of the strain
> That justice dare defend, and will the age maintain."

Yet we know, all over this country, men of integrity, capable of action and of affairs, with the deepest sympathy in all that concerns the public, mortified by the national disgrace, and quite capable of any sacrifice except of their honor.

Faults in the working appear in our system, as in all, but

they suggest their own remedies. After every practical mistake, out of which any disaster grows, the people wake and correct it with energy. And any disturbances in politics, in civil or foreign wars, sober them, and instantly show more virtue and conviction in the popular vote. In each new threat of faction the ballot has been, beyond expectation, right and decisive.

'T is ever an inspiration, God only knows whence; a sudden, undated perception of eternal right coming into and correcting things that were wrong; a perception that passes through thousands as readily as through one.

The gracious lesson taught by science to this country is, that the history of nature from first to last is incessant advance from less to more, from rude to finer organization, the globe of matter thus conspiring with the principle of undying hope in man. Nature works in immense time, and spends individuals and races prodigally to prepare new individuals and races. The lower kinds are one after one extinguished; the higher forms come in. The history of civilization, or the refining of certain races to wonderful power of performance, is analogous; but the best civilization yet is only valuable as a ground of hope.

Ours is the country of poor men. Here is practical democracy; here is the human race poured out over the continent to do itself justice; all mankind in its shirt-sleeves; not grimacing like poor rich men in cities, pretending to be rich, but unmistakably taking off its coat to hard work, when labor is sure to pay. This through all the country. For really, though you see wealth in the capitals, it is only a sprinkling of rich men in the cities and at sparse points; the bulk of the population is poor. In Maine, nearly every man is a lumberer. In Massachusetts, every twelfth man is a shoemaker, and the rest, millers, farmers, sailors, fishermen.

Well, the result is, instead of the doleful experience of the European economist, who tells us, "In almost all countries the condition of the great body of the people is poor and miserable," here that same great body has arrived at a sloven plenty, — ham and corn-cakes, tight roof, and coals enough have been attained; an unbuttoned comfort, not clean, not thoughtful, far from polished, without dignity in his repose; the man awkward and restless if he have not something to do, but honest and kind, for the most part, understanding his own rights and stiff to maintain them, and disposed to give his children a better education than he received.

The steady improvement of the public schools in the cities and the country enables the farmer or laborer to secure a precious primary education. It is rare to find a born American who cannot read and write. The facility with which clubs are formed by young men for discussion of social, political, and intellectual topics secures the notoriety of the questions.

Our institutions, of which the town is the unit, are all educational, for responsibility educates fast. The town meeting is, after the high school, a higher school. The legislature, to which every good farmer goes once on trial, is a superior academy.

The result appears in the power of invention, the freedom of thinking, in the readiness for reforms, eagerness for novelty, even for all the follies of false science; in the antipathy to secret societies, in the predominance of the Democratic party in the politics of the Union, and in the voice of the public even when irregular and vicious, — the voice of mobs, the voice of lynch law, — because it is thought to be, on the whole, the verdict, though badly spoken, of the greatest number.

All this forwardness and self-reliance cover self-government; proceed on the belief that as the people have made a government they can make another; that their union and law are not in their memory, but in their blood and condition. If they unmake a law, they can easily make a new one. In Mr. Webster's imagination the American Union was a huge Prince Rupert's drop, which will snap into atoms, if so much as the smallest end be shivered off. Now the fact is quite different from this. The people are loyal, law-abiding. They prefer order, and have no taste for misrule and uproar.

America was opened after the feudal mischief was spent, and so the people made a good start. We began well. No inquisition here, no kings, no nobles, no dominant church. Here heresy has lost its terrors. We have eight or ten religions in every large town, and the most that comes of it is a degree or two on the thermometer of fashion; a pew in a particular church gives an easier entrance to the subscription ball.

We began with freedom, and are defended from shocks now for a century by the facility with which, through popular assemblies, every necessary measure of reform can instantly be carried. A congress is a standing insurrection, and escapes the violence of accumulated grievance. As the globe keeps its identity by perpetual change, so our civil system, by perpetual appeal to the people and acceptance of its reforms.

The government is acquainted with the opinions of all classes, knows the leading men in the middle class, knows the leaders of the humblest class. The President comes near enough to these; if he does not, the caucus does, — the primary ward and town meeting, and what is important does reach him.

The men, the women, all over this land shrill their exclamations of impatience and indignation at what is short-coming or is unbecoming in the government, — at the want of humanity, of morality, — ever on broad grounds of general justice, and not on the class-feeling which narrows the perception of English, French, German people at home.

In this fact, that we are a nation of individuals, that we have a highly intellectual organization, that we can see and feel moral distinctions, and that on such an organization sooner or later the moral laws must tell, to such ears must speak, — in this is our hope. For if the prosperity of this country has been merely the obedience of man to the guiding of nature, — of great rivers and prairies, — yet is there fate above fate, if we choose to speak this language; or, if there is fate in corn and cotton, so is there fate in thought, — this, namely, that the largest thought and the widest love are born to victory, and must prevail.

The revolution is the work of no man, but the eternal effervescence of nature. It never did not work. And we say that revolutions beat all the insurgents, be they never so determined and politic; that the great interests of mankind, being at every moment through ages in favor of justice and the largest liberty, will always, from time to time, gain on the adversary and at last win the day. Never country had such a fortune, as men call fortune, as this, in its geography, its history, and in its majestic possibilities.

We have much to learn, much to correct, — a great deal of lying vanity. The spread eagle must fold his foolish wings and be less of a peacock; must keep his wings to carry the thunderbolt when he is commanded. We must realize our rhetoric and our rituals. Our national flag is not affecting, as it should be, because it does not represent the population of the United States, but some Baltimore or Chicago or Cincinnati or Philadelphia caucus; not union or justice, but selfishness and cunning. If we never put on the liberty-cap until we were freemen by love and self-denial, the liberty-cap would mean something. I wish to see America not like the old powers of the earth, grasping, exclusive, and narrow, but a benefactor such as no country ever was, hospitable to all nations, legislating for all nationalities. Nations were made to help each other as much as families were; and all advancement is by ideas, and not by brute force or mechanic force.

In this country, with our practical understanding, there is, at present, a great sensualism, a headlong devotion to trade and to the conquest of the continent, — to each man as large a share of the same as he can carve for himself, — an extravagant confidence in our talent and activity, which becomes, whilst successful, a scornful materialism, — but with the fault, of course, that it has no depth, no reserved force whereon to fall back when a reverse comes.

That repose which is the ornament and ripeness of man is not American. That repose which indicates a faith in the laws of the universe, — a faith that they will fulfil themselves, and are not to be impeded, transgressed, or accelerated. Our people are too slight and vain. They are easily elated and easily depressed. See how fast they extend the fleeting fabric of their trade, — not at all considering the remote reaction and bankruptcy, but with the same abandonment to the moment and the facts of the hour as the Esquimaux who sells his bed in the morning. Our people act on the moment, and from external impulse. They all lean on some other, and this superstitiously, and not from insight of his merit. They follow a fact; they follow success, and not skill. Therefore, as soon as the success stops and the admirable man blunders, they quit him; already they remember that they long ago suspected his judgment, and they transfer the repute of judgment to the next prosperous person who has not yet blundered. Of course this levity makes them as easily despond. It seems as if history gave no account of any society in which despondency came so readily to heart as we see it and feel it in ours. Young men at thirty and even earlier lose all spring and vivacity, and if they fail in their first enterprise throw up the game.

The source of mischief is the extreme difficulty with which men are roused from the torpor of every day. Blessed is all that agitates the mass, breaks up this torpor, and begins motion. *Corpora non agunt nisi soluta;* the chemical rule is true in mind. Contrast, changes, interruption, are necessary to new activity and new combinations.

If a temperate wise man should look over our American society, I think the first danger that would excite his alarm would be the European influences on this country. We buy much of Europe that does not make us better men : and mainly the expensiveness which is ruining that country. We import trifles, dancers, singers, laces, books of patterns, modes, gloves and cologne, manuals of Gothic architecture, steammade ornaments. America is provincial. It is an immense Halifax. See the secondariness and aping of foreign and English life, that runs through this country, in building, in dress, in eating, in books. Every village, every city has its architecture, its costume, its hotel, its private house, its church, from England.

Our politics threaten her. Her manners threaten us. Life is grown and growing so costly, that it threatens to kill us. A man is coming here as there to value himself on what he can buy. Worst of all his expense is not his own, but a far-off copy of Osborne House or the Elysée. The tendency of this is to make all men alike ; to extinguish individualism and choke up all the channels of inspiration from God in man. We lose our invention and descend into imitation. A man no longer conducts his own life. It is manufactured for him. The tailor makes your dress ; the baker your bread ; the upholsterer — from an imported book of patterns — your furniture ; the Bishop of London your faith.

In the planters of this country, in the seventeenth century, the conditions of the country combined with the impatience of arbitrary power which they brought from England, forced them to a wonderful personal independence and to a certain heroic planting and trading. Later this strength appeared in the solitudes of the West, where a man is made a hero by the varied emergencies of his lonely farm, and neighborhoods must combine against the Indians, or the horse-thieves, or the river rowdies, by organizing themselves into committees of vigilance. Thus the land and sea educate the people, and bring out presence of mind, self-reliance, and hundred-handed activity. These are the people for an emergency. They are not to be surprised, and can find a way out of any peril. This rough and ready force becomes them, and makes them fit citizens and civilizers. But if we found them clinging to English traditions, which are graceful enough at home, as the English Church, and entailed estates, and distrust of popular election, we should feel this reactionary and absurdly out of place.

Let the passion for America cast out the passion for Europe. Here let there be what the earth waits for, — exalted manhood. What this country longs for is personalities, grand persons, to counteract its materialities. For it is the rule of the universe that corn shall serve man, and not man corn.

They who find America insipid,— they for whom London and Paris have spoiled their own homes, can be spared to return to those cities. I not only see a career at home for more genius than we have, but for more than there is in the world.

The class of which I speak make themselves merry without duties. They sit in decorated club-houses in the cities, and burn tobacco and play whist; in the country they sit idle in stores and bar-rooms, and burn tobacco, and gossip and sleep. They complain of the flatness of American life; "America has no illusions, no romance." They have no perception of its destiny. They are not Americans.

The felon is the logical extreme of the epicure and coxcomb. Selfish luxury is the end of both, though in one it is decorated with refinements, and in the other brutal. But my point now is, that this spirit is not American.

Our young men lack idealism. A man for success must not be pure idealist, then he will practically fail; but he must have ideas, must obey ideas, or he might as well be the horse he rides on. A man does not want to be sun-dazzled, sun-blind; but every man must have glimmer enough to keep him from knocking his head against the walls. And it is in the interest of civilization and good society and friendship, that I dread to hear of well-born, gifted and amiable men, that they have this indifference, disposing them to this despair.

Of no use are the men who study to do exactly as was done before, who can never understand that to-day is a new day. There never was such a combination as this of ours, and the rules to meet it are not set down in any history. We want men of original perception and original action, who can open their eyes wider than to a nationality, — namely, to considerations of benefit to the human race, — can act in the interest of civilization; men of elastic, men of moral mind, who can live in the moment and take a step forward. Columbus was no backward-creeping crab, nor was Martin Luther, nor John Adams, nor Patrick Henry, nor Thomas Jefferson; and the Genius or Destiny of America is no log or sluggard, but a man incessantly advancing, as the shadow on the dial's face, or the heavenly body by whose light it is marked.

The flowering of civilization is the finished man, the man of sense, of grace, of accomplishment, of social power, — the gentleman. What hinders that he be born here? The new times need a new man, the complemental man, whom plainly this country must furnish. Freer swing his arms; farther pierce his eyes; more forward and forthright his whole build and rig than the Englishman's, who, we see, is much imprisoned in his backbone.

'T is certain that our civilization is yet incomplete, it has not ended, nor given sign of ending, in a hero. 'T is a wild democracy; the riot of mediocrities and dishonesties and fudges. Ours is the age of the omnibus, of the third person plural, of Tammany Hall.

Is it that nature has only so much vital force, and must dilute it if it is to be multiplied into millions? The beautiful is never plentiful. Then Illinois and Indiana, with their spawning loins, must needs be ordinary.

It is not a question whether we shall be a multitude of people. No, that has been conspicuously decided already; but whether we shall be the new nation, the guide and lawgiver of all nations, as having clearly chosen and firmly held the simplest and best rule of political society.

Now, if the spirit which years ago armed this country against rebellion, and put forth such gigantic energy in the charity of the Sanitary Commission, could be waked to the conserving and creating duty of making the laws just and humane, it were to enroll a great constituency of religious, self-respecting, brave, tender, faithful obeyers of duty, lovers of men, filled with loyalty to each other, and with the simple and sublime purpose of carrying out in private and in public action the desire and need of mankind.

Here is the post where the patriot should plant himself; here the altar where virtuous young men, those to whom friendship is the dearest covenant, should bind each other to loyalty, where genius should kindle its fires and bring forgotten truth to the eyes of men.

Let the good citizen perform the duties put on him here and now. It is not possible to extricate yourself from the questions in which your age is involved. It is not by heads reverted to the dying Demosthenes, or to Luther, or to Wallace, or to George Fox, or to George Washington, that you can combat the dangers and dragons that beset the United States at this time. I believe this cannot be accomplished by

dunces or idlers, but requires docility, sympathy, and religious receiving from higher principles ; for liberty, like religion,
is a short and hasty fruit, and like all power subsists only by
new rallyings on the source of inspiration.

Power can be generous.   The very grandeur of the means
which offer themselves to us should suggest grandeur in the
direction of our expenditure.   If our mechanic arts are unsur-
passed in usefulness, if we have taught the river to make
shoes and nails and carpets, and the bolt of heaven to write
our letters like a Gillott pen, let these wonders work for honest humanity, for the poor, for justice, genius, and the public
good.   Let us realize that this country, the last found, is the
great charity of God to the human race.

America should affirm and establish that in no instance
shall the guns go in advance of the present right.   We shall
not make *coups d'état* and afterwards explain and pay, but
shall proceed like William Penn, or whatever other Christian
or humane person who treats with the Indian or the foreigner,
on principles of honest trade and mutual advantage.   We can
see that the Constitution and the law in America must be
written on ethical principles, so that the entire power of the
spiritual world shall hold the citizen loyal, and repel the
enemy as by force of nature.   It should be mankind's bill of
rights, or Royal Proclamation of the Intellect ascending the
throne, announcing its good pleasure, that now, once for all,
the world shall be governed by common sense and law of
morals.

The end of all political struggle is to establish morality as
the basis of all legislation.   'T is not free institutions, 't is not
a democracy that is the end, — no, but only the means.   Morality is the object of government.   We want a state of things
in which crime will not pay, a state of things which allows
every man the largest liberty compatible with the liberty of
every other man.

Humanity asks that government shall not be ashamed to be
tender and paternal, but that democratic institutions shall be
more thoughtful for the interests of women, for the training
of children, and for the welfare of sick and unable persons,
and serious care of criminals, than was ever any the best government of the old world.

The genius of the country has marked out our true policy,
— opportunity.   Opportunity of civil rights, of education, of
personal power, and not less of wealth ; doors wide open.   If

I could have it, — free trade with all the world without toll or custom-houses, invitation as we now make to every nation, to every race and skin, white men, red men, yellow men, black men ; hospitality of fair field and equal laws to all. Let them compete, and success to the strongest, the wisest, and the best. The land is wide enough, the soil has bread for all.

I hope America will come to have its pride in being a nation of servants, and not of the served. How can men have any other ambition where the reason has not suffered a disastrous eclipse? Whilst every man can say I serve, — to the whole extent of my being I apply my faculty to the service of mankind in my especial place, — he therein sees and shows a reason for his being in the world, and is not a moth or incumbrance in it.

The distinction and end of a soundly constituted man is his labor. Use is inscribed on all his faculties. Use is the end to which he exists. As the tree exists for its fruit, so a man for his work. A fruitless plant, an idle animal, does not stand in the universe. They are all toiling, however secretly or slowly, in the province assigned them, and to a use in the economy of the world; the higher and more complex organizations, to higher and more catholic service. And man seems to play, by his instincts and activity, a certain part that even tells on the general face of the planet, drains swamps, leads rivers into dry countries for their irrigation, perforates forests and stony mountain-chains with roads, hinders the inroads of the sea on the continent, as if dressing the globe for happier races.

On the whole, I know that the cosmic results will be the same, whatever the daily events may be. Happily we are under better guidance than of statesmen. Pennsylvania coal mines, and New York shipping, and free labor, though not idealists, gravitate in the ideal direction. Nothing less large than justice can keep them in good temper. Justice satisfies everybody, and justice alone. No monopoly must be foisted in, no weak party or nationality sacrificed, no coward compromise conceded to a strong partner. Every one of these is the seed of vice, war, and national disorganization. It is our part to carry out to the last the ends of liberty and justice. We shall stand, then, for vast interests ; north and south, east and west, will be present to our minds, and our vote will be as if they voted, and we shall know that our vote secures the foundations of the state, good-will, liberty and security of traffic and of production, and mutual increase of good-will in the great interests.

Our helm is given up to a better guidance than our own; the course of events is quite too strong for any helmsman, and our little wherry is taken in tow by the ship of the great Admiral which knows the way, and has the force to draw men and states and planets to their good.

Such and so potent is this high method by which the Divine Providence sends the chiefest benefits under the mask of calamities, that I do not think we shall by any perverse ingenuity prevent the blessing.

In seeing this guidance of events, in seeing this felicity without example that has rested on the Union thus far, I find new confidence for the future. I could heartily wish that our will and endeavor were more active parties to the work. But I see in all directions the light breaking. Trade and government will not alone be the favored aims of mankind, but every useful, every elegant art, every exercise of imagination, the height of reason, the noblest affection, the purest religion will find their home in our institutions, and write our laws for the benefit of men.

University Press: John Wilson and Son, Cambridge.